World Class
Quality
SECOND EDITION

World Class
Quality

SECOND EDITION

Using Design of Experiments to Make it Happen

Keki R. Bhote
Adi K. Bhote

AMACOM
American Management Association
New York • Atlanta • Boston • Chicago • Kansas City • San Francisco • Washington, D.C.
Brussels • Mexico City • Tokyo • Toronto

Special discounts on bulk quantities of AMACOM books are available to corporations, professional associations, and other organizations. For details, contact Special Sales Department, AMACOM, an imprint of AMA Publications, a division of American Management Association, 1601 Broadway, New York, NY 10019. Tel.: 212-903-8316   Fax: 212-903-8083

Library of Congress Cataloging-in-Publication Data

Bhote, Keki R., 1925–
    World class quality : using design of experiments to make it happen / Keki R. Bhote and Adi K. Bhote.—2nd ed.
      p. cm.
   Includes bibliographical references and index.
   ISBN 0-8144-0427-8 (alk. paper)
   1. Quality control—Statistical methods.   2. Process control—Statistical methods.   3. Experimental design.   I. Bhote, Adi K.   II. Title.
TS156.B563   2000
658.5'62—dc21   99-038804

Printing number

10   9   8   7   6   5   4   3   2   1

Contents

v

List of Figures

List of Tables

Foreword

The quality of Keki Bhote's career-long advocacies on quality enthuse me to invite your study of this inspiring and practical book.

World Class Quality is Keki's readily interpretable and challengingly embraceable reach out expectation. That expectation: singular superiority regarding everything we provide to customers, clients, and constituents.

The dimension, world, is additionally all encompassing. It intends, of course, much more than geography. Rather, he teaches performance superiority of every relevant initiative, objective, process, input, output, service, product that affects our institutions' earning the sustained loyalty of our customers, et al.

This doable, repeatable achievement will garner for all of us well-deserved, fair, honorable, self-interest rewards which in turn will stimulate a healthier, growing global economy with attendant elevation of the quality of life for so many of the world's deserving classes.

Keki has followed his overview of *World Class Quality* with a summary of ten quality tools designed for the 21st century. Even quality professionals are not aware of most of these tools. Using Design of Experiments as the centerpiece of these powerful tools, he describes their amazing simplicity, coupled with their cost effectiveness and statistical power. He developed and practiced these techniques in the crucible of Motorola's drive for a 10:1, 100:1, and 1000:1 quality improvement.

He has illustrated these techniques with numerous case studies and workshop exercises drawn not only from design and manufacturing, but from support services, farms, hospitals, and universities.

In the process, he has shown how Design of Experiments need not be the exclusive province of the professionals, but can be extended so that the whole factory can be turned loose on problem-solving, thereby fulfilling Dr. W. Edward Deming's vision of restoring "joy in the workplace."

Bob Galvin

Preface to the Second Edition

The first edition of *World Class Quality—Using Design of Experiments to Make It Happen* was published in 1991. In the intervening years, the book has sold more than 100,000 copies, has been translated into four European languages, and has made the list of best-selling business books in a few cities.

More important, we have received calls from hundreds of companies indicating that, in this book, they have finally found information on quality and, specifically, on design of experiments that did not leave them bewildered and lost after the first chapter. They have praised its simplicity, lack of technical jargon, practicality, and cost-effective solutions. It has shown them how to solve chronic quality problems in ways that are far more effective than the seven tools of quality control that are widely used in Japan and slavishly copied by many Western companies.

It has similarly shown them a methodology far easier, far less costly, and far more statistically powerful than the widely touted Taguchi design of experiments or the classical design of experiments, still used in certain segments of Western industry. Our consultancy has rescued companies that have tried the Taguchi and the classical methods, have been frustrated by difficulties in using them or by poor results, and have turned to us for effective solutions.

It is gratifying that several universities are using *World Class Quality* as a text in quality courses, at both the undergraduate and the graduate level. We have also conducted seminars lasting no more than one or two days in more than 350 companies in North America, Europe, Asia and Australia, teaching these elegant problem-solving techniques not only to engineers and those with technical skills, but also to technicians, blue-collar workers, and suppliers who do not want, much less need, sophisticated techniques that produce marginal results.

Why, then, is there a need for a revised edition? There are several reasons:

> At the strong urging of many of our clients from all over the world, we are adding more examples of problem solving, with both successful case studies to reinforce the power of the techniques and unsuccessful case studies to show how to avoid pitfalls. (It is a fact of life that people learn more from failures than from the mere emulation of success.)
> Another reason for the proliferation of case studies in this revised edition is to *facilitate the leap from classroom learning to practice.* Among the case studies in this book: both successful and unsuccessful, the practitioners will find parallels with their own specific problems and thus a ready guide for solutions.
> Although the use of these Design-of-Experiments (DOE) techniques can be learned just by reading this book and following the case studies—as has been the case in scores of companies—a mentor is an important factor in a company's success. Several years ago, a study determined that the dominant factor in producing excellent surgeons was the amount of internship time the student-surgeon spent under the guidance of a master-surgeon acting as a coach, a teacher. The authors have provided this coaching, this hands-on help to more than 100 companies, following introductory seminars.
> We have developed additional DOE techniques to make the total tool kit more comprehensive and more pervasive for a wider variety of applications.
> We are introducing a technique called Multiple Environment Over Stress Testing (MEOST) that achieves a breakthrough in reliability similar to DOE's breakthrough in quality. The combination of DOE and MEOST is a powerful way—in many cases, the only way—to solve chronic field problems and to prevent such problems early in design.
> We are also adding a chapter that summarizes related techniques, such as Quality Function Deployment (QFD), Total Productive Maintenance (TPM), benchmarking, Poka-Yoke, Next Operation as Customer (NOAC), Supply Management, Value Engineering (VE), and Cycle Time Reduction. These approaches round out DOE and MEOST and constitute a powerful new took kit for the 21st century.
> We are refining and embellishing the DOE techniques contained in the original edition to make them even more user-friendly and to

guide teams with dos and don'ts in the form of a questionnaire for each technique. Again, the emphasis is on coaching.

> We are extending DOE techniques to the service sector and to administrative applications.
> This revised edition can help companies that have achieved ISO-9000 and QS-9000 certifications go beyond simplistic quality practices and reach for truly world class quality.
> Each chapter has a summary page containing the highlights of that chapter for quick reference.
> In the all-important area of *top management* commitment, this new edition shows a practical way to secure and hold such commitment, with direct impact on organization, teamwork, bottom-line results, and the creation of a quality culture.

Acknowledgments

My first and eternal gratitude goes to my revered mother—a renowned author in India. She stressed, "When you have thought long and hard about a subject and researched it from all angles, you develop a yearning to write about it and make your world a better place." Her encouragement resulted in the first article I published in a magazine at age nine. To her, I owe everything.

The second great inspiration in my life is Bob Galvin, Chairman of the Board of Motorola, Inc., one of the giants of the industrial world. His vision to "blaze trails that none had explored before" is a true mark of leadership. This vision, his abiding faith in his "associates" as he called all his employees, and his helping them reach the never-ending maximum of their potential, has been a guiding light for me in the 50 years of my discipleship under him.

My revered "guru" has been Dorian Shainin, the foremost problem-solver in industrial quality. His admonition: "Talk to the parts; they are smarter than the engineers," has been the foundation of many designed experiments in this book. His guidance continues to this day. I am also grateful to his two worthy sons, Peter and Dick, for continuing the pioneering work of their father.

My son, Adi, has bestowed the greatest reward a fond father can hope for. He has not only followed my profession, but has also co-authored this book. His hands-on experience and practicality have been a perfect complement to the academic side of Design of Experiments (DOE).

In some ways, this book is a memorial to my late and esteemed colleagues Adolph Hitzelburger and Carlton Braun. The three of us were the young Turks that launched DOE 40 years ago. Together, we fought the bureaucracy, skepticism, and "not invented here" syndrome typical of many companies. I single out Bill Wiggenhorn, President of Motorola University, as the sugar daddy who funded worldwide training of our DOE. I must also thank my associates Dick Wendt, Rick Kiska, Bill

Schmidt, John Lupienski, and Thad Woronowicz, who solved problems declared to be unsolvable.

It took general managers, such as Simon Wong and S. K. Ko, to light the DOE torch at our international plants. My esteemed colleagues Oded Erlich (Israel), Shane Yemm (U.K.), Bernard Forgeot D'Arc (France), Y. F. Tan (China), and T. T. Yew (Malaysia) became enthusiastic DOE champions in these plants.

Following my retirement from Motorola in 1992 and the formation of my own consulting company, we extended DOE to 33 countries. Among the towering luminaries are Willy Hendrickx and Frans Wouters of Philips who spread the DOE gospel to 44 Philips plants all over the globe. They were ably supported by Brian Boling (U.S.), Sid Dasgupta (India), T. Van Der Hoek (The Netherlands), Mark Dale (U.K.), Chia Beng Chye (Singapore), Jeff Van Houdt (Belgium) and Alberto Chinen (Brazil). We salute them as dedicated DOE missionaries.

In the United States, recognizing all the stalwarts would fill several pages. Among the most notable are Mike Katzorke (Cessna), Ted Taber and Carl Saunders (Caterpillar), Wayne Stewart (Iomega), J. C. Anderson and Jeff Postl (Whirlpool), Bernie Sergesketter and Mary Rodino (AT&T), Chuck James (American Produce), Hemant Buch (Divicom), Dr. C. Jackson Grayson (American Production and Quality Center), Harvey Kaylie (Mini Circuits), Bill Beer, Jeff Winter, and Tony Hair (Maytag), and Doug Kilian (Siemens).

I also gratefully acknowledge the initiative of most of my 350 clients who have been the crucible for testing, honing, and polishing the practice of DOE. Without the encouragement and guidance of Ray O'Connor, Senior Acquisitions Editor at the American Management Association, and the inspirational Don Bohl, this book may not have seen the light of day. I would be totally remiss if I did not acknowledge the invaluable contribution of my associate, Jean Seeley, whose determined drive and uncanny computer speed produced the manuscript to beat the deadline.

Finally, my heartfelt thanks go to my family—my daughters Safeena and Shenaya and my sons Adi and Xerxes—for their faith in their father, and above all to my wife Mehroo, a tower of strength and sacrifice at every step of the long journey from concept to completion.

Keki R. Bhote

Part I

· ·

Introduction

1

The Need for and Objectives and Benefits of Design of Experiments

A. The Need

The Killing of Locusts Chinese Style

There is a story that at the height of Mao Zedong's cultural revolution in China, the fields of one village were being attacked by swarms of locusts. Seeing their crops decimated, the villagers turned to Mao's little red book for guidance in overcoming this catastrophe. But nothing the great helmsman wrote seemed to fit except one obscure sentence. Mao wrote that in the absence of any directive, people should devise their own solutions! Armed with that stupendous advice, the villagers rounded up all the able-bodied people and dispatched them to the fields to kill the locusts by hand, one by one. For seven days, hundreds of them labored long and hard until all the locusts lay dead. Had the same problem arisen in the United States, a few bags of insecticides would have done the trick in one hour!

Henley's Law

This Chinese story illustrates the power of tools—the right tools. What is wrong with many well-meaning problem-solving teams—be they Quality Circles, Kaizen, or Small-Group Improvement Activities—is weak tools. The principle is called Henley's Law (named after an industrial philosopher, Wes Henley). It states that the dominant characteristics of a team tend to grow exponentially. If the dominant characteristics are ignorance and misinformation, there will be an exponential growth of ignorance and misinformation. If the dominant characteristics are knowledge and sound information, there will be an exponential growth of knowledge and sound information. Even if a company has good leadership and dedicated and enthusiastic workers, weak tools will produce only confusion, frustration, and disenchantment.

The need for DOE (Shainin branch, specifically) is compelling and wide-ranging.

1. *Ninety percent of U.S. industries do not know how to solve chronic quality problems.* This statement does not apply to *all* problems. Some of the simplest problems can be solved with the seven tools of QC, engineering judgment, brainstorming, statistical process control or Kepner Tragoe approaches. But *chronic* problems that have festered for days, weeks, months, or even years cannot be solved with these traditional techniques. Design of Experiments specifically the Shainin DOE detailed in this book, is the only sure-fire way.

2. *Companies utilize the line workers' brawn but not their brains.* A second urgent reason to embrace DOE is its ability to be used by all workers—hourly workers, maintenance workers, and technicians as well as engineers and professionals. In a typical company, only the engineers are assigned to solving problems. The worker is supposed to use only his brawn. His brain is to be checked at the guard's gate. This is a colossal waste. In consulting with hundreds of companies, we have come to the firm conclusion that the direct labor worker has just as high an IQ as the engineer. He just has not had the same breaks in life as the latter.* Given the simple tools of our DOE approach, along with training, encouragement and coaching, the line worker frequently does extremely well. We have seen whole factories turned loose for problem solving, with a boost of morale that is pure joy to behold.

3. *Ninety percent of specifications and tolerances are wrong.* Engineers tend to pull specifications and tolerances out of the air. (This is known as atmospheric analysis.) Some are based on past drawings, supplier recommendations, conventional rules, and neighbor inputs. A few may use worst-case tolerancing or geometric tolerancing. Yet, almost all engineers are totally ignorant of the use of DOE to determine realistic specifications and realistic tolerances

---

*Throughout this book, the masculine is used as a neuter-gender word rather than the repetitious "he or she." We hope our readers will forgive us for taking this liberty.

that can achieve breakthroughs in quality and save months of production delays and millions of dollars in unproductive costs.

4. *Product/process characterization and optimization unknown.* At the design stage of a product or process, engineers guess at important parameters, through either a formula approach, computer simulation, circuit analysis, supplier inputs, or just plain experience. If they guess correctly, production could be launched with 100 percent yields. But that rarely happens. The best tools to separate important parameters from unimportant ones are Design of Experiments. Their use allows the tolerances of the important parameters to be tightened to maintain high yields and those of the unimportant parameters loosened to save money—a double whammy.

5. *Defects and variation are considered inevitable.* Industry has lived with defects so long that it looks on them as a fact of life, like breathing. Sorting and screening, detection and correction have grown into institutions. They are factored in by cost accounting and are passed on to customers in the form of higher prices. Similarly, variation is looked on as inevitable. "There is variation in nature, so why not in product" is the rationale.

   In the past, we have not had the tools to outlaw defects, to reduce variation in products and processes. With our DOE, we now have the ability to reduce defects from percentages to parts per million, even to parts per billion. We have the wherewithal to reduce variation with C_{pk}'s of 2.0 and more (see Chapter 4) and to move toward target values and yet effect enormous cost savings by reducing customer returns, scrap, analyzing, rework, inspection, and test.

6. *Brute force reliability testing is a recipe for unreliability.* Reliability is, perhaps, even more important than quality, because it has two additional dimensions—time and stress. Conventional reliability uses tools such as reliability prediction studies, Failure Mode Effects Analysis (FMEA) and Fault-Tree Analysis (FTA). These tools have about as much effect on reliability as do the seven tools of QC on quality—in other words, marginal at best! The U.S. Department of Defense has long used mass life testing to improve reliability, just as industry has used mass inspection to improve quality. The results are just as useless. Even today, the cost of maintaining military equipment in the field is 11 times the acquisition price! There has to be a better way. The combination of DOE and MEOST can simulate and prevent field failures at the design

stage to achieve orders of magnitude improvement in field reliability.

B. The Objectives

The objectives of this text are to:

1. Describe in simple, nonmathematical terms a variety of easy, practical, but statistically powerful techniques for solving any chronic quality problem that has resisted solution by traditional means. These techniques are applicable to a wide variety of fields, ranging from lettuce processing to nuclear energy, from microscopic semiconductor chips to macroscopic construction equipment.
2. Coach all levels in a company—from engineers and technicians to supervisors and line operators, from managers to customers and suppliers—in the use of these tools.
3. Progress from the current unacceptably high defect levels, e.g., 1 percent acceptable quality levels (AQLs) to parts per million (ppm), to parts per billion (ppb), to zero defects, and ultimately toward zero variation.
4. Prevent quality problems from reaching production or the field by using DOE at the design stage of a product and at the design stage of a process. When problems reach production, they become monuments to the failure of the engineering design! Such design flaws are the most insidious of all quality problems.
5. Prove that statistical process control (SPC) is not a problem-solving tool, but only a monitoring and maintenance tool, and show that within the world of SPC, control charts still widely used in the West are outdated, cumbersome, costly, and statistically weak. Instead, Pre-Control is explained as a viable alternative to control charts. It is simple, cost-effective, and statistically far more powerful than control charts.
6. Summarize the 10 powerful tools for the 21st century and show how, collectively, they contribute to world-class quality and productivity.
7. Advance reliability from elementary techniques, such as FMEA and brute-force testing, to elegant techniques that combine DOE with MEOST to achieve one to two order magnitudes of reliability improvement.
8. Add case studies, both successful and unsuccessful, as well as workshop exercises for the reader to practice, to reinforce the

right approaches to problem solving and to avoid the pitfalls of false starts.

9. Provide a checklist associated with each DOE technique for (1) avoidance of pitfalls, (2) detailed guidance of problem-solving teams, and (3) general guidance for management.
10. Address the all-important task of management support, involvement, and commitment to promote a quality culture throughout the corporation.

C. The Benefits

The very real benefits of these techniques have been attested to by more than two million practitioners in North America, Europe, Asia and Australia. More specifically, these benefits have been underlined by over 350 of our clients in 33 countries. They are:

1. Quality improvements from 2:1 to over 10,000:1 and achieved from one day to a maximum of six months.
2. Increased C_{pk}'s from 0.5 and 1.0 to 2.0 and 5.0.
3. Near-elimination of scrap and rework as well as drastic reduction in inspection and test; moving toward zero defects and 100 percent yields.
4. Steep reductions in the cost of poor quality (which historically runs from 10 to 20 percent of the sales dollar and from $100 to $200 per person per day) by an order of magnitude.
5. Field reliability increases by 10:1 and more than 100:1.
6. Enhanced customer satisfaction, customer loyalty, and long-term customer retention.
7. Moving from problem solving in production to problem prevention in product and process design.
8. Increased machine uptime, yields, and efficiencies within the framework of Total Productive Maintenance (TPM) to advance from Factory Overall Efficiencies (FOE) of less than 50 percent to more than 90 percent.
9. Significant reductions in cycle time by factors of from 10:1 to 50:1.
10. Improved employee morale. Success breeds success and enthusiasm, instead of a downward spiral of frustration and "give-up-itis" born of weak tools.
11. Extension of DOE benefits to suppliers to generate quality, cost, and cycle-time improvements; and to customers to generate partnerships and enhance perceived value to them.

12. Bottom-line improvements in business parameters: profitability, return on investment, market share, and overall productivity.

Figure 1-1 deals with the contribution of DOE* to total business excellence in 12 important areas:

1. ***Chronic Problem Solving (90 percent).*** DOE is the only tool that can successfully solve chronic quality problems that have been resistant to solution for a long time.
2. ***Profit/R.O.I. Improvement (60 percent).*** The cost of poor quality (COPQ) constitutes a loss of 10 to 20 percent of sales in a typical

Figure 1-1. Contributions of DOE to Business Excellence: A Spider Chart

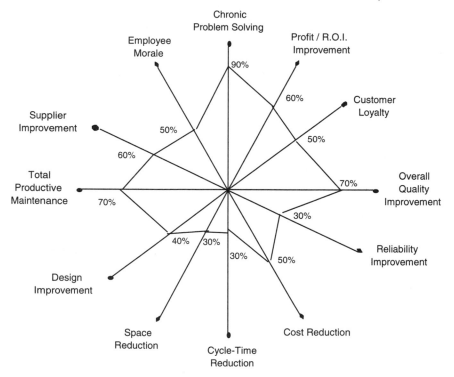

Note: A spider chart displays graphically the relative contribution of a particular technique to each of several parameters. The total length of each spoke in the spider chart represents 100%. The contribution of a particular technique (in this case DOE) is shown as a percentage of overall benefits.

*It must be understood in this context that DOE refers to the Shainin—not the less effective classical or Taguchi—DOE techniques (see Chapter 6).

company. If this cost can be cut in half, the profit of a company can be doubled. DOE can contribute 60 percent to such improvement.

3. *Customer Loyalty (50 percent).* Customer loyalty (retention) goes way beyond customer satisfaction. A 5 percent increase in customer retention can increase profits in a typical company by 35 percent to 120 percent. By focusing on quality not just for the sake of quality, but to fulfill the customer's requirements, DOE achieves more than this minimal increase in customer retention.

4. *Overall Quality Improvement (70 percent).* Only DOE, among all the techniques for quality improvement, can achieve breakthrough levels of improvement.

5. *Reliability Improvement (30 percent).* The addition of DOE to MEOST makes for a quantum leap improvement in reliability.

6. *Cost Reduction (50 percent).* Moving toward 100 percent yields with DOE is one of the best ways to reduce costs.

7. *Cycle-Time Reduction (30 percent).* DOE is an essential prerequisite to cycle-time reduction and lean manufacturing.

8. *Space Reduction (30 percent).* The resolving of all quality bottlenecks through DOE cuts down space for repair bays, inspection stations, and inventory banks.

9. *Design Improvement (40 percent).* Use of DOE at the design stage is the only sure way to prevent quality problems from getting to production and into the field.

10. *Total Productive Maintenance (70 percent).* Factory Overall Efficiency (FOE), as a TPM metric, consists of yield percentage times uptime percentage times machine-efficiency percentage. DOE has a strong impact on both yield and uptime percentages and a lesser influence on machine efficiency.

11. *Supplier Improvement (60 percent).* The development of partnership suppliers depends on their ability to implement a customer company's coaching in quality, cost, and cycle-time improvement. DOE is at the heart of all three disciplines.

12. *Employee Morale (50 percent).* Nothing frustrates production workers more than being given poor tools to solve problems. Nothing brightens their day more than the knowledge of being able to solve their own problems with the right tools. DOE—with its simple, powerful methodology—restores pride and joy in the workplace.

Before delving into the tools for quality improvement, we believe a brief history of the lurches, twists, and turns of the quality movement since its modern inception is in order.

2

....

Fads, Potions, Nostrums of the Quality Movement in the Last 50 Years

Lurching From Fad to Fad

The history of the quality movement—in its modern form—in the last half of the 20th century has a program-of-the decade flavor as it seeks quality salvation, with each new fad replacing a discarded one.

> *Sampling Plans.* In the 1950s, it was sampling plans, with their Acceptable Quality Levels (AQLs), Average Outgoing Quality Levels (AOQLs) and Lot Tolerance Percent Defectives (LTPDs). A host of such plans were developed, each claiming to be the alpha and omega of quality control. (This author, when requested to teach a course in quality control at a prestigious university, discovered to his horror that 14 weeks of a 16-week curriculum was devoted to nothing more than a variety of sampling plans.) Mercifully, sampling plans faded in popularity.
> *Zero-Defect Movement.* In the 1960s, it was the zero-defect movement. Born out of the Soviet success of Sputnik, where their space shots soared into the heavens, while U.S. shots flopped into the Atlantic after launch, the U.S. Department of Defense championed zero defects. If only workers would pledge themselves to zero defects, it stressed, quality would be guaranteed. There is a story of a company where all the workers were asked to sign a card pledging themselves to zero defects. One lone worker refused. His foreman pleaded with him to sign, to no avail. The works manager then tried. Again, the worker's answer was no. Finally, the man got hauled off to the company president, who bluntly told him: "John,

you either sign or you're fired." Whereupon John promptly signed. At that point, the president asked: "John, why did you give us so much hassle before signing?" John's reply: "Mr. President, until this moment, nobody pointed out the advantage of signing!" The zero-defect movement turned out to be all show and no substance.

> *ISO-9000.** In 1987, ISO-9000 was launched by a consortium of countries. This is, at best, a very elementary quality system—the least common denominator of 45 squabbling nations. It is a bureaucratic burden, with hide-bound procedures; contractual quality levels, rather than a philosophy of continuous improvement; little attention to the customer; and a goal of "freezing" defects at existing levels rather than eliminating them. As one wit said: "If you want to produce scrap, ISO-9000 will enable you to do it consistently!" It is being pushed down the throats of businesses today, making it a passport to do business with customer companies who are equally pressured to comply. And yet, almost no company has seen bottom-line benefits from ISO-9000. In fact, it has set the quality movement back 20 years.

> *Malcolm Baldrige Award.** In 1988, the Malcolm Baldrige Quality Award was established by the U.S. Congress as America's answer to the global quality challenge, in general, and the Deming Prize of Japan, in particular. Its guidelines are considerably superior to those of ISO-9000. But it is far from a world class quality system. Its wording is ambiguous and confusing—even to quality professionals—and has the effect of impoverishing companies that attempt to use it, while making external consultants richer! It does not pay sufficient attention to powerful tools that can translate high-sounding goals into results. It is weak in its sections on suppliers; customer loyalty (as distinguished from customer satisfaction); leadership (which is treated only superficially); and bottom-line business results. Further, because the Baldrige award is optional for a company, whereas ISO-9000 is becoming compulsory, especially those wanting to do business with the European Union, it is becoming less and less relevant. The number of applications for the award, which reached a modest peak of 100 a few years ago, has dropped by more than 50 percent.

> *European Quality Award.** In 1990, the European Quality Award was established in the European Union. With the Malcolm Baldrige Award as its prototype, it includes a few structural and cos-

---

*ISO-9000, the Malcolm Baldrige Award, QS-9000, and the European Quality Award are all being revised periodically. Some of their glaring weaknesses are in the process of being corrected.

metic improvements. Of particular significance is its emphasis on results.

> *QS-9000.** In 1995, QS-9000 was established by the "Big 3" U.S. automotive companies to unify quality systems required of their suppliers. It is a decided improvement on ISO-9000, with emphasis on the reduction of variation, a minimum C_{pk} of 1.33, system audits, and tie-in with product quality. Its weaknesses—similar to those of the Baldrige Award—are its wordiness, a dictatorial tone, insufficiently detailed tools, weak treatment of leadership and employee motivation, and the absence of a win-win partnership with the very suppliers it is trying to improve. The Big 3 suppliers are being herded into compliance, with little regard for the exorbitant costs they may have to incur and the dubious cost-effectiveness of the system. Many of these suppliers complain that the Big 3 are preachers, not practitioners, of QS-9000 and would flunk if it were to be applied to their own plants.

> *Total Quality Management.* In the 1980s and 1990s, TQM became the latest in the long succession of fads, potions, and nostrums of the quality movement. It was heralded as the much acclaimed savior—the final solution—when launched 15 years ago. But it too has produced disenchantment. Table 2-1 is a summary of several recent surveys conducted by prestigious organizations on the effectiveness of TQM.

Effective Quality Systems

> *Six Sigma.* In 1987 Motorola introduced its renowned Six Sigma process† as an alternative to the C_p, C_{pk} metric (see Chapter 4). Its main raison d'etre was a clarion call to reach for hitherto unattainable heights in quality levels, within the context of the company's

---

*ISO-9000, the Malcolm Baldrige Award, QS-9000, and the European Quality Award are all being revised periodically. Some of their glaring weaknesses are in the process of being corrected.

†There is a large difference between the statistical meaning of six sigma (a defect level of 2 parts per billion [ppb]) and Motorola's interpretation of "Six Sigma" as 3–4 ppm, assuming that the process is noncentered by 1.5 sigma. Motorola also escalates the defects (numerator) by adding the total number of defects from start to finish of an entire line, but then it waters down such challenging ppm levels by dividing these total defects not only by the number of units, but multiplying the latter (denominator) by the number of parts in that unit, and multiplying the denominator further by the number of opportunities for defects in each part. One reason for this is to make it possible to compare any product or line or plant fairly against another, regardless of product complexity, by this "normalizing" process.

Table 2-1. Surveys of TQM Ineffectiveness

Surveyor	
American Electronics Association[1]*	Seventy-three percent had TQM under way. Of these, 63 percent had lowered quality defects by less than 10 percent.
Arthur Little[2]	Only one-third of the companies stated that TQM was improving their competitive position.
McKinsey and Co.	Sixty-seven percent of the companies had stalled or fallen short of real improvements.
American Quality Foundation[3]	Seventy-seven percent of the companies had failed to achieve results and business objectives.
Quality Magazine[4]	"Companies have trained thousands of employees, launched numerous quality processes, but have been disappointed in the results. Despite their best intentions, these companies have floundered. They recognize the need for annual quality improvement at a revolutionary rate but have not achieved what they set out to achieve."

*Throughout the book, superscript numbers refer to the references at the end of the text.

drive for "Total Customer Satisfaction." It became a unifying symbol that knit all levels of employees together in an assault on defects.

Motorola's Six Sigma success has spawned a number of "baby six sigma" programs—notably at General Electric, ABB, Allied Signal and Polaroid. Even the American Society of Quality is attempting to clone these baby six sigma programs on the cheap. These programs require a lot of investment—in the millions of dollars for outside consultants alone and multiples of such figures for internal costs. Yet, these companies claim a 2:1 to 4:1 return on their quality investment. Insiders, however, suspect that much of this is accomplished with creative accounting. In any case, these baby six sigma programs fall short in terms of bold imagination, scope execution, and results.

> *The Ultimate Six Sigma—"The Big Q."* Even Motorola's Six Sigma process is in need of improvement in a number of significant areas. After we won the very first Malcolm Baldrige National Quality Award, this author felt that resting on our quality laurels could lead to complacency. I started to research and develop a truly world class quality system, well beyond TQM and well beyond

Motorola's Six Sigma.[5] These latter programs are all hemmed in by the narrow confines of product quality (i.e., design and manufacturing). On a larger canvas, there should be a strong linkage between quality and the imperatives of a business. To paraphrase Barry Goldwater, the pursuit of quality for the sake of quality alone is no virtue. The pursuit of quality for the sake of customer loyalty and profit is no vice. My ultimate Six Sigma system,[6] focusing on total business excellence, "the Big Q," replaces the "Little Q" of just product quality, represented by all other quality systems. The Big Q system has already become "the bible" in a few enlightened companies as a guiding light for their whole approach to business excellence.

Table 2-2 compares the relative strengths and weaknesses of the various quality systems, along with an effectiveness rating for each, using a scale of 1 to 100, where 1 is the least effective and 100 the most effective.

Table 2-3 compares conventional TQM, the baby six sigma programs and my Big Q in each of 12 key areas of a business.

Table 2-2. The Relative Effectiveness of Various Quality Systems

Quality System	Strengths	Weaknesses	Effectiveness
> ISO-9000	> Now an international standard > Mandatory for most companies > A passport to "Fortress Europe"	> Bureaucratic, procedures frozen before defects can be eliminated > Contractual quality levels rather than continuous improvement > Areas of leadership, organization, tools, field, support services, and people not emphasized; poor bottom-line results	5
> QS-9000	> Uniform quality requirements from U.S. "Big 3" automotive companies > Reduction of variation stressed	> C_{pk} of 1.33 a step forward, but inadequate > Dictatorial, wordy > Big 3 do not meet their own QS-9000 standard > Areas of leadership, employees, organization tools, and support services not emphasized	10
> Malcolm Baldrige Guidelines	> Leadership and customer areas emphasized	> Mandatory ISO-9000 compliance has eclipsed this voluntary but superior system > Wording ambiguous and confusing > Pursuit of narrow quality at the expense of business exellence in all areas	25
> European Quality Award	> Builds on Malcolm Baldrige > Emphasis on results	> Same as Malcolm Baldrige weaknesses, but less intense	30
> TQM	> Management emphasized	> See Tables 2-1 and 2-3	35

Table 2-2. (Continued)

Quality System	Strengths	Weaknesses	Effective- ness
> Six Sigma	> Reach out goals > Very good results at Motorola	> Cloning by other major companies has not captured full spirit of system	50
> The Ulti- mate Six Sigma— The Big Q	> Emphasis on total busi- ness excellence over narrow product quality > Akin to a constitution for a world class com- pany	> Newly introduced > Full-blown text in prep- aration, but not yet published	90

Note: Effectiveness Scale: 1 = lowest; 100 = highest.

Table 2-3. Conventional TQM versus Baby Six Sigma versus Big Q

Area	Conventional TQM	Baby Six Sigma— "The Little Q"	The Ultimate Six Sigma— "The Big Q"
1. Customer	Customer Satisfaction	Customer Satisfaction	Customer loyalty, employee loyalty, investor loyalty
2. Management	Leadership not stressed	Leadership mentioned in vague terms	Inspiring leadership to help people reach their full potential
3. Employees	Taylorism, fear-driven, drudgery	A few black belt experts Rest of people passive	True empowerment, freedom, joy in the workplace
4. Organization	Vertical structure Tall pyramid	Departments the norm	Flat pyramid, teams the building block
5. System	ISO-9000; QS-9000	Baldrige, quality-mindedness promoted	World-class system, business excellence a superordinate value
6. Tools	7 Q.C. tools, PDCA, 8-D	Classical DOE	Shainin DOE, MEOST, QFD, TPM, NOAC, VE, cycle time
7. Design	Design in isolation	Computer simulation	Design in half the time, half the defects, half the costs, half the manpower
8. Suppliers	Dictatorial, remote-control relationship	Laissez-faire	Win-win partnership, based on ethics, trust, active help
9. Manufacturing	SPC and control charts	Expensive 4-month long training for black belts	Turning entire factory loose on problem solving, not just black belts
10. Field	Service contracts to cover product weaknesses	FMEAs	MEOST, built-in diagnostics
11. Support services	Static business processes	Quality barely introduced as a metric	NOAC, flow charting; cycle time a key metric; and out-of-box thinking

Table 2-3. (Continued)

Area	Conventional TQM	Baby Six Sigma— "The Little Q"	The Ultimate Six Sigma— "The Big Q"
12. Measurement/ results	Quality improvement for its own sake	Encourages return on quality investment—2:1 to 4:1	Return on quality investment: over 10:1; profit improvement: minimum 2:1

3
A Powerful Tool Kit for the 21st Century

As with the entire quality movement, quality tools have also experienced a checkered history, ranging from the seven tools of QC, the seven quality management tools, the Ford 8-D problem-solving prescription, and the engineering approach. In this chapter, we describe an alternative—a collection of 10 powerful tools applicable far out into the 21st century, along with breakthrough results.[7]

Elementary Tools

The Seven Tools of QC—The Kindergarten Tools

For a whole generation, the West has slavishly copied what the Japanese collected and packaged into a set of quality techniques—the "seven tools of QC"—to solve production problems. Table 3-1 lists each of these tools, its objective, its methodology, and when and where it is used. In fairness, it must be said that the Japanese have succeeded in training their entire work force in these tools. Through their Quality Circles, Kaizen (improvement) teams and employee suggestions, they employ these tools to tackle everyday problems. As a result, a whole factory of workers—not just professionals—becomes involved. But seven tools of QC are capable of solving only the most elementary quality problems. They are totally useless in solving chronic quality problems, hence the disenchantment in the West with these methods.

The Seven Quality Management Tools—Another Needless Complication

The Japanese have an amazing penchant for making simple things complicated. In the 1980s, for example, they borrowed a collection of planning

Table 3-1. Elementary SPC Tools

Tool	Objective	Methodology	When to Use	Typical Users
1. PDCA (Plan, Do, Check, Act)	Solve problems by trial and error	Plan the work; execute; check results; take action if there is a deviation between desired and actual results. Repeat the cycle until deviation is reduced to zero.	When more powerful tools are unknown	Mostly line workers
2. Data Collection and Analysis	˅ Assess quality ˅ Control a product ˅ Regulate a process ˅ Accept/reject product ˅ Interpret observations	Define specific reason for collecting data; decide on measurement criteria (attribute vs. variable vs. rank); assure accuracy of measuring equipment (min. 5 times greater than product requirement); randomize; stratify data collection (time, material, machine, operator, and type and location of defects); analyze data using several SPC tools. (Most data are voluminous, gathered haphazardly, unorganized, and of limited use.)	At all times	Universal
3. Graphs/Charts	˅ Display trends ˅ Condense data ˅ Explain to others	Select two or more parameters to be displayed; determine method of display (bar, line, or circle graphs are the most common); select the most appropriate scales of the parameters for maximum visual impact.	At all times	Universal

4. Check Sheets	› Transform raw data into categories	› Determine categories into which data are subdivided (e.g., types of defects, location of defects, days in the week, etc.). Enter quantities in each category.	In preparation for a histogram or frequency distribution	Universal
Tally Sheets	› Groups, cells in semipictorial fashion	› For tally sheets, divide variable being recorded into 10 levels or cells. Plot cell boundaries or midpoints. Make tally (with slash marks) of the number of observations in each cell.		
Histograms/ Frequency Distribution	› Translate data into a picture of the average and spread of a quality characteristic	› Convert tally sheet data into bar graphs (histograms) or line graphs (frequency distribution) showing the relationship between various values of a quality characteristic and the number of observations (or percentage of the total) in each value. (A minimum of 30 to 50 observations is required.)	For process capability studies in preproduction or production	Engineers, technicians, line workers

Table 3-1. (Continued)

Tool	Objective	Methodology	When to Use	Typical Users
5. Pareto's Law	Separate the vital few causes of a problem or effect from the trivial many. Concentrate attention on former.	Identify as many causes of a problem as possible and the contribution of each to a given effect (dollars, percentages, etc.), plot causes on X-axis, effects (cumulative) on Y-axis in ascending or descending order of magnitude. Prioritize action on the few causes that account for most of the effect (generally, 20 percent or less of causes contribute 80 percent or more of effect).	At all times	Universal—a fantastic tool for prioritization in manufacturing or white-collar work
6. Brainstorming	➢ Generate as many ideas as possible to solve a problem or improve a process, utilizing synergistic power of a group	➢ Gather group most concerned with problem; define problem precisely; ask each member to write down cause or problems or improvement ideas; then, open the floor for an outpouring of ideas, rational or irrational; no criticisms allowed; record ideas; narrow down the list to the most worthwhile ideas; vote on the most likely cause and work on it. (This is known as problem solving by democracy.)	➢ Initial problem solving ➢ Process improvement	➢ Quality circles, ➢ Improvement teams

| Cause and Effect (Ishikawa; fishbone diagram) | > Organize problem causes into main groups and subgroups for total visibility of all causes and determine where to start corrective action | > Define the problem; construct a "fishbone" diagram with the major causes (e.g., material, machine, method, and man) as the main "branches" and add detailed causes within each main cause as "twigs." Quantify the spec. limits established for each cause where possible, the actual value measured for each cause, and its effect upon the problem. If a relationship between cause and effect can be shown quantitatively, draw a box around the cause. If the relationship is difficult to quantify, underline the cause. If there is no proof that a cause is related to the effect, do not mark the cause. Prioritize the most important causes with a circle. Experiment with these in PDCA fashion until root cause is located. | > Initial attempt at problem solving. | Widely used, especially in Japan, by Quality Circles. Useful only in solving simple problems. |

Table 3-1. (Continued)

Tool	Objective	Methodology	When to Use	Typical Users
CEDAC (Cause-and-Effect Diagram with the Addition of Cards)	› Same as Cause-and-Effect Diagram and earlier identification of causes and better worker participation	› Workers, at their individual workplaces, identify causes on the spot. Cards used to identify such causes can then be readily changed by the workers.	› Same as Cause-and-Effect Diagram	Same as Cause-and-Effect Diagram
7. Control Charts	› *Maintain* a parameter with minimum variation *after* major causes have been captured and reduced	Detailed in the chapter on control charts.	› Not for problem solving › Production	Engineers, technicians, line workers

tools from organizational development disciplines and called them the Seven Quality Management Tools, which they touted as the next phase in problem-solving. Table 3-2 lists each of these tools, its objective, its brief methodology, and when and where it is used. Although these tools are useful in planning and correlation studies, they are not related to problem solving.

The 8-D Methodology—A Boondoggle

In the early 1990s, Ford Motor Company introduced its 8-D (eight disciplines) problem-solving technique for its plants and suppliers in eight steps. These are:

1. Use team approach.
2. Describe the problem.
3. Contain symptom.
4. Find and verify root cause.
5. Choose corrective action and verify.
6. Implement permanent corrective action.
7. Prevent recurrence.
8. Congratulate the team.

Many companies, attracted by the Ford name and/or pressured by its rigid, bureaucratic approach to quality, adopted 8-D as a problem-solving mantra, spending days and weeks in costly seminars. The results? Frustration and disillusionment.

The Ford 8-D discipline can be considered a doubling of the Deming PDCA (Plan, Do, Check, Act) cycle. At best, it provides a procedure and a generic structure within which problem solving can take place. *But it does not tell the team how to solve a given problem.* It is based on conjecture and guesswork, techniques that have been used for a century of problem solving with woeful effectiveness. As an example, in Step 4 (Find and Verify Root Cause), it asks the following questions:

Was an Ishikawa cause and effect diagram utilized? Has the true root cause been stated, not just a symptom or effect? Has a process root cause been listed? Has system root cause been listed? Has the true root cause been verified and listed? and Was the technique of asking "why" utilized until the root cause was identified?

Only two techniques—the Cause-and-Effect Diagram and the Five Whys—are mentioned. Both of these are of marginal value. Let us, therefore, dismiss 8-D as an empty skeleton.

Table 3-2. The Seven Quality Management Tools

Tool	Objective	Methodology	When Used	Where Used
1. The Affinity Diagram (K–J)	Rearranges disparate data into meaningful categories	Each piece of data is recorded on a card. The cards are then grouped into several categories or families.	Grouping categories of customer requirements, of quality problem causes, of reliability problem causes, etc.	⋗ QFD studies ⋗ Ishikawa Diagram users
2. Interrelationship diagram	Determines which idea influences another	An arrow is drawn in the direction of the influence. The ideas that have the most arrows coming in or out are then prioritized. The crucial root ideas are those with arrows coming out of them.	⋗ General planning ⋗ Root cause conjecture	⋗ Brainstorming sessions ⋗ General planning ⋗ Cause-and-Effect Diagram users ⋗ With Affinity Diagram as a parallel method

3. Tree Diagram	Breaks down categories in Affinity Diagram (primary) into secondary and tertiary subcategories	Resembling a sideways organizational chart, it takes the major component of an idea to see how it can be subdivided.	Determining and breaking down customer needs	> QFD studies > As a sequel to Affinity Diagrams
4. Matrix Diagram	Correlates two sets of ideas or data	Two groups of data or ideas are compared with each other to determine extent of correlation.	In QFD studies comparing the "what" to the "how"	> Scatter plots > Measuring equipment accuracy > QFD studies
5. Matrix Data Analysis Plot	Market and customer segmentation	Data on X and Y axes are divided into four quadrants to determine market and/or customer strategy.	At the start of business and/or customer strategies	> BCG Portfolio Analysis > Customer attractiveness vs. company competency
6. Process Decision Program Chart	Effect-cause-correction analysis	Similar to Fault Tree Analysis but with corrective action for each cause, along with a time sequency focus.	Early design	Field Service Planning
7. Arrow Diagram	Finding shortest time for a project	Similar to Program Evaluation Review Technique highlights	New product launch	Any complex activity planning

Source: Keki R. Bhote, "A Powerful New Tool Kit for the 21st Century."[7]

The Engineering Approach (Observe, Think, Try, Explain)

The observation step is okay, if the engineers "talk to the parts" detailed in subsequent chapters. But they don't know how to talk to the parts! The "think" step is guesses, opinions, hunches, fads, and theories that are ineffective for chronic problems. The "try" step is usually varying one factor (or variable) at a time, keeping all other factors constant. Besides the inordinate amount of time this takes, the method can miss significant interactions and can render the experiment weak or downright wrong. The "explain" step often attempts to explain and rationalize the results to fit the theory. There is no attempt to verify the improvement by turning the problem on and off.

Worker Involvement

Workers on the job know more about what is really going on than do engineers and managers who are too remote from the action. However, even workers have opinions and guesses that may prove to be wrong.

The authors have a rule: (1) Talk to the parts. (2) The next method is to talk to the workers on the firing line. (3) The least productive method is to talk to the engineers!

Behavioral scientists have indicated that the team concept is an excellent organizational building block. The Japanese, in particular, use teams under names, such as Quality Circles, Kaizen, and Small-Group Improvement Activities (SGIA). But for problem solving, workers in teams still need powerful tools. Without them, they spin their wheels and can get frustrated and demotivated.

The Ten Powerful Tools for the 21st Century[7]

If companies aspire to be world class, their leaders must understand, digest, disseminate, and direct the implementation of new, simple, but powerful tools that go well beyond the seven tools of QC, the seven Quality Management tools, the engineering approach, worker involvement, and 8-D. They are:

> ➤ Design of Experiments (DOE)
> ➤ Multiple Environment Over Stress Tests (MEOST)

> Quality Function Deployment (QFD)
> Total Productive Maintenance (TPM)
> Benchmarking
> Poka-Yoke
> Next Operation as Customer (NOAC)
> Supply Management
> Total Value Engineering
> Cycle-Time Reduction

Because the first tool—Design of Experiments—is the focus of the whole text, with almost all of the later chapters devoted to it, DOE will not be discussed in this chapter. Nor will the second tool—Multiple Environment Over Stress Test—be discussed in this chapter. It is so important a technique that it deserves a chapter by itself. The remaining eight tools are summarized in this chapter. A detailed treatment of each is beyond the scope of this book, but a brief treatment can guide the reader. For each tool, we highlight the applicable area, the need, the objective, the benefits, and the methodology, along with notes of caution, based on our own experience in using it.

Tool 3: Quality Function Deployment (QFD)—Capturing the Voice of the Customer[8]

Applicable Area

The customer-marketing-design interface at the concept stage of new products/services.

The Need

Product designs have been governed too long by the voice of the engineer and the voice of management, rather than by the voice of the customer. As a result, eight out of 10 new products end up on the ash heap of the market place. There is a saying: "You may have the best dog food in the world, but if the dogs don't eat it, what good is it?"

Objectives

1. Determine the customer's needs, requirements, and expectations before conceptual design is translated into prototype design.
2. Let the customer rate each requirement in terms of importance

and in terms of your performance on similar products versus those of your best competitors.

3. Based on the "House of Quality" matrix, determine the important, the difficult, and the new aspects of your design.
4. Deploy product specifications into part specifications, process specifications, and production specifications using similar House of Quality matrices.

Benefits

1. Design in half the time, with half the defects, half the cost, and half the manpower of previous comparable designs.
3. Move from customer disenchantment and mere satisfaction to customer excitement and loyalty.
3. Excellent evaluation of competitors.
4. Effective linkage between customer, design, manufacturing, and supplier.
5. Quick transfer of knowledge to new engineers.

Methodology

In QFD, the working tool is the House of Quality, depicted in Figure 3-1. On the far left, the customers' most relevant requirements (the what) are listed in order of importance. On the far right are the customers' evaluations of each requirement, with a rating of your company's performance versus competition. In the middle is a relationship matrix, comparing the linkage (strong, medium, or weak) between each customer requirement and each design specification (the how). A simple calculation then pinpoints those engineering specifications that must be concentrated on to meet both customer requirements as well as competitive strengths. At the bottom, there is a comparison of each specification against a target value and against competition, based on reverse engineering (competitive analysis). On the roof is a correlation matrix that shows whether each pair of engineering specifications has a reinforcing correlation or a conflicting correlation.

Similar House of Quality matrices are developed to translate the *what* of engineering specifications into the *how* of parts specifications, with similar translations cascading from parts to process, from process to production, from production to test, and from test to quality requirements.

Notes of Caution

1. Most QFD studies do not tap the requirements of core customers, which may be highly individual. Focus groups and clinics are not

Figure 3-1. House of Quality (Contact Lens)

NOWs vs. HOWs

Strong positive:	●	9
Weak positive:	○	3
Weak negative:	✖	–3
Strong negative:	✹	–9

WHATs vs. HOWs

Strong Relationship:	●	9
Medium Relationship:	○	3
Weak Relationship:	▲	1

		Power (Quality)	Optical Quality	Base Curve	Diameter	Thickness Profile	Edge Form	Surface Quality (Cosmetic)	Tint Centration	Tint Consistency	Engraving	Modulus	Flux	Deposit Resistance	X H2O (Dehydration)	Tear Strength	Peel Force	Saline PH, Toxicity	Degree of Importance	Company	Competitor 1	Competitor 2	
		1	2	3	4	5	6	7	8	9	10	11	12	13	14	15	16	17	1	2	3	4	
Good Vision	1	●	●	▲	▲			▲				▲	●	○					4.700	2.700	4.000	1.200	1
Comfort	2	○	▲	○	▲	○	▲	▲				▲		●	●			●	3.900	2.900	5.000	2.500	2
Physiology	3			○		○	▲	▲					●	●	○			●	3.800	2.000	2.000	2.800	3
Appearance	4								○	●									3.500				4
Handling	5					●					○					●			2.900	1.900	1.000	1.300	5
Convenience	6												●	○		○			2.300				6
Durability	7					▲	▲	▲						▲		○			0.800	1.600	2.000	0.900	7
Practitioner (Ease of Fit)	8	●	▲	●	○	○	▲	●	○	▲	▲	○											8
		1	2	3	4	5	6	7	8	9	10	11	12	13	14	15	16	17	1	2	3	4	

Source: Bhote, "A Powerful New Tool Kit. . . ."[7]

the answer. *The new discipline of mass customization is the best approach.* It determines the unique requirements of each core customer and then customizes its production, with information technology and computer integrated manufacturing where a quantity of one can be produced almost as cheaply as in mass production.

2. There is a tendency to concentrate mostly on performance requirements. Customers may be more interested in reliability, delivery, service, price, or other issues.
3. Too many QFD studies draw up a long and unmanageable "laundry list" of 40 to 70 requirements. The list should not exceed 20.
4. There is frequently more than one customer group, e.g., consumers, OEM manufacturers, and distributors. There may be conflicting requirements, necessitating separate QFD studies on each group.
5. The mechanics of filling in the House of Quality can be a "turnoff" for first-time QFD practitioners, who may be discouraged by the seeming complexity of this tool.
6. Ninety percent of QFD practitioners stop at the first cascade—translating the *what* of the customer requirements into the *how* of engineering specifications. Other cascades involve translating engineering specifications into arts, process, and test specifications.
7. Most QFD practitioners do not return to determine changing customer requirements and expectations as the design progresses from concept through prototype to pilot run. That can be a major "disconnect." There should be several QFD studies with the customer—at concept stage, prototype stage, and preproduction stage.

Tool 4: Total Productive Maintenance (TPM)—Improving Equipment Productivity[9]

Applicable Area

Manufacturing processes/equipment.

The Need

1. Maintenance costs range from 9 percent to 15 percent of the sales dollar.

2. "If it ain't broke, don't fix it" mentality is still widespread in industry.
3. Factory Overall Efficiency (FOE) (yield % × uptime % × machine efficiency %) is 40 to 50 percent in most U.S. companies. Machine efficiency is defined as run time divided by (run time + setup time).
4. Maintenance personnel in 50 percent of U.S. plants still spend more than half of their time fixing problems instead of preventing them.

Objectives

1. Radically improve process/equipment quality and productivity.
2. Improve plant throughput; reduce cycle time and inventories.
3. Establish worker-maintenance teams for preventing, not correcting, equipment problems.
4. Reduce life-cycle equipment costs.
5. Characterize and optimize processes and freeze key parameters with Positrol.

Benefits

1. Labor productivity increased by 40 to 50 percent.
2. Equipment breakdowns reduced by 90 percent.
3. Line capacity increased by 25 to 40 percent.
4. FOE increased to more than 85 percent.
5. Cost per unit of maintenance reduced by 60 percent.
6. Overall savings of 5 percent to 14 percent of the sales dollar.

Methodology

1. Improve product yields using Design of Experiments.
2. Improve uptime (i.e., reduce downtime) by using four important DOE tools: (a) Variable Search to characterize processes, (b) Scatter Plots to optimize processes, (c) Positrol to freeze processes, and (d) Process Certification to eliminate "noise" factors.
3. DOE experiments to increase process speed without sacrifice of product quality or equipment life.
4. Improve machine efficiency (i.e., run time/(run time and setup

time)) by setup time reductions of 50:1 or more, using well-established setup time reduction methods, such as flow charting, videotaping, intensive practice runs (as done by crew pits in auto racing), etc.

5. Establish operator-maintenance personnel teams to run DOE and other experiments to continuously increase FOE.
6. Encourage operators to perform more routine preventive maintenance, such as cleaning, lubrication, record-keeping, Positrol logs, and precontrol.
7. Train operators and maintenance personnel in problem-solving techniques, especially DOE, and in value engineering.
8. *Practice, practice, practice** to characterize and optimize key process parameters, reduce setup time, and run stress tests.
9. Establish good metrics to track FOE, mean-time-between failures (MTBF), and spare parts usage.
10. Promote predictive maintenance with diagnostics and alarm signals that can monitor key process variables, such as temperature, vibration, noise, and lubrication.

Notes of Caution

1. Give operators and maintenance workers powerful problem-solving tools, such as DOE, not weak tools, such as Cause-and-Effect diagrams, CEDAC, PDCA, etc.
2. In team-building, make sure up front that each member has a clear idea of benefits he or she will receive as a result of team progress.
3. Work with the suppliers of new equipment/processes in running joint DOE experiments on the factory floor and do not pay suppliers until very high yields are achieved before the start of full production. The suppliers will benefit by the joint improvement on their equipment, which could enhance their appeal to other customers.
4. Start process development at least six months to a year ahead of product development.

---

*A team of surgeons visited us at Motorola during our Six Sigma presentations, wanting to improve their productivity. One of the techniques discussed was benchmarking (tool 5). In examining who were the best in speed, the surgeons then visited a pit crew team at the Indy 500 car races, where they changed four tires in 12 seconds. The secret of their success was, they claimed, "practice, practice, practice." The surgeons then went back and examined every step of their surgical procedure. The result—a doubling of the number of surgeries per day, with actual increases in good health.

Tool 5: Benchmarking—Learning and Adapting From the Best[10]

Applicable Areas

Universal—manufacturing, business processes, services, public sector, and government.

The Need

1. Internal target setting and progress using internal goals is inadequate in terms of level and time.
2. A company is generally unwilling to learn from others—a "not invented here" (NIH) syndrome.
3. Benchmarking has not been perceived as an important corporate discipline.

Objectives

1. Benchmarking tied to key corporate strategies.
2. Closing the gap between a company and a "best-in-class" company in a key function, discipline, or technique.
3. Becoming "best in class" in a key function, discipline, or technique
4. Institutionalizing benchmarking as a way of life.

Benefits

1. Leap-frogging competition.
2. Shortening the cycle time of learning.
3. Excellent tool for quality, cost, and cycle-time improvement in products and services.
4. Converting tunnel vision into a global outlook.

Methodology: Twelve Steps in a Benchmarking Roadmap

1. Determine why and what to benchmark—tie in with key corporate strategies.
2. Establish your own company's performance as a baseline.
3. Conduct pilot runs in your own company (other divisions) and in nearby companies.
4. Determine whom to benchmark—nationally and globally.
5. Pay site visits to benchmark companies.

6. Determine the gap in performance between the benchmark company and your own.
7. Secure corporate commitment and buy-in by affected groups.
8. Establish goals and action plans.
9. Implement plans and monitor results.
10. Recalibrate/recycle the process.
11. Redesign the process *using "out of box" thinking*.
12. Become the benchmark.

Notes of Caution

1. Without a corporate steering committee and a benchmarking czar, the effort could lack focus and there could be organizational "disconnects."
2. There must be linkage between benchmarking and key business outcomes.
3. Involve the "internal customer" of the benchmarking study and secure cooperation and help from support services.
4. On-the-job training on benchmarking is more important than classroom training for team members.
5. It is mandatory to know your own company's baseline before benchmarking others.
6. Careful research is needed on which companies to benchmark. Noncompetitor companies are preferred, but do not hesitate to benchmark competitors as well.
7. A prior questionnaire should be pilot tested, and telephone interviews should precede site visits.
8. Make sure the right people are interviewed at the benchmark company. Pay attention to that company's failures as well as its successes.
9. Recycle the benchmarking process at least every one or two years.
10. Use the benchmark output as a spring board for further research and action on your own. There is always a way to improve another company's best performance.

Tool 6: Poka-Yoke—Eliminating Operator Controllable Errors[11]

Applicable Areas

Line operators in manufacturing.

The Need

1. All human beings make mistakes, no matter how much threatened or how well paid.

2. Line operators can cause quality problems in labor-intensive operation.

Objectives

Provide sensors—electrical, mechanical, or visual—that warn an operator that a mistake has been made or, preferably, is about to be made and can be avoided.

Benefits

1. Direct, fast, nonthreatening, nonupbraiding feedback to the operator.
2. Improved quality, throughput, and customer satisfaction.
3. The need for statistical process control virtually eliminated.
4. Better designs for easier manufacturability.

Methodology

This is best illustrated with an example (Figure 3-2).

Notes of Caution

1. The sensors should be simple, not complex Rube Goldberg designs.
2. The ingenuity of workers should be tapped to help design the sensors.
3. The best Poka-Yoke solutions are achieved through design of experiments to reduce variation or through design changes.

Before

Teflon powder was poured into a forming machine. The inner and outer diameters of the pressed powder pellets were consistent, but the thickness varied. A single worker had three machines to watch and could not control the thickness of the pellets as they passed through a chute.

After (Poka-Yoke Solution)

The specified thickness of the Teflon powder pellets is 10 mm ± 0.5 mm. A gauge/guide A is attached to the upper end of the chute. The

Figure 3-2. Example of Self-Check System

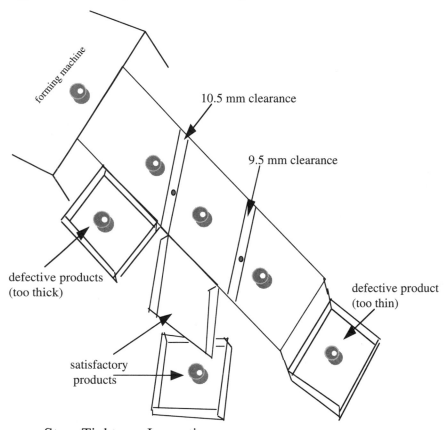

10.5 mm clearance

9.5 mm clearance

forming machine

defective products
(too thick)

defective product
(too thin)

satisfactory
products

Stem Tightener Inspection

Source: Bhote, "A Powerful New Tool Kit. . . ."[7]

space between gauge and the chute is set at 10.5 mm. Gauge/guide B is
attached to the lower end of the chute. The space between this gauge and
the chute is set at 9.5 mm. When the pressed pellet traveled down the
chute, pellets thicker than 10.5 mm cannot pass under gauge A and are
led by A into a defective bin at the left of the chute. Products thinner than
10.5 mm go onto gauge B, which passes pellets thinner than 9.5 mm into
another defective bin. Pellets between 10.5 mm and 9.5 mm are stopped
by gauge B and go on into a bin of acceptable parts.

Best Solution

Perform a DOE experiment to see why there is variation in pellet
thickness at the forming machine and prevent such variation.

Tool 7: Next Operation as Customer (NOAC)—White Collar Quality, Cost, and Cycle-Time Improvement[12,13]

Applicable Areas

All service organizations and support services in manufacturing companies.

The Need

1. Productivity in services is less than 40 percent (versus over 80 percent in manufacturing).
2. Quality is "off the screen" for most white-collar personnel.
3. Cycle time is "a foreign word" in any service operation.
4. U.S. national productivity is dragged down by the service sector.

Objectives

1. Improve quality, cost, and cycle time in all service operations.
2. Transform vertical management into horizontal management.
3. Break down departmental walls with cross-functional teams.
4. Revolutionize business processes.
5. In performance appraisals, replace boss evaluation with internal customer evaluation.

Benefits

1. Higher profits, ROI, market share, and productivity.
2. Greater customer satisfaction and loyalty through happy, productive workers.
3. Employee satisfaction and job excitement.
4. Greatly improved business processes.

Methodology: The 10 Step Roadmap for NOAC

1. Establish steering committee, process owner, and improvement teams.
2. Identify business/white-collar process problem; quantify impact on quality, cost, cycle time, and morale.

3. Identify major internal customers and their priority requirements; get agreement on internal suppliers' ability to meet these
   requirements from the methods of measurement.
4. Determine feedback frequency from internal customer as score-
   keeper as well as consequences of meeting or not meeting customer requirements.
5. Flow chart the entire "macro" process.
6. Determine the average cycle time for each step in the process and
   the total cycle time.
7. Separate the non–value-added steps from the value-added steps
   and estimate the reduction in steps and cycle time if the non–
   value-added steps could be removed.
8. Eliminate or reduce the non–value-added steps, using process
   improvement tools such as force field analysis, value engineering, DOE, process redesign, and job redesign.
9. *Using "out-of-box" thinking, value engineering, and creativity tools,
   examine the feasibility of a totally different approach to the business
   process or service, including its elimination.*
10. Conduct management reviews of internal customer scores and
    track progress against well-established business parameters.

Notes of Caution

1. NOAC is a step toward Business Process Re-engineering (BPR).
   But BPR is too far-out a concept to implement in its entirety. It
   means a virtual revolution in the way people are hired, evaluated,
   compensated, rewarded, and promoted. As a result, BPR is at least
   10 to 15 years away from full adoption by companies. NOAC is a
   practical bridge to this future and has been adopted by several
   leading companies.
2. Not much time should be spent on Steps 6, 7, and 8, because a
   totally different and revolutionary approach to the problem (Step
   9) could even eliminate the old process in its entirety.

Tool 8: Supply Management—Breakthrough for Supplier Quality, Cost, and Cycle-Time Improvement*,[14]

Applicable Areas

Key suppliers to form win-win partnerships.

*In its partnership dimensions, Supply Management is a management initiative,
but in its quality, cost, and cycle time dimensions, it is every bit a tool for supplier
development and growth.

The Need

1. Over 50 percent of the sales dollar is in materials from external suppliers, while only 3 percent is from direct labor.
2. Outsourcing is a trend as companies recognize that their concentration should be in *core competencies*, not in *all* areas of business activity.
3. The average price erosion in the marketplace is 2 percent to 7 percent per year (much higher in hi-tech products). Yet supplier charges to customer companies keep escalating at 5 percent per year. Eventually, this is a recipe for going out of business.
4. Companies confine purchases to piece parts. There is a much greater need to find subassembly and subsystem suppliers that can reduce valuable design-cycle time and costs.

Objective

1. Form real partnerships with key suppliers (over 90 percent of so-called partnerships are in name only) to fulfill mutual benefits.
2. Provide active, concrete help to suppliers to improve their quality, cost, and cycle time in return for reduced prices each year and early supplier involvement in design.

Benefits

1. Improve quality of partnership suppliers by factors of 10:1 and 100:1.
2. Reduce partnership supplier prices by an average of 5 percent per year, while helping them increase their profit margins.
3. Reduce partnership supplier lead time and raw material inventories by a factor of 10:1.
4. Enhance all-important customer-supplier mutual loyalty and retention.

Methodology

1. Establish a top management steering committee to guide this major corporate initiative of Supply Management.
2. Establish firm, meaningful, and mutually acceptable specifications with the partnership suppliers.

3. Establish an interdisciplinary commodity team for each major commodity to help the associated partnership suppliers in improving quality, cost, and cycle time in return for continued price reduction for the company.
4. Facilitate moves from "make" to greater "buy" piece-part procurement to "black box" procurement.
5. Facilitate early supplier involvement (ESI), parallel design development with the supplier, and cost targeting.

Notes of Caution

1. The company must not drive for supplier cost reduction by squeezing it out of the supplier. It must be a win-win solution, with continued lower prices for the company year by year and higher profits for the supplier year by year.
2. Both the company and the supplier should adhere to the highest standards of integrity and full trust.
3. Commodity team members must be thoroughly professional in quality, cost, and cycle-time improvement tools if they are to help in supplier development.
4. The partnership supplier should not be dumped at the first sign of weakness, but should be nurtured back to economic health.

Tool 9: Total Value Engineering—Going Beyond Traditional Value Engineering[15]

Applicable Areas

Design, Manufacturing, Services, and Suppliers. In fact, value engineering is so versatile that it can be applied to any economic activity.

The Need

1. Customers want value, not just price.
2. Spiraling labor, materials, and overhead costs.
3. Anemic profits.
4. Traditional cost reduction is mostly ineffective, because it keeps the product/service configuration the same.

Objectives

1. Go beyond cost reduction and beyond traditional value engineering.

2. Go beyond quality improvement to enhance all aspects of customer delight.
3. Strengthen every function within a company, a university, a government.
4. Provide an organizational framework for continuous, never-ending improvement.

Benefits

1. An average of 25 percent lower costs, a minimum of 10 percent.
2. A 10:1 return on investment.
3. Improved quality, reliability, and other elements of customer delight.
4. Conservation of resources and environment.

Methodology

A variety of disciplines, including value research, function analysis, the value engineering job plan, the "5 whys," job redesign, process redesign, and "out-of-box" thinking.

Notes of Caution

1. In the drive for lower costs, quality should never be sacrificed.
2. True customer requirements must be carefully assessed; specifications should not be blindly accepted.
3. All aspects of customer enthusiasm should be enhanced; the focus should not be on costs alone (Figure 3-3).
4. The suppliers should be made full partners in the total value engineering effort.

Tool 10: Cycle-Time Reduction—The Integrator of Quality, Cost, Delivery and Effectiveness[14]

Applicable Areas

Manufacturing, business services, and design.

The Need

1. There is wasted *time* in all areas of a company that translates into wasted *costs*.

Figure 3-3. Network of Elements of Customer Enthusiasm

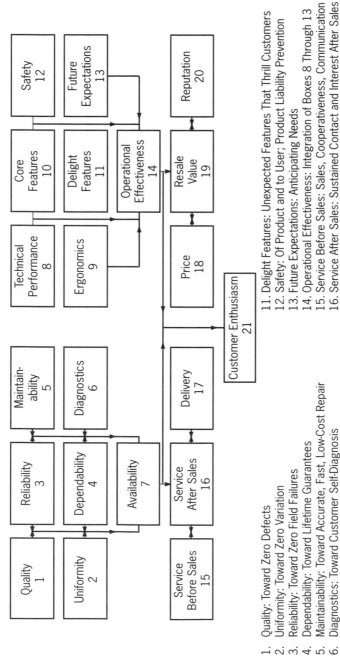

1. Quality: Toward Zero Defects
2. Uniformity: Toward Zero Variation
3. Reliability: Toward Zero Field Failures
4. Dependability: Toward Lifetime Guarantees
5. Maintainability: Toward Accurate, Fast, Low-Cost Repair
6. Diagnostics: Toward Customer Self-Diagnosis
7. Availability: Toward 100% Uptime
8. Technical Performance: State-of-the-Art Technology
9. Ergonomics: Styling, Color, Ease of Operation—"User Friendly"
10. Core Features: Expected by Customer
11. Delight Features: Unexpected Features That Thrill Customers
12. Safety: Of Product and to User; Product Liability Prevention
13. Future Expectations: Anticipating Needs
14. Operational Effectiveness: Integration of Boxes 8 Through 13
15. Service Before Sales: Sales, Cooperativeness, Communication
16. Service After Sales: Sustained Contact and Interest After Sales
17. Delivery: Short Cycle Time
18. Price: Cost Below Competition
19. Resale Value: High Percent of Purchase Price
20. Reputation: Image, Perceived Quality
21. Customer Enthusiasm: Value, Delight, Loyalty

Source: Keki R. Bhote, *Going Beyond Customer Satisfaction to Customer Loyalty,* New York: American Management Association, 1997.

2. Inventory reduction and cycle-time reduction have not been important to companies in the past because they do not show up in a P&L statement.
3. Companies protect delivery to customers with large safety stocks.

Objectives

1. Examine all areas of wasted time—waiting, setup, transport, storage, approval, inspection, test, etc. It is a war on all waste.
2. Use process mapping (flow charting), but more important, use "out-of-box" thinking to revolutionize manufacturing, business, and design processes.
3. Go to a "pull" versus "push" system.

Benefits

1. A company that gets a new product out to the marketplace faster has a decided edge over its competition.
2. Cycle time reductions of 10:1, even 100:1.
3. Inventory turns increased from 3:1 and 6:1 as much as 100:1.
4. When cycle time is reduced, quality, cost, delivery, and effectiveness are simultaneously improved.
5. As cycle time decreases, forecasting becomes less necessary and the old MRP-II system for scheduling is rendered obsolete.

Methodology

1. Reduce product defects, with techniques such as DOE, to reduce inspection time, test time, rework time, and "fire-fighting" time.
2. Improve factory overall efficiency using total productive maintenance (detailed in Tool 4 of this chapter).
3. Use a spider chart to plot the physical flow of product in a plant, and convert from a wasteful process flow to a productive flow.
4. Utilize a focused factory concept for concentration on a narrow range of customers, with a narrow range of products, with dedicated equipment and dedicated people.
5. Go to small lot sizes, with setup/changeover times reduced by a factor of 10:1, or even 100:1.
6. Utilize a "Kanban" pull system instead of master schedules and MRP-2.
7. Utilize manufacturing cells and u-shaped layouts.
8. Incorporate level-loading
9. Develop multiskilled operators.

10. Incorporate similar cycle-time reduction techniques with suppliers and with customers.

Notes of Caution

1. Start small in a limited area of the factory—the Wee Willy approach of a hit almost every time at bat versus the Babe Ruth occasional home run.
2. Clean up quality as a prerequisite to cycle-time reduction.
3. Practice, practice, practice setup time/changeover time reductions.
4. Cast off the shackles of MRP-II, master schedules, and an overreliance on the computer.
5. Measure bottom-line results—cycle time reductions, inventory turn improvements, return on investment (ROI) enhancements.

Awareness and Implementation of These 21st Century Tools

Here, then, is a powerful tool kit for companies that aspire to world class status. But what is the awareness of these tools and their percentage of implementation in average companies and among leading companies? An unscientific, but nevertheless perceptive, estimate conducted by the authors is shown in Table 3-3. Awareness of these powerful tools is dismal, even for the so-called leading companies, while implementation is downright pathetic. Industry, as the saying goes, "has a long, long way to go, baby!"

Table 3-3. Awareness and Implementation of the 21st Century Tool Kit

	Average Company		Leading Company	
Tool	Percent Aware	Percent Implementing	Percent Aware	Percent Implementing
1. Design of Experiments*	0.01	—	10.00	1.00
2. Multiple Environment Over Stress Tests	—	—	1.00	0.05
3. Quality Function Deployment	1.00	0.01	10.00	1.00
4. Total Productive Maintenance	5.00	0.02	15.00	3.00
5. Benchmarking	10.00	0.50	50.00	20.00
6. Poka-Yoke	1.00	—	10.00	1.00
7. Next Operation as Customer	0.10	—	3.00	0.10
8. Supply Management**	10.00	1.00	40.00	10.00
9. Total Value Engineering***	2.00	0.01	20.00	4.00
10. Cycle-Time Reduction	5.00	0.20	30.00	5.00

Source: Bhote, "A Powerful New Tool Kit. . . ."[7]
Notes:
*Design of Experiments refers to the Shainin approach, as outlined in this book, not the less effective classical or Taguchi approaches.
**Supply Management refers to true win-win partnership with key suppliers, and genuine, concrete, active help to them.
***Total Value Engineering goes beyond traditional value engineering (which concentrates on cost reduction) to include an enhancement of *all* elements of customer enthusiasm.

Part II

Preamble to the
Design of Experiments

4
....

The Measurement of
Process Capability

Why Variation Is Evil

Variation is inherent in Mother Nature. So it once seemed logical to believe that variation was equally inherent in the world of industry; that it
was inevitable; that nothing could be done about it. Yet today, we have a
new paradigm—that variation is evil, at least in industry; that it can be
drastically reduced with the new tools of design of experiments; that such
reduction can reduce costs, not add costs; and that it can enhance customer satisfaction.

A Football Analogy

Figure 4-1A is the old paradigm. As long as a unit was within an upper
specification limit and a lower specification limit, it was assumed that the
customer was satisfied. A football analogy is apropos. When kicking a
field goal, it does not matter where the ball lands, as long as it is between
the two goalposts. It could be close to one post or the other or in the
middle. The kicking team still gets the full field-goal point. We have this
football mentality in industry. Specifications become goalposts. If a unit
falls within specification limits and close to one edge, we assume that
a customer is satisfied. If another unit happens to fall just outside that
specification limit, we assume that customer satisfaction drops to zero. In
actual practice, there is nothing so digital about customer satisfaction.
Both units are on the ragged edge, marginal, unacceptable.

Figure 4-1B is the new paradigm. Customers want uniformity and
consistency in products they receive. A target value (usually in the middle
of a specification width) is the best. Any departure from such a target
value or design center represents an increasing economic loss, as a unit
moves toward one specification limit or the other—an economic loss to a

Figure 4-1. Specifications Limits versus Target Values

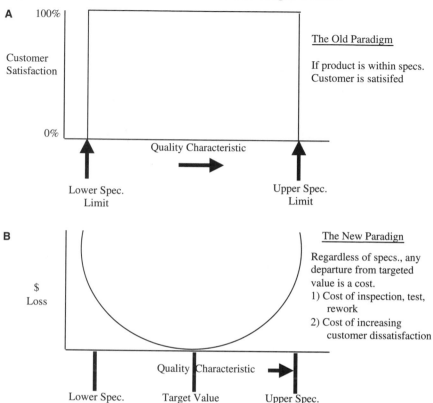

company, an economic loss to the customer, even an economic loss to society.

Case Studies

The Ford versus Mazda Case Study

This paradigm is illustrated by a famous Ford case study, now made into a videotape for training. Several years ago, Ford had a severe problem with its automatic transmission. It was noisy, had poor shifting characteristics, and generated many customer complaints and high warranty costs. Ford decided to compare its automatic transmission with Mazda's, which had exactly the opposite results—low noise, smooth shifting, no customer complaints, and very low warranty costs. Ford decided to take the two transmissions apart and compare them. They both had the same design, and the same specifications. Further, every Ford part met specifications. Then what was wrong? Ford found that its parts were all over the lot, some at one end of the specifications, some at another end, some in the middle. The Mazda parts, by contrast, were clustered tightly around a target value, a design center. As a result, Donald Peterson, then Ford Chairman, issued an edict to Ford engineers that they should design to a target value and not hide behind broad specification limits.

The Nippon Telegraph and Telephone Case Study

Nippon Telegraph & Telephone (N.T.T.), one of the largest government-owned companies in Japan, had six Japanese and one American supplier for its pagers. The maximum specification for sensitivity was 12 microvolts. The American supplier easily met that specification, its sensitivity ranging from 2 microvolts to 11. (The lower the number, the better.) N.T.T., however, wanted a consistent sensitivity level, regardless of specifications, so that every pager would have the same listening range. It indicated that two of its best Japanese suppliers had a narrow range—from 4 to 8 microvolts. N.T.T. stated flat out that if the American supplier could not match this narrow range for sensitivity, it would be forced to cancel the contract. In panic, the U.S. supplier set up a band-aid 100-percent sorting operation to select only those units with sensitivities between 4 and 8 microvolts—at a cost of $2 million! It then began a systematic effort, with this author's help, to reduce the sensitivity spread to 5 to 6.5 microvolts, using DOE techniques. The result? The U.S. supplier beat its six Japanese competitors and was declared N.T.T.'s No. 1 and preferred supplier.

The F-16 Fighter Jet Case Study

In recent years, a political decision was made to allow Japanese companies to build some of the F-16 fighter jets for the U.S. Defense Department. The specifications were exactly the same for suppliers in both countries. Yet, the field history has shown that the Japanese F-16s have a reliability (mean-time-between-failures) twice as high as the U.S. F-16s! The reason is that the U.S. units use the full spectrum of specification tolerances, while the Japanese strive for near zero variation. In fact, one of the lessons being learned in reliability is that the reduction of defects and of variation in production is an excellent way to assure reliability, even though there may not be an absolute, mathematical correlation between line defects and field reliability.

The Build-Up of Tolerances

If only a single part were to be considered, barely meeting specification limits might be marginally acceptable, but if two parts each occupy the full specification width, the total tolerance of the subassembly would exceed the allowable specification width. The reject level would be progressively worse in a subassembly of 5, 10, 20, or 50 parts. Unfortunately, just meeting specifications is so ingrained in the manufacturing psyche that it perpetuates a culture of needless inspection and test as well as costly rework and scrap.

The Enormous Cost of Inspection, Test, Rework, and Scrap

Aside from the huge loss of customer satisfaction, variation is evil because of the horrendous loss caused by poor quality. Eighty percent of companies are unaware of this metric, 15 percent do not measure it, 4 percent analyze it but do not reduce it, leaving 1 percent to turn it into bottom-line profit. The most basic elements of the cost of poor quality (COPQ) include warranty, scrap, analysis, rework, inspection, and test. None of them add value. They represent 10 to 20 percent of the sales dollar of a company. A study conducted by this author indicates that for a company that has not started the quality revolution, the cost of poor quality is $100 to $200 per employee per day. What a colossal waste. The best way to reduce these costs is by reducing variation through the design of experiments.

Introduction to Process Capability: C_p

Before examining the sources and causes of variation and their reduction, we must measure variation. Two yardsticks, C_p (meaning capability of a process) and C_{pk} (capability of a process, but corrected for noncentering) have become the standard language of quality at its most basic or parametric level in the last 20 years. Yet, even today, 30 percent of companies and 20 percent of quality professionals are unacquainted with C_p and C_{pk} or do not use it systematically to measure and reduce variation.

C_p is defined as the specification width (S) divided by the process width (P) or range. It is a measure of spread. Figure 4-2 depicts six frequency distributions comparing the specification width (always $40 - 20 = 20$) to varying process widths.

Process A in Figure 4-2 has a process width of 30, giving a C_p of 0.67. It is a process that is out of control, with 2.5 percent defect tails at both ends. This used to be the norm for companies (the very few that measured

Figure 4-2. C_p—A Measure of Variation

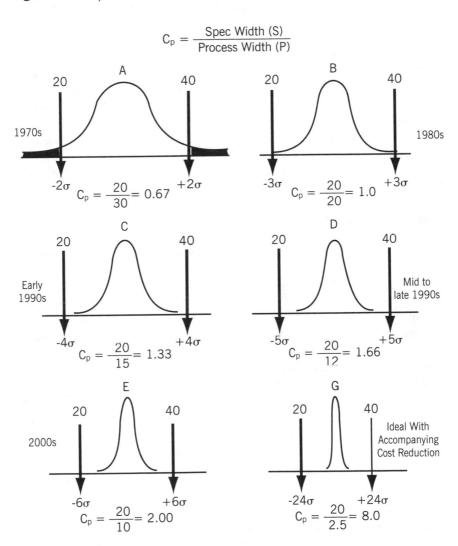

$$C_p = \frac{\text{Spec Width (S)}}{\text{Process Width (P)}}$$

A

1970s

20   40

$-2\sigma \quad C_p = \frac{20}{30} = 0.67 \quad +2\sigma$

B

1980s

20   40

$-3\sigma \quad C_p = \frac{20}{20} = 1.0 \quad +3\sigma$

C

Early 1990s

20   40

$-4\sigma \quad C_p = \frac{20}{15} = 1.33 \quad +4\sigma$

D

Mid to late 1990s

20   40

$-5\sigma \quad C_p = \frac{20}{12} = 1.66 \quad +5\sigma$

E

2000s

20   40

$-6\sigma \quad C_p = \frac{20}{10} = 2.00 \quad +6\sigma$

G

Ideal With Accompanying Cost Reduction

20   40

$-24\sigma \quad C_p = \frac{20}{2.5} = 8.0 \quad +24\sigma$

Note: (Upper spec. limit = 40; lower spec. limit = 20)

them) in the 1970s, before the age of Statistical Process Control (SPC). Sadly, even today 30 percent of companies are at or below a C_p of 0.67 for important parameters. They compensate for such an out-of-control condition with brute-force sorting, scrap, and rework.

Process B has the process width equal to the specification width to give a C_p of 1.0. It is a marginal condition, at best, for two reasons: (1) It still has a defect tail of 0.13 percent or 1,300 parts per million (ppm) at each end. In today's competitive world where companies are establishing upper limits for their rejects at 100 ppm, 10 ppm and even parts per billion (ppb), 1,300 ppm is a statistic for the dark ages. (2) Any slight shift in centering the process will cause a marked rise in reject levels. Process B was typical of companies in the 1980s. SPC was the rage. The U.S. automotive industry embraced SPC wholesale in its quest for quality. Yet, until the mid-1990s, it was mired in C_p's of 1.0. So much for our much-vaunted SPC.

Process C, with a C_p of 1.33, is somewhat better, in that it has a guard-band between the tighter process limits and the specification limits. It is typical of moderately progressive companies in the early 1990s. QS-9000—the quality standard developed by the Big 3 U.S. automotive companies—requires a C_{pk} of 1.33 as a minimum from their automotive suppliers, even though their own plants fail to meet that requirement! Hypocritical? You bet.

Process D, with a C_p of 1.66, has an even wider safety margin between process limits and specification limits. Only a few companies have reached this level in the mid-to-late 1990s.

Process E, with a C_p of 2.0 allows the process width to be only half the specification width. It is rapidly becoming the universal standard for quality for the first decade of the 21st century, even though only a handful of world class companies have achieved it today. (This author, while at Motorola's Automotive and Industrial Electronics Group, achieved a C_p of 2.0 on important quality parameters as far back as 1984.)

Another metric directly related to C_p is Sigma (or standard deviation). Table 4-1 shows the relationship between C_p, Sigma and the associated defects levels. This is the true statistical meaning of Six Sigma, not the statistical dribble of 3.4 ppm for an unknowing public, but a goal of two parts per billion (ppb).

Process F, with a C_p of 8.0 (or $\pm 24\sigma$) is not only the ideal, but it is also

Table 4-1. C_p, Sigma, and Defect Levels

C_p	Sigma (s)	Defect Levels
0.67	$\pm 2\sigma$	5%
1.0	$\pm 3\sigma$	0.13%
1.33	$\pm 4\sigma$	60 ppm
1.66	$\pm 5\sigma$	1 ppm
2.0	$\pm 6\sigma$	2 ppb
		(parts per billion)

Source: Motorola: Six Sigma Seminars.

attainable and lower in overall cost. In fact, there is no limit to higher and higher C_p's which can reach 10, 15, and more, as long as there are not recurring costs added to the product or process and only the cost of DOE is incurred—as an investment. *It has been our experience that, with higher C_p's, not only are costs not added, they are actually reduced. Furthermore, the time it takes to go from C_p's of 1.0 or less to C_p's of 2.0 or more is not measured in years and months, but in weeks and days, generally with no more than one, two, or three well-constructed DOE.*

C_{pk}, A Better Measure of Variation and Process Capability

C_p is used only as a simple introduction to the concept of process capability. It does not take into account any noncentering of the process relative to the specification limits of a parameter. Such noncentering reduces the margin of safety and therefore has a penalty imposed, called a K or correction factor. The formulas are:

$$C_p = S/P$$

$$K = \frac{D - \overline{X}}{X/2} \text{ or } \frac{\overline{X} - D}{S/2} \text{ (whichever makes } K \text{ positive)}$$

$$C_{pk} = (1 - K) C_p$$

where:
S = specification width; P = process width ($\pm 3\sigma$ limits);
D = design center (D need not be at the midpoint of the specification width); $\overline{X}$ = process average.

When the process average, $\overline{X}$, and the design center, D, or target value, coincide, K is reduced to zero, making C_p and C_{pk} equal. If, however, the process average is skewed toward one end or the other of a specification limit, away from the design center, the value of K increases, causing a decrease in C_{pk} relative to C_p.

This is illustrated in Figure 4-3. In it, Panel A has a wide spread, with a C_p of 0.71. Because its design center, D, and its average $\overline{X}$, coincide, the C_p and C_{pk} values are the same at 0.71. Panel B has a narrow spread, with a respectable C_p of 2.5. But because it is located close to the lower specification limit, the K factor penalizes it to give a poor C_{pk} of 1.0. Panel C has a broader spread than Panel B, with a lower C_p of 1.67. But it is closer to the design center, D, than is Panel B and so the K factor has less of a penalty, resulting in a C_{pk} of 1.33, better than that of Panel B. Panel D is ideal, with both a very narrow spread and a centered process, to give a C_p and C_{pk} of 5.0.

Figure 4-3. Process Capability

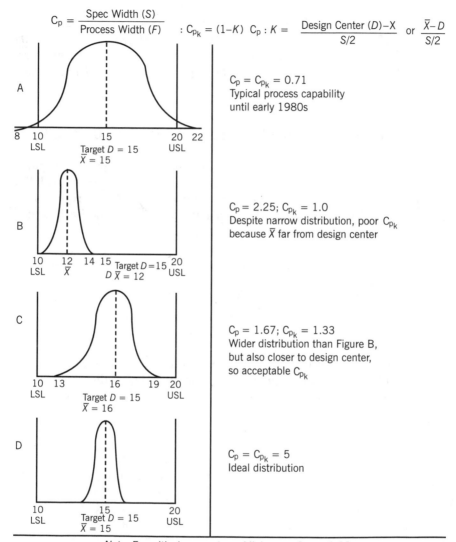

$$C_p = \frac{\text{Spec Width }(S)}{\text{Process Width }(F)} \quad : C_{p_k} = (1-K)\ C_p : K = \frac{\text{Design Center }(D) - X}{S/2} \quad \text{or} \quad \frac{\bar{X}-D}{S/2}$$

A

8   10   15   20 22
LSL   Target $D = 15$ USL
        $\bar{X} = 15$

$C_p = C_{p_k} = 0.71$
Typical process capability
until early 1980s

B

10   12 14 15 Target $D = 15$ 20
LSL $\bar{X}$ $D\ \bar{X} = 12$ USL

$C_p = 2.25;\ C_{p_k} = 1.0$
Despite narrow distribution, poor C_{p_k}
because $\bar{X}$ far from design center

C

10 13   16   19 20
LSL   Target $D = 15$ USL
      $\bar{X} = 16$

$C_p = 1.67;\ C_{p_k} = 1.33$
Wider distribution than Figure B,
but also closer to design center,
so acceptable C_{p_k}

D

10   15   20
LSL   Target $D = 15$ USL
     $\bar{X} = 15$

$C_p = C_{p_k} = 5$
Ideal distribution

Note: For critical parameters: Minimum $C_{p_k} = 1.33$
                              Desirable $C_{p_k} = 2.0$
                              Ideal $C_{p_k} = 5.00$

A simpler formula for C_{pk}, and one especially useful for a single-sided specification limit, is:

$$C_{pk} = \frac{\overline{X} - \text{nearest specification limit}}{1/2 \text{ process width}}$$

or

$$= \frac{\text{nearest specification limit} - \overline{X}}{1/2 \text{ process width}}$$

whichever makes C_{pk} positive.

C_{pk} is an excellent measure of variability and process capability because it takes into account both spread and non-centering. (In process control, centering a process is much easier than reducing spread. Centering requires only a simple adjustment, whereas spread reduction often requires the patient application of design of experiment techniques.) As in C_p, the objective should be to attain a higher and higher C_{pk}, with a C_{pk} of 2.0 considered merely as a passing milestone on the march past zero defects to near-zero variation.

Pitfalls to Avoid in C_p, C_{pk} Measurements

Pitfall 1. Measuring All Parameters

A common mistake made by companies anxious to get started in a C_p culture is to measure all product parameters, regardless of their importance. This practice adds costs, not value. Only the most important parameters need a C_p of 2.0 and more. The rest do not matter. Their C_p's can be 1.0 or even 0.5 and, for the most part, do not even need to be measured. To distinguish between important and unimportant parameters, engineering guesswork is not the answer. A design of experiments, using Variables Search as the primary technique, should be conducted at the design stage of a product or process (see Chapter 13).

Pitfall 2. Measuring C_p, C_{pk} Constantly

Another overzealous weakness is to measure C_p, C_{pk} on a given set of parameters constantly. A C_p measurement is either good or bad—above 2.0 or well below 2.0. If the former, process capability has been proven and does not need to be constantly remeasured; it can be monitored with precontrol (see Chapter 21). If the C_p is much less than 2.0, the parameter is out of control. Measuring it repeatedly will not magically bring it within control. The technique to use is DOE.

A major, reputable manufacturer, enamored of C_p measurements, dictated that each of its several plants measure C_p and C_{pk} on over 200 parameters every week and report them to corporate headquarters. The C_p's were in the range of 1.0 to 1.3—all well below their minimum of 1.66. If a particular C_p dropped from 1.3 to 1.2, the plant would have to come up with a tortured explanation of what had gone wrong! This author, as a consultant to the company, was instrumental in replacing the program with a major DOE effort, which saved the company hundreds of thousands of dollars and reduced variation (and only on parameters that were truly important).

Pitfall 3. If Specification Limits Are Not Correct, C_p and C_{pk} Are Meaningless

C_p and C_{pk} are based on specification limits. If the latter are not correct, C_p and C_{pk} values are wrong and meaningless. As will be shown in the chapter on Scatter Plots, 90 percent of specifications developed by engineers are either too tight or too loose, and invariably wrong. When qualifying a product or process, the important parameters must be separated from the unimportant ones, using Variables Search. Next, the required tolerances and specification limits for the important parameters must be determined using Scatter Plots. Only then can C_p and C_{pk} be realistically determined.

Pitfall 4. Extending C_p Measurements to Suppliers Without Doing So in Your Own Company

There is a saying: "Those who can, do. Those who can't, teach." Several companies require high C_p's from their suppliers when they themselves do not measure C_p's or reach the C_p levels they demand from their suppliers. The Big 3 automotive companies are a notorious case in point. Under QS-9000, they require a minimum C_p of 1.33 from their first tier automotive suppliers. (Moves are afoot to revise QS-9000 to demand C_p's of 1.66, and even 2.0.) Yet, most of their own automotive plants do not measure C_p's or reach a C_p level of 1.33. Ford especially is known within the supplier industry for its attitude of "Do as I say, not as I do!"

Workshop Exercise 1: The Press Brake

A press brake is set up to produce a formed part to a dimension of 3" ± 0.005". A process capability study reveals that the process limits are at

3.002″ ± 0.006″, i.e., at a minimum of 2.996″ and a maximum of 3.008″. After corrective action, the process limits are brought under control to 3.001″ ± 0.002″.

Questions

> *Question 1.* Calculate the C_p and C_{pk} of the old process.
> *Question 2.* Calculate the C_p and C_{pk} of the corrected process.

Answers

> *Question 1.* Specification width (S) = 0.010″; process width (P) = 0.012″

$$\text{So } C_p = S/P = 0.10/0.012 = 0.833$$
$$\overline{X} = 3.002″; \text{ design center } (D) = 3.000″$$
$$\text{So } K = \frac{\overline{X} - D}{S/2} = \frac{3.002 - 3.000}{0.005} = \frac{0.002}{0.005} = 0.4$$

> *Question 2.* Specification width (S) = 0.010″; process width (P) = 0.004″

$$\text{Therefore } C_{pk} = (1 - 0.4)\,0.833 = 0.5$$
$$\text{So } C_p = S/P = 0.10/0.004 = 2.5$$
$$\overline{X} = 3.001″; \text{ Design Center } (D) = 3.000″$$
$$\text{So } K = \frac{\overline{X} - D}{S/2} = \frac{3.001 - 3.000}{0.005} = \frac{0.001}{0.005} = 0.2$$

Therefore $C_{pk} = (1 - K)\,C_p = (1 - 0.2)\,2.5 = 2.0$

Using the simpler and alternate formula for C_{pk}:

$$\text{In Question 1: } C_{pk} = \frac{3.005 - 3.002}{0.006} = \frac{0.003}{0.006} = 0.5$$

$$\text{In Question 2: } C_{pk} = \frac{3.005 - 3.001}{0.002} = \frac{0.004}{0.002} = 2.0$$

Workshop Exercise 2: Supplier Tolerances versus Cost*

A manufacturer placed an order with his supplier for a part with a tolerance of ± 5 percent. The manufacturer's management had instructed the

*This workshop exercise was the result of the problem being presented by the company to this author. The solution recommended by me was carried out brilliantly by the DOE team working with the supplier.

purchasing department to find the lowest price. Accordingly, in negotiations with the supplier, the latter offered a price reduction per part of 10 percent if the tolerance could be opened up to ± 10 percent and a price reduction of 25 percent if the tolerance could be further expanded to ± 20 percent. The supplier's rationale and current process spread is shown in Figure 4-4.

The engineering department insisted, however, that the ± 5 percent tolerance was sacred in order to meet customer requirements. The customer concurred. What course of action should be followed?

1. Accept the tolerance of ± 5 percent at the higher price?
2. Challenge the engineering department to prove that ± 5 percent is essential?
3. Ignore the engineering department and accept the higher tolerance of ± 10 percent for a 10 percent reduction?
4. Ignore the engineering department and accept the higher tolerance of ± 20 percent for a 25 percent reduction?
5. Any other action?

Answer

There are two approaches in resolving the dilemma of the purchasing department.

First, it is always appropriate to challenge any engineering specification and tolerance. A Scatter Plot (see the chapter on Scatter Plots) should be conducted to determine the broadest parameter tolerance that would accommodate the specification tolerances established by the customer.

Figure 4-4. Supplier Tolerances versus Cost

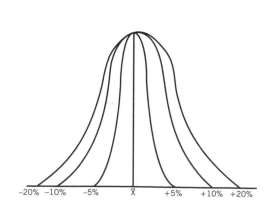

Tolerance
± 5%
± 10%
± 20%

Price
Y
Y − 10%
Y − 25%

−20% −10%   −5%   X̄   +5%   +10% +20%

Second, assuming that the tolerance of ±5 percent indicated by engineering is correct, Figure 4-4 clearly indicates that the supplier has too much variation in his product. The only way to give the customer tighter tolerances is through testing and sorting, detection and correction, scrap and rework—all non–value-added operations.

The solution was for the manufacturer to go to the supplier, train him in DOE techniques and work with him on the process associated with this part, so that a tolerance of ±5 percent was easily attained. Then the company asked for a reduction of not just 25 percent but 30 to 35 percent in cost. The rationale was that the supplier was able to eliminate his scrap and rework, drastically reduce his inspection and test, reduce his cycle time and work in process inventory, reduce his space requirement, and increase his throughput. The profits were equitably divided.

Workshop Exercise 3:
Customized Matching of Light Emitting Diodes (LEDs)

A supplier of light emitting diodes (LEDs) had a very wide variation in the LEDs. To match this variation in the LEDs, the customer had to segregate the supplier's LEDs into:

1. Five bins for varying light intensity.
2. Three bins for varying forward voltage—V_f.
3. Two bins for temperature variations.
4. Three bins for varying wavelength (color).

This meant that the customer had to store a total of 90 bins, from which LEDs had to be selected to meet the customer's end requirements! What actions should the customer and supplier take to eliminate this excessive customization?

Answer

This travesty perpetuated by the supplier on the customer should not be allowed to continue. There is too much variation in these LEDs on all four outputs (or Green Y's, as will be explained in the next chapter). The customer must either find a better supplier or, if this is the state of the art for this type of LED and there is no better supplier, the customer must train the supplier in DOE techniques. Then they must conduct DOE experiments at the supplier's facility on each Green Y to reduce variation and produce an LED with uniform intensity, uniform forward voltage, uniform temperature, and uniform wavelength—with a C_{Pk} of 2.0 minimum for each of these quality characteristics. *The final outcome should be a price reduction for the customer* and no more than one or two bins versus the current 90.

Questions for Top Management

1. Are the specifications truly derived from customer requirements?
2. Are target values (design centers) a long-term objective in reducing variation?
3. Is a minimum C_{pk} of 2.0 a goal for important parameters?
4. Are C_p, C_{pk} measurements made just once or twice to determine if a process is capable or not capable?
6. If the process is capable, is SPC (precontrol) the next step?
7. If the process is not capable, is DOE undertaken?
8. Are C_{pk}'s of 2.0 specified as a minimum on supplier drawings and specifications?
9. Are suppliers given active, concrete help in reducing variation?
10. In return for the above help, are supplier cost reductions demanded and obtained, while achieving higher supplier profits at the same time?

5

Variation: An Industrial Epidemic

The Many Sources of Variation

Chapter 4 quantified variation with the introduction of C_p and C_{pk}. But measuring variation does nothing to reduce it. The many causes of variation in industry should be described before a systematic attack on variation is mounted. Variation is so widespread in industry that it can be likened to an epidemic. The new quality mission, therefore, is to inoculate products and processes against variation. In fact, the main duty for all technical people—development engineers, process engineers, quality professionals, technicians, and maintenance personnel—is the systematic reduction of variation.

This chapter will outline the many sources of variation, their underlying causes, and the general approaches to variation reduction. Table 5-1 presents a capsule summary. The major sources of variation can be grouped into six categories: (1) poor management, (2) poor product/process specifications, (3) poor component specifications, (4) inadequate quality system, (5) poor manufacturing practices, (6) poor supplier materials, and (7) "operator" errors.

Poor Management

Deming and Juran assert that 85 percent of quality problems are caused by management and only 15 percent by workers on the line. They are being kind to management: The split is actually closer to 95 to 5. Although there are many dimensions to the quality problems caused by management, the following are some of its sins of omission and commission with respect to variation.

Table 5-1. Sources, Causes, and Reduction of Variation

Source	Causes of Variation	Variation Reduction
Poor Management	> No knowledge of or policy on variation reduction > No resources or time allocated to DOE > No championship or involvement in DOE > No DOE training or implementation > SPC and control charts, especially for problem solving	> Top management training in DOE overview > Management steering committee for DOE > DOE training and workshops for tech. population > Monitoring the DOE process rather than just goals and results
Poor Product/Process Specs.	> Not capturing the voice of the customer > Selling over marketing > Pushing state-of-art designs > Wide tolerances vs. target values > Reliability not a specification > No DOE in systems testing	> Quality function deployment and mass customization > Evolutionary vs. revolutionary designs > Target values and DOE to achieve them > Optimizing old equipment, not junking it > Multiple environment over stress tests for reliability > Extension of DOE in customer application > Total productive maintenance
Poor Component Specs.	> Fascination with technology > Indiscriminate and tight tolerances > Boilerplate specs; supplier-published specs. > Monte Carlo and worst-case analysis > Formulas linking variables nonexistent, wrong, or unable to determine interaction effects	> DOE techniques at pilot run stage to separate important variables from unimportant ones > Realistic tolerance parallelogram (scatter) plots

Inadequate Quality Tools and System	> ISO-9000, QS-9000, Malcolm Baldrige, European Quality Award, and TQM are all inadequate > Quality peripherals overlooked	> Infrastructure of a "Big Q" quality system > Positrol, Process Certification, Pre-Control
Poor Manufacturing Practices	> Standard operating procedures: inadequate/too difficult > Inadequate preventive maintenance > No environmental controls > Metrology inadequate	> Worker involvement in formulation of standard operating procedures > Total Productive Maintenance > See Chapter 19
Poor Supplier Materials	> Too many suppliers > Control by negotiations and table pounding > AQL, incoming inspection	> "Best in class" partnership supplier > Physical proximity, continuous help > DOE training > C_{pk} of 2.0 as a minimum
"Operator" Errors	> Poor instructions, training > Poor processes, materials, equipment > Design for nonmanufacturability > External inspection > "Pair of hands" syndrome	> Training in DOE > Encouragement, support, management involvement > Self-inspection and poka-yoke (mistake proofing) > Gain sharing > Empowerment

> Lack of knowledge about the impact of variation on overall quality, costs, cycle time, and profit.
> No coherent policy on variation reduction.
> No resources or time allocated to DOE, but unlimited quantities of both expended on fire fighting.
> No leadership in variation reduction in terms of goals, sponsorship, championship, or involvement.
> No DOE training or no follow-up of training with implementation.
> Equating of quality progress with SPC and control charts.

How very different from an enlightened management philosophy, as illustrated by an internal memo from William Scollard, vice-president of engineering and manufacturing at Ford: "Our new quality thinking should be reduced process variability around the nominal as an operating philosophy for never-ending quality improvement."

The attack on variability in management must begin with an understanding of the economics of variation reduction. It requires a top management steering committee to launch training in DOE, followed by workshops and "learning by doing" for the technical people. The committee should also be involved in the DOE process for improvement and not just limit itself to formulating high-sounding goals and tracking results in sterile operation reviews.

Poor Product/Process Specifications

Most product specifications are either vague, arbitrary, or wrong. Occasionally, an important quality characteristic requirement is missing, its relevance never even having been suspected. Process specifications are even worse!

A major cause of this variation lies in the difference between selling and marketing. In selling, management or the engineer determines product requirements in isolation and then forces the product down the throats of customers through slick advertising and other high-pressure tactics. In marketing, the company first makes a painstaking effort to explore what the customer wants and then designs products to fit those needs. It is tragic that 80 years after Julius Rosenwald and Robert Wood laid the foundations of marketing and on them built Sears Roebuck into a giant merchandiser, most American companies still "sell" rather than "market" their products. The worst crime in this source of variation is to design and build products efficiently, even with zero defects, that the customer does not want!

"The voice of the engineer" must be replaced by the "voice of the customer." The latter is then translated into meaningful product specifications through use of tools such as quality function deployment (QFD) and mass customization.

Other reasons for poor product/process specifications are:

> The engineer's ego in creating a state-of-the-art design with his name etched onto it in perpetuity;
> Use of broad specification limits and tolerances rather than a focus on target values or design centers for product/process parameters;
> Infrequent use of reliability—in mean time between failures (MTBF) or mean time between assists (MTBA)—as a specification; and
> Lack of systems testing in the customer's application with a DOE approach to identify important and interacting variables.

The variation reduction antidotes are to:

> Use an evolutionary, rather than a revolutionary, approach to product/process design, one in which no more than a fourth of the design is changed at a given time;
> Establish target values;
> Save and optimize old processes through DOE, rather than junk them in favor of capital-intensive new equipment with its own host of problems;
> Utilize multiple environment overstress tests as the most powerful tool in reducing product/process variations in reliability; and
> Extend DOE to field testing at the customer's site.

Poor Component Specifications

Even assuming that product specifications have been optimized as shown above, there is another major pitfall, the inadequate conversion of product specifications into component specifications. The reasons are:

> Engineering's fascination with technology;
> Engineering's proclivity for tight tolerances;
> Engineering's reliance on previous component drawings, boiler-plate requirements, or supplier's published specifications;
> Reliance on the computer for determining component's tolerances. This can only be done if the formula governing the relationship between the output (or dependent variable) and the independent component variables is known. In many complex designs, involving scores of independent variables, developing a formula is well-

nigh impossible. This is a major weakness in many Monte Carlo simulation exercises.

➢ A worst-case analysis and design with an extremely low probability of occurrence in actual practice. This is an appreciable addition to cost with no value added.

➢ No way of having knowledge of an unknown, synergistic interaction effect between or among component variables, even when there is a mathematical formula for the relationships between variables.

All these excess variations can be overcome—at the prototype, engineering pilot run, or production pilot run stage—by well-designed experiments, fully detailed in Part III, that can pinpoint the important variables, their ideal values (or levels), and their realistic tolerances.

Inadequate Quality Tools and Systems

The inadequacy of more traditional quality tools has been discussed in Chapter 3. Table 5-2 is a list of both the traditional quality tools and the three DOE tools in terms of effectiveness (1 = worst, 100 = best). It indicates that the Shainin DOE tools are at least 20 to 40 times as effective as the traditional tools and 3 to 5 times as effective as the classical and Taguchi DOE tools. Similarly, the inadequacy of various quality systems has been described in Chapter 2.

Poor Manufacturing Practices

This category is so important that a whole chapter—Process Certification—is devoted to it. *In fact, we strongly recommend that a Process Certifica-*

Table 5-2. Relative Effectiveness of Various Quality Tools

Quality Tool	Effectiveness Scale
Seven Tools of QC	3
Seven Management QC Tools	2
SPC	5
Design of Experiments	
Classical	30
Taguchi	20
Shainin	100

Note: Scale: 1 = worst; 100 = best.

tion "scrub"—an audit, along with remedial action—be initiated both before the start of a DOE project and at the end of such a DOE study.

Poor Supplier Materials

Next to design, variations in supplier materials contribute the most to poor quality. The traditional approach of having multiple suppliers for the same part to assure quality, delivery, and cost is obsolete and counterproductive. So are negotiations, table pounding, and quality improvement by fiat and by remote control. So are AQL, sampling plans, quality audits, and incoming inspection. The only way to improve supplier quality and to reduce variability is to adhere to the following steps:

> ➤ Ascertain that the supplier is both committed to improvement and capable of entering into a long-term partnership with you;
> ➤ Demonstrate, first, that your own company is highly professional in the field of quality in general and in DOE in particular;
> ➤ Select a supplier who is near you and is small enough and hungry enough to accept your professional coaching in DOE techniques;
> ➤ Specify minimum C_{pk}'s of 2.0 and more for important parameters, bypassing the useless milestones of AQLs, ppms, sampling plans, and postmortem incoming inspection; and
> ➤ Provide active, concrete help in quality, cost, and cycle-time improvement in return for continuous price reductions.

Operator Errors

Operator variations and inconsistencies are the causes of quality problems most frequently cited by orthodox management. Such citations, however, almost always reflect a general ignorance of quality—management at its quality worst. Worker defects are only the effects. The underlying causes are more likely to be:

> ➤ Poor instructions, goals, training, and supervision;
> ➤ Poor processes, materials, and test equipment;
> ➤ Poor design for manufacturability;
> ➤ Use of external inspection as a crutch; and
> ➤ Assumption that workers are but "pairs of hands," hired from the neck down.

When these roadblocks to quality work are removed, workers—ninety-nine percent of whom are well-motivated to begin with—will almost always come through with sterling performance. The steps to variation reduction in this area, in general terms, are encouragement, support, the elimination of fear, and management's mingling among and active involvement with the workers. Financial incentives for improved performance, such as gainsharing, should also be given serious consideration.

In specific terms, there should be a concerted move from external inspection to neighbor inspection and eventually, self-inspection, aided by poka-yoke (mistake proof) methods, such as the use of automatic equipment and sensors to buttress visual checks. More important, workers can skip being trained in seven tools of QC as practiced widely by Japanese line workers; instead, they can be trained in the even easier DOE tools described in Part III. It has been our experience that some of the most adventurous and rewarding DOE work has been conducted by line workers and technicians, once trained, rather than by their more cautious and conservative engineering counterparts.

6

The Three Approaches to DOE: Classical, Taguchi, and Shainin

Ineffective Approaches to Problem Solving and Variation Reduction

Chapter 4 measured variation. Chapter 5 outlined the sources of variation. But measuring variation does nothing to reduce it. Using an analogy from the world of dieting, thousands get on their weight scales each day to fight the battle of the bulge. But if measurement alone could do the trick, Americans would be the thinnest people on earth! Weight reduction is much harder. So is variation reduction.

There have been several traditional approaches to variation reduction; all ineffective.

1. *Engineering judgment* has been used for nearly a century. But if it is that effective, why have we had chronic quality problems, some lasting for weeks, some for months, some for years? Some of these problems have two to four birthday candles lit on them. Some are old enough to vote! One of our clients had a quality problem so old that it could have applied for Social Security!

2. *Computer simulation* is the latest fad in problem solving. We have the older Monte Carlo simulation, the E-chip, and a host of other software programs, all purporting to get to root-cause solutions. But for computers to be effective, the mathematical equation governing the relationship between independent variables and the dependent variable must be known. If that equation or formula is unknown, the computer cannot be programmed. Unfortunately, for many complex products or processes, even an Einstein could not develop such an equation. As an example, some

scientists, with their mathematical models, predict that temperatures will rise in the next 100 years and create global warming catastrophes. Other scientists, with their "crystal ball" models, predict another ice age in the same time period. The chances are, between all these computer simulation predictions, that we earthlings will continue to be comfortable for the next 100 years!

3. *Statistical Process Control (SPC)* has been perceived as the silver bullet for improving quality. But SPC is only a monitoring tool, not a problem-solving tool. It is like hanging a meter on a process. The meter is only a visual indicator. It does not problem-solve or improve a process. SPC should only be used after a problem has been solved, not before.

4. *Ford 8-D,* detailed in Chapter 3, provides, at best, an administrative framework for problem solving. It is woefully lacking in the "how to" of problem solving. It does not provide the specific tools required to do the job. The famous PDCA cycle is an even more primitive framework.

5. *Kepner-Tragoe.* Some companies have latched on to so-called detective methods, taught by Kepner-Tragoe facilitators. Kepner-Tragoe may be an acceptable method of writing detective novels, but it is no substitute for industrial problem solving.

Background on the Three Approaches to DOE

That leaves Design of Experiments as the best way to solve chronic quality problems and reduce variation. There are three approaches.

Classical DOE

This approach is based on the pioneering work of Sir Ronald Fisher, who applied DOE to the field of agriculture as early as the 1920s. It is difficult to conceive of an application that has as many variables as agriculture—soil, rain, water, sun, climate, seed, fertilizer, terrain, etc. Yet Fisher, using only the full factorial method, improved the productivity of the British farm and was knighted for his great contribution. In fact, Fisher, who used DOE to reduce variation, was the real father of modern-day quality control. Walter Shewhart, who is credited with the title, was Fisher's student.

Fisher's robust full factorial approach was watered down to a much weaker fraction factorial—called the classical approach—by his successors. But it was confined to the agriculture and chemical industries. Beyond these applications, it remained—until recently—in the province of academia, where university professors crank out its dreary dribble, with little expectation that their students would use it in the "real world."

Taguchi DOE

Genichi Taguchi of Japan adapted the classical approach, simplifying it with his orthogonal arrays. However, he has not had much success in his own country. In fact, the executive director of the Japanese Union of Scientists and Engineers—the primary training institution in Japan—remarked to this author that "Taguchi is for export!" Taguchi had a better reception in the U.S. He offered his services to the Bell Laboratories of AT&T for free, in return for the help America had rendered to Japan. Thus was born the Taguchi cult in the 1980s, with companies like AT&T, Ford, Xerox, and ITT becoming the missionaries. Thousands went to Taguchi seminars in the vain hope that "if it is Japanese, it has to be good." But the Taguchi approach has had modest success, at best, and downright failure, at worst, for reasons explained later in this chapter.

Shainin DOE

The third approach is a collection of simple, but powerful techniques invented or perfected by Dorian Shainin of the United States, a consultant to more than 800 leading companies. Shainin is easily the world's foremost quality problem solver. An American icon, he has won every major prize and medal granted by the American Society for Quality. In fact, we have a saying at Motorola: "Without Deming, the U.S. would not have had a quality philosophy; without Juran, it would not have had a quality direction; without Shainin, it would not have solved quality problems!" That sums up the contributions of America's three greatest quality gurus.

Unfortunately, the Shainin techniques have not received the wide publicity and use they deserve because the companies that used these techniques and experienced excellent results were unwilling to share them with others. In fact, this author was allowed to publish them in the first and only text on these methods, because his company, Motorola, won the Malcolm Baldrige National Quality Award,* which stipulates that its methods be shared with other U.S. companies.

*Motorola was the first company to win the Malcolm Baldrige Award in 1988, and the only large company to win the award for the corporation as a whole, in the 11-year history of the award. The company has been most generous in sharing its reasons for success in its famous "Six Sigma" seminars conducted for thousands from other companies.

The Motorola Case Study: 10:1, 100:1, 1,000:1 Quality Improvement

In the 1970s, Motorola faced stiff competition from the Japanese. They were in every business we were in and were aiming to eat our market share for lunch. "Meet the Japanese Challenge" became our rallying cry. Bob Galvin, the chairman of the board at Motorola, decided that quality was to be the focus of that challenge.

In 1981, he established a quality improvement goal of 10:1 in five years. Motorola's previous quality record was respectable and had been improving at the rate of 10 percent per year. Now, Bob Galvin's challenge was to improve it—not by 50 percent or 100 percent but by 1,000 percent in five years. Many skeptics thought it was an impossible goal. But by 1986, most of Motorola's divisions had met that goal. This author, then the Group Director of Motorola's automotive sector, achieved a 10:1 improvement in three years. We, then, benchmarked ourselves vis-à-vis the Japanese and found that they were still ahead in quality. So Bob Galvin established another 10:1 quality improvement in 1987, but this time in two years—by 1989. And in 1989, he increased the height of the quality bar by yet another 10:1 improvement in two years—by 1991. So, starting in 1981, Motorola had to improve quality by 1,000:1. The goal was not completely achieved throughout Motorola's far-flung operations, but the average improvement was an incredible 800:1, starting from an already respectable base in 1981.

The Pot of Gold

Many in the media were critical of Motorola's "obsession" with quality. "Would not there be a severe cost penalty for such a magnitude of quality improvement?" they smirked. The fact of the matter was that quality did not cost (it never does), it paid, and paid handsomely. Since 1979, Motorola had been tracking its cost of poor quality (see Chapter 4). In 10 years, it saved more than $9 billion by reducing its cost of poor quality! That is the pot of gold that has enabled it to pass some of the savings on to its loyal customers in the form of lower prices, some to its employees (among the highest paid in its industry) and some to its stockholders in the form of its 24:1 stock appreciation in 13 years! Several years later, a leading news journal asked: "Mr. Galvin, you have led the company to many quality peaks and have won many honors, including the Malcolm Baldrige Award. What is it that you most regret in your quality drive?" Bob Galvin's amazing answer: "I did not set high enough goals!"

Bob Galvin's Inspiring Leadership

There are many reasons for Motorola's spectacular quality achievement. Success has many fathers; failure is an orphan. First and foremost, were Bob Galvin's leadership and complete dedication to quality. Without his vision, his inspiration, and his charisma, we would have been mired in mediocre improvements. He led the quality charge. But Bob Galvin was not prescriptive in the approach to be used to achieve these quality heights. He freely admitted that he did not know how to reach the goals he set. But he had abiding faith in his people, that by leading them into areas where no one had ventured before and by pointing out the direction, he would inspire them to develop a roadmap to success.

Tools

A second reason for this success was our embracing the tools, which were outlined in Chapter 3. Of these, the most important was the Design of Experiments. Early in 1982, the vice president of Training and Education (now Motorola University) approached this author on what could be done to achieve the difficult 10:1 quality improvement goal, knowing that the usual methods of improvement would not be equal to the task. We needed, he said, to break out of the mold. I advised that the Shainin DOE be adopted, not piecemeal and intermittently as in the past, but wholesale. Thus was born the DOE era.

The Arcade Pilot DOE

Two months later, the first Shainin DOE pilot was conducted in Motorola's plant in Arcade, New York. Sixty people, drawn from technical disciplines as well as from line operators, were given a three-day training in DOE. At the end of that seminar, 12 teams were formed to tackle 12 major quality problems. Two months later, we reviewed their results and, more important, the DOE methods they had used. All teams did well, but the best team had members drawn entirely from direct labor. It had reduced a thick-film substrate defect rate from 12.5 percent to 0.5 percent in just one experiment.*

That was the first time that this author was able to reinforce his conviction that DOE (Shainin) need not be the exclusive province of development and process engineers. The intelligence and receptivity of line

---

*It is most heartwarming to know that one of the line workers of that team started using DOE so regularly in her work that she went on a meteoric career path—to lead operator, to group leader, to supervisor, to manager. She is now the popular and highly respected plant manager of over 1500 people!

operators to new ideas and techniques has always been slighted by management. I have proved, in at least a dozen companies that opened DOE to their direct labor pool, that line operators, given training, encouragement, and support, do as well as engineers—perhaps better—because they are in a hurry to solve problems and are not bogged down by the conservative skepticism of technical types.

The Five-Plant Pilot Run in the U.S.

The Arcade success spawned DOE pilot runs in five of Motorola's other U.S. plants. They were all successful, but the accounting department objected to the high costs of the projects. To counter this negativism, the Corporate Training and Education Department that had sponsored the projects brought in an independent auditing firm to monitor the results. The audit did reveal high costs for the training—$328,000—but the total savings were more than $7 million, greater than 20:1 return on investment. From that day forward, we got no more flak from the 19th-century accounting department!

The Worldwide Spread of DOE

Armed with this success, we launched DOE in all of our U.S. plants and then in our European and Asian plants—a total of more than 50 facilities. Several years later, Motorola developed its famous Total Customer Satisfaction (TCS) competition, in which as many as 5,000 teams incorporating 65,000 of its 140,000 employees strive for continuous improvement in quality, cost, cycle time, and other key measures. DOE continues to be one of the major tools used by these empowered teams. Each year, the winning teams are awarded six gold medals and 12 silver medals in the worldwide finals. Many of these prizes are awarded for diligent DOE projects. The corporation estimates that this TCS competition has resulted in savings of $2.4 billion a year, a savings that is essential given that its "high-tech" products have a 15 to 35 percent price erosion in the marketplace each year!

Fundamental Weaknesses in Classical and Taguchi Approaches

All three approaches to DOE—classical, Taguchi, and Shainin—are superior to the traditional problem-solving techniques of engineering judgment, computer simulation, SPC, 8-D, and Kepner-Tragoe. All three approaches are also far superior to old-fashioned experiments that used to be taught in universities and are still widely practiced by traditional engineers, in which only one variable is varied at a time, with all the other variables held constant. Besides the inordinate amount of time needed for such experimentation, the central weakness of this approach is the chronic inability to separate the main effects from their interaction effects. The results are frustration, the endless chasing of one's own tail, and high costs.

Nevertheless, there are also major structural and other weaknesses in both the classical and the Taguchi approach to DOE. Table 6-1 summarizes the weaknesses of each and the strengths of the Shainin approach in 10 categories. Table 6-1 also rates classical versus Taguchi versus Shainin on a scale of 1 to 10 (with 1 being the worst and 10 being the best) for each of the 10 categories.

1. Techniques: Limited and Ineffectual for Classical/Taguchi; Versatile and Powerful for Shainin

> - Classical DOE uses, for the most part, only the fraction factorial approach (although the full factorial approach is used in both classical and Shainin DOE) for problem-solving and a response surface methodology for optimization.
> - Taguchi DOE uses solely the orthogonal array—both inner arrays for parameters and outer arrays for noise factors. In both the classical and the Taguchi methods, if these single approaches fail, you are up a creek without a paddle.
> - Shainin DOE uses 10 distinct techniques, each suited for a particular problem or application. If one approach is inappropriate, there are many others to fall back on.

2. Clue Generation: "The Parts Are Smarter Than the Engineers!"

This is one of the most important distinctions that separate the Shainin approach from the classical/Taguchi approach.

> - In classical and Taguchi DOE, the engineers and/or teams guess at the possible causes of a problem. They use brainstorming. They vote, with a show of hands, on which are the most likely causes. This is known as problem solving by democracy! If the guesses are wrong, the experiments are a failure.
> - In Shainin DOE, *"we talk to the parts. The parts and the process are smarter than the engineers!"* This is not a putdown of the engineers. We want their knowledge. But we ask them to postpone their guesses, hunches, opinions, biases, and theories until they have talked to the parts—meaning *that they must first get some powerful*

Table 6-1. The Three Approaches to the Design of Experiments: A Comparison

Characteristic	Classical	Rating*	Taguchi	Rating*	Shainin	Rating*
1. Techniques	One or two approaches—fraction factorial and response surface method	3	One approach—orthogonal array	2	Minimum of 10 approaches (see Fig. 7-1)	10
2. Clue-generation ability	Poor: guesswork	1	Poor: guesswork	1	Powerful: "talk to the parts"	10
3. Effectiveness	➤ Moderate-improvement range: 2:1 to 10:1 ➤ Retrogression possible	3	➤ Low-improvement range: 2:1 to 5:1 ➤ Retrogression likely	2	➤ High-improvement range: 5:1 to 100:1 ➤ No retrogression	10
4. Cost	➤ High: 30 to 60 trials	4	➤ High: 50 to 100 trials	2	➤ Low: 2 to 30 trials	8
5. Complexity	➤ Difficult concepts ➤ Full ANOVA required	2	➤ Difficult concepts ➤ Inner and outer array multiplication; ANOVA; S/N	1	➤ Easy, simple, logical concepts ➤ Experiments done by line operators and engineers	8
6. Time (a) To understand (b) To do	(a) Long: three days or two weeks (b) Long: weak clues mean starting all over again	2	(a) Long: One to two weeks (b) Long: Weak clues, poor results require several trials	1	(a) Short: One day (b) Short: Experiments finished in one day to three weeks	9

7. Statistical validity	• Weak • Interaction effects confounded with main effects	2	• Very weak • No randomization • Interaction effects confounded with main effects	1	• Strong • Clear separation and quantification of main and interaction effects	8
8. Applicability	• Requires hardware • Main use in production	2	• Can be used in paper study with computer simulation, but danger of wrong results	4	• Requires hardware • Has universal applicability in product/process design, production, field, suppliers, and administrative processes	8
9. Ease of implementation	• Difficult • Wrong results if interactions are strong	2	• Difficult • Wrong results likely because of high degree of fractionation	1	• Easy • With clue-generation techniques, repeating experiment not needed	9
10. Disruption of production	• Stoppage of production during experimentation	1	• Stoppage of production during experimentat on	1	• No stoppage in clue-generation experiments, which can solve 70% of chronic quality problems	8

*On a scale of 1 to 10, 1 = worst, 10 = best.

and meaningful clues from one or more of four clue generation techniques that are more relevant and have far, far greater detective power than engineering guesses.

3. Effectiveness: Low Success Rates for Classical/Taguchi; High for Shainin

> Classical DOE: Modest improvements ranging from 2:1 to 10:1 and averaging 4:1, are possible if strong interaction effects are not present, but a slide back to square one is likely, since there are no follow-on validation experiments. Further safeguards such as Positrol and Process Certification are unknown.

> Taguchi DOE: Modest improvements, ranging from 1.5:1 to 5:1 and averaging 2:1, are possible if strong interaction effects are not present. (Taguchi DOE is worse than classical DOE because of the greater fractionation of the designed experiment.) But a slide back to square one is likely because of the absence of validation experiments. Here again, safeguards such as Positrol and Process Certification are unknown.

> Shainin DOE: An order magnitude (10:1) improvement is commonplace. 20:1 improvement is average. 50:1, 100:1, even 1,000:1 improvements can be and have been attained. And retrogression is avoided because of "B versus C" validation experiments and safeguards such as Positrol and Process Certification.

4. Cost: High Cost of Failure in Classical/Taguchi versus Lower Costs of Success in Shainin

> Classical DOE uses the fraction factorial as a preliminary screening tool. If the experiment is not a success, it has to be repeated. There can be 30 to 60 trials, using combinations of main factors and interacting factors, adding to costs. In addition, since production is always disrupted, there can be huge costs associated with line shutdowns.

> Taguchi DOE has even higher costs for two reasons: (1) The higher fractionation with the necessity of repeated trials. (2) The inner array and the outer array must be multiplied together, sharply escalating the total number of trials. There is the same disruption of production as in classical DOE.

> Shainin DOE is most economical in its sample sizes and the number of trials required. Since "talking to the parts" is better than guessing, its diagnosis of causes is much more accurate, and repeat trials are rarely needed. Most important, it does not disrupt production—a distinct advantage of the power of clue generation.

5. Complexity: Incomprehensible Statistical Jargon in Classical/ Taguchi versus Simple, Logical Concepts in Shainin

Classical DOE requires the full Analysis of Variance (ANOVA), and even after intensive training, it is difficult for engineers to understand, much less implement. The factors in the experiment are guesses and hunches. Taguchi DOE also requires the guessing not only of inner array factors but also of outer array factors and their multiplication. It, too, requires ANOVA, along with the calculation of signal to noise ratios (S/N) and graphical analysis. It, too, is so complicated that most engineers, after exposure, suffer from give-up-itis!

Shainin DOE, on the other hand, is so simple that line operators can understand and use it. (We sometimes joke that even engineers can understand and use it; and, once in a while, even management can understand and use it!)

6. Time in Instruction: Three Days to Two Weeks of Seminars for Classical/Taguchi versus One Day for Shainin; Time in Execution: False Starts in Classical/Taguchi versus Sure-Fire Clues in Shainin

> In terms of understanding, classical and Taguchi seminars require three days to two weeks. Even then, engineers have their eyes glazed over and lose comprehension. In terms of implementation, assuming they even get started (which most of them don't), it takes a long time to conduct the experiments, especially because the factors that are guessed at turn out to be blind alleys and the experiments have to be re-run.

> The Shainin seminars, conducted by us, require only one day for understanding the different approaches. On the second day, the participants actually design DOE experiments to start solving their own chronic quality problems. And the time is much shorter, because the clues—gained by talking to the parts—are far more sure-fire.

7. Statistical Validity: Confounding and Saturation in Classical/ Taguchi versus Clear Separation of Main and Interaction Effects in Shainin

The main weakness of the classical and Taguchi DOE methods, from a statistical point of view, is the severe confounding (or contamination, in lay terms) between main effects and second-order, third-order, and higher order interaction effects. (For readers who are interested in a more statistical and technical treatment of the saturation that occurs, Chapter 13 offers a detailed explanation.)

> In classical DOE, the fractionation that occurs when only 3 percent to 25 percent of all the possible combinations of independent variables are made part of the experiment, we can get marginal or downright wrong results because the main factor effects cannot be separated from the interaction effects. The apologists of the classical DOE school try to explain this weakness by stating that this fractionation, in a fraction factorial experiment, is only a screening mechanism and should be followed by a second experiment, and that the method does allow the purity of at least the second-order interaction effects, if not the higher order interaction. Both statements are wrong. If the fundamental design of the experiment is wrong, the conclusions are likely to be wrong. Second, there is no way of isolating the second order interaction effects from the main effects. The very foundation of the design approach is weak; as a result the edifice built on it is equally weak.

> In Taguchi DOE, the fractionation that occurs is even more pronounced and harmful than in classical DOE. As an example, if there are 10 factors to be examined, each with two levels (high and low), each factor must be tested with each level of each of the other factors in a full factorial design. This combination would require 2^{10}, i.e., 1,024, combinations, or 1,024 experiments. A Taguchi orthogonal array would only sample eight or sixteen such combinations. Which combinations would you select? Taguchites say, "Select the most important." But, if you don't know the most important factors, how can you determine the most important combinations of unknown factors? It is like playing Russian roulette;—in fact, worse than Russian roulette. Because, in Russian roulette, you have only one chance in six of being killed. With the Orthogonal Array you have a chance of being killed almost every time!

In Shainin DOE, after the clue generation experiments "allow the parts to tell you which are the significant factors," a full factorial or variable search neatly separates the main factors, second-order and higher order interaction effects, quantifying them in a factorial analysis. (See Chapters 13 and 14.)

8. Applicability: Shainin Best at the Design Stage of a Product or Process, in Production, at the Supplier, in the Field, Even in Administrative Applications

> Classical DOE does require hardware. It is not used as a preliminary paper study. Its main use is in production problem solving.

> Taguchi DOE has been used as a paper study, with computer simulation. But this approach is dangerous, because computer simula-

tion does require knowledge of the mathematical equations governing the relationship between independent and dependent variables. Most designs lack that knowledge.

> Shainin DOE has the same limitations as classical DOE in that it requires hardware—at the prototype stage of a design. But it has a distinct advantage over the other two approaches in evaluating new designs. It neatly separates the important variables from the unimportant ones. Further, it has universal applications beyond the design stage of a product or process—in production, at the supplier, at the customer, in the field, and in administrative processes.

9. Ease of Implementation: Classical/Taguchi—Difficult, Slow, Tedious; Shainin—Easy, Fast, Exciting

> Classical/Taguchi: This method takes a lot of preparation time. Production has to be stopped and samples of two levels for each factor have to be gathered. Further, if the results are poor—because of wrong guesses or interaction effects confounded with main effects—the experiments have to be repeated one or more times, with another 8, 16, 32, or 64 trials.

> Shainin: Since clue-generation techniques are far superior to engineering guesses and hunches, they can achieve desired results rapidly (at least 70 percent of the time, without the necessity for more formal experiments). Further, with its variable search technique, you can determine in one or two trials whether you are on the right track.

10. Disruption of Production: Classical/Taguchi—Disruptive; Shainin—Nondisruptive

> Classical/Taguchi: Production, concerned with shipments and meeting customer schedules, hates having lines stopped for experimentation. In classical/Taguchi methods, lines are forced to shut down for the duration of an experiment, which may not succeed the first time or even the second time. This means customer irritation, loss of cycle time, and high inventory costs.

> Shainin: There is no disruption of production at least 70 percent of the time, because only clue-generation techniques are used to sample ongoing product.

An Open Challenge

We are so convinced of the power of the Shainin DOE that we throw out a challenge. Any problem that can be solved by classical or Taguchi methods, we can solve better, faster, and less expensively with the Shainin methods.

7

A Synopsis of the 10 Powerful DOE Tools

Linking the 10 DOE Tools

As we stated in Chapter 6, a distinct feature of the Shainin DOE that differentiates it sharply from classical/Taguchi DOE is its versatility in utilizing 10 different DOE tools, each with a specific application in problem solving. This compares to only one or two straightjacket approaches in classical/Taguchi methods.

Figure 7-1 is an introductory block diagram. It links these 10 tools in a beautiful sequence of progressive problem solving. The start can be a problem with as many as 1,000 variables. (In this context, variables, causes, and factors are synonymous terms.) These variables can be systematically eliminated until only the top one, two, or three are distilled for corrective action and prevention control.

Clue-Generation Tools—Filtering Out Unimportant Variables

At the top are four primary clue-generation tools, the multi-vari, components search, paired comparisons, and product/process search, along with a fifth, derivative tool—the concentration chart. Their virtues are: (1) They provide clues—*by talking to the parts—that are far more effective than engineering guesses, theories, opinions, and biases, all the basis of the classical and Taguchi methods. (2) They do not disrupt production. They let it continue, drawing only small quantity samples from the production stream. (3) They reduce a large number of unknown, unmanageable variables—20 to 1,000—to a smaller number—1 to 20 families of manageable variables.*

Formal DOE Tools—Homing In on the Red X

From such meaningful clues, we can either fall back on engineering judgment to find the root cause problem or we can use formal DOE. If 5 to 20

Figure 7-1. An Introductory Variation Reduction Block Diagram

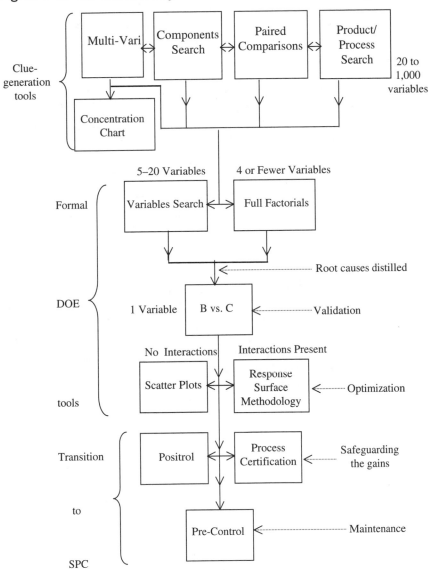

variables are still deemed significant, variables search is the best technique to use. If 2 to 4 variables are significant a full factorial is the preferred technique. If there is only one variable left, the root cause is known, and needs a B versus C DOE, the main purpose of which is to validate the effectiveness and permanence of corrective action. The next step is to optimize the important parameters, i.e., their ideal levels or values, and their realistic tolerances. If there are no interaction effects, the scatter plot DOE method is used. If there are interaction effects, response surface methodology is the correct approach.

Safeguards Against Retrogression

There are still two very important steps between the completion of DOE and the start of statistical process control in production. Ninety-nine percent of companies are totally unaware of these disciplines; among those who do know about them, fewer than 10 percent use the techniques. Their objective is to "freeze"the gains of previous DOE experiments and prevent a slide back into the earlier defects.

1. Positrol makes sure that important process parameters are always kept within their respective tolerances, as determined by DOE optimization experiments.
2. Process certification ensures that peripheral quality issues—such as operator-controllable problems, metrology, and environmental factors—are addressed and certified to prevent defects before and after DOE experiments.
3. SPC: Pre-Control. The last step is Pre-Control, which is far better, faster, and less expensive than the old control charts that are becoming, or should become, obsolete as a maintenance and monitoring technique in ongoing production.

A Generic Problem-Solving Framework

Table 7-1 shows an outline of a 10-step problem-solving framework that combines all the tools shown in Figure 7-1 to form a sequential, comprehensive way to solve a problem, especially a chronic one. It is far more profound than the empty slogan of PDCA or the vacuous dribble of 8-D, whose adherents mistakenly claim "finding the root cause."

A Capsule Summary of the Ten DOE Tools

Table 7-2 presents a short summary of the 10 DOE tools—their objective, where they are applicable, and when they are applicable. It also shows

Table 7-1. A Generic Problem-Solving Framework: A 10-Step Sure-Fire Approach

1. Define the problem (the Green Y)
2. Quantify and measure the Green Y
    - Measurement scatter plot (rather than Gage R&R)
    - Likert Scale to convert attributes into variables
3. Problem history (problem age, defect rate, cost)
4. Generate clues
    - Multi-Vari (including concentration chart)
    - Components Search
    - Paired Comparisons
    - Product/Process Search
5. Formal Design of Experiments
    - Variables Search
    - Full Factorials
    - B vs C
6. Turn the problem on and off—ensuring *permanence* of improvement
    - B vs C
7. Establish realistic specifications and tolerances (optimize)
    - Scatter Plots
    - Response Surface Methodology (RSM)
8. "Freeze" the process improvements
    - Positrol
9. Certify the process: Nail down all peripheral quality issues
    - Process Certification
10. Hold the gains with SPC
    - Pre-Control

the unbelievably small sample sizes used in the experimentation. The chapters that follow for each of these tools will make Table 7-1 more relevant as the reader gains familiarity with the tools.

The Green Y, Red X, Pink X, and Pale Pink X

The foundation of Shainin DOE rests on an old but universal theory—the Pareto Principle. Pareto was an Italian economist who studied the Italian economy and discovered that peoples' incomes were not evenly distributed, that a few people—the vital few—had a much larger collective sha:● of the total income than did the vast majority—the trivial many.

It was left to Dr. Juran to translate Pareto's Law to industry, with totally universal applications. Causes and effects are not linearly related. A few causes produce the preponderant percentage of an effect. This is

Table 7-2. The 10 DOE Tools

Tools	Objective	Where Applicable	When Applicable	Sample Size
Multi-Vari Chart	› Reduces a large number of unrelated, unmanageable causes to a family of smaller and related ones, such as time-to-time, part-to-part, within part, machine-to-machine, test position to test position › Detects nonrandom trends.	› Determines how a product/process is running; a quick snapshot without massive historical data that is of very limited usefulness. › Replaces process capability studies in some white-collar applications.	At engineering pilot run, production pilot run, in production, even in the field.	Min. 9 to 15 or until 80% of historic variation is captured.
Concentration Chart	Sequel to Multi-Vari. Pinpoints repetitive defects by location or component.	Same as Multi-Vari.	When the Red X is "within unit."	Same as Multi-Vari.
Components Search	From hundreds of thousands of components/subassemblies, homes in on the Red X, capturing the magnitude of all important main effects and interaction effects.	Where there are two differently performing assemblies (labeled "good" and "bad") with interchangeable components.	At prototype, engineering pilot run, production pilot run, or in field.	2
Paired Comparisons	Provides clues to the Red X by determining a repetitive difference between "good" and "bad" units with a high degree of confidence.	› Where there are matched sets of differently performing products (labeled "good" and "bad") that cannot be disassembled. › Many administrative and white-collar applications.	At prototype, engineering pilot run, production pilot run, or in field.	6 to 8 pairs of "good" and "bad" product.

	Purpose	When to Use	Where to Use	Number of Units
Product/Process Search	➤ To identify important product variables with Paired Comparisons. ➤ To identify important process variables associated with 8 good and 8 bad products.	Where it is difficult to isolate important process variables with Multi-Vari alone.	At prototype, engineering pilot run, production pilot run or in full production.	Sufficient units through a process to produce 8 "good" and 8 "bad" products and their associated process parameters.
Variables Search	Pinpoints Red X, Pink X, etc. Captures the magnitude of all important main effects and interaction effects. Open up tolerances of all unimportant variables to reduce cost.	➤ Where there are 5 to 20 variables to investigate. ➤ Excellent problem prevention tool. ➤ Applications in white-collar work	Excellent in R&D and development engineering, and in production for product/process characterization. Also for pinpointing Red X after Multi-Vari or Paired Comparisons.	1 to 20
Full Factorials	Same as Variables Search.	Practical only where there are 2 to 4 variables.	Same as Variables Search.	1 to 20
B vs. C	➤ Validates superiority of a new or better (B) product/process over a current (C) one with a desired statistical confidence (usually 95%). ➤ Evaluates engineering changes. ➤ Reduces cost.	➤ Follow-up of one or more of the above seven tools. ➤ When problem is easy to solve, B vs. C can bypass above tools in some white-collar applications. ➤ Can be used for more than 2 choices, i.e., B vs. C vs. D vs. E, etc.	At prototype, engineering pilot run, or production.	Usually 3 B's and 3 C's.

Table 7-2. (Continued)

Tools	Objective	Where Applicable	When Applicable	Sample Size
Scatter Plots: (Realistic Tolerances Parallelogram)	‣ Determines optimum values (levels) for Red X, Pink X, variables, and their maximum allowable tolerances.	When there are weak or no interactions between important variables.	At engineering pilot run, or product/process.	30
Response Surface Methodology (RSM)	Same as scatter plots.	When there are strong interactions between important variables.	Same as scatter plots.	5 to 25

the 20-80 law, which states that 20 percent or fewer of causes produce 80 percent or more of a given effect. The Pareto Principle is true in so many industrial and real-life situations that it is uncanny. Twenty percent or fewer parts account for 80 percent or more of total costs—a principle used in value engineering and in inventory control. In management, it is used to "manage by exception." Similarly in quality, 20 percent or fewer of causes produce 80 percent or more of the total magnitude of a given quality problem.

Figure 7-2 illustrates the Pareto Principle. There are a few terms that will be used throughout the text.

> The effect is called the Green Y. It represents the magnitude of the problem (or output or response) that must be solved.
> The No. 1 or dominant cause is called the Red X. It generally accounts for at least 50 percent of the total Green Y.
> The No. 2 cause is called the Pink X. It accounts for about 20 to 30 percent of the total Green Y.
> The No. 3 cause is called the Pale Pink X. It accounts for about 10 to 15 percent of the total Green Y.

Generally, with DOE finding solutions for the Red X, Pink X, and Pale Pink X of a given Green Y, variation can be reduced by anywhere from 75 percent to 95 percent. Let us assume a C_p of 1.0 at the start. If the variation in this process is reduced by 75 percent, a C_p of 4 can be achieved—twice the world class standard companies strive to achieve. If the variation is reduced by 95 percent, a C_p of 20.0 can be achieved—10 times the world class standard. This is another way to quantify the advantages of the Shainin approach—of C_p's up to 20—contrasted with the anemic results of the classical/Taguchi approach, with C_p's barely reaching 2.0.

The block diagram in Figure 7-1 shows how the DOE tools are linked. To solve problems systematically, however, a more detailed roadmap is needed to guide teams in the search for the Red X. Figure 7-3 is such a roadmap, with a starting point at the Green Y and proceeding, with the progressive use of each tool in solution-tree fashion, to distill the Red X; it then monitors and controls it with pre-control. (In this roadmap, variables search and full factorials are bracketed together because they have the same objective. Variables search is the more versatile tool because it can handle five or more variables, while full factorials can best handle four or fewer variables.)

As we proceed along the road to the Red X, each step will be highlighted in Figure 7-3. The start is defining the Green Y (shaded area).

Figure 7-2. The Pareto Principle: The Green Y and the Red X

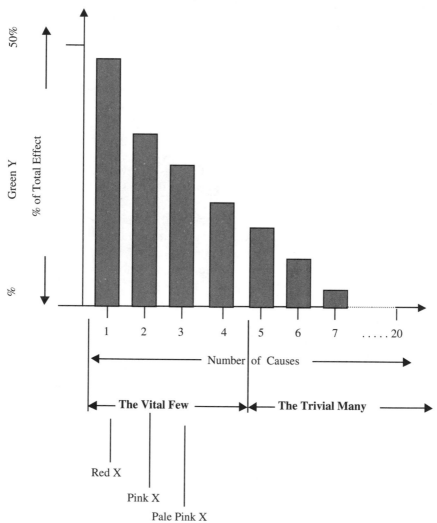

Note: Solving the Red X, Pink X, and Pale Pink X can:
> Reduce variation
> Achieve C_{pk}'s of 2 to 10 with one, two, or three experiments

Figure 7-3. The Search for the Red X: A Problem-Solving Roadmap

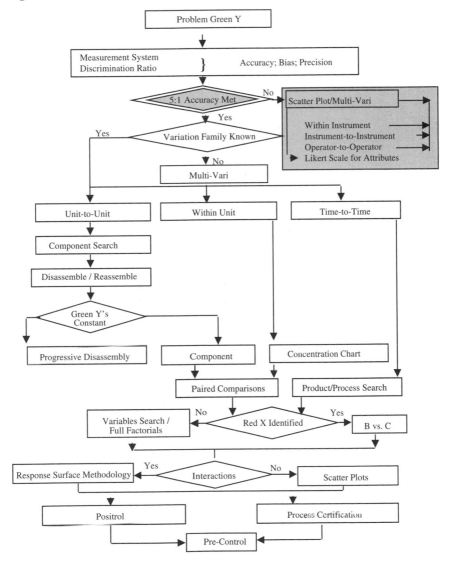

Defining and Quantifying the Problem: The Green Y—A Checklist

Before the start of DOE, it is important to describe, define, and quantify the problem, i.e., the Green Y. The following checklist should be used by the DOE team as a starting point to make sure that all the bases are covered. It can also be used by management in DOE project reviews.

1. Has the problem been clearly stated—in one sentence (or one paragraph) as a maximum? If a problem cannot be stated succinctly in such a short space, the chances are that the team is floundering at the very start.

2. Has the Green Y been defined and quantified, in terms of:

> Defect levels (percentages or ppms or C_p, C_{pk}) or field failure levels?
> Cost, safety, or environmental impact?
> Longevity (weeks, months, years)?

3. If the Green Y is an attribute (go/no go), can it be transformed into an artificial variable on a scale, say, of 1 to 10—with 1 being the worst and 10 being the best. This is known as a Likert scale.

4. Is there more than one Green Y? (In rare cases, there may be as many as seven.)

5. Is there an earlier Green Y, or an easier Green Y, that has a close correlation with the final Green Y? As an example, retail stores were complaining about food from a processing plant becoming prematurely stale. Staleness tests, however, take 14 days—too long for designed experiments. An earlier Green Y than staleness was leakage in the bags in which the food was contained and sealed. Leakage became the Green Y. But leakage is hard to measure. So the location of the food particles trapped in the seal area of the bag became an easier and an earlier Green Y, and the DOE experiment yielded the Red X cause within three days, as opposed to several weeks, of testing.

6. Has the Green Y been detected as early in the process flow as possible to catch the problem at its source rather than the accumulation of the problem further down the line? Has the process flow been charted?

7. If the problem is a field, rather than a plant, Green Y:

> Has a multiple environment over stress test been devised to accelerate the Green Y in a short time? Is it capable of duplication in the long term?

> Has the external customer or customers been identified and contacted?
> Has the customer application been examined?
> Where in the customer chain is the Green Y located—in transportation, installation, distributor, dealer/retailer, servicer, or consumer?
> How valid and realistic are the customer specifications and tolerances?
> Have internal specifications and tolerances been derived from customer requirements?

8. If the problem is reliability-oriented (time plus stress, as distinguished from quality-oriented, which is at time zero and at zero stress):

> Has a bathtub curve been drawn to determine if the failure is "infant mortality" (within one month in the field), constant failure rate (within one to three years in the field), or a wear-out problem (well beyond a warranty period)?
> Is the problem intermittent? If so, are stress tests designed to force an intermittent failure into a permanent failure?
> Have similar reliability failures occurred in the plant before shipment or during stress tests in the plant?
> Can the problem be accelerated with stress tests, with the Green Y becoming stress level to failure or stress time to failure?

It may seem that many of these questions are obvious and do not need to be part of a checklist. Yet, many DOE projects have been shipwrecked because the Green Y has not been precisely defined, quantified, or thought through.

Measurement Accuracy

Before proceeding to Part III—the powerful clue-generation DOE tools—the pitfalls in the measurement system associated with products should be highlighted. More frequently than is thought possible, the Red X, i.e., the No. 1 problem associated with a Green Y, is the weakness and variation of the measuring system rather than the variation within a product.

The first questions that should be asked after defining the Green Y are: How good is the measuring instrument? What is its variation vis-à-vis the product variation? Various rules have been established as guides. One guideline stipulates a 10:1 ratio as a minimum for product variation: instrument variation. Other guidelines indicate that a range of 4:1 to 6:1 is adequate.

Total variation (or total tolerance, T_T) has two components: Product tolerance, T_P, and instrument tolerance T_I. Tolerances do not add up arithmetically. They follow the root-mean-square (RMS) law, governed by the formula:

$$T_T = \sqrt{T_P^2 + T_I^2}$$

As an example, if a product tolerance (T_P), is five units, and the instrument tolerance (T_I) is one unit—a 5:1 ratio—the total tolerance is:

$$T_T = \sqrt{5^2 + 1^2} = \sqrt{26} = 5.1$$

If now, the instrument tolerance is reduced to zero, the total tolerance will still remain high, at 5.0—a change of only 0.1 in 5, or two percent. In other words, a 5:1 product:instrument tolerance ratio means that 98 percent of the total tolerance would come from the product and only two percent from the instrument, an inaccuracy that could be considered negligible.

If, however, the instrument tolerance, in the above example was 3 (i.e., a ratio of 1.66:1 of product tolerance : instrument tolerance) the total tolerance would be $\sqrt{5^2 + 3^2} = \sqrt{34}$ or 5.83, a change of 0.83 in 5; or a 16.6 percent inaccuracy that would be unacceptable.

In summary, a product : instrument tolerance ratio of 10:1 would be too difficult for instrument accuracy to achieve, especially with product tolerances getting tighter and tighter in industry. A 1:66 ratio would result in unacceptable inaccuracies. A 5:1 ratio is a reasonable industry norm. Another feature of tolerances adding up according to the root-mean-square law is that *the dominant tolerance* (in this case, the product tolerance) among two or three or four tolerances that have to be combined unduly influences the total tolerance.

Precision, Bias, Accuracy, Discrimination in Metrology

Precision is defined as the spread of a frequency distribution around its average. It can be called the range, R, in the distribution, or C_p, if measured against a specification width. *Bias* is defined as the deviation of the average, in a frequency distribution, from the target value or design center. It is the noncentering $(\overline{X} = D)$, where $\overline{X}$ is the average and D the design center) in a C_{pk} calculation. *Accuracy* combines precision and bias. It can be called C_{pk}, if tied to a specification width. *Discrimination* is the ratio of product spread to measurement spread, with a minimum ratio of 5:1. Figure 7-4 depicts these terms pictorially.

Panel A shows four frequency distributions with constant precision

Figure 7-4. Metrology: Bias, Precision, Accuracy

Precision = Repeatability; spread; range, C_p (with specs.)
Bias = Deviation from design center, D; X - D, where
D = Design center or target
X = Average; R = Range
Accuracy: combines precision and bias; C_{p_k} (with specs.)
Discriminating: ratio of product spread: measurement spread

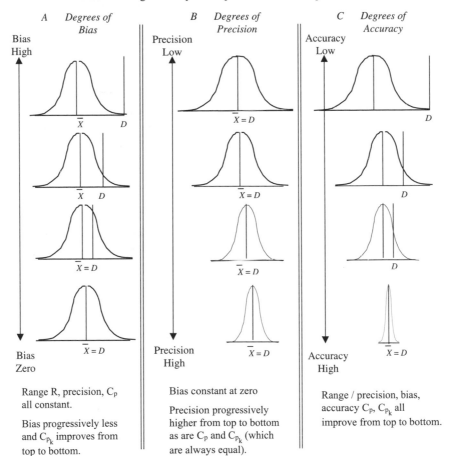

A *Degrees of Bias*	*B* *Degrees of Precision*	*C* *Degrees of Accuracy*
Range R, precision, C_p all constant. Bias progressively less and C_{p_k} improves from top to bottom.	Bias constant at zero Precision progressively higher from top to bottom as are C_p and C_{p_k} (which are always equal).	Range / precision, bias, accuracy C_p, C_{p_k} all improve from top to bottom.

(range) and constant C_p, but with bias ranging from high at the top to zero at the bottom; C_{pk} also improves.

Panel B shows four frequency distributions, all with zero biases, and with precision, C_p and C_{pk} (which are always equal) improving from poor at the top to very good at the bottom. Panel C shows four frequency distributions with varying accuracies—poor at the top, excellent at the bottom—because precision, range, bias, an C_p, C_{pk} all keep improving.

Reducing Instrument Variations

As indicated earlier, reducing inherent variations in the measuring instruments should precede reducing variations in the product if the total discrimination ratio is less than 5:1. The total instrument tolerance T_t is made up of three factors— within-instrument tolerance (T_{wi}), instrument-to-instrument tolerance (T_{i-i}), and operator-to-operator tolerance (t_{o-o}).

The total tolerance,

$$T_t = \sqrt{T_{wi}^2 + T_{i-i}^2 + T_{o-o}^2},$$

as governed by the root-mean-square law. Since these three tolerances are not likely to be equal (Pareto's law is universal), the dominant tolerance among these three would be the overwhelming influence on T_t and would be the one to attack and reduce.

Reducing Within-Instrument Variation

There are a number of causes for variation within the same instrument, assuming, of course, that variations in operator techniques have been ruled out. These include:

> Differences in ambient temperatures, humidity, etc., during successive measurements.
> Influence of electromagnetic fields, transient voltages, line voltages, extraneous noise, setup, materials, vibration.
> Hysteresis (example, gear backlash) with increasing versus decreasing inputs.
> Nonlinearity.
> Fixturing: connections, pins, mechanical linkages, loading, positioning, etc.
> A Multi-Vari study (concentration chart to pinpoint within unit variation) or a B versus C could be the DOE tools to use to pinpoint and correct the specific cause.

Reducing Instrument-to-Instrument Variation

The causes of variation between two or more instruments of the same type include: different manufacturers; lack of calibration; and differences in materials, components, circuitry, mechanical assemblies; connections, etc.

The applicable DOE techniques would be Components Search (if the instruments can be disassembled and reassembled and their original Green Y's remain the same) between the best and worst unit, and Paired Comparisons.

Reducing Operator-to-Operator Variation

The causes of variation between two or more operators include: lack of instruction; nonuniform procedures and sequence in steps; lack of skill; parallax errors; and physical differences (eyesight, height, dexterity, etc.).

The applicable DOE technique would be a flow chart, recording every step and looking for differences with paired comparisons.

Measurement Accuracy Checklist

The following checklist on the accuracy of the measuring equipment should be consulted by the problem-solving team before the start of DOE.

> - Is the Green Y measurable?
> - Can the measurement—if an attribute (i.e., go/no go, pass/fail)—be converted into a variable, using a Likert scale (see the following case study).
> - Can the consistency of such a Likert scale between different operators be assessed?
> - Has a scatter plot study been conducted to determine a minimum discrimination ratio of 5:1?
> - Have the variations (tolerances) within instruments, between instruments, and between operators been quantified relative to the product tolerance?
> - Have experiments been conducted on the causes of the largest of these three sources of variation, and have permanent solutions been instituted?
> - If the state of the art precludes attaining a 5:1 ratio, is there an alternate Green Y that is earlier, easier, and more consistently measurable?

Skipping this checklist and not assessing the adequacy of the measurement system can derail a problem-solving project at the very start.

Converting an Attribute into a Variable

Another important step in any quantification and measurement of the Green Y is the desirability of converting an attribute into a variable. There are three types of data—variables, attributes, and rank.

> *Variables data* can include a very large, almost infinite, number of readings of a parameter, depending on the scale used. Examples of variables data are dimensions, voltage, weights, tensile strength, etc. In a narrower sense, even the number of defects, yield percentages, and ppms can be approximated to variables.

> *Attribute data* are digital—either good or bad, pass or fail, accept or reject—with no readings in between these extremes. Examples of attributes could include cosmetic defects, such as paint, plating, bubbles, corrosion, color, solder defects, blow-holes, and tool marks.

> *Rank data* variables are not recorded by exact value, but graded by rank—from smallest to largest, lowest to highest, best to worst (or vice versa). The use of rank data is discussed in Chapter 11 under the section on Tukey Test.

Likert Scale

Since attribute data have no gradations between the extremes of good and bad, the challenge is to convert an attribute artificially into a variable and give it a gradation. This is done with a Likert numerical scale, where 1 is the worst and 10 is the best. A committee consisting of the customer, sales, engineering, manufacturing, and quality would grade 10 physical samples, ranging from an unacceptable 1 to a perfect 10. These physical samples (sometimes photographs can suffice) would not constitute a "variables scale" to determine the appropriate score for a similar defect in production. This takes the subjectivity out of the arbitrary judgment of different inspectors. It prevents the eternal battle between production wanting acceptance of, say, a cosmetic defect and inspection wanting to reject it. Sometimes a truncated scale from 0 to 5 or 1 to 6 can suffice. The Likert scale can also be reversed with 0 being the best and 5 (or 10) being the worst. Figure 7-5 is an example of a Likert scale applies to tool marks on a cam end bearing; with 0 as best and 5 as worst.

Likert Scale Achieves Smaller Sample Sizes

Another advantage of a Likert scale is to reduce large sample sizes in DOE work, which would otherwise be required to calculate percentages of defects, yield percentages, etc. For example, if one wanted to distinguish between two yield percentages—say, at 70 percent vs. 80

Figure 7-5. Likert Scale: Cam End Bearing Rating

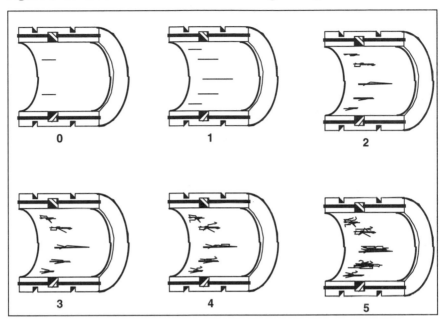

percent—a large number of units (generally 30 to 50 of each yield as a minimum) would be required in a DOE test to determine the difference in this attribute. Use of a Likert scale, by contrast, would require sample sizes of only three to 10 of each yield to detect the difference and even to quantify it (see Tukey test and B versus C in Chapters 11 and 15).

Measurement Case Study: Electric Razor

In one of the plants of a global company, the product—an electric razor—made excessive noise. But before determining the Red X cause, an accurate measurement system had to be established. Typical measurement tools for noise are frequency spectrum analyzers and decibelmeters. These, however, turned out to be inconsistent in their readings, with low discrimination ratios.

A listening test was suggested. After some trial and error, a Likert scale of 1 to 10—with the 1 worst and 10 the best—was established. Ten operators were trained for the listening test. The average for the noisy razors turned out to be 3, with a range of only 0.2. The average for the silent razors was 8.6, with a range of 0.3. The discrimination ratio was well over 5:1 in both cases. The managers were amazed that a subjective listening test, by trained operators, could be more consistent and accurate than more sophisticated instruments.

Part III

····································

"Talking to the Parts"— A Set of Clue-Generating Tools

Continuation of the Journey to the Red X

Chapter 7 saw the start of the journey to the Red X with the definition and quantification of the problem—the Green Y. Next, it was stressed that a viable measurement system whose accuracy was at least 5:1 relative to the accuracy of the product tolerance, or specification width (whichever was larger), was necessary for a successful solution of a given Green Y.

Part III consists of a set of five clue-generation tools—the Multi-Vari, the Concentration Chart, Components Search, Paired Comparisons, and Product/Process Search. These are the tools that collectively constitute "talking to the parts"—tools that are infinitely superior to the guesses, hunches, biases, opinions, and judgments of classical and Taguchi experimenters. The clues they provide are solid. Further, these tools do not disrupt production, because they let production run uninterrupted, drawing samples only for examination.

The five tools are treated in-depth in the next five chapters, each of which contains:

1. A detailed description of a given tool and a step-by-step procedure.
2. Successful case studies.
3. Unsuccessful case studies and lessons to be learned from them.
4. Workshop exercises, with answers for the reader to practice.
5. Applications to white-collar administrative problems, where applicable.
6. Questions as guidelines for DOE teams.
7. Questions for management during DOE project reviews.

8
··

The Multi-Vari Analysis:
Homing In on the Red X

Purpose and Principles

The main objective of a multi-vari study is to reduce a large number of unknown (or merely suspected) and unmanageable causes (causes, factors, and variables are synonymous terms) of variation to a much smaller family of related variables containing the Red X, i.e., the dominant cause. It is a graphical technique that homes in on the most likely cause of a problem by eliminating noncontributing causes of variation. Find its place in the problem-solving roadmap of Figure 7-1.

A Card Trick to Illustrate Homing In on the Red X With a Multi-Vari Analysis

The authors have made the multi-vari come to life at DOE seminars with a card trick. It goes as follows:

1. Ask a person in the audience to help you (the card dealer) by selecting any 27 cards from a deck of cards.
2. Ask your helper to choose any card from the ones selected and show it to the audience without your seeing the card. The trick is for you to guess the Red X card by asking him or her three identical questions. Let us say the card picked is the ace of clubs.
3. Ask your helper to shuffle the selected 27 cards and hand the pack to you.
4. You then arrange the 27 cards, face up, in three columns of nine cards each, as shown in Figure 8-1, Panel A.
5. Then ask your helper to indicate the column containing his or her selected card. He or she will point to column two.

Figure 8-1. The Card Trick: To Illustrate Multi-Vari Principles

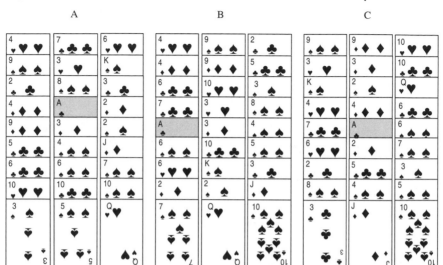

6. Then pick up the cards by columns, with the designated column always picked up second.
7. For the second arrangement, lay the cards out in rows (see Figure 8-1, Panel B).
8. Ask question number two: "Which column is the card in now?" Your helper will point to column one. Again, pick up all 27 cards by columns, with the designated column picked up second.
9. For the third arrangement, lay the cards out again in rows (see Figure 8-1, Panel C).
10. Finally, ask question number three: "Which column is the card in now?" Your helper will point to column two.
11. With a flourish, you pull out the fifth row (always the middle row) card in column two and declare the ace of clubs as the Red X card.

The Multi-Vari Principle Behind the Card Trick

Let us say that the 27 cards represent 27 possible variables in a given problem; any one of which could be the Red X. Guessing that it is the Queen of Hearts would give you odds of only 1 in 27 of being correct—which incidentally are better odds than those for engineers who may be right 1 in 50 or 1 in 100 times!

> ➤ In arrangement one (Figure 8-1A), when the helper from the audience pointed to column two as containing the selected card, you

immediately got a signal that the card was not in columns one and three—eliminating 18 variables and narrowing the Red X to just nine cards of column 2.

› In arrangement two (Figure 8-1B), the nine cards of the original column two were the three middle rows, namely 4, 5, and 6 of Figure 8-1B. When your helper next pointed to column one, you again got a signal that the Red X could only be in column one and rows 4, 5, and 6, eliminating the six cards in rows 4, 5, and 6 associated with columns two and three. The Red X was then narrowed down to just three cards out of 27.

› In arrangement three (Figure 8-1C), those three cards of column one and middle rows 4, 5, and 6 are now in the middle, or fifth, row. And when your helper pointed to column 2 after question number three, the Red X was firmly established as the ace of clubs.

This is the principle of the multi-vari study. It is a filtering technique through which a large number of noncontributing causes of variation are eliminated until, systematically, the Red X can be distilled. In most applications, the multi-vari acts as the first filter and is generally followed by:

› Other clue-generation techniques, if there are still too many remaining relevant variables.
› Variables search, if the remaining relevant variables are between five and twenty, or the full factorial, if they are two to four.
› B versus C if the relevant variable is only one and the improvement has to be confirmed as permanent.
› Engineering judgement—now that its confused clutter of guesses has been substantially reduced.

The Futility of the Cause-and-Effect (Ishikawa) Diagram

Many experimenters start with a cause-and-effect diagram, listing every conceivable cause of a given effect that is dredged up by a brainstorming team. But the huge number of causes can be bewildering. Figure 8-2 is an example of a mind-boggling cause-and-effect diagram used in an attempt to solve the variability associated with a fired resister in a microcircuit. More than 80 causes were meticulously listed! But where would you start? What causes would you select for further experimentation? A typical approach for the brainstorming team is to vote with a show of hands on which causes to select. Democracy may be a viable political institution, but it is useful in solving chronic quality problems in manufacturing.

Figure 8-2. Cause-and-Effect Diagram of a Fired Resistor Value Variability

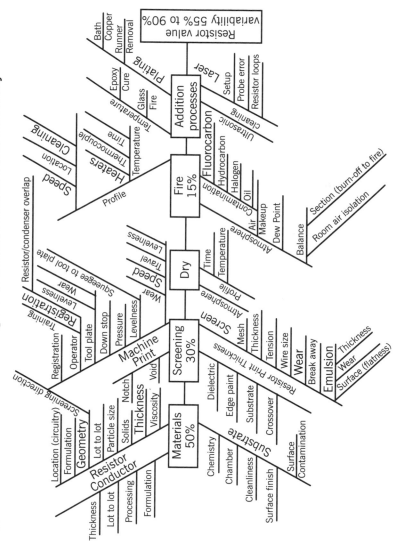

Source: An early Motorola microcircuit experiment.

Based on the 80-odd strands of assorted guesses in Figure 8-2, a Taguchi experiment was tried at this company. It failed to identify the problem.

By contrast, a progressive multi-vari study, used with other clue-generation tools, would have neatly pinpointed the Red X, Pink X, and Pale Pink X causes and reduced the fired resistor variability from its 55 to 90 percent figure to less than 2 percent.

Three Major Families of Variation: Positional, Cyclical, and Temporal

The card trick broke the total variability of the 27-card pack into three families—column 1, column 2 and column 3. However, in industry management would undoubtedly frown on cards as a problem-solving occupation! The most generic breakdown of a problem is into three families: positional—or within-unit variation; cyclical—or unit-to-unit variation; and temporal—or time-to-time variation.

If the largest variation is temporal, the several causes associated with positional or cyclical variations can be either ruled out or given a much lower priority for further investigation. Examples of variation in each family are:

Positional Variation (Within Unit Family)

> Variations within a single unit (e.g., left side versus right side, top versus bottom, center versus edge, taper, out-of-round, run out, or casting-wall thickness).
> Variations across a single unit containing many parts (e.g., a semiconductor wafer with many chips; a printed circuit board with repetitive defects of one component type or value).
> Variations by location or position in a batch loading process (e.g., cavity-to-cavity variations in a mold press).
> Machine-to-machine variations.
> Variations in test position to test position and fixture to fixture.
> Operator-to-operator variations.
> Line-to-line and plant-to-plant variations.

Cyclical Variation (Unit to Unit Family)

> Variation between consecutive units drawn from a process in the same general time frame.
> Variation among group of units.

> Batch-to-batch variations.
> Lot-to-lot variations.

Temporal Variations (Time to Time Family)

> Hour to hour.
> Shift to shift.
> Day to day.
> Week to week.

Preamble to Any DOE Study

The authors have seen far too many examples of companies drawing Pareto charts that depict defects across a broad spectrum of models and a broad section of defect types. Then they get overwhelmed with the size and scope of problem solving. It is essential, in such situations, to follow four simple rules:

1. Select, as a starting point, only the model with the largest number of defects.
2. Select, within that model, the defect mode with the largest number of defects.
3. Solve the problem with one or more DOE tools.
4. Repeat steps 1, 2, and 3 for the model with the second largest number of defects . . . and so on.

Designing, Conducting, and Analyzing a Multi-Vari Study: A Roadmap

A number of steps must be undertaken in designing, running, interpreting, and analyzing a multi-vari study. These are summarized as follows:

A. Designing the Multi-Vari Study

1. Identify the Green Y (the problem to be solved). If the Green Y is an attribute, try to convert it into a variable using a Likert scale.

2. Make sure that the accuracy of the measuring instrument is at least five times the accuracy of the product (i.e., its allowed tolerances).

3. Determine the number of families of probable variation.

4. Draw a family tree.

5. Estimate the number of time-to-time samples required.

6. Determine the number of unit-to-unit samples to be drawn consecutively from the process (generally three to five consecutive units).

7. Determine the number of samples for each subfamily of within-unit families; e.g., the number of locations, machines, cavities, etc.

8. Multiply the quantities in steps 3, 4, and 5 to determine the total number of units to be studied.

9. Design a table to facilitate gathering the multi-vari data.

B. Running the Multi-Vari Experiment

1. Do not mix up models within a given product. Run only the worst model in that product.

2. Run the multi-vari study, extending the time-to-time samples until at least 80 percent of the historic variation or specification tolerance—whichever is less—is captured.

3. Minimize the number of adjustments to be made on the process during the multi-vari run.

4. Pay particular attention to any discontinuities, such as coffee breaks, lunches, shift changes, operator changes, setup changes, tool changes, preventive maintenance, etc., that cannot be avoided during the multi-vari run. In the time-to-time samples, choose the time before and after such discontinuities, whenever possible.

C. Interpreting and Analyzing the Multi-Vari Chart

1. Determine the family with the greatest variation. (*Note: the Red X can only be in one of several families*, although the Pink X and the Pale Pink X can be in other families).

2. If the Red X family is time-to-time, examine changes with temperature, humidity, tool wear, break and lunch periods, adjustments made during the multi-vari, and any process parameter changes. A follow-up with Product/Process Search might be in order. (See Chapter 12.)

3. If the Red X family is unit-to-unit, examine cyclical patterns, dust, dirt, housekeeping, etc., that might affect one unit and not other consecutive units. A follow-up with a Components Search and/or Paired Comparisons might be in order.

4. If the Red X is within-unit, construct a concentration chart (see Chapter 9) to determine repetitive locations or components of the Green Y.

5. Look for nonrandom trends and other clues.

6. Look for one or a few samples that may exhibit an unusual pattern. Unequal sensitivity may be an indication of interaction effects.

7. On the family tree, list all possible causes under each family of variation, to start a series of follow-on investigations.

Case Study 1:
Designing the Multi-Vari—Printed Circuit Board Drilling

The Green Y was excessive debris from the printed circuit boards during drilling. A Likert scale (see Chapter 7) was used to measure the printed circuit board debris, with the quantity of debris graded from one (no debris) to 10 (maximum debris).

The various families of variation were then identified.

> It was decided to run the experiment for just one day in the expectation that one day would be sufficient to capture at least 80 percent of the historic variation.
> Each day had three shifts.
> There were 13 identical drilling machines.
> Each machine had four machine heads.
> Eight operators per shift manned the machines.
> Each machine had three panels, stacked up, of printed circuit boards.
> Each machine had 10 drill sizes.

These three major families of variation and the seven subfamilies are shown linked together in the family tree of Figure 8-3. As the multi-vari investigation proceeds, the subfamily not contributing to debris variation can be ruled out and crossed off.

Determining Sampling Frequency and Number of Units Required

How long should a multi-vari study continue? As mentioned earlier, *an empirical rule states that periodic samples should continue to be taken from the process until at least 80 percent of historic variation or the specification tolerance—whichever is less—is captured.* If a lower figure, such as 50 or 60 percent, is used, the chance of finding the Red X quickly is reduced. Multi-

Figure 8-3. The Family Tree of a Multi-Vari Plan

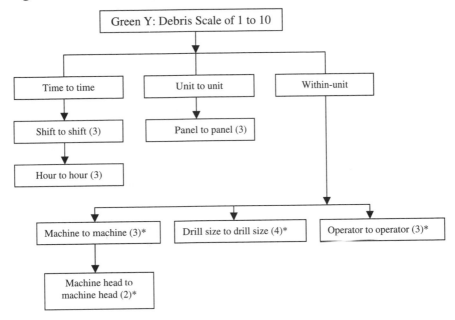

Source: Lika Corporation, Stockton, Calif.
*Sample size.
Note: It is not necessary to take the total number of units in a given subfamily (unless a minimum of 80 percent of the historic variation is not reached). Here, only three of the 13 machines are sampled; only two of the four machine heads are sampled; only four of the 10 drill sizes are sampled; and only three of the eight operators are sampled.

vari studies can range from one hour or less, in total, up to four weeks or more in order to capture 80 percent or more of the historic variation. Typically, however, multi-vari studies need not last more than one to three days. How many samples are needed? In the unit-to-unit family, the sample size is three to five consecutive units.

In the within-unit family, the sampling can either be 100 percent in each subfamily or a reasonable sample taken from each subfamily. The object is to keep the total number of units required to a practical upper limit, while allowing enough opportunities for the Red X to be captured.

For instance, in the printed circuit board example, if we selected three as the sample size for the unit-to-unit variation and took such samples from each of 10 machines, four machine heads, eight operators, and 10 drill sizes, the total number of units required each hour would be 3 × 10 × 4 × 8 × 10, or 9,600 units each hour. Multiply that by three hours and three shifts, and the total would be an unwieldy 86,400 units. So a decision can be made to sample just three of the 10 machines—historically the worst, the best, and one in-between. Similarly, only three operators, three drill sizes, and two machine heads could be selected. This would reduce the total number of units per hour to 3 × 3 × 3 × 3 × 2, or 162 units. Multiply that by three shifts and three samples per shift, and the total number of units required would be only 1,458 units. These smaller quantities in each subfamily are shown in Figure 8-3.

An alternative would be to start with just one shift. If 80 percent or more of the historic variation is captured, the second and third shifts could be deleted, reducing the total number of units to just 162.

We have deliberately chosen a case study with many families of variation and many units within each family. The absolute minimum for a multi-vari would be three units and three time periods, or a total of nine for the whole experiment. Very rarely would the total number of units exceed 100. Table 8-1A and B depicts tables for gathering data, by families of variation, with Table 8-1B being a subset of Table 8-1A. Such a table can easily be given to an operator or inspector to log.

Workshop Exercise 1: Semiconductor Wafer Multi-Vari Plan

On a semiconductor wafer (containing several hundred chips or dies), thickness measurements were made to determine which families of variation contributed the most to thickness differences in a multi-vari study. The Green Y is variation in thickness. Assume that the accuracy of the measuring instrument is more than six times the specified thickness tolerance. Design a multi-vari plan to address the following questions from aspects of the plan listed below.

    1. Identify the major families of variation (i.e., time-to-time, unit-to-unit, within-unit) for each of the following eight aspects of the plan.

    1. On each wafer, five dice were measured (north, south, east, west, and center).   _____

    2. Three wafers were sampled from each batch exiting the deposition process.   _____

    3. Wafers were selected from three locations in the batch process: left, center, and right locations in the chamber.   _____

    4. Two deposition chambers were used.   _____

Table 8-1. Multi-Vari Preparation Table: Printed Circuit Board Drilling

Table 8-1A

Variation Family																										
Day 1																										
Shift #	Shift 1									Shift 2									Shift 3							
Hour #	Hour 1			Hour 2			Hour 3			Hour 1			Hour 2			Hour 3			Hour 1			Hour 2			Hour 3		
Unit #	1	2	3	1	2	3	1	2	3	1	2	3	1	2	3	1	2	3	1	2	3	1	2	3	1	2	3

Table 8-1B

Variation Family																										
Unit 1																										
Machine #	1									2									3							
Machine Head #	1			2						1			2						1			2				
Operator #	1	2	3	1	2	3				1	2	3	1	2	3				1	2	3	1	2	3		
Drill #	1 2 3	1 2 3	1 2 3	1 2 3	1 2 3	1 2 3				1 2 3	1 2 3	1 2 3	1 2 3	1 2 3	1 2 3				1 2 3	1 2 3	1 2 3	1 2 3	1 2 3	1 2 3		

Source: Lika Corporation, Stockton, Ca.

5. Each batch took two hours, with four batches per shift.   _____

6. Samples were taken from two consecutive batches on shift 1 and shift 2.   _____

7. Sampling was done on Monday, Tuesday, and Wednesday.   _____

8. Wafers were sampled over the three consecutive weeks.   _____

(The answers to each workshop exercise are given immediately following the exercise throughout the text.)

2. Draw a family tree.

3. How many wafers should the total multi-vari run include?

4. What reductions could be made in the total samples of wafers required if previous history indicates few significant variations occurred from week to week, day to day, or shift to shift.

Answers

> Question 1

1. Five dice on each wafer N, S, E, W, and Center	Within-unit
2. Three wafers from each bath	Unit-to-unit
3. Three locations in each batch	Within-unit
4. Two deposition chambers	Within-unit
5. Four batches per shift	Unit-to-Unit
6. Batches from shift 1 and 2	Time-to-time
7. Sampling on Monday, Tuesday, and Wednesday	Time-to-time
8. Samples from three consecutive weeks	Time-to-time

> Question 2
    See Figure 8-4.

> Question 3

Weeks	Day/s per week	Shifts per day	Batches	Wafers per batch	Deposition chamber	Locations per batch
3	× 3	× 2	× 4	× 3	× 2	× 3

= 1,296; number of readings = 1,296 × (5 dice per wafer) = 6,480

Figure 8-4. Multi-Vari Family Tree

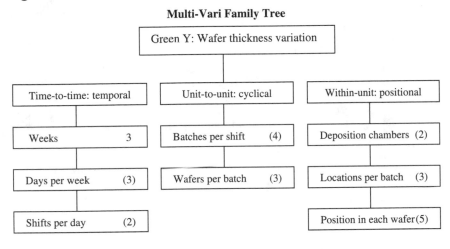

Multi-Vari Family Tree

> Question 4
>
> If the time variations (week, day, shift) were minimal, the total number of wafers would be: $1{,}296/(3 \times 3 \times 2) = 1{,}296/18 = 72$ and the number of readings would be: 72×5 (i.e., 5 dice) $= 360$

Constructing a Multi-Vari Chart

Tabular data can always be used to interpret and analyze a multi-vari study. However, the human eye cannot digest such data easily. Hence, a graphical plot is necessary to make interpretation easier and to quantify the effects of each family of variation.

The horizontal line represents time—either week-to-week, day-to-day, shift-to-shift, or hour-to-hour. However, since only samples are taken periodically from each time period—three to five units at a time—the horizontal axis should be divided into stratified and discrete time periods.

The vertical axis represents the Green Y that is under investigation and the variations within unit (say, from top to bottom or from side to side) are shown as small vertical bars. The multi-vari is not an artificial experiment. It does not disrupt production—a signal advantage. It is, in a sense, a snapshot of variation at a given time or over a short time period. It can be likened to an EKG plot of a patient's heart, where various sensors monitor different portions of the chest to determine a total profile of the heart's performance. Figure 8-5 shows three types of variation that are possible in measuring a quality characteristic. A few units, generally

Figure 8-5. Multi-Vari Charts: Separation by Major Family

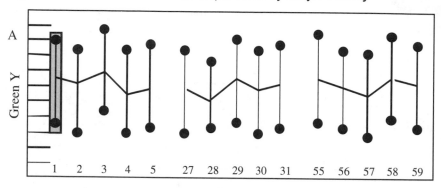

Within-Unit Variation (Positional)

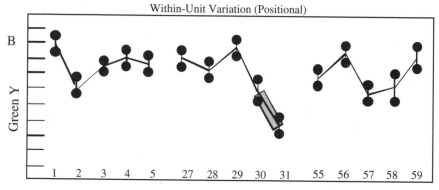

Unit-to-Unit Variation (Cyclical)

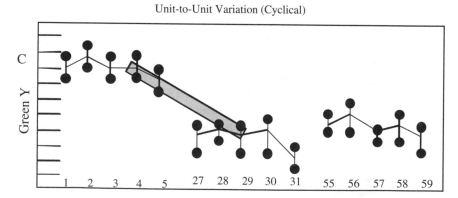

Time-to-Time Variation (Temporal)

three to five, are monitored consecutively at any given time. Figure 8-5 shows five consecutive units. Then an hour or two later, another five consecutive units are monitored. The sampling is repeated periodically until capture of at least 80 percent of the historic variation of the process or of the full specification tolerance, whichever is smaller. (See the section "Running the Multi-Vari Experiment.")

By plotting the results of the multi-vari run, you can determine if the largest variation is positional (within unit) as in Figure 8-5A, or cyclical (unit-to-unit) as in Figure 8-5B, or temporal (time-to-time) as in Figure 8-5C. The multi-vari is one of the few DOE techniques that *should not be randomized*. It is sequential. Many people, exposed to the multi-vari chart for the first time, may confuse it with a control chart. But a control chart can distinguish only time-to-time variations. It cannot probe unit-to-unit or within-unit variations or their subfamilies.

Case Study 2: The Rotor Shaft

A manufacturer producing cylindrical rotor shafts with a diameter requirement of 0.0250" ± 0.001" was experiencing excessive scrap. A process capability study indicated a total spread of 0.0025" against a requirement of 0.002", i.e., a C_{pk} of only 0.8. The foreman was ready to junk the old turret lathe that produced the shaft and buy a new one (for $70,000) that could hold a tolerance of ± 0.008", i.e., a C_{pk} of 1.25. But the works manager, on the advice of a consultant, directed that a multi-vari study be conducted before the purchase of a new lathe.

Figure 8-6 shows the results of the multi-vari in chart form. Three shafts were run at 8 A.M., another three at 9:00 A.M., 10:00 A.M., 11:00 A.M., and 12:00 noon. There was no need to go beyond noon because the rule—the capture of at least 80 percent of the historic variation of 0.0025"—had been met by 11:00 A.M. For each shaft, there were four measurements—two on the left side and two on the right side. Going from left to right measured taper on each shaft; going from top to bottom measured the out-of-round condition as the shaft was rotated to measure the point of maximum diameter and the point of minimum diameter. So, there were two subfamilies in this within-unit variation, namely, taper and out-of-round.

The cyclical, or unit-to-unit, variations are shown by the thin lines connecting the average of the four readings within each shaft. The temporal, or time-to-time, variations are shown by the double-dotted lines.

A quick reading of the chart reveals, even to a person unfamiliar with the multi-vari technique, that the largest variation seems to be time-to-time. The diameter decreased from 8:00 A.M. to 9:00 A.M. and further by

Figure 8-6. The Rotor Shaft: A Multi-Vari Chart

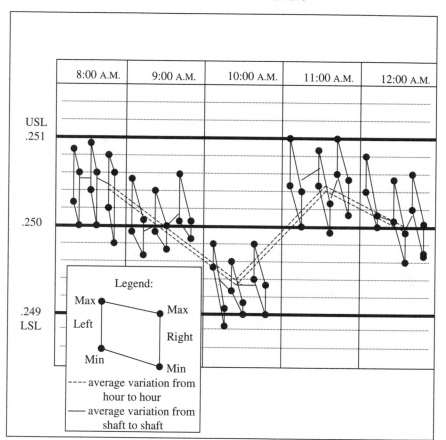

10:00 A.M. Between 10:00 A.M. and 11:00 A.M., however, it reversed direction. What could cause time-to-time variations? The foreman suspected tool wear. But if tool wear could be the cause, the readings would have risen from 8:00 A.M. to 10:00 A.M. They went down instead. So the tool wear clue was rejected. The reversal in direction from 10:00 A.M. to 11:00 A.M. provided the foreman with a strong clue. What happens, generally, around 10:00 A.M.? A coffee break! When the next sample of three shafts was taken at 11:00 A.M., the readings were similar to those at the start of production at 8:00 A.M. The foreman was then able to equate time variations with temperature variations. As the lathe warmed up from 8:00 A.M. to 9:00 A.M. to 10:00 A.M., the readings got lower. But after the machine had been shut down at the coffee break, its cooler condition resulted in higher readings at the 11:00 A.M. sampling. The foreman then guessed that the temperature rise could be caused by insufficient coolant in the tank. He confirmed that the coolant was low. When he added coolant to the prescribed level, the time-to-time variation, which accounted for 50 percent of the allowed variation, was reduced to almost zero. This illustrates how the time clue led to a temperature clue that led to the level of coolant—a Red X!

The unit-to-unit variation, accounting for only 5 percent of the total tolerance allowed, was not worth investigating. However, the within-unit or positional variation showed two significant subfamilies of variation—an out-of-round condition accounting for 30 percent of the allowed variation; and taper, contributing about 10 percent of the allowed variation. The out-of-round condition in each shaft was traced to a worn bearing guiding the chuck axis. New bearings were installed for a cost of $200, including labor, eliminating another 30 percent of the former variation.

The taper in each shaft showed a significant *nonrandom variation*, with the left side consistently higher than the right side on all 15 shafts. (It is important that every multi-vari chart be scanned for such nonrandom trends to provide strong clues.) This led to the conclusion that the cutting tool, as it traversed the shaft from left to right, was not parallel to the axis of the shaft. A slight adjustment to the guide rail reduced taper to almost zero, allowing another reduction of 10 percent of the former variation.

Quantification of Each Family and Subfamily of Variation

It is important that the variation of each family and subfamily of variation be quantified.

> ➤ The time-to-time family variation is the difference (or range) between the highest-time average and the lowest-time average.
> ➤ The unit-to-unit family variation is the difference (or range) between the highest within-unit average and the lowest within-unit average.
> ➤ The within-unit family variation is the height of the longest vertical bar of a given unit.

A more rigorous analysis of the average $\overline{X}$ and standard deviation(s) of each family is sometimes used, but is not necessary in most applications.

Table 8-2 is a summary of each family and subfamily variation of the rotor shaft case study—the percentage of variation, the cause, the correction made, and the percentage of variation reduced.

Figure 8-7 is a family tree depiction of the rotor shaft case study.

Table 8-2. Rotor Shaft Case Study: A Quantification of Variation

Variation family	Variation subfamily	% of total variation (initial)	Variation cause	Variation correction	% of variation reduced
Time-to-time	Hour-to-hour	50%	Low level of coolant	Coolant added	Nearly 50%
Within-unit	Out-of-round	25%	Worn bearings	New bearings	Nearly 25%
Within-unit	Taper	15%	Nonparallel setting	Guide rail adjusted	Nearly 15%
Unit-to-unit	Shaft-to-shaft	5%	?	—	—

In summary, the following results were achieved in the rotor shaft multi-vari study. The total variation in subsequent production was reduced from 0.0025″ down to 0.003″ and the new C_{pk} was 0.002/0.0003 or 6.7—way above the world standard C_{pk} of 2.0. The benefits: zero scrap and a cost avoidance of $70,000 in not investing in a new machine.

There is a moral in this story. Too often, industry is prone to throw out an old machine or process as "not being capable" before investigating the underlying causes of variation. Our experience indicates that in more than 90 percent of such cases, these causes can be identified and corrected without the crushing burden of capital investment. The Japanese, on the other hand, painstakingly search out the causes of variation in the old machines, while selling the West newer and costlier ones! But the techniques they use for variation reduction are crude methods, such as cause-and-effect diagrams—nowhere as elegant or comparable to the multi-vari or the other clue generation techniques to be discussed in the following chapters.

Two Types of Multi-Vari Charts

In multi-vari charts, different families of variation can be combined into one chart or each family and/or subfamily can be charted separately.

The former approach is best when the total number of families and subfamilies is no greater than three or four. Otherwise, the chart becomes too complex and too busy to dissect the separate families of variation.

Figure 8-7. The Rotor Shaft: A Family Tree

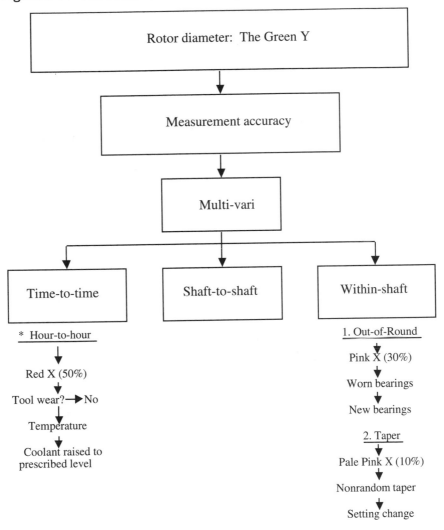

Even Figure 8-6, with four families of variation, may seem too complex for an individual constructing a multi-vari chart for the first time.

Showing each family of variation separately is the preferred method when the total number of families and subfamilies of variation exceeds three or four. Figure 8-8 depicts this for the rotor shaft case study, where the Red X family (time-to-time variations), the Pink X family (the within-unit out-of-round and taper variations)—are split into separate graphs.

Figure 8-8. An Alternate Multi-Vari Chart: The Rotor Shaft

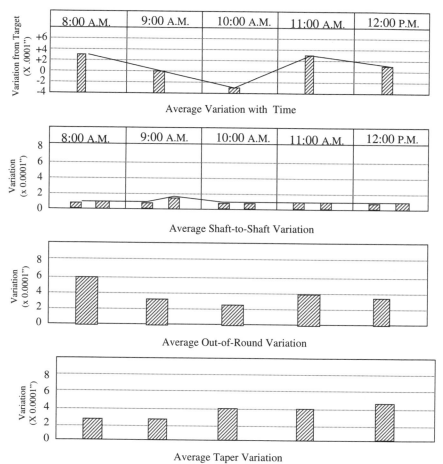

Figure 8-8 shows that the smallest (and negligible) variation is shaft-to-shaft—less than 0.0001″.

Case Study 3:
Radio Rejections—"No Trouble Found" Category

A few years ago, radios in a large electronics factory were tested for several electrical parameters by computer test positions. The rejects from these tests were then sent to analyzers to determine the cause of the rejects. The analyzers could not find anything wrong with about 22 percent of these rejects and would return the radios to be retested at the computer test positions. Most of the returns would still be rejected by the computer test positions. Back they would come to the analyzers; back again to the test positions. The units would go back and forth, round and round, until they developed enough kinetic energy to go out the door!

To stop this merry-go-round, a multi-vari team was formed. It selected 100 radios each day and examined the no-trouble-found (NTF) radios among the following multi-vari families: days (3), shifts (2), analyzers (2), test positions (7), radio bands (3), and electrical parameters (12).

Figure 8-9 shows the multi-vari chart for all of the above families except the electrical parameters. It clearly demonstrates that there was practically no variation in the number of NTFs from day 1 to day 2 to day 3, or from shift 1 or shift 2 each day, or from the two analyzers in each shift. However, among the seven computer test positions, stations A and C had 10 times as many NTFs as stations B and E—definitely a Red X. In addition, radio bands A02 and A03 had five times as many NTFs as radio band A01—a Pink X.

Investigation of the test positions revealed that stations A and C had nonstandard power supplies. Stations A, C, and D had defective test pins. Stations F and G had defective coaxial cables. When all these faults were repaired, Positrol, process certification, and pre-control (see Chapters 18, 19, and 21) were instituted to assure control. Investigation of radio bands A02 and A03 determined that three of the 12 electrical parameters—Page Sense, I-VB, and Antenna Tune) required minor redesign.

The result: The NTF's dropped from 22 percent to 2 percent, yielding a savings of $150,000 per year. Further investigations continued for another two weeks, resulting in an NTF of only 0.5 percent and an overall savings of over $500,000 per year!

The lessons learned from this case study:

1. Do not be satisfied with small, marginal, incremental improvements. (If you are satisfied with small improvements, use classical or Taguchi methods!) If you don't get 5:1, 10:1, 50:1 improvements, you've barely scratched the surface.

2. How could a classical DOE or a Taguchi DOE have gone about solving the problem? Guessing at the causes? What a waste!

3. The time actually spent on the multi-vari was only three days, plus one week in preparation. And production was not disrupted at all.

Workshop Exercise 2:
Paint Defects on a Washing Machine Tub

On a washing machine production line, paint defects were the largest category of defects. The company decided to use a multi-vari chart to isolated the families of variation. The historic variation was running

Figure 8-9. Multi-Vari Chart: NTF Case Study

Problem: 22% of radios rejected at computer test station are NTF at
              analyzing position

Stratifications: (1) Day to day   (3) Band to band   (5) Test parameter
                (2) Shift to shift   (4) Station to station   to test parameter

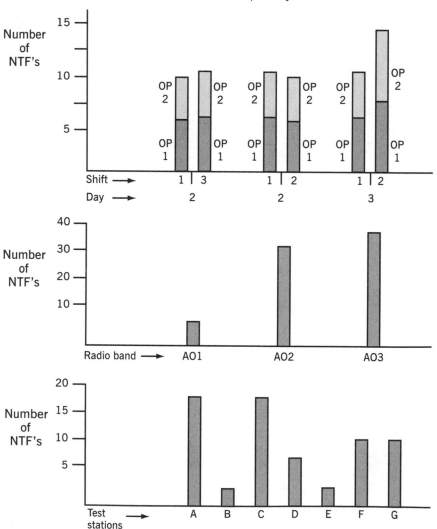

(100 radios tested per day)

Source: Motorola, Boyton Beach, Florida.

around 7 percent. The company decided that one day's data would be sufficient to capture a minimum of 80 percent of this historic variation. The production rate was 250 machines per hour. The company took 100 percent of the inspection data accumulated each hour and separated the defects into three areas of each tub—top, middle, and bottom—as well as the circumference of the tub—at twelve, three, six, and nine o'clock positions.

The defects, by family, are shown in Figure 8-10. What conclusions would you draw? What were the mistakes made in the multi-vari analysis?

Conclusions and Mistakes Made in the Tub Paint Defects Exercise (right method: ✔; wrong method: X)

✔ 1. The one-day multi-vari run was sufficient to capture more than 80 percent of the historic variation of 7 percent.

X 2. However, the Green Y was left as an attribute—just the total number of paint defects. It could have been converted into a variable, with a Likert scale, based on the size, color, or shape of the defect in order to give greater sensitivity to the defect.

X 3. The time-to-time family of variation was tracked every hour, but it was based on 100-percent inspection. The total sample size was 2,000 units, a huge expenditure. The total number of samples could have been reduced to 400 units, which would have yielded about 28 defects. In addition, if a Likert scale of 1 to 100 had been used, the weighted defects could have been expanded to a maximum of 200. This would have provided sufficient differentiation between families of variation. Fifty units could have been sampled every hour, five at a time, so that there would be 10 time samples of five units each every hour.

X 4. The unit-to-unit family—three to five consecutive units—was not identified; therefore, a key family clue was missing.

✔ 5. In the within-unit family, two subfamilies were properly identified: the top, middle, and bottom of the tub; and location within the inner diameter of the tub.

✔ 6. The variations with time and top-to-bottom variations were not significant.

✔ 7. The Red X—the 12 o'clock position—was correctly identified.

Workshop Exercise 3: Tile Adhesion

In a multi-vari study on the adhesion of tiles mounted on a strip, Table 8-3 shows the variation within each strip, from strip to strip, and from time to time. (The higher the reading, the stronger the adhesion.)

Figure 8-10. Multi-Vari Chart: Paint Defects in Washing Machine Tub

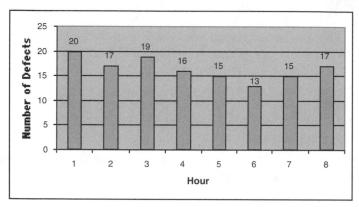

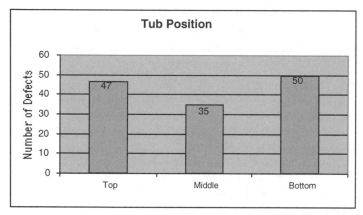

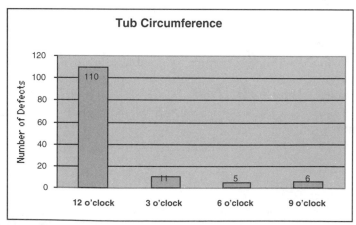

Source: Vitromatic Co., Celaya, Mexico.

Table 8-3. Multi-Vari Study: Tile Adhesion

	8:30 A.M.			1:00 P.M.			3:00 P.M.		
Strip #'s	11	12	13	267	268	269	314	315	316
Tile #									
1	66	59	54	60	57	47	38	14	56
2	56	58	32	53	37	45	09	43	39
3	58	56	59	44	46	48	54	08	60
4	65	48	48	50	44	49	57	38	58
5	67	63	72	58	52	56	60	60	60
Strip Avg.	62.4	58.8	53.0	53.0	47.2	51.4	43.6	32.6	54.6
Time Avg.		58.1			50.5			43.6	

A plot of the data is also shown in Figure 8-11. (H and L are the highest and the lowest pull force, respectively, within each strip. X is the average for each strip, 0 is the average of all three strips for each time interval.)

Questions

1. What is the family of the Red X? Justify your choice.
2. What is the family of the Pink X? Justify your choice.
3. What nonrandom trends do you detect? Pick up at least three or four clues, using Figure 8-11.

Answers

1. The within-strip variation is the family of the Red X, with a maximum variation of 61 units (see Table 8-3 and Figure 8-11).
2. The strip-to-strip variation is the family of the Pink X, with a maximum variation of 22 units (between strips 2 and 3 at 3:00 P.M.).
3. Trends and clues:

> In the Red X family (within-strip), the most pronounced nonrandom trend is the adhesion of tile 5 (generally the highest) and tile 2 (generally the lowest)
> There is a fair degree of consistency among the highest adhesions within each strip (a range from 60 to 70 units), whereas the lowest adhesions show great variations (ranging from 8 to 56).
>> This points to the great applicability of design of experiments.

Figure 8-11. Multi-Vari Study—Tile Adhesion

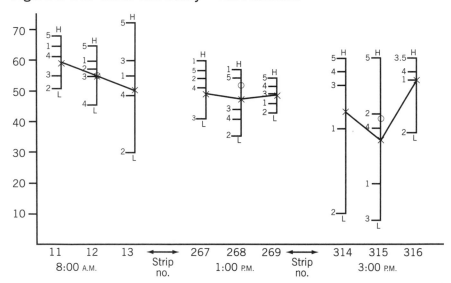

Legend
O = Average tile strength of 15 tiles at one time
X = Average tile strength of each strip
1, 2, 3, 4, 5 = Strength of each tile

Why, supposedly, with the same design, the same process, the same materials, the same operators, and the same measuring devices, do we get good units and bad? What is the difference between the good and bad units? Engineers and problem solvers traditionally investigate only the bad units—the 1, 5, or 10 percent associated with defects. Their knee-jerk reaction is to change the design, change the process, change suppliers, and berate the poor operators without bothering to investigate why with the same "recipe," there are 99, 95, or 90 percent good units. They never bother to investigate the difference between good and bad units.

Yet, this distinction between good and bad units forms the basis of three later clue-generation techniques—Components Search, Paired Comparisons, and Product/Process Search.

› The time-to-time variation is the family of the Pale Pink X, with the greatest variation at 3:00 P.M. and the least variation at 1:00 P.M. (This also points to an interaction between the within-strip and 3:00 P.M. readings.)

> Strips 1 and 2 have the same amount of variation, while Strip 3 is different. Figure 8-12 depicts the family tree of this workshop exercise.

Workshop Exercise 4: An Unsuccessful Outcome— Belt Passivator Multi-Vari Case Study

CVD silicon dioxide glass was used as insulation between two layers of metal interconnect on a product in the wafer fabrication area of a semiconductor factory. Control of the glass thickness was critical and the current process equipment was producing out-of-tolerance wafers.

There were three trays, each holding three wafers. The trays were mounted on a conveyor belt, which moved them through a reaction chamber. Inside the chamber, gases reacted, depositing a phosphorus-doped glass on the wafers. The rate of this chemical reaction was fairly constant and the glass thickness was assumed to be dependent on the speed at which the belt moved through the chamber.

Figure 8-12. Tile Adhesion: Family Tree

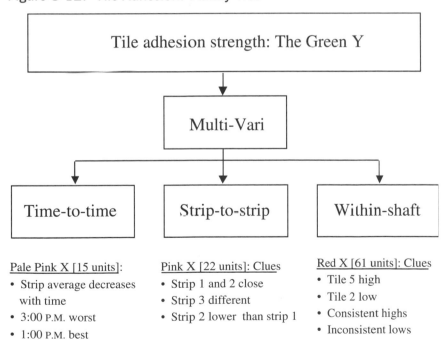

Pale Pink X [15 units]:
• Strip average decreases with time
• 3:00 P.M. worst
• 1:00 P.M. best

Pink X [22 units]: Clues
• Strip 1 and 2 close
• Strip 3 different
• Strip 2 lower than strip 1

Red X [61 units]: Clues
• Tile 5 high
• Tile 2 low
• Consistent highs
• Inconsistent lows

The process specification was 5,000 ± 1,000 angstroms.* The wafer from the middle position on the tray was measured once in the center. If this reading exceeded the specification limits of 4,000 to 6,000 angstroms, an adjustment was made in belt speed.

Past history showed considerable variation in passivation thickness. This variation was assumed to be due to changes in belt speed over time.

A multi-vari study was conducted. Three trays of wafers were measured every four hours for a whole day. Each of the three wafers on each tray was measured in two places, as shown in Figure 8-13. The tabular data are shown in Table 8-4. The multi-vari chart is shown in Figure 8-14.

Questions

1. What is the Green Y? Is it quantified and measurable?
2. Is the measurement system accurate enough to meet the 5:1 rule for specification width to instrument accuracy?
3. Was the multi-vari run long enough to capture a minimum of 80 percent of the historic variation or the specified tolerance?
4. What are the families of variation in this multi-vari study?
5. What is the Red X family of variation?
6. What are the Pink X and Pale Pink X families?
7. What are the quantifications of variation in each family?
8. What nonrandom trends can the multi-vari chart detect?
9. What was wrong with the way the experiment was conducted?
10. What would have been a better method to conduct the multi-vari experiment?

Answers

1. Glass thickness variability. It is quantified and measured in angstroms.
2. Yes. The thickness can be measured to the nearest 50 angstroms (see Table 8-4 separation of individual readings in increments of 50). The specification width is 2,000 angstroms (± 1,000 angstroms), giving a 40:1 accuracy.
3. Yes. The specified tolerance is ± 1,000 angstroms, i.e., a spread of 2,000 angstroms. The range in the multi-vari is from 3,750 to 6,400 angstroms, or 2,650 angstroms, which is greater than 100 percent of the specification width.
4. Time-to-time (4); tray-to-tray (3); wafer-to-wafer (3); within-wafer (2).

*One angstrom is one-hundredth of one-millionth of one centimeter.

Figure 8-13. Workshop Exercise 4: Belt Passivator

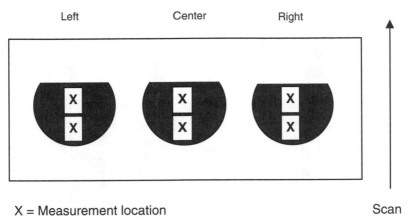

X = Measurement location

Scan

Direction

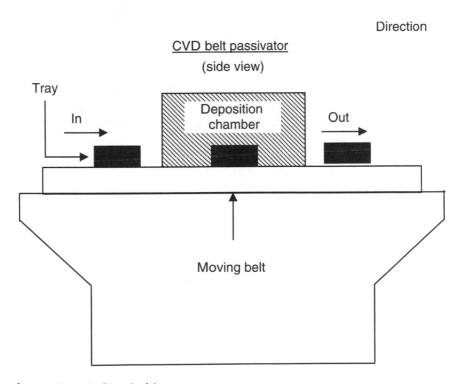

Source: Motorola, Phoenix, Ariz.

Table 8-4. Workshop Exercise 4: Belt Passivation Multi-Vari Tabular Data

Time	Tray order	Left			Center			Right			Tray average	Time average
		Up	Down	Average	Up	Down	Average	Up	Down	Average		
8:00 A.M.	1	5200	5350	5275	5000	5200	5100	5300	5350	5325	5233	
	2	4750	4950	4850	4900	5150	5025	5200	5300	5250	5042	5339
	3	4950	5350	5150	5750	6050*	5900	5950	6400	6175	5742	
Noon	1	4150	4300	4225	4050	4150	4100	4350	4550	4450	4258	
	2	4250	4300	4275	4250	4400	4325	4350	4550	4450	4350	4367
	3	4400	4650	4525	4200	4350	4275	4650	4700	4675	4492	
4:00 P.M.	1	3750	4050	3900	3950*	4250	4100	4700	5000	4850	4283	
	2	5350	5550	5450	5700	5750	5725	5650	5800	5725	5633	5211
	3	5450	5600	5525	5650	5350	5500	5800	5850	5825	5617	
8:00 P.M.	1	5800	5950	5875	5700	5950	5825	5850	6050	5950	5883	
	2	5400	5500	5450	5550	5600	5575	5500	5700	5600	5542	5608
	3	5250	5450	5350	5300	5400	5350	5450	5650	5500	5400	

Wafer position

*Whenever one of the measurements on the center wafer is out of specifications, an adjustment is made to the belt speed.
Source: Motorola, Phoenix, Ariz.

Figure 8-14. Workshop Exercise 4: Belt Passivation Multi-Vari Chart

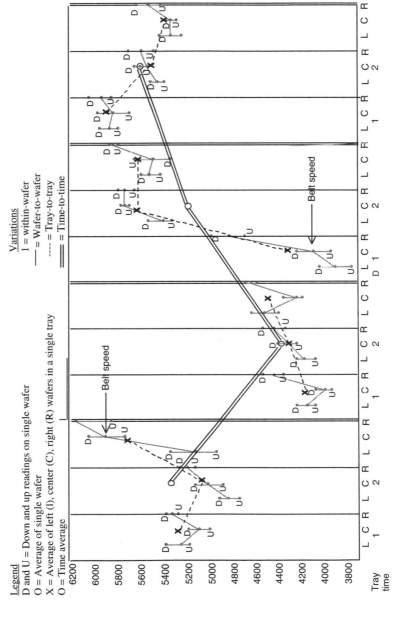

Legend
D and U = Down and up readings on single wafer
O = Average of single wafer
X = Average of left (l), center (C), right (R) wafers in a single tray
O = Time average

Variations
l = within-wafer
—— = Wafer-to-wafer
----- = Tray-to-tray
══ = Time-to-time

Source: Motorola, Phoenix, Ariz.

137

5. to 7. From Table 8-4 and Figure 8-14:

> The Red X is tray-to-tray—from 4,253 to 5,633 = 1,350 angstroms.
> The Pink X is time-to-time—from 4,367 to 5,608 = 1,241 angstroms.
> The Pale Pink X is wafer-to-wafer—from 5,150 to 6,175 = 1,025 angstroms.

8. Trends

> Within each wafer, the "down" reading is consistently higher than the "up" reading on 71 of 72 observations.
> The right wafer in each tray is consistently higher than the left and center wafers in 12 of 12 observations.
> There are wild swings in glass thickness each time the belt speed is adjusted, accounting for most of the differences in the time-to-time averages.
> Excluding the periods of belt-speed adjustment, the average tray-to-tray variations are relatively small.
> Two bad trays (#3 at 8:00 A.M. and #1 at 4:00 P.M.) were responsible for the belt-speed adjustment, and the trend across each of these bad trays is consistently from low thickness on the left side to higher thickness on the right side.

9. Mistakes in the Experiment

> The belt speed was adjusted too often. A good multi-vari study requires no adjustments or minimal adjustments to see the natural variations of the process. Belt-speed adjustments resulted in wild swings in thickness.
> The adjustment was based only on the center wafer reading. Because there was considerable variation from wafer to wafer (Pale Pink X), the adjustment—even if it was deemed necessary—could have been based on the average or median of all three wafers.
> There were only two readings—up and down—within each wafer. For a wafer with more than 100 locations, a sample of at least five locations should have been taken to determine within-wafer variations.

10. A Better Method

> The multi-vari need not have been run for a full 12 hours. Within four hours, over 100 percent of the specification variation or tolerance had been captured.

> The belt-speed adjustment at the very start—at 8:00 A.M.—should not have been made. It is a classic case of needless overcorrection. It disturbed the natural variation that should have been observed.
> The frequency of sampling—every four hours—was too low. A sampling of the three trays should have been made every hour to better determine the time-to-time family of variation.
> Two samples on each wafer were not enough. At least five points on each wafer—say, north, south, east, west, and center—should have been measured.
> The conclusions were that the Red X, Pink X, and Pale Pink X families were obscured by the artificial belt-speed variation. Had the adjustment not been made, a different conclusion would have resulted.
> Two obvious variations, regardless of belt-speed adjustment, should have been warning signals to take immediate action. Namely, (1) the right wafer in each tray being consistently higher than the left and center wafers, and (2) the "down" reading in each wafer being consistently higher than the "up" reading.

Case Study 4: "Tombstoning"

It often happens that the Red X in a long production line is buried somewhere in the various process sequences of that production line.

It became necessary, in such situations, to conduct a progressive multi-vari study at each step of the process chain after the initial multi-vari conducted at a given check point. An analogy of an EKG medical check, at a doctor's office or hospital, is appropriate. Several probes are placed in the region of the heart, arms, and legs to pinpoint the exact location of the malfunction. Similarly, a progressive multi-vari pinpoints where in the long process chain, the problem first appears and where it is the most frequent. Figure 8-15 is a typical example of a product flow where the main problem—the Green Y—was a component lead that was lifted off the motherboard at one end, somewhere in the long process chain. This phenomenon, where the component stands up like a tombstone instead of lying flat on the printed circuit board, is called "tombstoning." The reject rate was around 7,000 ppm.

In the above example, a progressive multi-vari study was conducted at each process station, following the initial multi-vari at the end of inspection and at the end of the two test positions (A, B, and C). These initial multi-vari studies had indicated that two types of capacitors in three locations on the printed circuit board were repetitive defects. The speculation was that the causes could be: capacitor lead diameter; de-

Figure 8-15. Sequence of Steps for a Printed Circuit Board

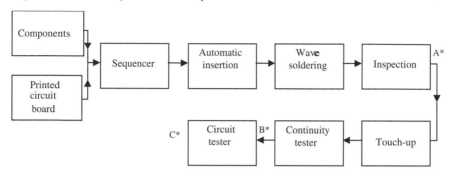

Source: Philips, Inc., Singapore.
*Check points.

formed capacitor leads; hole size in specific locations on the printed circuit board; warped circuit board; orientation of the capacitors in the sequencer; misalignment in the automatic insertion machine; program error in automatic insertion machine; parameter variations in the wave-solder machine; or unequal pressures in the pin contacts in the continuity (bed-of-nails) tester.

The progressive multi-vari indicated that there was little variation in any of the process stations in the chain until the automatic insertion machine, after which the defect level did not appreciably increase. The pipettes associated with the automatic insertion machine had to be readjusted for the capacitors and their associated hole locations, after which the defect rate dropped to zero. A regimen to calibrate the pipettes periodically, using Positrol (see Chapter 18) was established.

Multi-Vari Applications in Administrative Work

In the last 10 years, the authors have extended DOE to nonproduct applications and to administrative white-collar areas. Each DOE technique has applications in these areas.

In this chapter, dealing with the Multi-Vari technique, three examples are included. The three major families in product work—time-to-time, unit-to-unit, and within-unit—do not apply to administrative applications, where there are likely to be several more families of variation.

Case Study 5: Hospital Billing Errors

Hospitals are notorious for errors in invoices sent to discharged patients. Claims go back and forth from patients to hospitals, to medical insurance companies and to doctors, with some cases not settled for months.

One large hospital in a metropolitan area had billing errors on at least 30 percent of the bills sent to patients. As a preliminary investigation, the hospital decided to establish several families of variation that could contain the Red X in 300 disputed claims. These were subdivided into the following categories, or "families."

1. By patient's length of hospital stay
2. By patient's treatment—complex versus simple
3. By billing clerk
4. By doctor-in-charge
5. By nurse(s)
6. By insurance company
7. By billing dates
8. By prescription drugs

While there were variations in some of these families, the Red X family appeared to be differences in what tests the doctor in charge authorized and those the insurance company challenges, leaving the patient in the middle of this ping-pong match. The hospital established a set of ground rules that were fair to the doctor and the patient, while recognizing the insurance company's need to put a cap on escalating costs.

Case Study 6: Customer Service at a Hotel

Customer satisfaction surveys were a common practice at a large hotel. Forms requesting customer feedback were placed in every room. But the response was poor (fewer than 10 percent were returned), and the answers were sloppy and disjointed. The hotel's management decided to conduct in-depth interviews with its customers in person, using senior managers trained in interview techniques. The sample size was 200. The responses were divided into 10 categories, as follows:

1. Approaches/access to hotel/parking
2. Front desk
3. Concierge
4. Room amenities/housekeeping
5. Room service (food and beverages)
6. Restaurants
7. Hotel facilities (including entertainment)
8. Business services
9. Climate of caring
10. Unexpected/unanticipated experiences

The free-flowing interviews were then summarized using the above categories, with each given an importance rating of 1 to 3 by the customer, who then gave the hotel a rating of 1 to 5 on each category.

The survey resulted in a customer satisfaction profile that was similar to the survey forms that had previously been used, except for two categories—climate of caring and unexpected/unanticipated experiences—that were rated far above the others, both in importance and in rating. The fact that the hotel's management took the time and trouble to conduct a personal interview was an expression of the hotel's caring for its customers. It was also an unexpected-delight factor. Another unexpected-delight factor was the front desk's inquiry to the hotel guest 10 minutes after check-in as to whether everything in the room was to his or her satisfaction. A third delight factor was the ready willingness of the hotel staff to bend its rules somewhat to accommodate the customer's needs.

The long-term results of this caring and unanticipated delight was a dramatic increase in occupancy rates and in repeat customers.

Case Study 7: High Employee Turnover

In a company in a labor-intensive business, employee turnover was deemed excessive by its management. This was particularly disturbing because the direct labor pool was fairly stable, with a low degree of mobility. Furthermore, the company's reputation as a worthy employer was good.

The personnel department decided to conduct a multi-vari study on its departing employees and divided the gathered data into the following multi-vari families or categories:

1. By age
2. By marital status
3. By commuting distance to work
4. By length of service in company
5. By stated reason for quitting
6. By pay grade
7. By shift
8. By department type

The multi-vari study did not show significant variations by age, marital status, commuting distance to work, stated reason for quitting,* or

---

*There is a natural tendency in exit interviews for ex-employees to be circumspect and guarded, so that they don't burn bridges behind them. Often, the real reason for quitting is not uncovered.

shift. The largest variations were in length of service, with a six-month to one-year stay as the dominant period; pay grade; and department type.

Of these three reasons, pay grade was understandable, with the largest concentration of resigning employees in the lowest pay grade. The company decided not to change its wage policy, because it was already among the highest paying industries in the area. In the department type category, the paint shop stood out like a sore thumb. This was caused by poor working conditions and health problems. The company undertook strong measures—including, it must be noted, other DOE techniques—to improve housekeeping, environments, and morale.

That left the six-month to one-year service subcategory as the dominant factor to explore. The company undertook another DOE technique— paired comparisons—to determine the underlying cause (see Chapter 11).

We now conclude the chapter on the Multi-Vari technique with questions that a DOE team should ask of itself when launching a Multi-Vari study, as well as questions that senior management should ask when reviewing the DOE work of a team. The questions serve as memory joggers and guidelines to assure that the team does not go off down a blind alley. (Some of the questions pertain to the Green Y, which have been formulated in Chapter 7. They are repeated here for continuity and emphasis.)

Questions for DOE Teams

1. Has the Green Y been clearly defined, quantified, and measured?

2. Is the accuracy of the measuring instrument at least five times the range of the product spread or the specification tolerance, whichever is larger?

3. If the Green Y is an attribute, can it be converted into a variable with a Likert scale?

4. Is there an earlier, less expensive, or less complex Green Y that can serve as an approximate substitute for the original and more appropriate Green Y?

5. If it takes too long to determine the Green Y (typically when a problem is found only in the field several months after shipment from the plant), can a Multiple Environment Over Stress Test be advised to accelerate the Green Y (a field failure, as an example), so that it can be simulated within an hour or a day at the most, rather than waiting for weeks and months, in order to facilitate a meaningful DOE experiment? MEOST can also be used to convert an intermittent failure into a permanent failure before the application of DOE.

6. Is there more than one Green Y? If so, the multi-vari (or any other DOE technique) could select the most important Green Y among several.

7. If there is more than one Green Y, has the most important one been selected based on highest cost, highest defects and/or defect rates, and affected customers?

8. Is the Green Y (or problem to be solved) really important to the customer? Nothing can be more wasteful than spending money on a problem of little consequence to the customer. In the appliance industry, for example, cosmetic defects are a sacred cow. Yet, one of its studies revealed that it is typical to throw away 25 to 40 parts for every one that the customer would object to! Establishing cosmetic standard with customer inputs could have saved millions of dollars as well as throughput time.

9. If there is a Pareto distribution of causes for a high defect rate or poor yield, is the most prevalent defect mode selected for the Green Y as a first priority?

10. If there are many models in the particular product line being investigated, is the model with the highest reject rate singled out as the starting point of DOE experiments?

11. In the time-to-time family, has the total time for the experiment been determined by the 80 percent rule—i.e., running time samples until at least 80 percent of the historic variation or the specification tolerance (whichever is less) is captured? There is no point in tackling a wide variety of models and a wide variety of defect modes, as many novice problem-solvers attempt to do. That is a recipe for futility, frustration, and failure.

12. If it is known that the variation is from unit-to-unit in the same time period, bypass the Multi-Vari and conduct a Components Search, or Paired Comparisons.

13. In the unit-to-unit family, have the number of consecutive samples—generally, 3, 4, or 5—been determined?

14. In the within-unit family, have the number of lines, machines, cavities, testers, operators, and the number of locations within each unit been identified, so that suitable sample sizes can be designed for the family tree?

15. Are the total quantities required for the entire multi-vari study determined by multiplying the number of time samples by the number of consecutive units in each time sample and by the number of locations in the within-unit samples?

16. Is this total (in Item 15 above) a reasonable compromise between low cost and the necessity to continue until the 80 percent rule is met? A

suggested approach is to take just three samples in the time-to-time family and then extend the time samples, only if necessary, to fulfill the 80 percent rule.

17. Has a family tree been drawn to show the selected families and subfamilies?

18. Has a table been established to record the data gathered by major family and subfamily?

19. Is the use.of old, historic data discouraged in analyzing trends? Most historic data is suspect and of little value, except in gross percentages of defects. No one is sure who gathered the data, how it was gathered, under what conditions it was gathered, and over what length of time it was gathered. The purpose of a multi-vari is to start afresh and gather meaningful data under closely controlled conditions.

20. Have instructions been given to production maintenance personnel not to adjust any process controls during the multi-vari run but, if it is absolutely unavoidable, to record the exact nature and time of such an adjustment.

21. In determining the exact hour of time samples, the times associated with typical discontinuities, such as just before or just after coffee breaks, lunches, shift changes, etc., should be favored. Great variations can occur with such discontinuities.

22. Have nonrandom trends been examined for clues in analyzing the multi-vari chart?

Questions for Top Management During DOE Project Reviews*

1. What is the Green Y? Has it been quantified and measured? Is the ratio of the accuracy of the instrument five times the accuracy of the product?

2. How important is the Green Y to the customer?

3. What is the duration of the Green Y problem? What is the defect level? What is the cost impact to the company?

4. Who are the team members? Is there team synergy?

5. Why was this particular DOE technique selected in preference to other DOE techniques?

*These generic questions that top management should ask of their DOE teams are common to every DOE technique. They will not be repeated at the end of the succeeding chapters. At the end of each succeeding chapter, the top management questions will be confined to those related to a specific technique.

6. How were the subfamilies of variation selected?

7. Is the Green Y found in the plant as well as in the field? If only in the field, has a multiple environment overstress test been devised to accelerate and simulate the same failure mode in the plant, in order to detect and correct it much earlier?

8. How long has the DOE experiment taken? In preparation? In running time?

9. Are the Red X and the Pink X pinpointed? Or will follow-on DOE experiments be necessary, either in the plant or with the supplier, to pursue clues generated by the multi-vari? If so, which DOE technique is the most appropriate?

10. What stumbling blocks did the team experience? From management? From support departments?

11. Were the resources provided by management adequate?

12. What are the lessons to be learned from this project? For the team? For management?

9

The Concentration Chart: Pinpointing Locations of Repetitive Problems

Purpose

If the Multi-Vari shows that the largest major family of variation is within-unit, the next step would be to plot the exact location of the problem within the unit. This is best done with a concentration chart—or, as it is popularly termed—a "measles chart." Find its place in the problem solving roadmap of Figure 7-1.

A concentration chart can show either that: (1) there is no one specific location with repetitive problems (i.e., it is a random distribution) or (2) there does appear to be a concentration of defects in a particular location. Experience tells us, following the universal Pareto's Law, that the many causes of an effect are never equal. In similar fashion, it is almost universally true that there is bound to be a concentration of problems in a specific location within the unit, or a specific component or part within the unit, if the latter itself is an assembly.

In the Multi-Vari case studies described in the last chapter, we have already seen examples of the Red X family within-unit. In Case Study 2 of Chapter 8, the Red X family was in the computer test stations, with test stations A and C having 10 times the number of "no trouble found" radios as had test stations B and E. In Workshop Exercise 3 of Chapter 8, the Red X family was within-strip—specifically tile 5 (repetitively high) and tile 2 (repetitively low).

Constructing a Concentration Chart

1. Make a drawing or template of the unit containing repetitive defects.

2. Draw a grid, if needed, so that the exact locations of the problem can be plotted.

3. Ask the inspector, as each unit is being examined, to mark

> - the location of each defect type, with each defect type suitably coded, and
> - the number of defects of each type in each location. (It is not necessary to record the time of occurrence of each defect unless the time-to-time variation is deemed to be important.)

The Concentration Chart technique is best illustrated with a few case studies.

Case Study 1: Foam Leaks on Refrigerator Door

An appliance manufacturer had a problem of foam leaks during the process of filling the space between the door and its liner with foam insulation in its refrigerator product line. The problem had existed for months, with defect rates of about 8 percent. Rework costs were in excess of $120,000 a year. Operators had been blamed for the problem. The second and third shifts were particularly suspected.

This author was called in to solve the problem. A Multi-Vari study was run for three shifts, divided into the time-to-time family, door-to-door family and within-door family. There were no significant variations in either the time-to-time family (including shift-to-shift and hour-to-hour samples) or in the door-to-door family. There were, also, no significant variations from operator to operator. The most frequent foam leaks were within-door. There was hardly any foam leak at the top right, bottom right, or bottom left corners of the door where foam was inserted. The concentration chart pinpointed the top left corner location. It was determined that the operators always started the foam process at the top left corner of the door and went clockwise to fill in the other three corners. This led to an investigation of the foam start process and a discovery that there was a two-second programming delay in the foam application at that corner. When the program delay was eliminated, the defects dropped to zero. The total experiment, including correction, took less than two weeks.

Case Study 2: Wave Solder Defects

The author, following a DOE seminar in his company's Australian plant, was requested to solve solder defects that were occurring on one of the high-volume printed circuit boards. The defect rate was around 1,500 ppm. Even in those days, over 10 years ago, the company had established a maximum allowable defect rate of 500 ppm on its processes.

A multi-vari study was started, with (1) three time samples at 9:00 A.M., 9:30 A.M., and 10:00 A.M.; (2) 10 panels, each containing five boards for each time period; and (3) a concentration chart depicting the distribution of solder defects within each board. A well-qualified inspector was chosen to note the location and number of defective solder connections. Figure 9-1 shows a family tree of the variables considered.

The inspector reported that the total defect rate for solder defects— from 9:00 A.M. to 10:00 A.M.—was 1,450 ppm. Thus, the guide rule of capturing 80 percent or more of the historic defect level of 1,500 ppm, was met in just one hour. The multi-vari study revealed that there was no significant variation between the 9:00 A.M., 9:30 A.M., and 10:00 A.M. boards. Nor was there any significant variation from panel to panel or from board to board.

The largest variation was within the board, in three specific locations. The first were pinholes in the solder connections, clustered around the middle of one edge of the printed circuit board, as shown in the concentration chart of Figure 9-2. The others were in two locations of poor solder connections, both associated with two intermediate-frequency (I.F.) cans (Figure 9-3). The remaining 990 odd solder connections were perfect.

The concentration chart shown in Figure 9-2 raised the obvious question—why were there no poor solder connections on the other three sides of the board? The Multi-Vari team decided that the fixtures on which the panels were placed, while going over the solder wave, were not perfectly horizontal, but tilted to one side, causing poor solder wetting on that

Figure 9-1. A Multi-Vari Family Tree on Printed Circuit Solder Connections

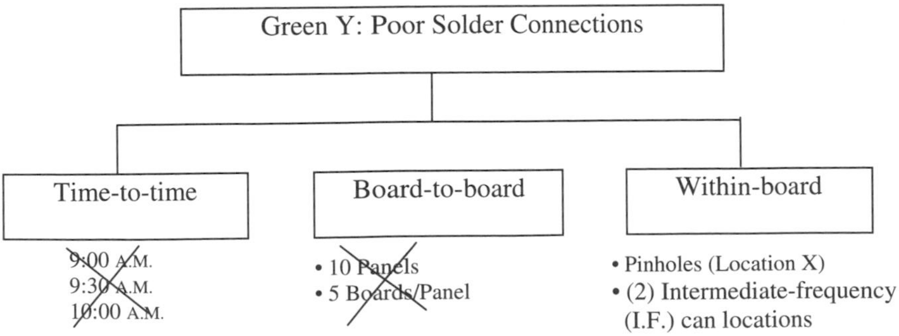

Source: Motorola Inc., Melbourne, Australia.

Figure 9-2. Pinholes in Solder Connections (Board Underside)

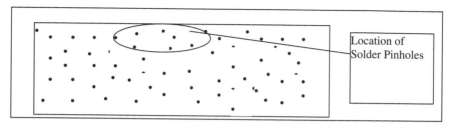

Source: Motorola Inc., Melbourne, Australia.

side. Straightening the fixtures eliminated the pinhole problem. A second Multi-Vari, following the correction, showed a reduction of the solder defect level from 1,450 ppm to around 500 ppm. A 3:1 reduction in defects had been achieved by lunchtime in just three hours!

Attention then centered on the poor solder connections associated with the two I.F. can components. The holes in the board, as shown in Figure 9-3, permitted the solder to wick up through the hole and collapse again. Two solutions were tried. The first was presoldering the I.F. can leads. The second was prefluxing the leads.

Neither solution yielded any appreciable reduction in the newly established 500 ppm level. The ratio of hole size to lead size is an important parameter in board design. Production prefers a maximum ratio to facilitate automatic insertion of components. Quality control prefers a minimum ratio for good solder connections.

In the case of the I.F. cans, it was felt that this ratio was too large (see Figure 9-3A). An experiment was tried to double up the I.F. lead onto itself and reduce the ratio (see Figure 9-3B). The result was zero defect. A

Figure 9-3. Solderability of Intermediate-Frequency (IF) Cans in the Printed Circuit Board

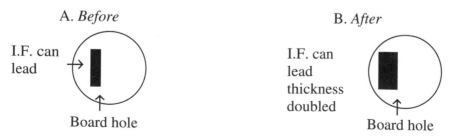

Source: Motorola Inc., Melbourne, Australia.

Multi-Vari run was performed. It showed zero defects. A production run, continued for the next half-day, confirmed zero defects! One wonders what approach a classical or a Taguchi DOE experiment would have used to solve this problem and how many fruitless weeks it would have taken, versus the Multi-Vari Concentration Chart that took a day and a half!

Workshop Exercise 1: Paint Defects

In a paint process on a panel, the yield was averaging only 82 percent. Each 1 percent yield improvement could save the company $45,000 per year. A Multi-Vari experiment was run. It determined that the largest variation was not time-to-time or panel-to-panel, but within-panel. A concentration chart was constructed, as shown in Figure 9-4, depicting four defect types (as examined under a microscope and cross-sectional detection) and the location and number of defects of each type.

1. What conclusions would you draw from the concentration chart in terms of the distribution of each defect type?
2. Could you speculate, from the type of defects, the underlying causes of each?

Answers

1. The Inconel defects were not only the most frequently occurring defect type, accounting for 75 percent of all defects, but were concentrated in the middle of the top edge of the panel, as clearly indicated in the concentration chart. The DOE team recognized that the panels were suspended from the middle of the top edge with hooks made of the Inconel alloy. Lack of periodic cleaning of these hooks led to chips being dislodged from the hooks to the panel. A preventive maintenance schedule—cleaning once every two weeks instead of once per quarter—and a redesign of the hooks reduced the overall defect rate from about 19 percent to 4.8 percent.

2. The other defect categories—glass, organic, and iron—accounted for about 25 percent of the defect totals, and there was no concentrated location for any of them. The DOE team traced the "glass" defects to enamel running from the panels to the suspension of the panels. Even though there was no repetitive pattern in these defects, the redesigned smaller hooks helped reduce this category of defects by 3:1.

Figure 9-4. Concentration Chart on Paint Defects

			I : 9	I : 16	I : 8			
								G : 2
		G : 2 O : 2						
	F$_E$: 1							
					G : 1			
			O : 2					
							F$_E$: 1	

Defect code		Total defects
I =	Inconel defects	33
G =	"Glass" defects	5
O =	Organic defects	4
F$_E$ =	Iron defects	2

3. The organic defects—presumably caused by outgassing during the ground coat or finish coat—and the iron defects, supposedly caused by reworked panels, were not followed up.

4. The concentration chart aided in a yield improvement of almost 20 percent for a savings of approximately $900,000 per year.

Workshop Exercise 2: Shaft Distortion After Heat Treat

In a machine shop, shafts were distorting after the heat treat operation and quenching. Ten shafts were placed in a container at one time, as shown in Figure 9-5, and sent to the heat treat chamber at 1500°F for one hour. The shafts were then quenched for approximately three minutes. The Green Y was the run-out, which was within specifications before heat treat but exceeded specifications afterwards. Further, there were changes in the direction of run-out after heat treat and quenching.

A DOE team studied the concentration chart shown in Figure 9-5. It concluded

1. That the heat treat caused the direction of the run-out to change in half the shafts, but not in the other half.
2. It suspected several causes for the change:

Figure 9-5. Placement of Shafts in Heat Treat; and Run-Out Direction Before and After Heat Treat

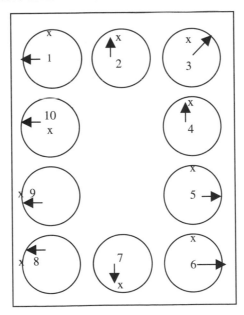

Legend:
"X" indicates run-out direction before heat treat
↑ Indicates run-out direction after heat treat
Source: Caterpillar, Decatur, Ill.

> Quench: quenching solution, quench time, and quench temperature.
> Heat treat: heat treat time and heat treat temperature.

The quenching solution was thought to be a prime suspect. A B versus C (see Chapter 15) experiment was run, but it showed no improvement in the run-out differential before and after heat treatment. Similarly, heat treat parameters of time and temperature were changed, with no improvement.

Question

What strong clue from the concentration chart did the team overlook? What action should have been taken?

Answer

It is true that the run-out direction did change on five shafts, but not on the remaining five, as seen in Figure 9-5. However, the direction of the run-out on nine of the 10 shafts pointed to the outer perimeter of the container—a strong clue that the temperature of the shafts on the outer edges was different than the temperature of the inner sides. Actual temperature measurements confirmed the temperature differential. The heat treat chamber was modified with a blower to achieve a uniform temperature within the chamber. This brought the run-out to well within specifications after heat treat.

Applications in Administrative Work

As in multi-vari studies, the concentration chart is useful in pinpointing locations of repetitive problems in administrative work.

Case Study 3: Shorted Horizontal Output Transistor

A television company was faced with a deluge of field problems that were traced to a shorted horizontal output transistor. The failure analysis indicated a massive short, caused by some unexplained phenomenon. Attempts to recreate the short in the laboratory were unsuccessful. To pick up clues, the company decided to make a plot of the exact geographic location of each failure.

A concentration chart was prepared showing the locations of field failures in various parts of the United States. The chart clearly showed that the coastal areas were prone to far more failures than were the interior locations. The coastal areas are subject to far more lightning strikes and electrical storms than further inland. As a result, the horizontal output transistor had to be redesigned to withstand these power surges, and a vexing field problem was resolved.

Case Study 4: A University Recruitment Drive

A small university, with a relatively low endowment, wanted to increase the number of applicants. Rather than lower its admission standards, it wanted to target its slender recruitment resources to those areas of the region where it would have greater success in attracting the largest number of applicants. It divided its student population of the last five years into 20 geographical areas. It then developed a concentration chart to determine which of the 20 geographical areas had been the source of the largest number of students.

Contrary to the university's expectations, the concentration chart showed that three of the 20 areas that had attracted the largest percentage of students were the furthest distance away from the university's locations. In researching the reasons for this concentration, they discovered two causes. The first was the recommendations of the high school admissions counselors in those three areas in directing students toward the university. The second was the tendency of students to select the same university that their friends had selected.

Questions for DOE Teams

1. In the Multi-Vari study, is "within-unit" the Red X family?
2. Is there more than one Green Y (defect modes) to consider?
3. Is there a drawing or template or schematic prepared in advance to determine the location of each Green Y (defect mode)?
4. If the Green Y(s) is an attribute, can it be converted into a variable, using a Likert scale?
5. Is the frequency of repetitive locations or repetitive parts recorded?
6. Is the Concentration Chart followed up with engineering judgment or other DOE experiments to distill the Red X?

Questions for Top Management During DOE Project Reviews

1. Was the Concentration Chart technique preceded by a full-fledged Multi-Vari study and was the "within-unit" family the Red X?

2. Over what length of time was the study conducted to assure that 80 percent or more of the Green Y was captured in the "within-unit" family?
3. Was there a concentration of locations or parts associated with the Green Y?
4. What is the follow-up action?

10

Components Search:
Simple, Smooth Swapping

Introduction

Components Search is the third of our clue-generation techniques for "talking to the parts." As in the case of the Multi-Vari technique and its satellite—the Concentration Chart—Components Search does not disrupt production, nor does it require any depth of technical knowledge of the product. It can, therefore, be taught to and practiced by line operators with less than one hour of coaching. Further the sample size is unbelievably small—two units, one "good" and one "bad."

A Humorous Analogy: Incident on a British Train

The principle of Components Search can be illustrated by the story of four passengers on a British train travelling from London's Euston Station to Newcastle. The four passengers in the private compartment of the train, as shown in Figure 10-1, were an old lady (L); a young woman (YW), sitting next to the old lady; an army general, sitting opposite the young woman (G); and an army private, sitting next to the general (P).

The British are a formal people and will not talk to anyone without proper introduction. So all was quiet in the train compartment. As the train was speeding through a long tunnel, the lights went out for some strange reason. Soon thereafter, all four in the compartment heard the sound of a kiss, followed by a tight slap! Now all four started to speculate about who was responsible.

> The old lady thought: "It has to be the general, old goat that he is. He kissed the young woman and the young woman slapped him back." That was her theory.
> The young woman thought: "Damn, I'm the pretty one. This hand-

157

Figure 10-1. Four Passengers in a Train's Private Compartment

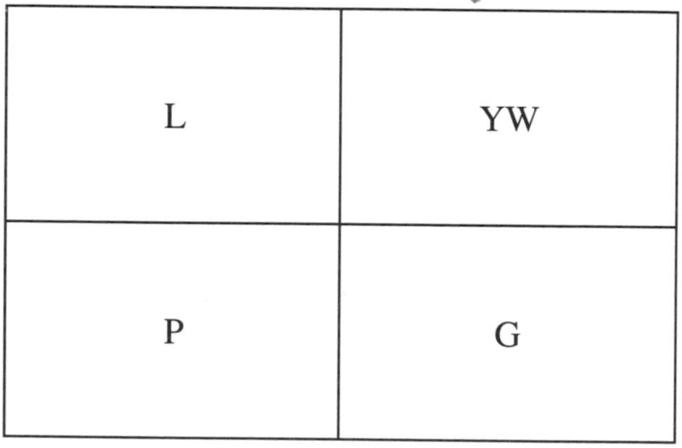

L	YW
P	G

some private tried to kiss me, but missed me and got the old bag instead, who returned the favor with a slap." That was her theory.

> The general was the one who got slapped. As he ruefully rubbed his cheek, he thought: "It's got to be this young punk of a private—the scum of the army. I wonder how he even got into the army; should have stayed in the National Guard, like former Vice President Dan Quayle. Preferably, he should have stayed out of the National Guard like President Clinton! In any case, he is the culprit. He kissed the young woman and I got the brunt of the attack because I was sitting opposite her and she suspected me." That was the general's theory.

> Only one person in that whole compartment knew the true story, and that was the private. As things were quiet and then became dark, he seized his moment of opportunity. He kissed his own hand, slapped the general and got away with it!

That is the principle of Components Search, except that you don't swap theories. You actually swap parts and/or subassemblies from the good unit to the bad unit and vice-versa, and see if the problem follows the swapped part or remains in the rest of the unit. The mechanics of Components Search are that simple!

Bypassing the Multi-Vari With Components Search

A Multi-Vari study generally determines three major families of variation—time-to-time, unit-to-unit, and within-unit. But what if the dominant family of variation is already known to be unit-to-unit? What if, in the same run and at the same time, there are both "good" and "bad" units?* Then, the multi-vari can be bypassed and the components search process begun. This is depicted in Figure 10-2, which is a reproduction of Figure 7-1, with the components search steps highlighted.

Disarming the Critics of Components Search

1. Components Search uses an unbelievably small sample size of just two units, as widely separated as possible in their respective Green Y's. Many practitioners of classic DOE object to this small sample size. "How could you determine the distribution of a given parameter (Green Y) with just two units," they ask? Their laborious, time-consuming and costly method would be to run control charts over a period of two to three days, with 50 to 300 units to determine the spread.

In Components Search, only the extremes of a distribution need be considered, as shown in Figure 10-3. By capturing the two extremes, the full range of the Green Y variation is captured, and the causes can then be systematically distilled by swapping components and/or subassemblies.

2. A second concern of traditionalists is repeatability of the culprit component found in components search. "How can you be sure, if a different pair of good and bad units are selected, that the same culprit component (or components) is likely to surface?" they ask. The answer lies in selection of the extreme good and bad units. As long as we are investigating the same Green Y, the Red X will invariably surface from that extreme variability. Many hundreds of Components Search experiments have borne this out. Only twice, in our experience, has a different Red X emerged from a second Components Search experiment, and that was caused by a time factor.

3. Some critics of Components Search consider it to be another form of fractional factorials. This indicates a fundamental lack of knowledge of the elegance of Components Search and its diagnostic power. Fraction factorials suffer from their inability to separate the main effects from their interaction effects. These "confounding aliases" can lead fraction factorials to weak, marginal, and even downright wrong results!

Rather than merely confirming or denying a preselected set of causes, as attempted in classical or Taguchi DOE, components search actually talks to the parts. Its systematic and symmetrical design unearths

---

*"Good" and "bad" units in this and subsequent chapters need not be "accept" and "reject" units. They could both be acceptable, but they must be widely separated in terms of the Green Y measurement(s). The "good" and "bad" units are only labeled as such for brevity.

Figure 10-2. The Search for the Red X: A Problem-Solving Roadmap Highlighting Components Search

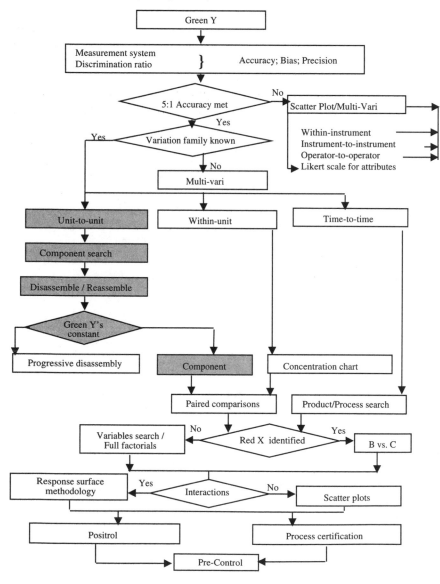

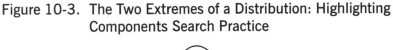

Figure 10-3. The Two Extremes of a Distribution: Highlighting
Components Search Practice

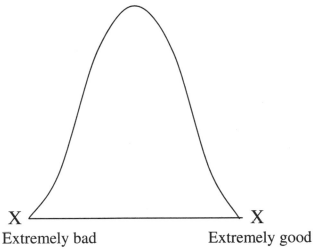

X ————————————————————→ X

Extremely bad   Extremely good

unexpected controlling causes, be they main causes or higher order interactions.

The Four Stages of Components Search

Understanding the four stages in Components Search experiments will
greatly help in overcoming the misunderstanding of its critics. Table 10-1
lists each of the stages, along with its objective.

Stage 1: Ballpark Stage. This stage determines whether the right variables have been chosen among the components to be investigated, i.e., are
they in the ballpark? If Stage 1 is successful there is a statistical confidence
of 95 percent and that enables the experimenter to proceed to Stage 2.

Stage 2: Elimination Stage. The purpose of Stage 2 is to eliminate not
only all the unimportant main causes or factors but also the interaction
effects associated with each of these unimportant causes. This goal is
achieved by using pairs of interchanged tests. With each interchange, a
large number of potential interactions and the main effect (the single factor changed) are simultaneously "energized." Again, with 95 percent statistical confidence, at each test pair, only the absence of a Red X eliminates
that large host of main effects and their associated interactions.

Stage 3: Capping Run Stage. This stage verifies or validates that the
important causes selected in Stage 2, when combined, continue to be im-

Table 10-1. The Four Stages of Components Search

Stage	Objective
1 Ball Park	Determine if the Red X and Pink X have been included among the variables* considered. It also assures the repeatability of the disassembly/reassembly process.
2 Elimination	Eliminates unimportant causes and their associated interaction effects.
3 Capping Run	Verifies that the important variables are truly important and the unimportant variables are truly unimportant.
4 Factorial Analysis	Quantifies the magnitude and direction of the important causes and their interaction effects.

*Throughout this text, variables, causes and factors are synonymous terms and are used interchangeably.

portant, and that the unimportant causes identified in Stage 2, are confirmed as unimportant.

Stage 4: Factorial Analysis. This stage is not another experiment but an analysis drawn from Stages 1, 2, and 3 in a full factorial matrix to quantify and neatly separate the *magnitude and direction* of the important main effects and their interaction effects.

The methodology of each of the four stages will be clarified in the case studies that follow.

Components Search: Prerequisites

> The technique is applicable primarily in assembly operations, as distinguished from process-oriented operations (although it can be used where there are identical processes or machines with a varying Green Y and where parts of the process can be interchanged between these machines).
> The performance (output or Green Y) must be measurable, with the accuracy of the measuring instrument at least five times the specification tolerance or product spread.
> Both "good" and "bad" units must be capable of disassembly and reassembly without a significant change in the original output.

A Procedure in 12 Steps

1. Select a sample size of just two units (assemblies) from a day's production as far apart as possible with respect to the Green Y being investigated—one very good unit and one very bad unit. (In shorthand language, one BOB, i.e., *Best of the Best*, and one WOW, i.e., *Worst of the Worst*.) The farther apart the BOB and the WOW, the easier it will be to find the Red X). Measure their respective Green Y's.

2. Stage 1. Disassemble and reassemble the BOB and the WOW twice and measure their respective Green Y's twice more.

3. Test of Significance: There are two parts to this test to determine if the difference between the BOB and the WOW is statistically significant.

> The three Green Y's of the BOB must all rank better than the Green Y's of the WOW, with no overlap.
> The $D/\bar{d}$ ratio must be greater than or equal to a minimum of 1.25. (D is the difference between the medians of the BOBs and the WOWs, while $\bar{d}$ is the average difference within the ranges (or non-repeatability) of the three BOB measurements and the three WOW measurements. The next case study will explain the test of significance further.)

4. If the $D:\bar{d}$ ratio is less than 1.25, Stage 1 of Components Search has failed. It means that the Green Y's do not remain constant; in that case, the problem is in the assembly process (i.e., the sequence in which the components are assembled) rather than in the components themselves). This calls for a progressive step-by-step disassembly and reassembly to determine which assembly process step is the Red X (see Figure 10-2). If the $D:\bar{d}$ ratio is greater than or equal to 1.25, the Red X is in one or more of the components and/or subassemblies. In that case, Stage 1 is successful and the swapping of components/subassemblies can begin.

5. Starting with the most likely subassembly, rank the subassemblies in descending order. If there are no significant subassemblies, rank the components in descending order of likelihood.

6. Stage 2. Switch the top-ranked subassembly or component (call it component A) from the BOB to the WOW and its counterpart from the WOW to the BOB. Measure and record the two new Green Y's.

7. There are three outcomes possible in Step 6:

(a) The BOB remains a BOB, i.e., good, and the WOW remains a WOW, i.e., bad. This result means that the switched component A is unimportant.

(b) The BOB becomes a WOW and the WOW becomes a BOB. This outcome means that the switched component A is important and is a solid Red X; Components Search is over.
(c) The BOB deteriorates *partially* moving toward a WOW but does not quite get there and the WOW improves *partially* toward a BOB but does not quite get there. This result means that the switched component A may be important, but is not the only problem component. Some other component that can also cause a partial change needs to be discovered in subsequent swaps. Such a partial change is also an indication of an *interaction* of A with another component.

To determine the extent of whether such a partial change is important or not, the decision limits (described in the next section) must be calculated. Any swap that results in a point outside a home decision limit—for either the BOB or the WOW—means that component A is now definitely important, along with one or more other components yet to be discovered.

8. In each of the three possible outcomes of Step 7, restore component A from the original BOB back to the rest of the BOB and component A from the original WOW back to the rest of the WOW to ensure that the original Green Y's of the BOB and WOW are restored. If this does not happen, the disassembly/reassembly process is suspected and should be investigated.

9. Repeat Steps 6, 7(a) or 7(c), and 8 with the next most likely subassembly, or component B, then C, then D, etc.

10. Once two or more components are identified as important in Step 7(c) and Step 9, switch them simultaneously between the BOB and a WOW until a complete reversal occurs, i.e., a BOB becomes a WOW and vice-versa. The Red X is now a combination of these important components and their interaction effects.

11. Stage 3. A capping run is then performed by testing all of the untested and unimportant subassemblies/components as a group as WOWs, against all of the important subassemblies/components as a group as BOBs. The outcome should be close to Stage 1 BOBs. Then flip-flop, with the unimportant components as BOBs and the important components as WOWs. The result should be close to Stage 1 WOWs.

12. Stage 4. Finally, a full factorial analysis, using all the data generated in Stages 1 and 2, is conducted to determine, quantitatively, the magnitude and direction of the main effects and interaction effects. Stage 4 is only a calculation, not a new experiment.

Case Study 1: The Hourmeter

An hourmeter, built by an electronics company, had to meet the customer's reliability requirement of remaining operational clear down to −40°C. The reject rate, however, was in the double digits, and the problem had not been solved after several months. The worst units had lock-up even as high as 0°C.*

The hourmeter consists of a solenoid cell with a shield to concentrate the electrical charge that pulses at regular intervals. The pulse triggers a solenoid pin, which in turn causes a verge arm, or bell crank, to trip the counter, advancing it by one unit. The counter is attached to a numerical shaft containing numerical wheels. These numeral wheels are separated from each other by idler gears, which rotate on an idler gear shaft. Both the idler gear shafts and the numeral shafts are attached to the main frame, which is made of hard white plastic. The pulsing rhythm is provided by an electronics circuit board.

Stage 1: Disassembly and Reassembly

Two units—one very good (at −40°C) and one very bad (at 0°C) were selected for the components search investigation. Table 10-2 shows the results of Stage 1 disassembly and reassembly.

Test for Significant Repeatable Differences

(a)   The three Green Y's of the BOB should be better than the three Green Y's of the WOW. Test 1 passes.

(b)   D:d̄ ratio should be ≥1.25,† where

Table 10-2. Stage 1: Establishing Significant Repeatable Differences

Results	High (good) assembly	Low (bad) assembly
Initial	−40°C	0°C
First Disassembly/Reassembly	−35°C	−5°C
Second Disassembly/Reassembly	−37°C	−7°C

Source: Motorola Automotive, Schaumburg, Ill.

*This case study is more complex than most Components Search projects. It is selected to show the full range of techniques that can be utilized.
†Based on the 0.05 Classical F Table, with three builds of each assembly.

D = difference between median* values of the
three highs and the three lows

$$\text{and } \overline{d} = \frac{\left(\begin{array}{c}\text{range of nonrepeatability of the high assembly } + \\ \text{nonrepeatability of the low assembly}\end{array}\right)}{2}.$$

Here D = $-37° - (-5°) = -32°$

$$\overline{d} = \frac{(-40° - 35°) + (-7° - 0°)}{2} = \frac{(-5°) + (-7°)}{2} = -6°$$

So D/$\overline{d}$ = $-32°{:}-6° = 5.33{:}1$ which exceeds 1.25.

Conclusion

Tests for significance (a) and (b) are met. Therefore, Stage 1 is success-ful. This means that the Red X, Pink X, etc., are among the components and not in the assembly techniques.

Table 10-3 shows the ranking of suspect components/subassemblies of the hourmeter, in descending order of likelihood. This is, of course, engineering judgment, which may or may not be correct. But we do know, having passed Stage 1, that one or more of these components/subassem-blies definitely will be the Red X, Pink X, etc.

Table 10-3. Ranking of Components (in Descending Order of Likelihood)

Rank	Component	Label
1	Solenoid, pin, and shaft	A
2	Idler gear shaft	B
3	Numeral shaft	C
4	Mainframe	D
5	Bill crank	E
7	Idler gears	F
7	Numeral wheels	G
8	Electronic circuit board	H
9	Remainder of components	R

Source: Motorola Automotive, Schaumburg, Ill.

*Average values can be used, but median values (where there is an equal number of readings on either side of the median) are more accurate.

The Graphical Plot

Stage 2: The next step is to swap each component/subassembly from the good hourmeter to the bad and vice-versa, starting with component A—the solenoid, pin, and shaft. Since the good remains good and the bad remains bad, A is not important. The swap must be followed by restoring the components to their original good and bad units, respectively. (This is not shown in Figure 10-4, so as not to clutter the chart excessively. The same is true for the other switched components—B, C, D, etc.).

Figure 10-4 shows that components/subassemblies B, C, E, F, and H, when swapped, do not show a reversal from good to bad and vice-versa, and are, therefore, unimportant. But D and G do produce a partial reversal and must be considered important. Whenever there are two or more such components/subassemblies with partial reversals, they are switched simultaneously from good to bad and vice-versa.

Stage 3: Capping Run. Here, the important components, D and G, are deliberately kept at their good (high) levels, with the rest of the components, R, kept at their bad (low) levels. The symbols are D_H G_H R_L. The original good levels in Stage 1 should be reproduced. Next, the important components, D and G, are deliberately kept at their bad (low) levels, with the rest of the components, R, kept at their good (high) levels. The symbols are D_L G_L R_H. The original bad levels in Stage 1 should be reproduced.

Decision Limits

The purpose of decision limits, in Stage 2, is to determine whether a component (when swapped) and its associated interaction effects are important (outside of the decision limits) or unimportant (inside the decision limits), and therefore, eliminated as unimportant.

The decision limits for Stage 2, and derived from Stage 1, are given by the formula:

$$\text{Decision limits} = \text{median (H or L)} \pm t_{0.95}\, \overline{d}/\overline{d}_2 \text{ where}$$

> median high (h) is the median value of the high assembly in Stage 1: (see Table 10-1);
> median low (l) is the median value of the low assembly in Stage 1 (see Table 10-1);
> t is the value corresponding to a 0.95 or 95 percent confidence; and
> $\overline{d}/d_2$ is an estimate of sigma, σ. ($\overline{d}$—as defined in the test for significant repeatable differences—is the average range of nonrepeatability of the high and low assemblies added together.)

Figure 10-4. Components Search Case Study: Hourmeter
              Experiment—A Graphical Plot

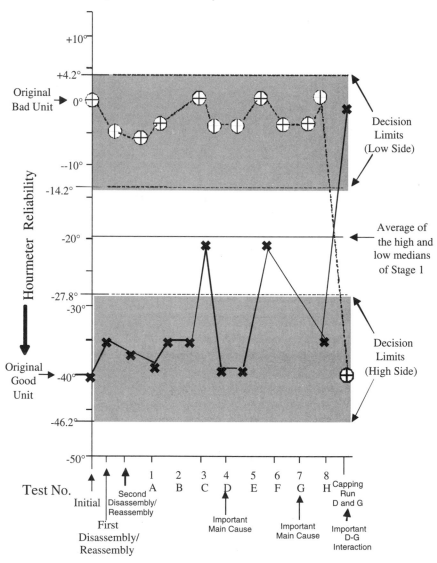

Source: Motorola Automotive, Schaumburg, Ill.

With three disassemblies/reassemblies for both good and bad units, we have two degrees of freedom for each of them, or a total of four degrees of freedom. From the Student's t table,[16] with four degrees of freedom, t, for a 2-tailed 95 percent confidence, is 2.776:$\bar{d}_2$ is the statistical constant of 1.81.

Therefore decision limits (high) = median (high) ± 2.776 d/1.81,
and decision limits (low) = median (low) ± 2.776 $\bar{d}$/1.81.

In the hourmeter case study:

Median (high) = -37; median (low) = $-5°$; $\bar{d} = -6°$.

So, decision limit (high) = $-37 + 2.776 \times \dfrac{-6}{1.81} = -46.2°$ and $-27.8°$,

and decision limits (low) = $-5° \pm 2.776 \times \dfrac{-6}{1.81}$ - $+ 4.2°$ and $-14.2°$.

Figure 10-4 shows not only the effects of swapping components A through H, but also the decision limits for the high levels of these components, i.e., $-46.2°$ and $-27.8°$, and the decision limits for the low levels of these components, i.e., $+ 4.2°$ and $-14.2°$.

> It shows that components A, B, C, E, F, and H stay within their decision limits, both high and low. Therefore, they are not important.
> However, components D and G go beyond the high decision limit but not the low decision limit. Therefore, D and G are important.

(Even if a component goes beyond one decision limit—say high—and not the other, it is considered important and its interaction effects are also considered important.)

Table 10-4 summarizes stages 1, 2, and 3 of the hourmeter case study. It includes the decision limits (derived from Stage 1), the analysis, and the conclusion.

An Alternative "Rule of Thumb" to Assess the Importance of a Component Exchange in Stage 2

Many practitioners find the statistical calculations associated with determining these decision limits tedious. The authors have developed an em-

Table 10-4. Components Search: The Hourmeter Case Study

Test No.	Component Switched	High Assembly	Results	High Decision* Limits	Low Assembly	Results	Low Decision* Limits	Analysis
Initial		All Comp. High	−40°		All Comp. Low	0°		
No. 1		All Comp. High	−35°		All Comp. Low	−5°		
Disassembly/ Reassembly								
No. 2		All Comp. High	−37°		All Comp. Low	−7°		
Disassembly/ Reassembly								
1	A	$A_L R_H$	−40°	−27.8° and −46.2°	$A_H R_L$	−5°	−14.2° and +4.2°	A Unimportant
2	B	$B_L R_H$	−35°	−27.8° and −46.2°	$B_H R_L$	0°	−14.2° and +4.2°	B Unimportant
3	C	$C_L R_H$	−35°	−27.8° and −46.2°	$C_H R_L$	−5°	−14.2° and +4.2°	C Unimportant
4	D	$D_L R_H$	−20°	−27.8° and −46.2°	$D_H R_L$	−5°	−14.2° and +4.3°	D Important
5	E	$E_L R_H$	−40°	−27.8° and −46.2°	$E_H R_L$	0°	−14.2° and +4.3°	E Unimportant
6	F	$F_L R_H$	−40°	−27.8° and −46.2°	$F_H R_L$	−5°	−14.2° and +4.2°	F Unimportant
7	G	$G_L R_H$	−20°	−27.8° and −46.2°	$G_H R_L$	−5°	−14.2° and +4.2°	G Important
8	H	$H_L R_H$	−35°	−27.8° and −46.2°	$H_H R_L$	0°	−14.2° and +4.2°	H Unimportant
Capping Run	R	$D_H G_H R_L$	−40°	−27.8° and −46.2°	$D_L G_L R_H$	9°	−14.2° and +4.2°	R Unimportant

Source: Motorola Automotive, Schaumburg, Ill.

*Decision Limits = Median ± d/1.81

Median for High Assemblies = −37°; Median for Low Assemblies = −5°

$\bar{d}$ = (Range for High Assemblies + Range for Low Assemblies)/2 = (7 + 5)/2 = 6

Decision Limits (High Side) = −37° ± 6/1.81 = 27.8° and −46.2°

Decision Limits (Low Side) = −5° ± 6/1.81 = −4.2° and −14.2°

CONCLUSION:
1. Components A, B, C, E, F, and H are within the high and low control limits. So they are unimportant.
2. Components D and G are outside the high control limits. So they are important.
3. The capping run confirmed that D and G combined go outside both the high and the low control limits. So D and G and their interaction effects are important.

pirical approach to assess whether a component swap in Stage 2 is important or not. It is not as accurate as decision limits, but can serve as a "rule of thumb."

1. Take the high median and low median in Stage 1. In the hour-meter case study, these are $-37°$ and $-5°$, respectively.

2. Calculate the average value between these two medians. Here, it is $-21°$.

3. In Stage 2 swaps, if a component crosses this average value or comes very close (within 10 percent) to crossing it, that component is important. If not, it is not important. In Stage 2 of the case study, A, B, C, E, F, and H are nowhere near this average value of $-21°$. But, when swapped from high to low, D and G, at $20°$, are very close to the average value of $-21°$ (within 5 percent) and are, therefore, deemed important, as are their interaction effects. So are D and G, when both the swapped together in the capping run—both from high to low and low to high—way over the average value. So D and G are now confirmed important; full reversal takes place and the D-G interaction effect is important.

Main Effects and Interaction Effects

Before a discussion of Stage 4—the factorial analysis—an explanation of main effects and interaction effects is in order. A simple analogy might help. A person who consumes alcohol may feel no adverse effect. He may not have any reaction to drugs either. But alcohol and drugs taken together may result in death. That is an interaction effect—a consequence that occurs only when two items are combined.

Another example would be a "mad" scientist experimenting with a jar of hydrogen and a jar of oxygen. He lights a match in these two separate jars and nothing happens. So he mixes the two jars together in the right proportions, then lights a match. He is immediately blown to "kingdom come" in one fell swoop. That is an interaction effect.

In the world of human relations, there are similar interaction effects. Ordinary people, with limited skills, working and pulling together, often achieve extraordinary results. In the world of sports, a team that has been fired up sometimes outperforms a superior team that does not pull together. That is an interaction—a synergistic effect. In the finals of the 1998 World Cup of soccer, the French team was a decided underdog. Brazil, on the other hand, had a dazzling array of stars, including superstar Renaldo—the Michael Jordan of soccer. Yet France left Brazil in the dust with an unbelievable 3–0 victory. That is team interaction, team synergy, team symbiosis.

In a product context, we can quantify interactions. Take two assemblies, A and B, with variations of 3 and 7 units, respectively. When joined together, the sum of the variation would normally be 10. A and B would be considered independent variables with each contributing independently to the result 10, which is called a main effect. However, if A and B are joined together and the total variation is 16, that is called an interaction effect, actually an additive interaction, where the whole is greater than the sum of the parts. A catalyst in a chemical reaction is an example of an additive interaction. On the other hand, if A and B are joined together and the total variation is 2, that is known as a subtractive interaction effect, with the whole being less than the sum of its parts. In the world of politics and industry, we see many examples of both additive and subtractive interaction effects. In the rare examples of a Democratic President and a Republican Congress working together, we see an additive interaction and the country prospers. More often, the two are at loggerheads, so the interaction is subtractive and the country is the loser.

Interactions can also be portrayed graphically. In Figure 10-5A, let us say that the output—Green Y—goes up from 5 to 15 units as an input variable A goes from low to high. For convenience, in later algebraic calculations, low is designated minus (−) and high is designated plus (+). This is under a condition in which another input variable B is kept constant at a low (minus) value. Now, if B is changed from a low (−) to a high (+) value, the Green Y goes up further—by 5 units. The contribution of A to the Green Y remains constant at 10 units, regardless of whether B is (−) or (+). And the contribution of B to the Green Y remains constant at 5 units regardless of whether A is (−) or (+). In other words, A is independent of B and B is independent of A; i.e., the AB interaction is zero. Graphically, whenever two lines are parallel, the interaction is zero.

In Figure 10-5B, as variable A goes from (−) to (+), the Green Y goes

Figure 10-5A. Main Effects: A and B, No Interaction

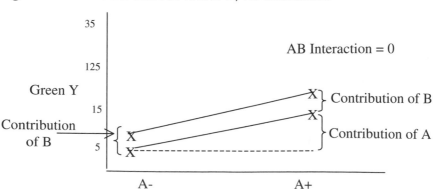

Figure 10-5B. Main Effects: A and B, With Interactions

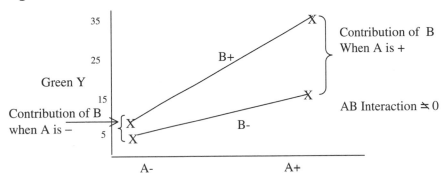

from 5 to 15 units, as before, when B is (−). However, when B is changed from (−) to (+), the Green Y barely increases to 8 when A is kept (−), but shoots up to a whopping 35 when A is (+). The contribution of B to the Green Y is only 3 units when A is (−), but is 20 units when A is (+). Now, the AB interaction is not zero. This is graphically portrayed by two nonparallel lines. The greater the nonparallelism, the greater is the interaction effect.

It is such interaction effects, when not isolated from the main effects, that make the fraction factorial approach—be it classic DOE or Taguchi DOE—give weak, marginal, or downright wrong results.

Stage 4: Factorial Analysis

A factorial analysis* is not a new experiment. It takes data from the 3 previous stages, 1, 2 and 3, in order to quantify the magnitude and direction of important main effects and interaction effects identified in Stages 2 and 3 of Components Search.

The simplest factorial analysis is a 2×2 factorial—i.e., two factors, with two levels. Figure 10-6 shows the two factors—D and G—identified as important in Stages 2 and 3 of the Hourmeter case study. There are two levels for factor D—D_L and D_H—and two levels for factor G—G_L and G_H. A 2×2 factorial is sometimes designated as a 2^2 where the "lower" 2 stands for two levels and the "power" 2 represents the number of variables. Hence there are four combinations, or four cells, in Figure 10-6 that need to be filled.

In the $D_L G_L$ cell (both low), there are a total of 10 Green Y's—three from Stage 1, six from low assembly Stage 2, and one from the capping

*A factorial analysis is common to Components Search, Variables Search, and the Full Factorial.

Figure 10-6. Factorial Analysis: The Hourmeter

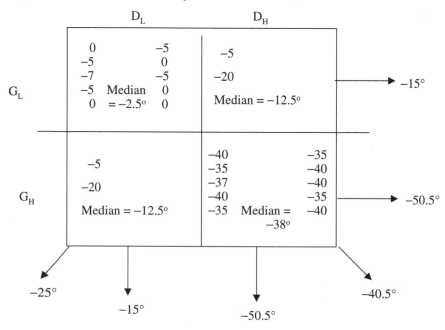

$$\text{Main Effect D} = -50.5° - (-15°)/2 = -35°$$
$$\text{Main Effect G} = -50.5° - (-15°)/2 = -35°$$
$$\text{DG Interaction Effect} = -40.5/2 - (-25°) = 15.5°/2$$

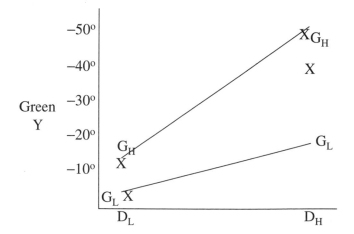

Source: Motorola Automotive, Schaumburg, Ill.

run, where D and G are both low. A reference to Table 10-4 would indicate that these readings are 0° from the initial "low" assembly, $-5°$ and $-7°$ from the replicated low assembly, with all three readings from Stage 1. In Stage 2, there are also six combinations in which D and G are both low.

These readings are $-5°$, 0°, $-5°$, 0°, $-5°$, and 0°. In Stage 3—the capping run—there is one more combination in which D and G are both low, at 0°.

In similar fashion for the D_H, G_L cell, there are two readings in Stage 2 where G is low and D is high. These are $-5°$ and $-20°$. For the D_LG_H cell there are also two readings in State 2 where D is low and H is high: $-5°$ and $-20°$. Finally, in the D_LG_H cell, there are 10 readings—three from Stage 1, six from High Assembly Stage 2 and one from the capping run, Stage 3, where D and H are both high. These are $-40°$, $-35°$ and $-37°$; $-40°$, $-35°$, $-35°$, $-40°$, $-40°$, and $-35°$; and $-40°$, respectively.

Next, the medians in each cell are determined, as shown in Figure 10-6. In the factorial matrix of Figure 10-6, if the medians in the D_L column are added, the result is the contribution of D_L alone to the Green Y, since the contribution of G_L and G_H balance and effectively cancel one another. Similarly, the medians of the D_H column, when added, give the contribution of D_H alone to the Green Y. The difference, then, between D_H and D_L is called the main effect of factor D. in the same manner, adding up the medians in the G_L row and G_H row, and then subtracting G_L from G_H gives us the main effect of factor G. To determine the interaction effect of D and G, the diagonal medians D_LG_H and D_HG_L are added together and subtracted from the diagonal medians D_LG_L and D_HG_H. This interaction effect is shown in the graphical plot of Figure 10-6. The D_LG_L cell reading (median) is $-2.5°$; the D_HG_L cell reading (median) is $-12.5°$; the D_LG_H cell reading (median) is 12.5°; and the D_HG_H cell reading (median) is $-38°$. When these four points are plotted and connected by the G_L and G_H lines, there is a nonparallel effect indicating the presence of a moderate interaction between factors D and G.

"Talking to the Parts"

The reliability engineer who conducted the Components Search study on the hourmeter wrote the following postscript to his report:
    "The problem has been with us for 18 months.

> We talked to the suppliers.
> We talked to the engineers and designers.
> We talked to the engineering managers.
> But we never talked to the parts!

With the Components Search technique, we identified the problem in just three days . . ."—Rick Kiska

The Final Solution to the Hourmeter Case Study

Clue Generation—Components Search

Mainframe and numeral wheels cause drop in performance.

Engineering Analysis

> $60\times$ life-size model built.
> Isolated first numeral wheel and main frame as the problem.
> Made measurement at critical points at critical temperatures.

Results

> Mainframe shrunken by up to 0.002", bringing numeral wheel and idler shaft too close.
> First numeral wheel off-center by 0.005".
> Counter jammed when shrinkage coincided with eccentricity.

Alternative Solutions

> Redesign mainframe (cost $50,000)—this alternative rejected.
> Change numeral wheel specification and tolerance (low cost)—this alternative accepted.

Let the Parts, Not the Engineers, Determine the Correct Specifications

In traditional problem solving, defective parts are sent back to Incoming Inspection or to the supplier to be checked vis-à-vis their specifications. More often than not, the stereotyped answer is that the parts are within specifications. End of investigation! Start of frustration!

Components Search (and the companion technique of Paired Comparisons detailed in the next chapter) is a much better way of establishing correct specifications than is engineering judgment. It is the authors' view, supported by many years of association with engineers, that most specifications are arbitrary and pulled out of the air. As a result, specifications are too tight, too loose and, in any case, invariably wrong.

In Components Search, the parts tell us which is a good component and which is a bad one. It is from the good component, or components, that correct specifications must be determined. The authors have seen example after example in which the bad parts meet specifications and the good parts do not meet specifications. What, then, should one do? Why, change the arbitrary specifications, of course, to conform to the readings on the good parts!

Case Study 2: The Nonfiring Burner

In a medium-sized international company making boilers, an oil-fired burner was not firing on approximately 3 percent of production units. Various components had been examined and found to be functional, yet the burners would not fire.

A components search was then launched, with only a go/no go Green Y, namely a burner that fired and another that did not fire.

Stage 1

The BOB and WOW units were disassembled and reassembled, with no change in their respective Green Y's, as shown in Figure 10-7.

Figure 10-7. Components Search Case Study: The Burner

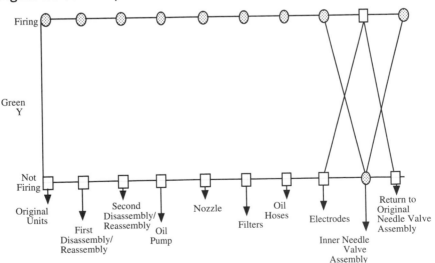

Source: Thermax, Pune, India.

Stage 2

The ranking of suspect components, in descending order of likelihood, was as follows:

> - Oil pump;
> - Nozzle;
> - Filters;
> - Oil hoses;
> - Electrodes; and
> - Inner needle valve assembly.

As often happens, when each of the above components was swapped, the least suspected component—the inner needle valve assembly—turned out to be the Red X. The other components showed no contribution to the problem—and, hence, no interactions. Consequently, Stages 3 and 4 were not needed.

A follow-up components search (not shown) was performed on the inner needle valve assembly, with its components ranked in descending order of likelihood, as follows:

> - Spring;
> - Needle valve;
> - Nozzle holder; and
> - Seat.

Luckily, the very first swap—the spring—produced a complete reversal of the BOB and WOW units, so it was not necessary to swap the remaining components. The springs were sent to the supplier for further investigation. (It would have been more productive to examine good and bad springs at the company itself, using paired comparisons, as discussed in the next chapter. Often, suppliers who have little or no knowledge of DOE do not know how to solve a chronic problem. Technical know-how alone is not enough.)

Workshop Exercise 1: A Car Company's Ice Cream Fiasco!

Several years ago, a car company was experiencing a peculiar problem on new cars, under certain combinations of circumstances. Typical was the experience of a young lady who drove her new car to her local ice cream shop and bought a cone of vanilla ice cream. She returned to her car with the vanilla ice cream cone and tried to start the car. It would not start. After some waiting, she managed to coax the car to start.

A few days later, she drove the car to the same ice cream shop and bought another cone of vanilla ice cream. She returned to her car with the cone and, again, it would not start. After another wait, she did get the car started. Now, she was convinced that the vanilla ice cream was the problem! So, on her third visit to the same ice cream shop, she switched flavors and ordered a cone of pistachio ice cream. After she returned to the car with the pistachio ice cream, the car started on the first try. Triumphantly, she told her husband: "I solved the problem. I knew something was wrong with the vanilla flavor." The husband was amused. But the wife challenged him: "If you're so smart, why don't you repeat what I did?"

Sure enough, each time the husband ordered the vanilla ice cream, the car would not start, but with the pistachio ice cream the start was instantaneous. Puzzled, the couple went to the dealer to voice their complaint. When the dealer heard the story, he muttered to himself about his town being filled with kooky people! But the dealer had the same problem. The next stop was the zone. By this time, the car company had so many similar complaints that the U.S. Department of Transportation was considering a demand for a massive recall campaign.

The car company, however, had done its DOE homework to solve this problem. In simple terms, the reason why the vanilla ice cream was a nonstarter for the car and the pistachio ice cream was a starter had nothing to do with the two flavors, but with the difference in the length of time it took the storekeeper to get them. The problem is known in the industry as a "hot crank" problem. It occurs when a brand-new car is run until it is hot, has the ignition shut down for just a short time and then does not have sufficient starting torque to restart. But when the engine is cooled somewhat, it can start again. The vanilla flavor, being readily available, took the storekeeper only a couple of minutes to deliver—too early for the hot crank problem to dissipate. Because the pistachio ice cream was an uncommon flavor, the storekeeper had to go to the back of the store, get the drum out, and thaw it out a bit. The five to ten extra minutes that it took to deliver the pistachio flavor provided enough time for the engine to cool off and start again.

Figure 10-8 is an actual Components Search conducted by the car company. The first step was converting an attribute Green Y—start versus no start—into a quantifiable, measurable Green Y. Water temperatures at the upper radiator hose were compared on "good" versus "bad" cars (with hot crank problems), but the correlation was cloudy. The oil temperature, however, turned out to be a more repeatable Green Y to monitor the engine temperature. Cars with oil temperatures around 240° to 250°

Figure 10-8. Components Search Workshop Exercise 1: The Hot Crank Car

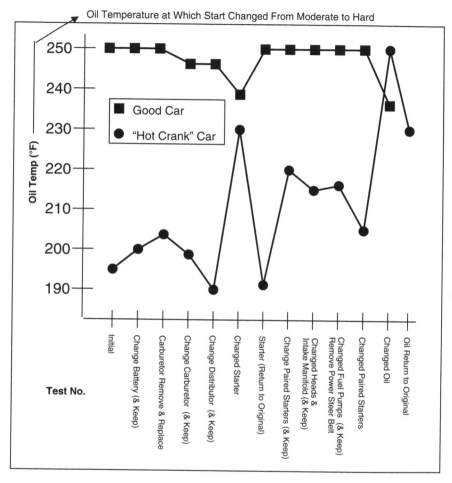

Source: General Motors Corporation.

had no hot crank problems, whereas those with oil temperatures around 190° to 200° consistently displayed hot crank problems.

Questions

Examine Figure 10-8 and answer the following questions:

1. Was the Green Y rightly quantified and measured?
2. Was Stage 1 of the Components Search performed correctly?

3. Stage 2 had 12 component swaps. Were they performed correctly?
4. What were the important components and what were the unimportant components in Stage 2? Use the average value between the good car oil temperature and the hot crank car oil temperature, as outlined in the section "Alternative Rule of Thumb to Assess the Importance of Component Exchange in Stage 2."
5. Was a capping run performed?
6. Was a factorial analysis conducted to determine the magnitude and direction of interaction effects?

Answers

Preamble. It must be stated at the outset that this Components Search experiment was not done according to the "textbook" roadmap. It was done in the early days of development of the Shainin DOE techniques and the approaches were tentative and empirical.

Answer 1: Most definitely "yes." The car company tried water temperature to distinguish the good cars and hot crank cars, but the correlation was not strong enough. Oil temperature proved to be a much more consistent differential between the good and hot crank cards—a differential of almost 60°F.

Answer 2: No. The good and hot crank cars were not disassembled and reassembled at all to assure that the problem was in the components and not in the assembly process. As it turned out, the experimenters were lucky. The problem was in one or more of the components and not in the assembly process.

Answer 3: No. When the battery; carburetor; heads and intake manifold; fuel pumps; and power steer belt were swapped, they were not returned to the original cars from which the swaps had taken place. This step is necessary to determine whether an interaction is present (if the original Green Y's are not reproduced). Again, the experimenters were lucky in that these components did not seem to produce significant changes when swapped and important interactions were not suspected to be present. On the other hand, when the starter swap showed a significant improvement in the hot crank car and the starters were returned to their original cars, the original conditions were reproduced. That return to the original cars should have been done with the other components too, regardless of the outcome of the swap.

Another mistake was replacing the starters in both cars with new ones. That introduced new variables and could have led to wrong conclusions. In this case, the hot crank car showed some improvement with new starters. Finally, swapping the engine oil caused a dramatic improvement in the hot crank car, with only a slight worsening in the good car. Returning the oil to the original cars, however, showed only a slight deterioration of the hot crank car, but the result of this last swap on the good car was not recorded.

Answer 4: The engine oil was the most important component—a quasi Red X—followed by the starter—a Pink X. There also appears to be a strong interaction effect between the oil and the starter. None of the other components were important, as judged by the "alternative rule of thumb" where the median line between the original oil temperatures of 250°F and 195°F would be at 222.5°F.

Answer 5: No. This is Stage 3, whose purpose is to verify that the important variables are truly important and the unimportant variables are truly unimportant. Here, the engine oil and the starters should have been swapped simultaneously, while the other components should have been kept in the opposite direction; i.e.: Test 1: O_G S_G R_B and Test 2: O_B S_B R_G, where O_G and O_B would be the oil of the good and bad cars, S_G and S_B would be the starters of the good and bad cars, and R_G and R_B would be the remaining components of the good and bad cars.

Answer 6: No. A factorial analysis (Stage 4) is necessary only when there is an indication of an interaction in Stage 2.

Further DOE Experiments

Even though the car company did not perform the Components Search according to textbook methodology, it conducted further designed experiments using full factorials (see Chapter 14). They showed the following results:

> ➤ The difference in oil was a 10W oil in the hot crank car versus a 20W oil in the good car, accounting for a 55°F difference in startability.
> ➤ Difference between a low-limit starter and a high-limit starter improved startability of the latter by 26°F.
> ➤ Raising the compression ratio from 1:9 to 10:5 improved startability by only 4°F.
> ➤ Advancing the spark from 6° to 13° improved startability by only 1°F.

Analysis

The thinner (10W) oil loses its lubricating ability and drains from the walls of the mating surfaces. Hot crank is most pronounced if the engine is turned off while hot and allowed to cool for only a few minutes. At running speeds, the mating surfaces are in a bath of oil, and the thinner oil becomes unimportant. Further, as a new engine is broken in after, say, the first 1,000 miles, the hot crank problem disappears because the torque required from the starter is reduced with use.

Conclusion

The hot crank phenomenon happens only under a combination of variables: a new car, thin oil, tight engine fits, and low torque on starters. But design of experiments got to the root causes.

Workshop Exercise 2: Oscillator Time Delay

An electronic instrument had a problem of a long time delay between the "power on" signal and when the unit actually started to function. A "good" unit had a time delay of around 16 milliseconds (ms), while a "bad" unit had around a 35 ms delay. The oscillator circuit was determined to be the source of the delay. Stage 1 and Stage 2 (for the 10 suspect components) are shown in Table 10-5. R represents the assembly, minus the component switched.

Questions

1. Stage 1. Determine if there is a significant difference between the high (H), or good, assembly and the low (L), or bad, assembly.

2. Calculate the $D:\overline{d}$ ratio. What does Stage 1 prove?

3. Plot the results shown in Table 10-5 and calculate the high and low decision limits. What are the unimportant components? What conclusions would you draw?

4. Was the capping run successful?

5. Construct a factorial analysis. Determine the main and interaction effects of the important components. Draw a graphical plot to show the extent of such interaction.

Answers

1. There appear to be fairly consistent readings on the high readings—13, 16, and 15; as well as on the low readings—34, 38, and 35. This will be verified by the answer to question 2—the $D:\overline{d}$ ratio.

Table 10-5. Components Search Workshop Exercise 2: Oscillator Time Delay

Stage 1	High Assembly (H)		Low Assembly (L)	
	Configuration	*Results (m.s.)*	*Configuration*	*Results*
Initial	All Comp. High	13	All Comp. Low	34
First disassembly and reassembly	All Comp. High	16	All Comp. Low	38
Second disassembly and reassembly	All Comp. High	15	All Comp. Low	35

Stage 2 Tests	Components	Configuration	Results	Control Limits High	Configuration	Results	Control Limits Low
1	A: Crystal	$A_L R_H$	16		$A_H R_L$	19	
2	B: Microprocessor	$B_L R_H$	16		$B_H R_L$	35	
3	C: Transistor	$C_L R_H$	14		$C_H R_L$	33	
4	D: Capacitor C_2	$D_L R_H$	15		$D_H R_L$	37	
5	E: Capacitor C_1	$E_L R_H$	16		$E_H R_L$	16	
Stage 3							
Capping Run	A and E	$A_L E_L R_H$	32		$A_H E_H R_L$	17	

Source: Motorola Inc., Arcade, N.Y.

2. The median in the three high assemblies is 15; the median in the low assemblies is 35. So, D = 35 − 15 = 20.

The range within the high assembly is 3. The range within the low assembly is 4. So $\bar{d}$, the average range (or lack of repeatability) is (3+4)/2 = 3.5. So the D:$\bar{d}$ ratio is 20:3.5 = 5.7:1 which exceeds the minimum required ratio of 1.25:1.

Stage 1 proves that the causes of the delay problem are not in the assembly process but are among the components alone.

3. Figure 10-9 is a graphical plot of Table 10-5. The decision limits (high) are:

Figure 10-9. Graphical Plot With High and Low Decision Limits

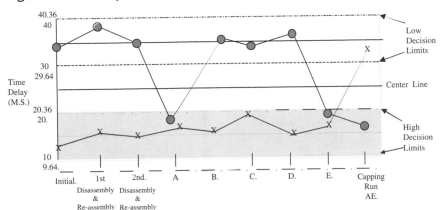

Legend: X = All high, except for designated component

● = All low, except for designated component

$$\text{Median (high)} \pm 2.776\,\overline{d}/1.81 = 15 \pm (2.776 \times 3.5/1.81)$$
$$= 15 \pm 5.36 = 20.36 \,\&\, 9.64$$

The decision limits (low) are:

$$\text{Median (low)} \pm 2.776\,\overline{d}/1.81 = 35 \pm (2.776 \times 3.5/1.81)$$
$$= 35 \pm 5.36 = 40.36 \,\&\, 29.64$$

Components B, C, and D are unimportant. They do not cause a reversal of the initial good and bad readings, nor do they go outside of either the high or the low control limits.

Conclusions drawn: (1) There is no significant change in any of the components swapped in Stage 2, when going from high to low, because A, B, C, D, and E do not go outside of their high decision limits. (2) On the other hand, components A and E do go outside their low decision limits when swapped in Stage 2. (3) Such one-way changes—playing within one set of control limits but going outside the other set of control limits—are a sure indication of interaction effects.

4. Yes. When components A and E were kept high and the rest (R) low, the results were high (beyond the high decision limits), and vice-versa.

5. Table 10-6 shows the two-factor factorial analysis of components A and E.

Conclusion

Further engineering investigation on this time delay problem revealed that the series impedance of the crystal was on the low side, while the

Table 10-6. Two-Factor Factorial Analysis

X	A_H	A_L
E_H	13 16 16 14 15 15 16 17 14 ---- Median = 15.5	16 19 ---- Median = 17.0
E_L	19 16 ---- Median = 17.5	34 37 38 32 35 35 33 ---- Median = 35.0

capacitor leakage was on the high side. When this condition was present in both components, the oscillator circuit loaded down the microprocessor, causing a longer time delay. Working with the capacitor supplier and using DOE to reduce capacitor leakage resolved the time delay at no extra cost to the company.

We can loosely call E a Red X, A a Pink X and the AE interaction a Pale Pink X. This result is unusual for its lack of great separation between the Red X, the Pink X, and the Pale Pink X.

From Table 10-6

$$\text{Main Effect A} = \frac{17.0 + 35.0}{2} - \frac{15.5 + 17.5}{2} = 26 - 16.5 = 9.5$$

$$\text{Main Effect E} = \frac{17.5 + 35.0}{2} - \frac{15.5 + 17.0}{2} = 26.25 - 16.25 = 10$$

$$\text{Interaction AB effect} = \frac{15.5 + 35.0}{2} - \frac{17.0 + 17.5}{2} = 25.25 - 17.25 = 8$$

Components Search Practices When Disassembly/Reassembly Is Not Repeatable

So far, our examples have involved cases where, following disassembly and reassembly, the good unit remained good and the bad unit remained bad. But what if this is not the case? Then, a step-by-step progressive disassembly and reassembly is in order to determine which specific step requires analysis and correction. A case study illustrates the technique.

Case Study 3: Refrigerator Door Gap

An appliance manufacturer was experiencing a gap between the cabinet and the door of its refrigerator line when the door was closed. It was not a functional problem, but a cosmetic defect, objectionable to the consumer. The problem had existed for months, requiring extensive rework.

Components search was the obvious DOE response. A BOB, with minimal door gap, and a WOW, with the most objectionable door gap, were selected. Upon disassembly and reassembly of each unit, however, the BOB became a WOW and the WOW became a BOB. This was most unusual in the long history of components search. The DOE team then outlined the sequence of disassembly/reassembly steps:

1. Unscrewing and rescrewing the brackets.
2. Removing and reinserting the hinges and hinge pins.
3. Removing and reinserting the flange angles on the door and cabinet.
4. Removing and realigning the doors into the hinges.

It was in Step 4—when the door was being set into the hinges—that the lack of consistency was discovered. The assemblers in production had their own unique assembly methods. A paired comparison of these methods revealed the correct procedure that had to be scrupulously followed by all assemblers. All the WOWs were converted to BOBs, with no more defective units.

Workshop Exercise 3: The "Walking" Machine

In another product line, a company was experiencing "machine walk" due to vibration in an accelerated life test. Since there were "good" and "bad" machines, Components Search seemed to be the logical DOE technique. A BOB and a WOW were selected from a day's production. But on disassembly and reassembly, the amount of "walk" was not repeatable. Several other machines were tried to repeat the amount of walk even before disassembly and reassembly, but the readings were not at all consistent. On a second or third try, the "walking" machines would stop and vice-versa. (Production's practice was to send the "walking" machines to the quality test laboratory. If they passed—no walk—they would be shipped to customers. Yet, field complaints on "walking" continued to plague the company.)

Questions

1. What DOE technique should have been used ahead of components search?

2. Should a progressive disassembly and reassembly have been conducted to see which disassembly step contributed the most to the "walk" problem?

Answers

1. The Green Y was correctly quantified in terms of the magnitude and direction of "walk" on the machines. However, the second step in a DOE investigation was not followed—namely, the measurement system requiring an accuracy five times the "walk" tolerance. The measurement system was most erratic, with no consistency in the "walk" readings on the specified "floor," either in production or in the quality test laboratory. To add to the problem, the engineering "floor" could find no walking units, even though field complaints kept coming in.

When these inconsistencies within the test stations were uncovered, the first order of business was to establish a test platform that was consistent. A new test method was devised where the force on each foot of the machine was accurately measured on the X, Y, and Z axes. With the new measurement, the difference between the BOBs and the WOWs disappeared. The "walk" on all the machines was consistent and worse than that of comparable machines from competition. This meant a serious design problem that had to be resolved with a Variables Search experiment (see Chapter 13).

2. No. When the correct test method revealed that there were no units that did not walk, the absence of BOBs rendered the disassembly/reassembly step unnecessary.

Components Search Applications in Processes/Machines/Lines

Components Search is a natural and powerful DOE tool for assemblies, as described throughout this chapter. Yet, it can also be used to compare two seemingly identical processes or machines or lines—one good, one bad. The methodology may not be as rigorous as it is for assemblies. As an example, there may not be several BOBs or WOWs—only one of each.

Also, disassembly/reassembly may not always be possible, but the general principles of Components Search do apply.

Case Study 4: Spring Torque Differences on Two Lines

Two identical lines were producing springs. The flow chart was as follows:

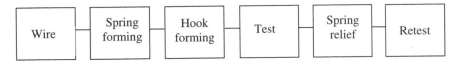

There was only one shift; Line 1 was reporting a high defect rate on torque at the last retest station, while Line 2 had virtually zero defects. Management's first thought was the difference in supervisors. The Line 2 supervisor blamed the workers, who in turn blamed the forming machines. If the machines could talk, they would probably have pointed to the wire material!

A Components Search between the two lines found the Red X. Switching supervisors, operators, forming machines, and even the stress relief equipment revealed that the problem torque remained in Line 2. Finally, the retest fixtures in the two lines were swapped. Line 1 became the problem line, while Line 2 now became perfect. It was found that the Line 2 fixture had not been maintained or calibrated for correct torque readings.

Case Study 5: Operator Performance Differences

In a laser trimming operation on a resistor, two identical machines with two operators were giving vastly different results. The first machine produced zero defects; the second had high defect levels. The laser trim machine parameters were checked and found to be identical. The untrimmed resistors were also uniform in value. Next, the two operators were switched. Now, both laser trim machines reported zero defects.

Further investigations centered on the machine-operator interface. The surprising result? Operator 2, who had an excellent quality record in other work, but was creating defects on Machine 2, was short and was therefore viewing the laser trim resistance removal through a window at an angle. The parallax error was causing her to miss the target area. On Machine 1, the window was six inches lower and Operator 2 had no difficulty in achieving zero defects. The solution was to give Operator 2 a higher stool on Machine 2 or to move her to Machine 1. She elected to move to Machine 1.

Components Search Applications in Administrative Work

Case Study 5 showed how Components Search can be used to differentiate between two operators. The same principle can be used in administrative work to differentiate between two dealers, two installers, two servicers, two clerks, two bank tellers, two branch managers, etc., as long as there is a notable Green Y difference between one who is good and another who is poor. In many such cases, we have found that the WOW human being is less to blame than the WOW system.

Workshop Exercise 4 (Game): Find the Red X Ball (1)

There are 80 steel balls. All weigh the same except one, which is heavier. You have a weighing scale with two pans (no measurements). Identify the Red X ball in no more than four tries on the weighing scale.

Workshop Exercise 5 (Game): Find the Red X Ball (2)

There are 12 steel balls. All weigh the same except one, which may be heavier or lighter than the rest. You have a weighing scale with two pans (no measurements). Identify the Red X ball in no more than three tries on the weighing scale.

Answer to Workshop Exercise 4: Find the Red X Ball (1)

A common tendency is to start by dividing the 80 balls into two groups of 40. That will lead to a minimum of five, not four tries. The correct method is to divide the 80 balls into three groups of 27, 27, and 26. (One clue is $3^4 = 81$, which suggests the initial split of 3 groups and 4 trials.) (See Figure 10-10.)

Answer to Workshop Exercise 5: Find the Red X Ball (2)

Hint: Number the balls 1 to 12. (See Figure 10-11.)

Components Search Questions for DOE Teams

As with the Multi-Vari technique, the following questions act as a memory jogger and guideline for DOE teams conducting a Components Search study. The first 10 questions in the chapter on the Multi-Vari deal with determining the Green Y and assuring the accuracy of the measuring

Figure 10-10. Answer to Workshop Exercise 4

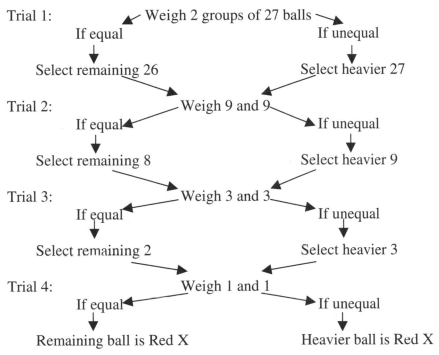

Trial 1: Weigh 2 groups of 27 balls

If equal → Select remaining 26

If unequal → Select heavier 27

Trial 2: Weigh 9 and 9

If equal → Select remaining 8

If unequal → Select heavier 9

Trial 3: Weigh 3 and 3

If equal → Select remaining 2

If unequal → Select heavier 3

Trial 4: Weigh 1 and 1

If equal → Remaining ball is Red X

If unequal → Heavier ball is Red X

instrument. The same 10 questions should be asked by a DOE team for all DOE techniques. (In the interest of saving space and time, they are not repeated here.)

General

1. If it is known that the largest family of variation is unit-to-unit (not time-to-time or within-unit), has the multi-vari been bypassed and components search selected to investigate differences between units that are run at the same time?

2. Is the product/assembly capable of disassembly and reassembly without damaging or destroying or radically changing it?

3. Has every attempt been made to select the very best and the very worst units, say, over a day's time or even a week's time? (The greater the difference between these units, the easier it is to find the Red X.)

Stage 1

4. Have the BOBs and the WOWs been disassembled and reassembled twice, after their initial Green Y's, to meet two rules: 1) The three

Figure 10-11. Answer to Workshop Exercise 5

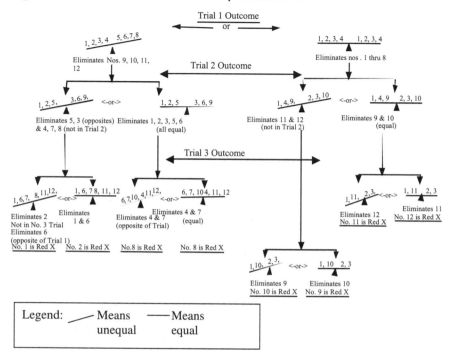

```
Legend:   ╱ Means        ── Means
            unequal         equal
```

Note: The scale shows tipping in one direction. The same logic would apply if the scale shows tipping in the opposite direction.

BOB readings must outweigh the three WOW readings; 2) the D:d̄ ratio must exceed 1.25.

5. If the above two rules are not met, is there a step-by-step disassembly and reassembly step as a possible Red X?

Stage 2

6. Has a list of parts to be swapped been made in descending order of importance?

7. Are the swapped parts, from the BOB to the WOW and vice-versa, returned to their original BOB and WOW units after each swap?

8. If there is only a partial change from a BOB to a WOW and vice-versa, is Components Search continued to other parts not yet swapped?

9. If a BOB becomes a WOW but the WOW remains a WOW (or vice-versa), is an interpretation made that components search should continue and that the presence of an interaction between the swapped and unknown part is indicated?

10. Is components search continued with one or more part swaps until a complete reversal of BOB and WOW occurs?

11. Are decision limits for BOBs and WOWs calculated to see which component swap goes outside its decision limits?

12. As an alternative to decision limits, will the median line between the BOBs and WOWs of Stage 1 be used to determine component importance?

Stage 3

13. Is a capping run conducted where all important parts are kept at their high levels and unimportant parts at their low levels, and vice-versa?

Stage 4

14. Is a factorial analysis conducted to quantify main and interaction effects?

Questions for Top Management

1. Why was Component Search chosen as the DOE technique?

2. Did Component Search follow an earlier DOE technique, such as the Multi-Vari?

3. How long did it take to find the truly best (BOB) unit and the truly worst (WOW) unit to start Components Search?

4. Was the gap between the BOB and the WOW large enough? (It is a common failing among DOE teams that the gap is not large enough.)

5. Was there only a single cause discovered? A single Red X?

6. Or were there several important causes?

7. Was a capping run performed to confirm and separate the important factors from the unimportant ones?

8. If there were several important factors, was a factorial analysis done to quantify interaction effects?

11

· ·

Paired Comparisons: An Elegant, Versatile Tool

Introduction

In Chapter 10, we stated that whenever there were good and bad units being produced, at more or less the same time, the multi-vari could be bypassed and Components Search could be used instead. But what if one of the prerequisites of Components Search—that both good and bad units must be capable of disassembly and reassembly—is not met? What if disassembly damages, destroys, or radically changes the good and bad units? Then, Components Search is not the answer.

Fortunately, the fourth clue-generation technique for "talking to the parts" can be employed in such circumstances. It is Paired Comparisons. Like the three previous techniques, it does not disrupt production and its methodology is based on an extremely simple arrangement of data on 12 to 16 units—generally six or eight good units and six or eight bad units—in rank order. Yet, it provides a high degree of confidence (90 percent or greater) when a parameter or quality characteristic associated with the unit is declared to be important. (Refer to Figure 7-1 to see where this step fits into the appropriate roadmap.)

Paired Comparisons is so versatile a technique that it can be used in new product and process designs, production, field, support services, administrative work, farms, hospitals, and schools—in short, in any economic activity. Paired Comparisons is also the logical sequel to Components Search, when the Red X, distilled from systems, subsystems, and subassembly Components Searches, cannot be disassembled any further.

Prerequisites

> The performance (output or Green Y) must be measurable, with the accuracy of the measuring instrument at least five times the specification tolerance or product spread.

> Every attempt should be made to select the very best units (BOBs) and the very worst units (WOWs) within a more or less constant time frame.
> If the quality characteristic or parameter is an attribute, it should be converted into a variable—if at all possible—using the Likert scale, as discussed in Chapter 7.

Methodology Alternative A

1. Select a sample size of six or eight good units (BOBs) and a like number of bad units (WOWs) as far apart as possible with respect to the Green Y being investigated. The farther apart the BOBs and the WOWs are, the easier it will be to find the Red X.

2. List *as many* parameters, or quality characteristics, that might explain the difference in the Green Y's of a BOB and a WOW. Something is causing the good unit to be good. Something is causing the bad unit to be bad. *So a difference in some parameter or the other is bound to be there.* (Some DOE experimenters, using Paired Comparisons, lose patience and give up after exploring four or five parameters and finding no differences.) The differences could be visual, dimensional, cosmetic, mechanical, electrical, chemical, metallurgical, etc. The measurement techniques could be the eye, a ruler, an x-ray, a scanning electron microscope, a CAT scan, a finite element analysis, or a test-to-failure (using MEOST).

3. Select one pair—one good, one bad. Note the differences, as indicated in Step 2.

4. Select a second pair—one good, one bad. Note the differences in this second pair.

5. Repeat this search process with a third, fourth, fifth, sixth (and if necessary, with a seventh and eighth) pair until one or more parameters shows *a repeatable difference in the same direction.*

6. Generally by the fifth or sixth pair, consistent, repeatable differences will appear in a few important parameters that will provide strong clues on the major causes of variation.

Methodology Alternative B

Although this alternative method uses group comparisons (of good and bad units) rather than comparison by pairs, the generic name of paired comparisons has been retained.

> An alternative procedure is the same as Steps 1 and 2. But instead of selecting six or eight separate pairs, note the readings of each quality parameter for all six or eight good units and six or eight bad units. Arrange them in rank order from the smallest reading to the largest (or vice-versa), regardless of whether they are good or bad.
> Apply the Tukey test (procedure and example explained below).
> If the total end-count is six or more, there is 90 percent or greater confidence that that particular quality parameter is important in explaining the difference between good and bad units.
> If the total end-count is five or less, there is not enough confidence that such a quality parameter is important in explaining the difference between good and bad units.

The Tukey Test

The purpose of this test, named after its famous originator, John Tukey of Princeton University, is to determine whether a particular quality parameter is important, with a high degree of confidence. It is used in DOE work in Paired Comparisons, in Full Factorials, and in B versus C as a nonparametric comparative technique, where data is organized by rank, not by absolute values as in variables data, or by the totally inadequate nondiscriminating attribute data.

Tukey Test Procedure

> Rank a group of readings associated with a specific quality characteristic or parameter from the lowest to the highest (or vice-versa), regardless of good or bad.
> Designate each of the 12 or 16 ranked readings as either a good unit (G) or a bad one (B) from the original data.
> Draw a line starting from the top of these readings, when the "all bad" change to the "all good" (or vice-versa) *for the first time.* This is the top end-count.
> Similarly, draw a line starting from the bottom of these readings, where the "all good" change to the "all bad" (or vice-versa) *for the first time.*
> Add the top and bottom end-counts to determine the total end-count. (Note: if the top end-count contains only "all good," then the bottom end-count must contain only "all bad" (or vice-versa). If the top end-count and the bottom end-count both have the same designation, i.e., both all good, or both all bad, then the total end-count drops to zero.)

Total End-Count and Confidence Levels

Based on the combination formulas, the Tukey test shows the following relationship between total end-count and confidence levels:

Number of Total End-Counts	Confidence
6	90%
7	95%
10	99%
13	99.9%

Tukey Test—An Example

The simplicity and power of a Tukey test is best illustrated with an example. In an investigation of a thrust plug seal for oil leaks, eight non-leakers (good = G) and eight leakers (bad − B) were measured for a number of parameters, such as worm end-play, oil leaks, worm surface finish, seal height, and washer thickness. The following readings were compiled for worm end-play.

.015 B	0.019 B	0.017 B	0.024 G
0.018 B	0.018 G	0.019 B	0.023 G
0.014 B	0.016 G	0.011 B	0.021 G
0.022 B	0.023 G	0.007 B	0.017 G

1. Construct a Tukey ranking on these 16 worm end-play readings.
2. Determine top, bottom, and total end-counts.
3. What is the confidence level that worm end-play is important in distinguishing between leakers and non-leakers?

Statistical Principles in the Tukey Test

1. *The Combination Formula*
The statistical foundations of the Tukey Test are the combination formulas:

$$\text{Number of combinations (without any repetition)} = \frac{n!}{(n-r)!\, r!}$$

where n is the total number of units in the data; r is the number of good units; (n − r) is the number of bad units.

Therefore, the total number of combinations
without any repetition.
$$= \frac{16!}{(n-r)!\, r!}$$

$$= \frac{\left(\begin{array}{c}16 \times 15 \times 14 \times 13 \times 12 \times 11 \times 10 \times \\ 9 \times 8 \times 7 \times 6 \times 5 \times 4 \times 3 \times 2 \times 1\end{array}\right)}{8 \times 7 \times 6 \times 5 \times 4 \times 3 \times 2 \times 1 \times 8 \times 7 \times 6 \times 5 \times 4 \times 3 \times 2 \times 1}$$

$$= 12.870$$

Given these combinations, there are only two ways in which there can be no overlap entirely by chance: Either all eight good outrank all eight bad, or vice-versa. So the risk of a false conclusion is only 2 out of 12,870 or 0.016 percent. Therefore, the confidence of a total end-count of 16 is 99.984 percent—in short, very, very high.

2. *Confidence Levels Are Largely Independent of Sample Size*
Surprisingly, the confidence levels associated with the Tukey test are, for the most part, independent of the sample sizes of good and bad units, provided the numbers are not less than six and six respectively. If the sample sizes are 12 good and 12 bad units, for example, a larger overlap zone does not matter. It is always the sum of the top and bottom end-counts that determine the confidence levels. If the total end-count is larger, say 20, the confidence level is even higher than 99.9 percent, and its increase from that very high level does not justify a larger sample size.

3. The statistical theory associated with the combination formula does require that the number of good units and bad units be within 20 percent of one another.

4. *Calculating End Counts at the First and Last Transitions From "Good" to "Bad."* In ranking a group of readings, what happens if the good and bad readings have the same value at the point of first transition from good to bad or at the point of the last transition from good to bad? Whenever there is a tie—each equal reading between good and bad at each of the two transition points—the end-count should be reduced from 1 to $1/2$. Let us consider the example of the worm end-play readings (Table 11-1). If, instead of the readings as shown in Table 11-1, they were:

Alternative A			*Alternative B*	
0.007	Bad		0.023	Bad
0.011	Bad		0.023	Good
0.014	Bad		0.023	Good
0.015	Bad		0.024	Good
0.015	Good			

Table 11-1. A Tukey Test Ranking

Bad	Good	
0.007 0.011 0.014 0.015		Top end-count (all bad) = 4
0.017 0.018 0.019 0.022	0.016 0.017 0.018 0.019 0.021	Overlap region
	0.023 0.023 0.024	Bottom end-count (all good) = 3

Total end count = 4 + 3 = 7. So, confidence is 95 percent that worm end-play is important in explaining the difference between leakers and nonleakers in the thrust plug seal.

> In Alternative A, the top end-count would not be 4, but $3 + 1/2 = 3^1/2$.
> In Alternative B, the bottom end-count would not be 3, but $2 + 1/2 = 2^1/2$.

Case Study 1: Micro-Motor Noise

In the production of a silent pager (where the person being paged is signaled through vibration rather than an audio signal), there was excessive noise. A components search had isolated the problem to a micro-motor from a Japanese supplier, but it was too small to continue the components search within the micro-motor itself. For a variety of legal reasons, the Japanese supplier would not accept responsibility for the problem and had been disqualified. In the meantime, 50,000 of these motors had become a bone-pile at $5 per unit.

A DOE team decided to conduct a Paired Comparisons experiment between eight of the best (quietest) and eight of the worst (noisiest) motors. Eight quality parameters were selected for study. The results are shown in Table 11-2.

Conclusion: Red X was a significant 40 percent difference in motor speed between the good and bad micro-motors.

Table 11-2. Paired Comparison: Micro-Motor

Parameter Compared	Repetitive/Nonrepetitive Differences
Multilayer pads	Differences slight and nonrepetitive
Oil bearings	Differences slight and nonrepetitive
Shimmed retainer	Differences slight and nonrepetitive
Shaft play—axial and radial	Differences slight and nonrepetitive
Bearing dimension front and back	Not tried
Counterweight mass	Not tried
Resistance and current drain	Not tried
Speed (rpm)	Repetitive differences: 4800 to 5000 on good units; 6900 to 7200 on bad units

Source: Motorola Inc., Boynton Beach, Florida.

Action Taken

To investigate the differences in motor speed between the good and bad units would still have required disassembly of the micro-motors. Since this was not possible, the DOE team decided to adopt an out-board fix for the noise problem in the bad motors. It added an 18 ohm resistor in series with the battery voltage of 1.3 to 1.5 volts on the bad motors to reduce the voltage to 1.0 volt, which in turn reduced the rpm to 4500 to 5000 V. and resulted in the required noise reduction. So, the addition of a one-cent resistor salvaged a $5 motor, for a total savings (including labor) of over $248,000.

Comments on Micro-Motor Case Study

1. Checking separate pairs of good and bad motors was not done, nor was it necessary.
2. The differences in the eight parameters listed were not quantified.
3. Without such quantification, the Tukey test could not be conducted.
4. However, there was a clear separation—with no overlap—between the good motors and the bad motors that would have resulted in an end-count of 16. So the confidence is over 99.9 percent that the motor speed is very important in explaining the difference between the good and the bad motors.
5. The root cause of the bad motors was not solved, because a new motor supplier had replaced the uncooperative Japanese supplier. The objective was to salvage the bad motors and drastically reduce scrap costs.

Workshop Exercise 1: Contact Lens Prescription Defects

A contact lens manufacturer found that three percent of his lenses were not meeting the required optical specifications in a certain model. Since a contact lens consists of two pieces of curved plastic joined together by a compound called "hema," it cannot be taken apart, once formed. So Components Search could not be employed.

A DOE team selected six of the lenses closest to the target value of the prescription (Rx) and six that were furthest out of the Rx tolerance. The quality parameters tested were:

1. Cylinder: Curvature of the front of the lens.
2. Cylinder BP side: Curvature on the back of the lens.
3. UV absorbence: Amount of ultraviolet light absorbed.
4. Polarizer: The pattern of light refracted through the lens.
5. Mold: The mold used in forming the lens.

Table 11-3 shows the results.

Questions

1. Determine the Red X and Pink X parameters. Justify your choices.

2. Apply the Tukey test on these parameters. Which parameters have a confidence of 90 percent and more in explaining the difference between the good and bad units?

3. How would you quantify the two parameters that are attributes instead of variables?

Answers

1. The Red X is the cylinder. The Pink X is the polarizer.

> For the cylinder parameter, all the good readings are lower than the bad. The highest good reading is lower than the lowest bad reading, with no overlap.
> For the polarizer—an attribute—there is only one light pattern common to both good and bad units. The other five good units have a light pattern all different than those for the bad.

2. See Table 11-4.

> The total end-count for the cylinder is 12, with a confidence of 99.7 percent that the cylinder is important in explaining the difference between good and bad lenses.

Table 11-3. Paired Comparison: Contact Lens Prescription Defects

		Parameters Measured			
	Cylinder	Cylinder BP Side	UV Absorbence	Polarizer	Mold
Good	.030 mm	.074 mm	9.8%	Rainbow/Left/No Pattern	Boss
Good	.020 mm	.043 mm	8.8%	Rainbow/Left/No Pattern	Nonboss
Good	.018 mm	.069 mm	10.9%	Rainbow/Left/No Pattern	Boss
Good	.016 mm	.058 mm	11.2%	Rainbow/Left/No Pattern	Boss
Good	.030 mm	.063 mm	9.9%	Rainbow/Left/No Pattern	Nonboss
Good	.026 mm	.072 mm	8.9%	Rainbow/Left/No Pattern	Nonboss
Bad	.055 mm	.053 mm	9.3%	Rainbow/Left/No Pattern	Nonboss
Bad	.053 mm	.048 mm	7.8%	Light/Left/Pattern	Nonboss
Bad	.051 mm	.049 mm	7.4%	Light/No Pattern	Nonboss
Bad	.048 mm	.049 mm	8.7%	Light/Right/Pattern	Boss
Bad	.051 mm	.077 mm	8.8%	Light/Left/Pattern	Nonboss
Bad	.056 mm	.070 mm	11.2%	Rainbow/All/No Pattern	Boss

Source: CIBA Corp., Atlanta, Ga.

> The total end-count for the cylinder BP side is 2. So there is little confidence that the cylinder BP side is important in explaining the difference between good and bad lenses.
> For the UV absorbence: The top end-count is $3 + \frac{1}{2}$ (a tie at 8.8 percent between a B and a $G = \frac{1}{2}$) and the bottom end-count is also $\frac{1}{2}$ (a tie at 11.2 between a B and a $G = \frac{1}{2}$) for a total end-count of 4. So, there is little confidence that the UV absorbence is important in explaining the difference between good and bad lenses.

3. For the polarizer, an arbitrary Likert scale can be established for the difference patterns, with rainbow/left/no pattern as 1; light/left/pattern as 2; light/no pattern as 3; light/right/pattern as 4; and rainbow/all/no pattern as 5. A Tukey test now reveals a top end-count of $5\frac{1}{2}$ (one tie between good and bad) and a bottom end-count of 5, or a total end-

Table 11-4. Tukey Test on Contact Lens Workshop Exercise

Rank	Parameter			
	Cylinder (mm)	Cylinder BP Side (mm)	UV Absorbence (%)	Polarizer (Pattern)
1	.016 G ⎫	.043 G Top end-count	7.4 B ⎫ Top end-count	1 G ⎫ Top end-count
2	.018 G ⎬ Top end-count	.048 B	7.8 B ⎬	1 G
3	.020 G ⎭	.049 B	8.7 B ⎭	1 G
4	.026 G	.049 B	8.8 B ⎫ EC = $^1/_2$	1 G
5	.030 G	.053 B	8.8 G ⎭	1 G
6	.030 G	.058 G	8.9 G ⎫ Over-lap	1 B ⎫ EC = $^1/_2$
7	.048 B ⎫	.063 G Over-lap	9.3 B ⎬ lap	1 G ⎭
8	.051 B ⎬ Bottom end-count	.069 G	9.8 G	2 B ⎫ Bottom end-count
9	.051 B ⎭	.070B	9.9 G ⎭	2 B
10	.053 B	.072 g	10.9 G	3 B
11	.054 B	.074 G	11.2 B	4 B
12	.056 B	.077 B Bottom end-count	11.2 G ⎬ Bottom end-count	5 B
Total End-Count	6 + 6 = 12	1 + 1 = 2	$3^1/_2 + ^1/_2 = 4$	$5^1/_2 + 5 = 10 ^1/_2$
Confidence	99.7%	No	No	99.2 %

count of $10^1/_2$. So there is a 99.2 percent confidence that the polarizer is very important in explaining the difference between good and bad lenses.

For the mold, if on a Likert scale, "boss" is a 1 and "no boss" a 2, a Tukey test (not shown in Table 11-4) would show that the overlap is almost total and the confidence simply not there to deem mold as important.

Case Study 2: The 4-Megabit Dynamic RAM

In a large semiconductor company, a 4-megabit dynamic random access memory (RAM) device was being developed in the design department, but the new product could not get into production because a qualification test was not being met. One of the qualification tests was a burn-in (a high-temperature soak) where approximately 7 percent of the devices were failing.

The failure mode indicated a catastrophic failure, such that half the memory—2 megabits—would be wiped out. To compound the problem, many of the failed devices would recover the moment the designers went to extract them from the burn-in rack. This meant that the problem was intermittent. Detailed failure analysis was proving futile. Management pressure on the designers was mounting because of a similar product developed by competition. The investigation stretched from days into weeks and from weeks into months, with no resolution. In desperation, two outside consultants were brought in. Neither could solve the problem. Finally, the designers contacted the author to see if DOE would help.

I ruled out the multi-vari because the massive 2-megabit failure did not have pinpointed location and because the units were both good and bad in the same time frame. That suggested a Components Search, but because the units were encapsulated, that method was not feasible. I recommended a Paired Comparison, with eight good and eight failed units, but the engineers said that it would be difficult to find eight failed units, since they would recover on extraction. I assured them that intermittency did not matter. Something in the bad units was different from the good units, and we had to persevere in finding it. The following list of the parameters to be checked for differences in the good and bad units was made:

1. Molding compound
2. Lead frame
3. Gold wire (the thickness of a human hair)
4. Bonding at the die end
5. Bonding at the substrate end
6. Sockets in the burn-in rack

The engineers went to work on these six parameters. If none showed any repetitive differences between the good and bad units, other parameters would have to be investigated.

Within a week, the Red X was found. There were no appreciable or repetitive differences in the first five parameters. The problem was in the sockets in the burn-in rack. The bad sockets had a thin film of insulation—seepage from somewhere—that was acting as an electrical barrier. But it was so thin that, the moment the units were touched, the barrier broke down and electrical contact was made. There was nothing wrong with the product. The problem was in the test equipment. This story has a moral: Talk to the parts. Talk to the parts. Talk to the parts! That is the refrain in this book.

Workshop Exercise 2: Out-of-Square Grills

An appliance manufacturer experienced a chronic problem in which the grills used on its products were out-of-square after welding. The problem had existed for seven years. Following our DOE seminar and consultation, a DOE team used a Paired Comparison approach to find the important sources of variation between good and bad grills.

Figure 11-1 is a flow chart of the fabrication and assembly process. Table 11-5 shows 17 parameters measured on six good and six bad parts. (Column 1 is the Green Y, where the out-of-square is measured as the difference between the C and D dimensions.)

Figure 11-1. Flow Chart of Grill Fabrication and Assembly

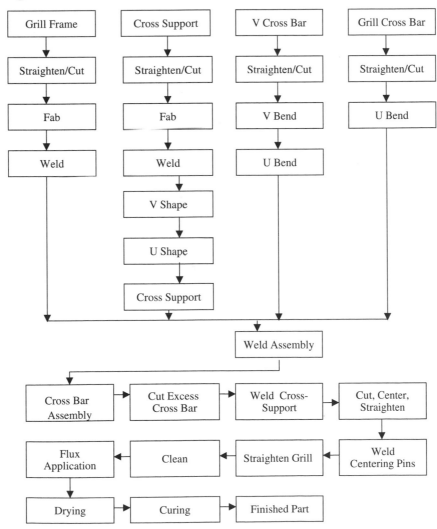

Source: Vitromatic Corp., Celaya, Mexico.

Table 11-5. Paired Comparison of Grill Parameters

Green Y Out-of-Square Δ of C vs. D Dimension	Distance From Hook Left	Right	Total Cross Length Front	Center	Back	Total Longitudinal Length Left	Center	Right	Straightness of Wire Frame Short Side Front	Back	Long Side Left	Right	Angle at 4 Corners 1	2	3	4	Direction of Bow
Good 0	25	45	217	216	216.5	484	484	484	X	V	S	S	89.5	89.5	90.5	90.0	N
Good −1	50	60	216	215	216	484	485	484	X	V	S	S	89.5	89.5	91.0	90.0	N
Good 1	28	28	216.5	215	216	484	484	484	X	V	S	S	89.5	90.0	90.5	90.0	N
Good 0	26	27	216.5	215	216	484	485	484	X	V	S	S	89.5	90.0	90.5	90.5	N
Good 0	45	60	217.5	216	216	484	485	485	X	V	S	S	89.5	89.0	90.5	90.5	N
Good 0	28	30	217	216	216	484	484	484	X	V	S	S	90	89.0	90.0	90.0	N
Bad 9	41	45	218	215	216	484	485	486	V	X	V	S	91	88.5	88	92	R
Bad 8	50	55	217	214	215	484	486	486	V	X	V	S	89	89.5	93	89.5	L
Bad 8	83	23	216	215	215	484	486	484	V	X	X	V	88.5	91	91.5	89.5	L
Bad 10	90	20	217	215	216	483	484	484	V	X	X	V	88	91.5	92.5	87.5	L
Bad 9	85	21	216	215	216	484	485	484	V	X	X	V	88.5	91	92.5	89	L
Bad 10	56	45	216	213	215	484	485	485	V	X	S	V	88.5	90.5	92.5	88.5	L

Note: 1. Straightness of Wire Frame
  X = Convex
  V = Concave
  S = Straight

2. Direction of Bow
  L = Left
  R = Right
  N = No Bow

Source: Vitromatic Corp., Celaya, Mexico.

1. Distance from hook—left and right;
2. Total cross length—front, center, and back;
3. Total longitudinal length—left, center, and right;
4. Straightness of wire frame: short side (front and back) and long side (left and right);
5. Angles at four corners; and
6. Direction of bow.

Question

Among the parameters measured, which are the important and unimportant parameters? Perform the Tukey test to determine the confidence level of each parameter.

Answer

Table 11-6 is a Tukey test compilation of the 17 grill parameters. It shows that the parameters in table 11-7 have a total end-count of 6 or more and, therefore, have a confidence of 90 percent and more that they are important in determining differences between good and bad units.

Comments

This DOE experiment was conducted largely by a direct labor team with only a smattering of English, in an international company, following our one-day seminar. It represents a fine example of "talking to the parts" and getting strong clues of where to focus the next stage in the elimination of the problem that has festered for seven years. *More important, it shows how grossly we underestimate the capabilities and effectiveness of direct labor people who are asked, by an uncaring management, to use only their brawn, not their brain.*

Tukey Test Ranking When the Center Is Good and the Tails Are Bad

The Tukey test ranking is generally based on a product quality characteristic or parameter ranging from smallest to largest or vice-versa, with the smallest being good and the largest being bad, or vice-versa. What happens, however, if in a rank order, the middle ranks are good and the ranks at both ends are bad? This is typical of a distribution of the parameter's data where the good ranks, reflecting actual variables data, are in the

Table 11-6. Tukey Test of 17 Parameters on Out-of-Square Grill

Distance from Hook		Total Cross Length			Total Longitudinal Length			Straightness of Wire Frame — Short Side		Straightness of Wire Frame — Long Side		Angle at 4 Corners				Bow Direction
Left	Right	Front	Center	Back	Left	Center	Right	Front	Back	Left	Right	1	2	3	4	
90 B	60 G	218 B	216 G	216.5 G	484 B	486 B	486 B	X G	V B	S G	S G	91 B	92 B	93 B	92 B	N G
85 B	60 G	216 G	216 G	216 B				X G	V B	S G	S G					N G
83 B	55 B	216 G	216 G					X G	V B	S G	S G					N G
56 B		215 B	215 B					X G	V B	S G	S G					N G
50 B								X G	V B	S G	S G					N G
50 G								X G	V B	S G	S G					N G
41 B								V B	X G	V B	V B					R B
28 G	27 G		215 G					V B	X G	V B	V B					L B
28 G	23 B							V B	X G	V B	V B					L B
26 G	21 B	214 B		216 G				V B	X G	V B	V B					L B
25 G	20 B	213 B		215 B	484 B	484 B	484 B	V B	X G	V B	V B	88 B	88.5 B	88 B	87.5 B	L B
Total End Count																
8½ = 5	0	0	2 + 3 = 5	1 + 1 = 2	0	0	0	12	12	12	12	0	0	0	0	6 + 5 = 11

Note: 1. Straightness of Wire Frame
X = Convex
V = Concave
S = Straight

2. Direction of Bow
L = Left
R = Right
N = No Bow

G = Good
B = Bad

It is not necessary to list all 12 readings in the rank order tabulations. It suffices to list them up to the first transition from good to bad (or vice-versa) and the last transition from bad to good (or vice-versa). A tie in readings between good and bad, at the transition, is counted as a half in the end-count. A bad (or good) reading at the top and at the bottom of the rankings reduces the total end-count to zero.

208

Table 11-7. Parameters With High Confidence Levels

Important Parameter	*Total End-Count*	*Confidence*
1. *Straightness of wire frame*		
a. Front: Convex better than concave	12	99.7%
b. Back: Concave better than convex	12	99.7%
c. Left: Straight better than concave	12	99.7%
d. Right: Straight better than concave	12	99.7%
2. Bow direction: No bow better than left bow	11	99.2%
3. Distance from left hook	8½	97%
Remaining 11 parameters	<6	No confidence

center and the bad ranks, reflecting those variables, are at the tail ends of that distribution. This is shown in Figure 11-2.

According to the general Tukey test guidelines discussed earlier, if both the tails of a rank order are bad (or both good), the end count is zero and there is no confidence that the parameter is important. There is a way, however, to convert a ranking in which the middle ranks are good and the two end ranks are bad into a Tukey format. In such a case, the ranking should be, not from smallest to largest, but from the deviation (plus or minus) of a parameter from its target value. Then the good units will tend to have the smaller deviations and the bad units the larger deviations. An example will illustrate this technique.

In Table 11-4, showing the Tukey test on contact lenses, let us assume that the rankings on the cylinder parameter were the same as before, but that the distribution of the good (G) and bad (B) lenses is as shown in

Figure 11-2. Distribution of a Parameter and Relationship to Rank

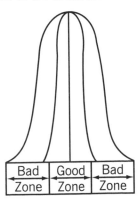

| Bad Zone | Good Zone | Bad Zone |

Column 1 of Table 11-8. Let us also assume that the target value for the cylinder is 0.040 mm. Then Column 2 would represent the deviation (plus or minus would not matter) from the target value of 0.040 mm of each observed lens. This deviation is then ranked in Column 3, which shows that the top five units with the lowest deviations are all good and the bottom five with the largest deviations are all bad. This gives a top end-count of five and a bottom end-count of five, for a total end-count of 10, with a confidence level of 99 percent.

Applications of Paired Comparisons in Administrative Work

As in the study of the Multi-Vari and Components Search techniques, Paired Comparisons can be used in nonproduct applications and in administrative work. It is so versatile a tool in these applications that it has become a workhorse in the entire clue-generation series. This author has used the Paired Comparison methodology in:

> Sales and marketing;
> Human resources;
> Dealerships, installation, and service;
> Hospitals; and
> Farms.

Table 11-8. Tukey Test Example: Center Good, Tails Bad

Original Rank	Column 1	Column 2 Deviation from Target of .040	New Rank Based on Deviation from Target
1	.016 B	.024 B	.008 G
2	.018 B	.022 B	.010 G
3	.020 B	.020 B	.010 G
4	.026 G	.014 G	.011 G
5	.030 G	.010 G	.011 G
6	.030 G	.010 G	.013 B
7	.048 G	.008 G	.014 G
8	.051 G	.011 G	.015 B
9	.051 G	.011 G	.016 B
10	.053 B	.013 B	.020 B
11	.055 B	.015 B	.022 B
12	.058 B	.016 B	.024 B
End-Count			5 + 5 = 10

The opportunities are endless! Two examples will suffice to illustrate the simplicity and power of the Paired Comparison techniques in such applications.

Case Study 3: Dairy Farm Bacteria Levels

A well-known international company that provides milking systems to dairy farms in the United States and abroad, had a subsidiary that provided chemical tablets that would clean the milking lines on dairy farms before the actual milking operation.

The company was receiving complaints from some of the diary farms that the chemical was not reducing bacteria levels sufficiently. These bacteria levels were all well below the maximum levels specified by U.S. government regulations. However, the dairy farms argued that the farm cooperatives (their customers) would pay them on a sliding scale depending on how low was the bacteria count. The complaining farms blamed the company's chemical for their loss of income.

This author, who had a long-standing consultation with the company on its milking systems, was asked to investigate the bacteria problem with the company's chemical subsidiary.

I devised a DOE Paired Comparison experiment in which six of the most frequently complaining dairy farms and six of the best farms with no complaints—all in Wisconsin, the dairy state—were selected. A trained company representative, whose family had run dairy farms for years, was selected to gather comprehensive data on these 12 farms, using the following 25 dairy farm parameters.

A. Green Y's (All six "bad" farms had higher counts than the six "good" ones.)

1. Bacteria counts
2. Pasteurized incubation counts (can cause rancidity and poor shelf life)
3. Red/white blood cell counts

B. Input Parameters: Where actual variables were not possible, a Likert scale of 1 to 10, with 1 = worst and 10 = best, was established.

1. *Cow/Teat Cleanliness*

1.1 Cleanliness of cow
1.2 Udder washing
1.3 Udder hygiene (pre and post)

1.4 Teat cleanliness after prepping
1.5 Milking unit cleanliness before milking
1.6 Milking unit cleanliness after milking
1.7 Milk filter cleanliness

2. *Water Analysis*

2.1 Hardness
2.2 Buffers (bicarbonate)
2.3 pH
2.4 Iron

3. *Systems Washing*

3.1 System configuration
3.2 Chemical type
3.3 Slugging
3.4 Cycles skipped
3.5 Pre-rinse temperature
3.6 Detergent cycle
3.7 Detergent wash temperature (start and finish)
3.8 Acid cycle
3.9 Acid rinse (start temperature and time)
3.10 Slope of line
3.11 Sanitizer

Tukey tests were conducted on each of the 25 parameters. The following total end-counts were observed on seven important parameters as shown in Table 11-9.

As was expected, the chemical type—the original source of the complaints—had an end-count of only one. The remaining 17 parameters with low end-counts, were not important.

Table 11-9. Tukey Test Results for Case Study 3

Parameter	Total End-Count
Slugging	12
Pre-rinse	12
Temperature	10
Milk filter	10
Detergent cycle	9
Teat cleanliness	9
Filter cleanliness	6½

The entire study, which took two to three months, revealed the necessity for the dairy farms to control their own operations much more closely. The company representative went back to the problem farms, pointing out the areas that needed correction. Four of these farms improved—and had no more complaints. The other two refused to change. They asserted: "I have been farming this way; my father has been farming this way. My grandfather was farming this way. Who are you to tell me how to farm!"

I persuaded the president of the parent company to capitalize on this "quality audit" of the dairy farms by turning it into a business and charging a fee for such service. He agreed, but modified my suggestion. He offered the audit service to the farms for free, provided they would buy his equipment and his chemicals. The result: The company captured 60 percent of its competitors' business!

Case Study 4: High Turnover of Temporary Employees

While conducting a DOE consultation at a well-known manufacturer of computer peripheral equipment, this author was approached by the human resources manager to see if DOE could be applied to a vexing problem in his area—namely, an unacceptably high turnover rate of temporary direct-labor employees. The estimated cost was $800,000 per year. The company had, by policy, a core of permanent direct-labor employees, with the balance labeled "temporaries." However, this company was growing so fast that no temporaries had ever been laid off. Yet the attrition rate among them was a matter of concern.

I suggested a Paired Comparison approach, with eight temporary employees (WOWs) who had quit the fastest after being hired and eight temporary employees (BOBs) who had stayed the longest for two years and more. The human resources team selected the people and established the following parameters for Paired Comparisons:

1. Commuting distance—home to work;
2. Driver's license;
3. Level of education;
4. History of turnover with other companies (churn rate);
5. Perceived quality of supervision;
6. Convenience of work schedule (the company had a rotating shift policy for all direct-labor employees);
7. Perception of pay relative to similar jobs in the community;
8. Perception of treatment relative to that of permanent employees.

Where actual variable measurements were not possible, a Likert scale of 1 to 10 (with 1 = worst and 10 = best) was devised.

A Tukey test of the 8 parameters showed only two parameters with an end-count of 6 or more.

1. Perception of treatment relative to that of permanent employees: End count of 7, with 95% confidence.
2. Commuting distance: End count of 6, with 90 percent confidence. (No one who commuted more than 15 miles stayed longer than six weeks.)

A third parameter—level of education—had only an end-count of 5, but was worth noting. (Persons with an associate degree or better seemed to have a higher turnover probability.)

The company could not do much to discriminate in hiring on the basis of commuting distance or level of education. But the treatment of temporaries versus permanent employees, which appeared to be a perception among the former, rather than a reality, was very much a challenge and an action item for the human resources team.

Questions for DOE Teams

1. Has the Green Y been quantified and measured, and is the accuracy of the measuring instrument at least five times the accuracy of the product tolerance?
2. If the Green Y is an attribute, has it been converted into a Likert scale variable?
3. Has Components Search—disassembly and reassembly without significant change in the Green Y—been ruled out, necessitating use of a Paired Comparison?
4. Have six or eight of the very best units (BOBs) and six or eight of the very worst units (WOWs) been elected for Paired Comparisons? (In unavoidable situations, where quantities are severely limited, it is possible to do a paired comparison with just three BOBs and three WOWs—with an end-count of 6—but then no overlap can be allowed.)
5. If it is not possible to have an equal number of BOBs and WOWs, are their respective counts within 20 percent of each other?
6. Is the separation between the BOBs and WOWs as large as possible, say, within a day's or a week's production?
7. If Paired Comparisons is being used to investigate field problems in customer hands, are the BOBs and WOWs being selected from comparable time periods of exposure in the field?
8. Has a list been drawn up of *all* possible quality parameters that

could possibly explain the difference between the BOBs and the WOWs?

9. Has this list been prioritized in descending order of probable causes of the difference?

10. Has the list been separated into nondestructive tests, which should be conducted first on the BOBs and WOWs, before proceeding with the destructive tests that may be necessary to probe differences?

11. Have the appropriate test methods to check for BOB and WOW differences been determined—e.g., SEMs, X-rays, hardness testers, frequency spectrum analyzers, finite element analyzers, morphology mapping, spectroscopy, etc.?

12. Has the Tukey test been applied to separate the important parameters, with an end-count of 6 or more (90 percent and greater confidence), from the unimportant parameters, with an end-count of 5 or less (less than 90 percent confidence)?

13. Have the parameters associated with the good parts been used to determine or revise the engineering specifications associated with such parts?

14. Have the parameters associated with the bad parts been used to challenge and modify the engineering specifications associated with such parts?

Questions for Top Management Review

In addition to the generic questions, associated with all DOE techniques, the following specific questions dealing with Paired Comparisons should be raised:

1. Are there good and bad units being produced, more or less at the same time?

2. Are the units incapable of disassembly and reassembly without damaging, destroying, or even changing their Green Y's?

3. Why was the Paired Comparison technique selected in preference to the other techniques?

4. Is there enough separation between the BOBs and the WOWs?

5. Has a list been made of as many parameters as possible that could account for the BOBs and the WOWs?

6. Are the nondestructive tests performed before the destructive tests?

7. Is there a follow-up to the Paired Comparisons, such as Variables

Search or Full Factorials, if there are several important variables identified?
8. Is a final follow-up performed with a B versus C to confirm the results of a Paired Comparisons experiment?

Sequel to Paired Comparisons Experiments: A Note of Caution

Paired Comparisons is a clue-generation technique. Sometimes, the clues—especially if a lone Red X is identified—will result in pinpointing the root cause and its correction. More often than not, however, a follow-on experiment is needed to determine the quantification of the important variables and their interaction on effects, such as a variable search or full factorials, and a B versus C confirmation. The Tukey test does not give 100 percent confidence. A 90 percent confidence means a 10 percent risk that a particular parameter labeled important may not actually be important. The experimenter must be prepared for such risks, even though they occur only occasionally.

12

Product/Process Search: Pinpointing Process Variables

Product/Process Search is the latest technique developed by the authors and constitutes another breakthrough in problem solving without disrupting a process. As such, it is the fifth of our clue-generation techniques.

Product/Process Search Objective

Just as Paired Comparisons separates important *product* parameters from unimportant ones, Product/Process Search separates important *process* parameters from unimportant ones.

Product/Process Search Principles

1. Any variation in a unit in production has two generic causes. Either there is variation in the product itself (causes by the material) or there is variation in one or more process parameters that is affecting the product.

2. If there is variation in the finished product, Components Search or Paired Comparisons could detect the causes of such product variations. This is the *product* part of Product/Process Search.

3. If, however, the causes are variations in process parameters that may shift, drift, fluctuate, or change with time, the *process* part of Product/Process Search can be employed. It uses the same principles as Paired Comparisons of six or eight good products and six or eight bad products,

but compares, instead, *the process parameters associated with the six or eight good products and the process parameters associated with the six or eight bad products.*

4. Product/Process Search is a natural sequel to a Multi-Vari study, where the time-to-time family is a Red X and where product fluctuations or variation with time are suspected. (See Figure 7-1 for the position of this technique in the roadmap.)

Product/Process Search Methodology

1. If process parameter variations are suspected as possible causes for good and bad finished products, make a list of these process parameters, *in descending order of likelihood.*

2. Determine how each process parameter is to be measured, who is to measure it, and where precisely it is to be measured.

3. Make sure that the accuracy of the measuring instrument is at least 5 times the accuracy (tolerance) of the process parameter. As an example, if the temperature in a furnace is to be kept at 1200°C ± 5 percent, the measuring instrument accuracy should be ± 1 percent maximum.

4. Make sure that the *actual* process parameters, *not just mere settings,* are measured.

5. If a particular process parameter does not vary at all while being monitored, it can be eliminated from further consideration.

6. Run a 100 percent sample of units (especially during a higher defect period, if the defects come and go), or a multi-vari sample of units; until:

> ➤ A minimum of eight good units and eight bad units are collected at the end of the process.
> ➤ The spread between the best unit and the worst unit is a minimum of 80 percent of the historic variation observed on the product produced by the process.

7. Measure all the designated process parameters associated with each unit (either 100 percent of the units or the chosen samples in a multi-vari).

8. As the units go through the process, a determination of whether the units are going to be good or bad cannot be made until the end of the process. This means that many potentially good units will have to be

measured, along with many potentially bad units, in order to obtain a minimum of eight eventually bad units, especially if the historic defect rate is low—say 1 percent. Then, 99 good units would have to be measured for each process parameter, on average, before one bad unit is likely to occur. Therefore, in order to get a minimum of eight bad units, approximately 800 to 900 good units will have to be measured, individually, as they go through the process.

This is tedious and time-consuming; but many modern processes now come equipped with automatic data acquisition and control systems that record the process parameters of each unit instantly and automatically.

9. A Paired Comparison of the *process parameters* associated with the eight good and eight bad units is then run. And a Tukey test is performed on each parameter, with a total end-count calculation. If the end-count is 6 or more, that particular process parameter is important, with 90 percent or greater confidence.

10. If there are several process parameters identified with 90 percent or greater confidence, run a "B versus C" test (see Chapter 15) to verify that the important parameters are truly captured. After all, a 90 percent confidence is not 100 percent confidence and there can be some parameters missing, or some included that may not repeat.)

11. Next, a variable search (see Chapter 13) or a full factorial (see Chapter 14) should be run to quantify the most important parameters and their interaction effects.

12. Further optimization, through Scatter Plots or Evolutionary Operation, followed by Positrol, Process Certification, and Pre-Control should be conducted (see Chapters 16, 17, 18, and 19).

13. The tolerances of the unimportant parameters in Step 8 can be expanded to reduce costs, although some experimentation may be necessary to determine how much to expand them.

Product/Process Search: When Process Parameters Cannot Be Measured on Individual Units

In certain processes, individual units of a product cannot be measured for their associated process parameters as they go through a process. Examples include batch processes or heats, as in foundries and glass fabrication. In that case, the process parameters associated with each batch as whole must be noted and paired comparisons made on the process parameter associated with eight good batches and eight bad batches of product. This method is not as sensitive as process readings on each individual unit, but—under these circumstances—is the only available option.

Case Study 1: Stale Lettuce/Bag Leakage

A company processing lettuce for a worldwide fast-food chain was receiving a chorus of complaints from several of the chain's restaurant outlets about lettuce that was stale when received. Lettuce spoils within a day when exposed to air—resulting in discoloration, sogginess, odor, etc.—and so has to be vacuum-packed in bags before delivery. This increases the shelf life of the cut-up lettuce from one day to two weeks.

The company's only customer was the fast-food chain. It became very concerned about losing its total business. This author received an emergency call from the company president to help solve the problem.

The Process

Lettuce arrives from farms in refrigerated trucks. In the processing plant, where the temperatures are kept at a chilling 34 to 37°F, it is cored, washed, rinsed, dried, and cut up in giant machines to exact customer size specifications. The next step is a comprehensive packaging operation in which the cut-up lettuce comes down a chute and a polyethylene bag descends from another chute. The bag is then filled to a $2/3$ level and a vacuum is drawn, after which the bag is heat-sealed and packed in cartons for shipment to the fast-food restaurants.

An Earlier Green Y

In the initial meeting with the company's management, my first task was to define and quantify the Green Y. The ultimate Green Y was stale lettuce, which is difficult to quantify and takes too long to measure. The company knew that the cause of the problem was vacuum leaks—an earlier Green Y. But, as we were in the process of quantifying that parameter, one of the managers determined a correlation between leaky bags and small pieces of lettuce in the area between the lettuce bed and especially at the top of the bag in the heat-seal area. So we settled on the number of loose pieces of lettuce in a bag as the earlier and easier Green Y.

A quick multi-vari run indicated variations with time and within bag. This pointed to a comprehensive Product/Process Search experiment, because (1) several variables in the packaging process were suspected to be fluctuating with time, and (2) the Concentration Chart revealed a large accumulation of pieces of lettuce in a specific location within the heat seal.

The DOE team drew up a list of primary process variables, as follows:

1. Snorkel position (depth of penetration into lettuce bed);
2. Vacuum time;
3. Snorkel speed;
4. Seal dwell time;
5. Seal heat;
6. Cooling time;
7. Machine PSI;
8. Dump delay; and
9. Snorkel-up delay.

Other process variables were kept in reserve in case the primary variables showed total end-counts of less than 6. These were

> Vacuum PSI;
> Vacuum pressure;
> Conveyor height;
> Seal width;
> Snorkel angle;
> Bag vibration;
> Bag weight; and
> Bag placement.

Results

Green Y: The number of pieces of cut-up lettuce found in each bag varied from none (good bags) up to two to four (bad bags). The Product/Process Search of the nine process parameters was continued until eight good bags and eight bad bags resulted. The Paired Comparisons of these process parameters are shown in Table 12-1.

There were end-counts of 16, 6, 6$^1/_2$, and 9 associated with snorkel position, vacuum time, snorkel speed, and machine PSI, respectively. These four process parameters were important (with 90 percent and higher confidence levels), of which the snorkel position (depth into the lettuce bed) was the Red X. This was logical because penetration of the snorkel into the bed of cut-up lettuce could suck pieces of lettuce into the Green Y area, whereas there would be no defects if the snorkel just kissed the lettuce bed. It was difficult to control the height of the lettuce within a bag, because lettuce density and moisture content vary from lot to lot.

Table 12-1. Product/Process Search: Case Study 1—Packaging Machine

Process Parameters	Snorkel Position	Vacuum Time	Snorkel Speed	Seal Dwell Time	Seal Temp.	Cooling Time	Machine Pressure	Dump Delay	Snorkel-up Delay
Parameter Range	0 to ½" Penetration Depth	.65 to .85 Minutes	90 to 105 Seconds	.6 to .9 Minutes	290 to 307 °F	.3 to .5 Minutes	95 to 105 PSI	.1 to .2 Minutes	.1 to .2 Minutes
Bag No.									
1	½ B	.85 B	100 B	.9 B	307 B	.5 G	95 G	.1 B	.1 B
2	½ B	.84 B	100 B	.9 G	307 G	.5 G	95 G	.1 B	.1 B
3	½ B	.84 B	99 B	.9 G	305 G	.5 B	95 G	.1 G	.1 G
4	½ B	.83 B	99 G	.9 B	305 B	.5 B	97 G	.1 G	.1 G
5	½ B	.81 G	98 B	.9 G	305 G	.5 B	96 B	.1 B	.1 G
6	¼ B	.80 G	97 G	.9 G	304 B	.5 G	98 B	.1 B	.1 G
7	¼ B	.77 B	97 G	.9 B	304 G	.5 B	100 G	.1 G	.1 B
8	¼ B	.77 B	95 G	.9 B	302 G	.5 G	100 G	.1 G	.1 G
9	0 G	.75 G	95 B	.9 G	300 B	.5 B	101 B	.1 B	.1 G
10	0 G	.75 G	95 B	.9 B	300 B	.5 B	103 G	.1 G	.1 B
11	0 G	.75 G	94 B	.9 B	300 G	.5 B	103 G	.1 B	.1 B
12	0 G	.72 B	93 B	.9 G	300 G	.5 G	104 B	.1 G	.1 G
13	0 G	.70 G	92 G	.9 G	300 B	.5 G	104 B	.2 B	.1 G
14	0 G	.69 B	92 G	.9 B	299 B	.5 G	105 B	.2 G	.1 G
15	0 B	.68 B	90 G	.9 G	298 B	.5 B	105 B	.2 G	.1 B
16	0 G	.68 G	90 G	.9 B	297 G	.5 G	105 B	.2 B	.1 B
End-Counts	8 + 8	4 + 2	2½ + 4	0	1 + 1	0	4 + 5	0	0
Total End-Counts	= 16	= 6	= 6½	= 0	= 2	= 0	= 9	= 0	= 0

Note: Readings of each parameter are arranged in descending or ascending order.
Legend: B = bad units; G = good units; shaded areas show end-counts.

But the supplier of the packaging equipment modified his process to assure zero penetration into the lettuce bed.

Follow-Up Experiments and Conclusion

A Variables Search experiment was the next step, with the above four variables, along with two other variables recommended by the packaging machine supplier. The final outcome was that the defect rate went from 12 percent to near zero, for a projected savings of $350,000 per year. More important, the company saved its business and retained a customer. It even made a presentation to the customer's top management at the latter's headquarters to demonstrate the simplicity and power of our DOE techniques.

Case Study 2:
Bubbles in Glass Screen

A multinational company's Latin American plant, which fabricated glass screens, was having a problem with bubbles in its final product that were objectionable to its customers. The defect level was around 13 percent.

A Taguchi experiment had been performed by the company's engineers. It showed an improvement from 13 percent to 6.2 percent, but the plant's management was still not satisfied with this incremental improvement. This author was asked to try his methods to eliminate the bubble problem.

Flow Chart

The process begins in a furnace, where glass is melted at very high temperatures, and then conveyed through two feeders to two presses, where the screens are formed. The screens are then transported to an annealing operation, after which they are tested.

An examination of the historic data indicated variations with time, with some periods producing zero defects and other periods showing 10 percent and higher spikes in defect percentages. This finding indicated that a multi-vari could be bypassed and a product/process search DOE experiment tried. This decision was supported by the fact that the plant had an excellent monitoring system of the key process parameters.

Because glass is a batch process, individual screens could not be monitored for their respective process parameters. The unit, therefore, was a batch rather than an individual screen. Eight process parameters were chosen:

Furnace / Feeder	Press
Crown temperature	Pressure #1
Bottom temperature	Pressure #2
Feeder temperature (in)	Box height #1
Feeder temperature (out)	Box height #2

The Green Y was the number of bubbles found in the total number of screens in each batch. (A Likert scale was established to distinguish bubble size; bubble depth; and number of bubbles. Eight good batches and eight bad batches were recorded; their respective process parameters are shown in Table 12-2.) The 16 readings for each parameter reflected not the actual readings, but the deviations (+ and −) from the expected best values. For the two furnace temperatures, the screens close to the expected best value were good and the screens at the temperature tails were bad, indicating that the end-counts had to be calculated by the alternate method, with the tails of the top (bad), bottom (bad), and the middle (only good)—added up. The same applied to box height #2. The other five parameters showed a one-way trend from bad to good as each parameter was increased in value, so that the standard Tukey test for end-count applied.

Results

Table 12-2 showed that:

> ⟩ The Red X was the bottom furnace temperature, with an end-count of 11, and should be maintained (in the good region) between 1353° and 1359°.
> ⟩ The Pink X was box height #2, with an end-count of 10, and should be maintained (in the good region) between 39 and 40 cm.
> ⟩ The Pale Pink X was the crown furnace temperature, with an end-count of 9, and should be maintained (in the good region) between 1567° and 1569°.
> ⟩ The Pale Pale Pink X was Pressure #2, with an end-count of 6, maintained around 520°.
> ⟩ A B versus C test indicated that the bubble defects on the B batch with these modified parameters had dropped to 0.4 percent as compared with the C batch at 6.1 percent.

Further DOE tests—a 2^4 Full Factorial to quantify interaction effects and a Scatter Plot or evolutionary operation to optimize the parameters—are still required to get the defect level down to zero.

Table 12-2. Product/Process Search: Case Study 2—Bubbles in Glass Screen

Process Parameters	Crown Temp.	Bottom Temp.	Feeder Temp. (In)	Feeder Temp. (Out)	Pressure #1	Pressure #2	Box Height #1	Box Height #2
Parameter Range	1555° to 1570° F	1350° to 1370° F	1098° to 1126° F	1030° to 1050° F	445 to 515 PSI	515 to 520 PSI	21 to 29 cm	36 to 44 cm
Expected Best	1565°	1360°	1126°	1040°	475	515	29	39
Bag No.								
1	−10 B	−15 B	−5 G	−2 G	−12 B	−4 B	−7 B	−3 B
2	−10 B	−13 B	−5 G	−2 B	−10 B	−4 B	−6 B	−3 B
3	−9 B	−13 G	−5 B	−2 B	−5 G	−3 B	−5 G	−2 G
4	−8 G	−12 B	−5 G	−1 G	−2 B	−2 G	−4 B	−2 G
5	−8 G	−10 B	−5 B	−1 G	0 G	−2 G	−4 G	−2 B
6	−5 G	−7 G	−5 B	−1 B	+5 G	−1 B	−4 G	0 G
7	−3 B	−6 G	−5 B	−1 B	+8 G	−1 G	−3 B	0 G
8	−1 G	−4 G	−5 G	−1 G	+12 G	0 G	−3 G	0 G
9	0 B	−4 G	−5 G	0 G	+12 B	0 B	−3 B	+1 G
10	+1 B	−2 G	−5 B	0 B	+14 G	0 B	−2 B	+1 G
11	+2 G	−1 G	−5 G	0 B	+20 G	0 G	−2 G	+3 B
12	+3 G	0 B	−5 G	0 G	+22 B	+2 B	−2 G	+3 B
13	+3 G	+1 G	−5 B	0 G	+25 B	+2 B	−2 B	+3 G
14	+4 G	+2 B	−5 B	0 B	+26 G	+3 G	−2 B	+4 B
15	+5 B	+3 B	−5 B	+1 G	+27 G	+4 G	−1 G	+5 B
16	+5 B	+5 B	−5 G	+1 B	+28 G	+5 G	−1 G	+5 B
End-Counts	3 + 2 + 4	2 + 3 + 6	0	0	2 + 3	3 + 3	2 + 2	2 + 3 + 5
Total End-Counts	= 9	= 11	= 0	= 0	= 5	= 6	= 4	= 10

Legend: B = bad units; G = good units. Shaded areas show end-counts.

225

Workshop Exercise 1: Plastic Injection Molding

A large toy manufacturer had a high reject rate (over 20 percent) on plastic parts produced on an injection molding machine. The Green Y was short shots. A product/process DOE experiment was conducted on eight selected process parameters:

> ➤ Mold temperature;
> ➤ Material temperature;
> ➤ First pressure;
> ➤ Back pressure;
> ➤ Injection speed;
> ➤ Screw speed;
> ➤ Mold vents; and
> ➤ Injection time.

The injection molding machine was equipped with an up-to-date automatic data acquisition system through which every shot's key parameters could be recorded. The results are shown in Table 12-3.

Questions

1. What are the end-counts on each of the eight process parameters?
2. Which of the process parameters are important? And which are unimportant?
3. Are the ranges of each of these parameters, as recommended by the machine supplier, reasonable?
4. If not, what ranges should the manufacturer try in the next round of experiments?

Answers

1. and 2. See Table 12-4.
3. and 4. For mold temperature, the supplier-recommended ranges of 80° to 110° appear to be too wide and too low. The ranges on the good units appear to be from 89° to 104°. A tightening—from 95° to 105°—would be in order. (See Table 12-5.)

Questions for DOE Teams as Guidelines for Product/Process Search

1. Has the Green Y been defined, quantified, and measured (instrument accuracy to exceed product tolerance by a minimum of 5:1)?

Table 12-3. Product/Process Search: Case Study 3—Plastic Injection Molding Machine

Process Parameters	Mold Temp.	Matl. Temp.	Pressure	Back Pressure	Injection Speed	Screw Speed	Mold Vents	Injection Time
Recommended Parameter Range	80° to 100° F	410° to 450° F	1000 to 1100 PSI	75 to 90 PSI	1"/Sec.	2"/Sec.	.0005 to .0015	2 Sec.
Actual								
1B	85	405	1055	82	1.0	2.0	0.0005	2.0
2B	88	420	1040	85	1.0	1.9	0.0005	2.1
3B	101	409	1060	83	1.0	1.9	0.0005	2.1
4B	103	403	1020	77	1.1	2.0	0.0005	2.0
5B	95	430	1010	85	1.0	2.0	0.0005	2.1
6B	90	416	1050	82	1.2	2.0	0.0005	2.0
7B	100	401	1095	84	1.2	1.9	0.0005	2.0
8B	101	406	1100	80	1.1	2.0	0.0005	2.0
9G	89	432	1190	77	1.0	2.0	0.0005	2.1
10G	104	416	1055	81	0.9	2.0	0.0005	2.0
11G	101	438	1075	76	1.0	2.0	0.0005	2.0
12G	93	408	1015	80	0.9	1.9	0.0005	2.1
13G	101	422	1075	78	1.0	2.0	0.0005	2.0
14G	104	418	1050	75	1.0	1.9	0.0005	2.0
15G	92	440	1055	79	1.0	2.0	0.0005	2.0
16G	99	445	1070	83	1.0	2.0	0.0005	2.0
End-Counts	4	8	0	0	6	0	0	0

Legend: B = Bad units; G = Good units.

Table 12-4. Process Parameters and Their Importance

Parameter	End-Count	Confidence	Importance
Mold temperature	4	—	Not important
Material temperature	8	97%	Important
First pressure	0	0	Not important
Back pressure*	$3^{1/2} + 2^{1/2} = 6$	90%	Important
Injection speed	6	90%	Important
Screw speed	0	0	Not important
Mold vents	No change	—	Not important
Injection time	0	0	Not important

*For back pressure, there were ties at the first and last transitions going from bad to good and from good to bad, resulting in two $1/2$ end-counts.

Table 12-5. Parameter Ranges

Process Parameter	Supplier Recommended Range	Comments	Range of Good Readings	Target for Next Round
Mold temperature	80° to 110°	Low end-count	89° to 104°	No change needed
Material temperature	410° to 450°	Too wide	408° to 445°	44°
First pressure	1000 to 1100	Zero end-count	1055 to 1090	No change needed
Back pressure	75 to 90	Too wide	75 to 83	77
Injection speed	1" / second	Too narrow	0.85 to 1.0	0.95
Screw speed	2" / second	Zero end-count	1.9 to 2.0	No change needed
Mold vents	0.001 to 0.0015	Zero end-count	0.0005	No change needed
Injection time	2 seconds	Zero end-count	2	No change needed

2. If the Green Y is an attribute, can it be converted into a variable, using Likert scale, so that the defects can be multiplied by the Likert scale to arrive at a larger, weighted defect score?

3. Is the family of variation time to time, in which case Product/Process Search would be a logical DOE technique to generate clues?

4. Has a list of process parameters, in descending order of likelihood of affecting the finished product, been drawn up? (Process parameters that show no change need not be further monitored.)

5. Has instrumentation been established to measure each process parameter accurately?

6. Are actual measurements, and not just settings, being monitored?

7. Is Product/Process Search being used during periods of high rejects, rather than when there are minimal or no defects?

8. Does the spread between the best finished units and the worst finished units cover a minimum of 80 percent of the historic variation of the finished product?

9. If each unit (product) cannot be monitored for its associated process parameters, can the next smallest batch or sample of time be used to get eight best and eight worst batches or samples of time?

10. If the process parameters tend to show a distribution of good units in the middle and bad units at the tails, is the alternate Tukey test method used to determine end-counts?

11. Once the important process parameters are identified, is a B versus C test conducted to validate the improvement?

12. Are subsequent tests such as Scatter Plots or Response Surface Methodology used to optimize the important process parameters?

13. Are further tests used to see how far the unimportant process parameter tolerances can be opened up to reduce costs?

14. Are Positrol, Process Certification, and Pre-Control put in place to assure the permanency of improvement in day-to-day production?

Questions for Top Management in Following DOE Team Progress

1. Why was the particular Green Y chosen? Could an earlier, easier Green Y have been chosen instead? Is the measurement accuracy of the Green Y assured (5:1 ratio)? Was a Likert scale established for an attribute Green Y?

2. Why was Product/Process Search chosen as the clue-generation technique?

3. Can the process parameters be measured (actuals, not settings) for each unit of product going through the process? If not, what is the smallest batch or time sample that can distinguish eight best and eight worst batches or time samples?

4. Is a B versus C test conducted following Product/Process Search to validate the improvement of the process?

5. Are other DOE disciplines—such as Scatter Plots and Positrol—used to optimize the process parameters and then "freeze" them in ongoing production?

6. Is Process Certification used to ensure that all quality peripherals,

such as good manufacturing practices, calibration, environmental factors, etc., are in place before the start of production (or, sometimes, even before the start of DOE)?

7. Is Pre-Control used as the best SPC tool to monitor the tightly controlled important process parameters?

Part IV
. . . .
Formal Design of Experiments Techniques to Characterize a Product/Process

13

Variables Search: The Rolls Royce in the Search for the Red X

From Clue Generation to Distilling the Red X

The previous chapters described the four clue-generation techniques that make it possible to talk to the parts—the Multi-Vari, Components Search, Paired Comparisons, and Product/Process Search. It has been the experience of the authors as well as many of our clients that 70 percent to 80 percent of chronic quality problems can be solved with one or more of these clue-generation techniques, performed either sequentially or simultaneously. These methods also have the unique advantage of not disrupting production.

Sometimes, however, after the clues have filtered out many variables as unimportant, they may leave two to 10, or even 15, important variables, requiring further distillation of the Red X, Pink X, and Pale Pink X, along with a quantification of their interaction effects. So, more formal DOE techniques are needed as follow-up, even though they do require disrupting production.

Formal DOE Techniques

Several formal DOE techniques are in vogue. The most frequently used ones are (in descending order of *accuracy but not practicality*):

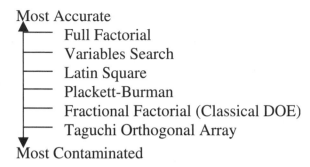

Most Accurate
- Full Factorial
- Variables Search
- Latin Square
- Plackett-Burman
- Fractional Factorial (Classical DOE)
- Taguchi Orthogonal Array

Most Contaminated

Of these, the Full Factorial is the purest because it neatly separates main effects from their interaction effects—compartmentalizing all second-order, third-order, fourth-order, and even higher order interaction effects. Why then, should not the experimenter use only the Full Factorial and forget about the less pure formal DOE techniques? The answer is practicality.

The Full Factorial

As will be seen in Chapter 14, the methodology in designing a Full Factorial is to select two levels for each factor—a high level and a low level. Then, each level of each factor is tested with each level of all the other factors, creating a 2^n matrix or 2^n combinations (i.e., experiments). If there are four factors and two levels for each factor, there are 2^4 or 16 combinations; which means 16 experiments. That is doable and practical. But what if there are 10 factors, each with two levels. Then, there are 2^{10} or 1,024 combinations (i.e., 1,024 experiments). Even a young experimenter could become an old person by the time he or she finished.

Limitations of All Types of Fractional Factorials

As a shortcut to the full factorial, the other formal DOE techniques test only a fraction of the number of combinations. On one end is the Latin Square—a neat DOE technique popular with this author in the 1960s and 1970s, but then abandoned because it generally tests three factors, each with two levels, with only four experiments instead of the required eight. This half-factorial—or half-replicate—is the least contaminated of the fraction factorial family.

Taguchi

On the other end, in terms of extreme contamination, is the Taguchi Orthogonal Array, in which as many as 10 factors would be tested with say, an L8 array or an L16 array, i.e., with only eight or 16 experiments. As will be shown in the next section, this means that the main effects can get severely contaminated—the statistical term is confounded—with the interaction effects, giving you marginal or plain wrong results. Taguchites counter by saying that they do include the most important interaction effects in an appropriate "L" array. But how would they select the most important combinations of unknown variables? That is like playing Russian roulette. In fact, it is much worse than in Russian roulette, where there is only one chance in six of being killed. With Taguchites, there is a chance of being killed every time!

Classical Fraction Factorials—Only Slightly Better Than Taguchi

The classical DOE school, which relies heavily on fraction factorials, uses a higher fraction of the total number of combinations or experiments required than does Taguchi's orthogonal array. So the contamination—or confounding—is a bit less severe, *but it is still a fundamental flaw in the very design of the experiment.* Here too, experimenters of the Classical school counter by saying that they use a Fraction Factorial approach as a "screening" exercise to identify at least the main effects and some second-order interaction effects, after which a full factorial can be employed to sort out the true variables. But, as will be shown in the next section, *if the basic construction of the experiment is flawed, the results will also be flawed.* A house erected on a foundation of sand is bound to collapse.

Confounding Main Effects With Interaction Effects— An Example

Let us say that there are four factors; A, B, C, and D, and that it is desired to quantify their main effects and true interaction effects. A Full Factorial, which is the purest technique, would require 16 experiments (see Table 13-1). For a balanced design that requires 15 contrasts—or 15 columns (The rule is that the number of contrasts is the number of experiments minus one):

> There would be four columns of main effects: A, B, C, and D.
> There would be six columns of two-factor interactions: AB, AC, AD, BC, BD, and CD.
> There would be four columns of three-factor interactions: ABC, ABD, ACD, and BCD.
> There would be one column of four-factor interactions: A, B, C, and D.

Table 13-1. A 2^4 Full Factorial Design

Cell* Group	Factors Main Effects A	B	C	D	2 Factor Interactions AB	AC	BC	AD	BD	CD	3 Factor Interactions ABC	ABD	ACD	BCD	4 F.I. ABCD	Results/ Output
1 (1)	−	−	−	−	+	+	+	+	+	+	−	−	−	−	+	
2 a	+	−	−	−	−	−	+	−	+	+	+	+	+	−	−	
3 b	−	+	−	−	−	+	−	+	−	+	+	+	−	+	−	
4 ab	+	+	−	−	+	−	−	−	−	+	−	−	+	+	+	
5 c	−	−	+	−	+	−	−	+	+	−	+	−	+	+	−	
6 ac	+	−	+	−	−	+	−	−	+	−	−	+	−	+	+	
7 bc	−	+	+	−	−	−	+	+	−	−	−	+	+	−	+	
8 abc	+	+	+	−	+	+	+	−	−	−	+	−	−	−	−	
9 d	−	−	−	+	+	+	+	−	−	−	−	+	+	+	−	
10 ad	+	−	−	+	−	−	+	+	−	−	+	−	−	+	+	
11 bd	−	+	−	+	−	+	−	−	+	−	+	−	+	−	+	
12 abd	+	+	−	+	+	−	−	+	+	−	−	+	−	−	−	
13 cd	−	−	+	+	+	−	−	−	−	+	+	+	−	−	+	
14 acd	+	−	+	+	−	+	−	+	−	+	−	−	+	−	−	
15 bcd	−	+	+	+	−	−	+	−	+	+	−	−	−	+	−	
16 abcd	+	+	+	+	+	+	+	+	+	+	+	+	+	+	+	

Note: **1. Cells**

Cell (1) indicates that A, B, C, and D are all at their (−) level.

Lower-case A (a) means that (A) is at its positive (+) level. Similarly, for B, C, & D.

Lower-case AB (ab) means that (A and B) are at their positive (+) level.

2. Interactions

The signs of A, B, etc., are multiplied algebraically.

- A as (−) and B as (−) produce AB as (+). $(- \times - = +)$
- A as (−) and B as (−) and C as (−) produce ABC as (−). $(- \times - \times - = = -)$

(See Chapter 14 for an explanation of the Full Factorial.)

Now let us assume that a decision is made to use a half-replicate Fraction Factorial—the least objectionable in the Fraction Factorial family—instead of the full factorial. Table 13-2 shows a typical example.

Weaknesses of a Half-Replicate Fraction Factorial

1. Only half the number, i.e., 8 experiments are run instead of 16, as in a Full Factorial.

2. Four main factors (A, B, C, and D) are included in the design, each with two levels—high (+) and low (−)—so each factor with four high level and four low level experiments.

3. But with eight experiments, there is room in the design for only seven contrasts. Four columns are used up for A, B, C, and D. That leaves room for only three interaction effects—say, AC, BC, and ABC. What happens to:

> - The remaining two-factor interactions: AB, AD, BD, and CD?
> - The remaining three-factor interactions: ACD, ABD, and BCD?
> - The one four-factor interaction: ABCD?

4. The stark reality is that the eight interactions, out of the 15, that are not included in the experiment can find their way into one or more of the four main factors or the three selected interactions and completely confound the results!

5. The interactions themselves, can be unbalanced in terms of an unequal number of highs (+) and lows (−), as seen in Table 13-2.

6. The net result is confounding, leading to frustration and disillusionment.

Table 13-2. A Half-Replicate Fraction Factorial Design

Test No.	A	B	C	D	AC	BC	ABC	Results
1	+	+	+	+	+	+	+	
2	+	−	+	−	+	−	−	
3	−	+	−	+	+	−	+	
4	−	−	+	+	−	−	+	
5	+	+	−	−	−	−	−	
6	−	−	−	+	+	+	−	
7	+	+	+	−	+	+	+	
8	−	−	−	−	+	+	−	

Statisticians speak of aliases, which mean assumed or false names. Fraction factorials are filled with aliases. For example, if there are seven factors with two levels each, a Full Factorial requires 2^7, or 128, experiments. If, instead, a Fraction Factorial with only eight experiments is used, the results are mass confounding, as seen in Table 13-3. This shows that each of the main effects could be confounded with 15 interaction effects, producing a total of 112 aliases!

This parallels a story of a Chicago woman who paraded around under 100 aliases (false names) in order to collect welfare checks from Uncle Sam. She was known as the Alias Queen of Welfare until she was

Table 13-3. Aliases Produced by Seven Factors With Only Eight Experiments

A	=	BD = CE = BCG = CDF = BEF = FG = DEG
	=	BCDEFG = ACEFG = ABDFG = ABCDE
	=	ADEF = ACDG = ABEG = ABCF
B	=	AD = EG = ACG = CDE = AEF = DFG
	=	ACDEFG = BCEFG = ABDEG = ABCDF
	=	BDEF = BCDG = ABFG = ABCE
C	=	AE = BF = ABG = BDE = ADF = DG = EFG
	=	ABDEFG = BCDFG = ACDEG = ABCEF
	=	CDEF = BCEG = ACFG = ABCD
D	=	AB = CG = BCE = ACF = EF = AEG = BFG
	=	ABCEFG = CDEFG = ABDEF = ABCDG
	=	BDEG = BCDF = ADFG = ACDE
E	=	AC = BG = BCD = DF = ABF = ADG = CFG
	=	ABCDFG = BDEFG = ACDEF = ABCEG
	=	CDEG = BCEF = AEFG = ABDE
F	=	BC = AG = DE = ACD = ABE = BDG = CEG
	=	ABCDEG = BCDEF = ADEFG = ABCFG
	=	CDFG = BEFG = ACEF = ABDF
G	=	ABC = CD = BE = AF = ADE = BDF = CEF
	=	ABCDEF = BCDEG = ACDFG = ABEFG
	=	DEFG = BCFG = ACEG = ABDG

112	Aliases
15	Lost Forever
127	Total Contrasts

caught and put in prison. In the tidy world of statistics, Fraction Factorials can be labeled the Alias King of DOE!

Variables Search: Its Advantages Over All Fraction Factorials

If the Full Factorial is too time-consuming and complex for factors beyond four, and if the whole family of fraction factorials is too statistically weak, what is the alternative? This is precisely where Variables Search comes to the rescue. It has the advantage of a small number of experiments—a maximum of 26, even for 10 factors—as well as the neat compartmentalization of all main effects, and all second-order, third-order, and most fourth-order interaction effects, as will be shown later in this chapter. Further, it economizes the cost of experimentation over the classical and Taguchi methods by factors of from 3:1 to 10:1. Its place in the detailed problem-solving roadmap is shown in Figure 7-1.

Variables Search Objectives

1. To reduce a residually large number of causes—up to a practical maximum of 20—from earlier clue-generation DOE techniques and distill the Red X, Pink X, and Pale Pink X. (As stated earlier, causes, variables, and factors are synonymous terms.)
2. To separate the important factors from the unimportant ones.
3. To open up the tolerances of the unimportant factors (i.e., the C_p and C_{pk} of these factors can easily be lowered to below 1.0) and smile all the way to the bank.
4. To quantify the magnitude and desired direction of the important factors and their interaction effects, and to tighten the tolerances of these important variables to a minimum C_p, C_{pk} of 2.0.
5. While Variables Search can be and is used as a problem-solving tool in production and as a sequel to the four clue-generation tools, *its indispensable function is at the design stage of a product or process, to prevent problems from reaching production* in the first place. When there is a quality problem in production, it is too late. When there is a quality problem in the hands of a customer, it is way to late. In fact, the existence of a problem in production is a sure reflection of the poverty of the design function.
6. There exists a number of paper and computer studies to identify important factors at the conceptual stage of a design. These include Monte Carlo simulation, E-chip, and circuit analysis, as well as other methods. But they all have a weakness in that they require

a knowledge of the mathematical equation or formula that governs the relationship between independent factors and a dependent variable (the Green Y). If that formula is not known, the computer and paper studies are guessing games at best and useless at worst! In such cases, Variables Search is the only answer.

7. Even if a formula governing the independent and dependent variables is known, *a follow-up of such computer simulation with Variables Search at the prototype stage is essential to verify the accuracy of the formula on which the computer model is based.* The experience of the authors indicates that, in at least 20 percent of these verifications, using the computer resulted in the wrong identifications of the important variables.

8. Variables Search can also be used to open up tolerances, to standardize products, and to reduce costs.

The Binary Search Principle

Variables Search is based on the binary search principle. This is best illustrated by the game 20 Questions. A person is asked to select any word whose meaning has to be found in a dictionary, of, say, 800 pages. He or she then writes down the selected word and notes the page number in the dictionary on which the word appears. The game is for the questioner to pinpoint the word selected with no more than 20 "yes" or "no" questions. Let us say that the person selecting the word has chosen it from page 272. The questions are shown in Table 13-4.

Generally, in no more than 11 questions, the page number is identified. The questioner then asks if the selected word is in the left column of

Table 13-4. The Binary Search Principle: 20 Questions

No.	Question	Answer
1.	Is the page number greater than 400?	No
2.	Is it greater than 200?	Yes
3.	Is it greater than 300?	No
4.	Is it greater than 250?	Yes
5.	Is it greater than 300?	No
6.	Is it greater than 275?	No
7.	Is it greater than 263?	Yes
8.	Is it greater than 269?	Yes
9.	Is it greater than 272?	No
10.	Is it greater than 271?	Yes
11.	Is it page 272?	Yes

the page. If the answer is no, it is in the right column. Next question: Is the word in the upper half of the right column? If yes, is it in the upper quartile of the column, and so on until the exact word is found in less than 20 questions.

This game illustrates the difference between an engineer guessing at the exact word out of a dictionary of over 100,000 words. He'd be at it all night! Instead the binary search is a process of systematic elimination. After the first question has been answered, 400 pages have been eliminated. After the second answer, 600 pages have been eliminated, and so on, until the 11th question when 799 pages are eliminated and the Red X, page no. 272, found.

This binary search principle, in modified form, is used in Variable Search. The methodology of Variables Search is similar to Components Search, which deals with discrete components, parts, or subassemblies that are good or bad (attributes), while Variables Search deals with process or material parameters that are continuously variable.

Variables Search Methodology

Like Components Search, Variables Search has four stages; these are shown in Table 13-5, each with a title and a stated objective.

Table 13-5. Stages of Variables Search

Stage	Objective
1 Ball Park	To determine if the right variables and right levels for each variable have been selected for the experiment.
2 Separation of important and unimportant factors	> To separate the important variables from the unimportant variables. > To eliminate the unimportant variables and their associated interaction effects.
3 Capping Run (Verification)	To validate that the important variables are confirmed as important and the unimportant ones confirmed as unimportant.
4 Factorial Analysis	To quantify the magnitude and desired levels of the important variables and their associated interaction effects.

Stage 1. Ball Park

1. *Green Y.* In the initial stage (Ball Park), the experimenter must first determine the Green Y (i.e., the problem, output, or response) to be investigated. In some investigations, there may be more than one Green Y. The maximum this author has used in a Variables Search experiment is seven Green Y's. The Green Y must be quantified and measurable, and the accuracy of the measuring instrument must be at least five times the specification tolerance of the Green Y. If the Green Y is an attribute, the experimenter should try to convert it into a variable, using a Likert scale. This conversion reduces the sample size required by expanding a narrow base of defects into an expanded scale of weighted defects. (See Chapter 7.) Every attempt should be made to locate an earlier Green Y in the process that may be easier to measure and that is likely to have a reasonable correlation with the final Green Y.

2. *Selection of the Variables in the Experiment.* This is an important part of Stage 1. Make a list of the most important input variables of factors—A, B, C, D, E, F, G, H, and so on, *in descending order of importance.* (The reason for this order is that, if it is reasonably correct, the experiment is considerably shorter.)

The best time to make the selection is after one or more of the four clue-generation techniques have narrowed the list from a large number of unknown, unmanageable factors to a smaller family of related, manageable factors. For example, the end-counts in a Paired Comparison or Product/Process Search would be a useful way to assign importance—the larger the endcount, the greater the likelihood of importance.

If, however, the product or process is new, at the prototype stage of design, and there are not sufficient quantities to run a Multi-Vari, Components Search, Paired Comparisons, or Product/Process Search, then:

> Use a computer simulation or circuit analysis to select the likely important factors. (Recognize, however, that in many complex products or processes, the formula that governs the relationship between independent and dependent factors is not known, in which case the mighty computer is reduced to guesswork! Even if the formula is known, it is always desirable to confirm the results of a computer simulation with a hardware Variables Search experiment.)

> Conduct a brainstorming session, using engineering, operator, maintenance, and supplier inputs to generate a list of likely factors. This is, however, the least productive method, because it is based on hunches, guesses, opinions, and theories.

3. *Best and Marginal Levels of Each Variable.* After selecting the factors for the experiment, assign two levels to each factor—a best level (B), which is likely to contribute to a best Green Y (hopefully, better than the current Green Y) and a marginal level (M), indicative of a likely deviation from the best level in day-to-day production with normal maintenance. (Sometimes the sign (+) is assigned to each best level and the sign (−) to each marginal level.) If Variables Search is conducted at the prototype design stage, the best level is generally the design center or target value of that factor. The marginal level is an engineering judgment of how far the factor can deviate (on either side) from the best level to register a large, repeatable difference, within practical limits. If the experimenters are not sure about which level, best or marginal, is better, they can assign the best and marginal levels somewhat arbitrarily. The Variables Search experiment will determine, in subsequent stages, which level is better.

Steps 1, 2, and 3 involve designing the Variables Search experiment. Next comes running the experiment.

4. *Sample Sizes.* As in Components Search, where sample sizes are unbelievably small—two to be specific; one "BOB" and one "WOW"— Variables Search sample sizes are also unbelievably small. Table 13-6 gives some guidelines.

5. *Early and Quick Evaluation of Trends.* Run two experiments, the first with all factors at their best levels, the second with all factors at their marginal levels.

(a) If there seems to be a large difference between the Green Y's of the all-best and the all-marginal combinations of factors, it is an early indication that you have captured the right factors in your list of factors. Proceed to the next step, No. 6.

(b) If the all best levels are better than the all marginal levels, but there seems to be only a small difference between them, the chances are that you have not captured (1) the right factors; or (2) the right levels of these factors; or that (3) the Red X is being cancelled by a strong Pink X; or (4) the Red X is an interaction among an even number of factors.

(c) If the all-best levels do show an improvement over the all-marginal levels but the difference is not much greater than the historic levels of the Green Y, the chances are that you have not gone far enough in capturing the right factors or the right levels of the selected factors.

> If the result of Step 5 is (b) or (c), the loss in Variables Search is only two experiments, whereas in a classical or Taguchi experiment, you do not know whether you have succeeded or not till the end of, say, 16 or 32 or 64 experiments!
> If the result of Step 5 is (b) or (c), the list of factors in Step 2 must

Table 13-6. Sample Sizes for Variables Search

Green Y	Factors	Conditions	Sample Size
A Variable	Components or Process Parameters	Components can be inserted and reinserted without disturbing the Green Y.	1
An Attribute Converted to a Variable with a Likert Scale	Components or Process Parameters	Same as above	5 to 10
An Attribute (e.g., no. of defects, % defects, % yields, etc.)	Components or Process Parameters	Same as above	16 to 502

Notes: If the same components cannot be reused in Stage 1 or Stage 2, a fresh set of components of the same value should be chosen.
- If the defect percentage is high, smaller sample sizes can detect difference.
- If the defect percentage is low, larger sample sizes are required.
- If the defects are 100 ppm or lower and cannot be converted to a Likert scale, variables search is not appropriate. Paired Comparisons or Product/Process Search should be used.

be reevaluated; first, to try different levels of some of the factors; or second, to delete some of the factors and insert new ones.

> If the result of Step 5 is (a), continue to Step 6.

6. *Replication.* Repeat Step 5, with two more all-best levels of all the factors and two more all-marginal levels of all the factors. This means that, altogether, there are now three all-best and three all-marginal levels. *Care must be taken, however, that the order (or sequence) of running three best and three marginal levels is randomized. Otherwise, biased readings may be introduced (see Chapter 15).*

7. *Tests of Significance.* To determine if the three all-best Green Y's are truly better than the three all-marginal Green Y's, two tests of significance are required.

(a) All three of the all-best Green Y's should be better than all three of the all-marginal Green Y's, *with no overlap.* (If the three all-marginal Green Y's turn out to be better than the three all-best—as frequently happens (!)—then, just change the headings of the all-best levels to the all-marginal, and vice versa.)

(b) The D:$\overline{\text{d}}$ ratio should be greater than or equal to 1.25:1 (the same rule as in Components Search), where

> D is the difference between the median values of the best and the marginal Green Y's.
> $\bar{d}$ is the average of the two differences (or ranges) within the all-best Green Y's and the all-marginal Green Y's (i.e., the lack of repeatability in each).

8. *Tests of Significance Met. If these tests of significance pass, Stage 1 is over; the right factors have been captured, even though the Red X, Pink X, etc., have not been pinpointed.* (That is determined in Stage 2.)

9. *Tests of Significance Not Met.* If either of the two tests of significance do not pass, switch one pair of the most likely factors from best to marginal and vice versa to see if a cancellation of influence was taking place. If there is still no significant difference, switch a second pair of factors. This step is rarely necessary, unless the engineering judgment of best and marginal levels have been reversed.

If the repeatability, $\bar{d}$, is poor, it is an indication that an important factor—possibly the Red X—has been left off the list in Step 2. Review the clue-generation process. Sloppy clue generation is a common reason for failing Stage 1. Look for a better clue—add one or two more factors to the list, and rerun Stage 1.

Stage 2. Separation of Important and Unimportant Factors

1. Run a pair of tests. (1) with the marginal level of the most important factor, A, i.e., A_M, along with the best levels of all the remaining factors, labeled R_B. (2) Then, a mirror image test with the best level of A, i.e., A_B, along with the marginal levels of all the remaining factors, labeled R_M. Calculate the high-side and low-side decision limits, using the same formula as in Components Search.

The decision limits are: median $\pm\ 2.776(\bar{d}/1.81)$. (These are similar to the decision limits in Components Search.)

2. Possible Results

(a) If both pairs of tests—i.e., $A_M R_B$ and $A_B R_M$—show results *inside* the low-side and high-side decision limits, *factor A, along with all of its associate interaction effects, is unimportant* and can be eliminated from further study.

(b) If there is a complete reversal—i.e., if $A_M R_B$ becomes the original all-best level and $A_B R_M$ becomes the original all-marginal level, *A is the only Red X. The rest of the factors, B, C, D, etc., are all unimportant* and can be eliminated. Variables Search has ended.

(c) If either or both pairs of tests—$A_M R_B$ and $A_B R_M$—show results *outside* the low-side and high-side decision limits, respectively, but not a complete reversal, factor A, along with its associated interaction effects, cannot be eliminated. A plus some other factor or factors must be considered, along with their interactions.

3. If the test results in Step 2 are (a) or (c), repeat Step 1 with factor B. If (a) results, B is unimportant and can be eliminated. If (b) results, B is the Red X; end of Variables Search. If (c) results, B cannot be eliminated. B plus some other factor or factors must be considered, along with their interactions.

4. If the result in Step 3 is (a), repeat Step 1 with Factor C. If (a) results, C is unimportant and can be eliminated. If (b) results, C is the Red X; end of Variables Search. If (c) results, C cannot be eliminated. C plus some other factor or factors must be considered along with their interactions.

Stage 3. Capping Run

1. If factors A and B display a partial reversal (results c), with readings outside the decision limits, run a capping run (i.e., a confirmation or verification test) with these factors—$A_BB_BR_M$ and $A_MB_MR_B$—to see if R, the rest of the factors, can be eliminated. One or more results outside of decision limits would indicate that the search is not yet complete. In that case, continue Stage 2 with the next single factor—C, then D, then E, etc.—in alphabetical order until another factor shows out-of-control results.

2. Now run a three-factor capping run. (Generally, a four-factor capping run is rare.)

Stage 4. Factorial Analysis

This is not a physical experiment, but only number-crunching to draw up a factorial analysis, using the data generated in Stages 1, 2, and 3, of the important factors that cannot be eliminated in Stage 2. It is similar to the factorial analysis technique explained in the case study on Components Search, to quantify the main effects and interaction effects of the important factors.

An Alternate "Rule of Thumb" to Assess the Importance of a Factor in Stage 2

This rule of thumb is similar to the one described in Components Search. Many practitioners find the statistical calculations associated with determine the decision limits tedious and confusing. The authors have developed the same empirical approach to assess whether a factor in

Stage 2 is important or not. It is not as statistically pure as decision limits, but can be used as an approximate guide.

1. First, take the best median and the marginal median in Stage 1.
2. Calculate the average value between these two medians as the center line.
3. In Stage 2, if a factor crosses this center line or comes very close to crossing it (within 10 percent), that factor is important. If not, it is not important. This alternate method will be shown in the case studies on Variables Search.

Interaction Effects in Variables Search

Skeptics of the Variables Search methodology claim that it is only a warmed-over version of the old method of varying one variable at a time while keeping everything else constant. Nothing can be further from the truth. Variables Search is an elegant method, in which:

1. All unimportant main factors and their associated interaction effects can be proven to be unimportant (see the first cast study).
2. All important main factors and their
   (a) second-order interaction effects are neatly compartmentalized,
   (b) third-order interaction effects are neatly compartmentalized,
   (c) 62.5 percent of all fourth-order interaction effects are neatly compartmentalized. If a full factorial can follow, the remaining 37.5 percent of fourth-order interaction effects can also be compartmentalized.
3. Fifth-order and higher order interaction effects can be confounded, but the presence of fifth order and higher interaction effects are present in only one out of 10,000 real-life experiments.

The proof of the above statements are as follows:

(a)   Two factors, A and B, with two levels each, can produce four combinations, as shown in the four corners of Figure 13-1. Does Variables Search cover all four corners (interactions)? The answer is yes:

> $A_M B_M$ and $A_B B_B$ are measured in the first two experiments of Stage 2.

Figure 13-1. Two-Factor Interaction Effects: A Schematic Diagram

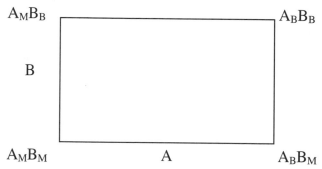

> If A and B are unimportant, the graphical response of Figure 13-1 will be two parallel lines, indicating zero (or near zero) interaction effects.
> If A and B are important, the graphical response of Figure 13-1 will be two nonparallel lines, indicating the presence of interaction.
> Similar conclusions can be reached on other factors, two at a time.

(b)   Three factors, A, B, and C, with two levels each, can produce eight combinations, as shown in the eight corners of Figure 13-2. Does Variables Search cover all eight corners (interactions)? The answer is yes.

> $A_BB_BC_B$ and $A_MB_MC_M$ are measured in Stage 1.
> $A_MB_BC_B$, $A_MB_MC_M$, $A_MB_BC_M$, $A_BB_MC_B$, $A_BB_MC_M$, and $A_BB_BC_M$ are all measured in the first six experiments of Stage 2.
> If A and B are unimportant, the graphical three-dimensional response surface (difficult to portray) will be parallel planes, indicating zero or near zero interactions.
> If A, B, and C are important, the graphical three-dimensional response surface will be nonparallel (twisted) planes, indicating the presence of interactions.
> Similar conclusions can be reached on the other factors, three at a time.

(c)   Four factors, A, B, C, and D, with two levels each, can produce 16 combinations as shown in Table 13-7.

Product/Process Characterization

As stated earlier in this chapter, even though Variables Search is a powerful DOE technique to follow one or more of the four clue-generation tools,

Figure 13-2. Three-Factor Interaction Effects: A Schematic Diagram

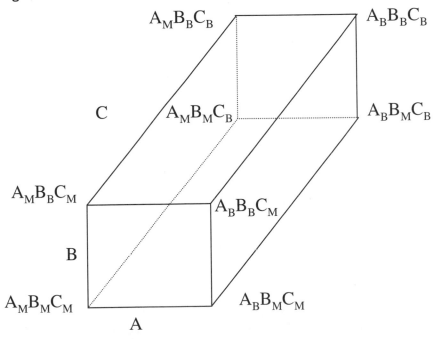

Table 13-7. Four-Factor Interaction Effects

Cell	Combination	
(1)	$A_M B_M C_M D_M$	> Variables Search measures cells (1) and abcd in Stage 1.
a	$A_M B_B C_B D_B$	
b	$A_B B_M C_B D_B$	> It measures cells a, b, c, abc, d, abd, acd and bcd in Stage 2.
ab	$A_M B_M C_B D_B$	
c	$A_B B_B C_M D_B$	> It does not measure cells ab, ac, bc, ad, bd and cd in Stage 1 or 2.
ac	$A_M B_B C_M D_B$	
bc	$A_B B_M C_M D_B$	> Therefore, if interaction effects are suspected among these six cells or combinations that have not been measured, Stage 3—the capping run—is not likely to succeed.
abc	$A_M B_M C_M D_B$	
d	$A_B B_B C_B D_M$	
ad	$A_M B_B C_B D_M$	
bd	$A_B B_M C_B D_M$	
abd	$A_M B_M C_M D_M$	> In that case, a full factorial experiment is in order among the four factors.
cd	$A_B B_B C_M D_M$	
acd	$A_M B_B C_M D_M$	> However, if Stage 3 is successful and the results of Stage 1 are closely repeated in Stage 3, the interaction effects among the six nonmeasured cells can be considered to be unimportant.
bcd	$A_B B_M C_M D_M$	
abcd	$A_M B_M C_M D_M$	

Note: Subscript B denotes best; subscript M denotes marginal.

its greatest use is as a design technique for a product or process, at the prototype stage of development.

In recent years, the term Product/Process Characterization has been used to describe design intent. This means

(a)   separating the important variables (or factors) from the unimportant ones;

(b)   tightening the tolerances of the important variables to C_{pk}'s of 2 and more; and

(c)   expanding the tolerances of the unimportant variables (a few more experiments may be required to see how far the tolerances can be expanded) in order to substantially reduce costs.

The best way to achieve these objectives is through Variables Search.

Case Studies and Workshop Exercises

Case Study 1: The Press Brake

In a metal stamping/forming operation, parts produced on the press brakes could not be held within a tolerance of 0.005" or a process width of 0.010". Variations were running as high as 0.010" (or C_{pk}'s of only 0.5). The foreman was adamant that the press brake was a "black magic" process. He railed against suppliers, with excessive variations in metal thickness and hardness. He railed against inconsistent and careless operators, and he had tried newer press brakes with little success.

A Variables Search was recommended to the company's management (much to the foreman's annoyance as a waste of time). The objective was to bring the process under control to a tolerance of 0.005" or less. Six factors were selected in descending order of perceived importance. The best and marginal levels for each factor were determined. (In the interest of company confidentiality, the precise levels are not shown.) Table 13-8 shows the results of Stages 1 and 2. The numbers are expressed in deviation from nominal in multiples of 0.001", with the lower numbers better and the higher worse.

Stage 1. Ball Park

The three all-best levels and the three all-marginal levels (run in random order sequence) indicate that (a) the three all-best are definitely better (lower deviations) than the three all-marginal. And, (b) the medians best and marginal are 4 and 61, respectively, and that the $D/\bar{d}$ ratio is

Table 13-8. Variables Search: The Press Brake Case Study

Factors	Best	Marginal
A. Punch and die alignment	Aligned	Not aligned
B. Metal thickness	Thick	Thin
C. Metal hardness	Hard	Soft
D. Metal bow	Flat	Bowed
E. Ram stroke	Coin form	Air form
F. Holding material	Level	At angle

Note: Results below are expressed in deviation from nominal in multiples of 0.001″.

STAGE 1	ALL-BEST LEVELS	ALL-MARGINAL LEVELS
Initial	4	47
First Replication	4	61
Second Replication	3	68

STAGE 2

Test	Combination	Results	Median	Decision Limits	Conclusion
1	A_M R_B	3	4	−12.87 to 20.87	A not important
2	A_B R_M	72	61	44.13 to 77.87	
3	B_M R_B	5	4	−12.87 to 20.87	B not important
4	B_B R_M	47	61	44.13 to 77.87	
5	C_M R_B	7	4	−12.87 to 20.87	C not important
6	C_B R_M	72	61	44.13 to 77.87	
7	D_M R_B	23	4	−12.87 to 20.87	D important with
8	D_B R_M	30	61	44.13 to 77.87	another factor
9	E_M R_B	7	4	−12.87 to 20.87	E not important
10	E_B R_M	50	61	44.13 to 77.87	
11	F_M R_B	73	4	−12.87 to 20.87	F important with
12	F_B R_M	18	61	44.13 to 77.87	another factor
Capping run	F_M F_M R_B	4	4	−12.87 to 20.87	➣ DR interaction important
Capping run	F_M F_M R_B	70	61	44.13 to 77.87	➣ Complete reversal ➣ End of test

Note: Medians for best and marginal assemblies are 4 and 61, respectively, so D = 61 − 4 = 57.
d = Average lack of repeatability in each assembly = (1 + 21)/2 = 11.
So D/d = 57:11 = 5.21, which is greater than 1.25:1. So Stage 1 is successful.
Control Limits = Median ±2.776 d/1.81 = Median ± 16.87.
So lower control limits = 44.13 to 77.87 and
    upper control limits = −12.87 to 20.87
Source: Qualitron Corp., Chicago, Ill.

57:11, or 5.21, which is greater than the minimum requirement of 1.25. So Stage 1 results indicate that the right factors, A through F, were chosen.

Stage 2. Elimination

The decision limits are:

1. median marginal—2.776 d/1.81 $=$ -12.87 to 20.87;
2. median best—2.776 d/1.81 $=$ 44.13 to 77.87.

> Factor A_M at 3 does not fall outside its marginal control limits, and A_B at 72 does not fall outside its best decision limits. Therefore, A is not important.
> Similarly, B, C, and E are not important.
> D_M at 23 falls outside its marginal decision limits of -12.87 to 20.87, and
> D_B at 30 also falls outside its best decision limits of 44.13 to 77.87.
> Therefore, D is important, but at 23 and 30, it shows partial but not complete reversal, so another factor must be involved and investigated.
> Similarly, F is important, but at 73 and 18, it does show even greater partial but not complete reversal. Therefore, D and F are important, with an interaction between them.

Alternative to Decision Limits

> The center line between the all-best and all-marginal levels of Stage 1 is $(4+61)/2 = 32.5$. The empirical rule says that if a factor crosses this center line in Stage 2, it is important; if not, it is not. Factors A, B, C, and E do not cross the center line for both their marginal and their best levels, so they are not important.
> Factor D does not cross the center line of 32.5 for D_M (23) but does cross the center line the other way for D_B (30). So D is somewhat important (indicative of a one-way interaction).
> Factor F crosses the center line of 32.5 for F_M (73) as well as for F_B (18), so F is quite important.
> Therefore, F and D should be considered for a Stage 3 capping run.

Stage 3. Capping Run

The capping run in Figure 13-3 shows that, with factors D and F at their best level and marginal level, respectively (while the other four fac-

Figure 13-3. A Factorial Analysis of the Press Brake

	D Best	D Marginal	
F **Best**	4 3 4 5 3 7 4 7 Median = 4	23 18 Median = 20.5	➤ 24.5
F **Marginal**	73 30 Median = 51.5	47 72 61 47 68 72 70 50 Median = 64.5	➤ 116.0

72.0   55.5   85.0   68.5

$$\text{Main Effect D} = \frac{(20.5 + 64.5) - (4.0 + 51.5)}{2} = \frac{(85 - 55.5)}{2} = 14.75$$

$$\text{Main Effect F} = \frac{(51.5 + 64.5) - (4.0 + 20.5)}{2} = \frac{(116 - 24.5)}{2} = 45.75$$

$$\text{DF Interaction} = \frac{(20.5 + 51.5) - (4.0 + 64.5)}{2} = \frac{(72 - 68.5)}{2} = 1.75$$

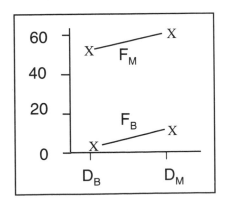

Note: The above results clearly show that the Red X is factor F, with a 45.75 main-effect contribution to process spread. Factor D is a Pink X, with a 14.75 main-effect contribution to process spread. And the DF interaction contributes 1.75 to the process spread. The graph shows the presence of a relatively weak interaction.

tors are marginal and best, respectively), the results of Stage 1 are closely approximated. Therefore, D and F are now confirmed as important.

Stage 4. Factorial Analysis

(Refer to the case study on Components Search in Chapter 10 for a refresher on constructing a Factorial Analysis.)
The Variable Search DOE experiment produced several results.

1. The metal bow had to be controlled flat (Pink X).
2. The metal thickness and hardness were not important, and their tolerances could be widened, and the punch and die alignment and the ram stroke, were unimportant.
3. The holding material (Red X) was so important that a fixture was devised to keep it level and to eliminate operator-related variation.
4. The press brake was now capable of meeting a tolerance of $+0.002$ instead of the original $+0.005$ to $+0.010$, with a respectable C_{Pk} of 2.5.

A Graphical Plot of Case Study 1, The Press Brake

As in Components Search, a graphical plot in Variables Search explains a thousand words in a single, simple picture. Figure 13-4 is a pictorial representation of the Stage 1, 2, and 3 results of the press brake case study depicted in Table 13-8. It clearly shows that:

> Factors A, B, C, and E have no influence in reversing the Green Y's of the best and marginal levels. This is further verified by these factors not falling outside either band of the best decision limits or the marginal decision limits.
> Factors D and F both show a partial reversal (F far more than D). They both fall outside the bands of the best and marginal decision limits.
> The alternative to decision limits shows that the center line is not crossed on factors A, B, C, or E, indicating that they are not important. But factor F does cross the center line, and factor D crosses it at its best level.
> All of this is so clear pictorially that the graphical approach adds greatly to an understanding of what goes on.

Common Mistakes Made by Variables Search Experimenters

Variables Search is a powerful DOE tool when performed correctly. Yet, the authors have found more mistakes made in Variables Search than in

Figure 13-4. Variables Search: Press Brake—A Graphical Plot

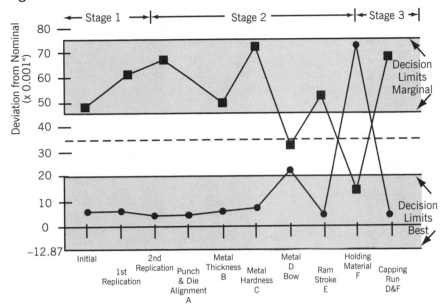

● All factors best, except A, B, etc., at their marginal levels in Stages 2 and 3.
■ All factors marginal, except A, B, etc., at their best levels in Stages 2 and 3.

any of the other DOE tools. The following list highlights common pitfalls to avoid.

Stage 1

1. Stage 1 is totally skipped and Stage 2 is used as a starting point.
2. Only one all-best and one all-marginal experiment is run instead of three each.
3. If the all-best Green Y is not as good as historic levels, no attempt is made to start all over, either with different levels of the same factor or with different factors.
4. If there is more than one Green Y, no attempt is made to resolve a situation in which one Green Y is optimized but the other is not.
5. The sequence of running three all-best and three all-marginal experiments are not randomized.
6. There is uncertainty in determining the marginal levels of a factor.
7. Stage 2 is performed even if the D:d ratio is less than 1.25.

Stage 2

8. There is confusion in determining the important and unimportant factors.
9. Decision limits are skipped as too tedious. (Here, the alternative approach of factors crossing a center line can be used as a rule of thumb.)

Stage 3

10. A capping run is not performed to verify and separate the important factors from the unimportant ones.

Stage 4

11. A factorial analysis is not computed to quantify the main and interaction effects of important factors.

Post Variables Search

12. Optimization, Positrol, and Process Certification disciplines are not practiced as a follow-up to Variables Search. (See Chapters 16 through 19.)

Workshop Exercise 1: Engine Control Module

A microprocessor-based engine control module (with 600 electronic components in its circuitry), was being developed by the engineering department of a large company for an important automotive customer. It was a sophisticated development, where the module monitored 20 to 25 engine parameters in a passenger car and optimized the engine for maximum gas mileage and minimum pollution.

One of the important specifications of the customer was idle speed current, which had to be between 650 milliamperes (ma) and 800 ma. The car company claimed that if the idle speed current dropped below 650 ma, the car would stall or stop. If it went above 800 ma, some of the components could burn up.

Since the module was only in the prototype stage, very few models had been built and these had variations in idle speed current that were unacceptable. So, clue-generation techniques could not be used. Variables Search was selected by the engineering team, which listed seven factors in descending order of importance—based on a circuit analysis—that could affect the Green Y, namely idle speed current. The best levels for each factor were deemed to be at the design center of each component or factor. The marginal levels were judged to be at one end or the other of the tolerances (whichever was thought to be the worse) for each component. The results are shown in Table 13-9.

Questions

1. Is Stage 1 successful? Have the right factors been selected? What is the D:$\overline{\text{d}}$ ratio? Can the experiment proceed to Stage 2?

2. In Stage 2, identify the important and unimportant factors. What are the decision limits of the best and marginal levels? Are there any significant interaction effects?

3. Draw a graphical plot of the Stage 1 and 2 results.

4. Are a capping run and a factorial analysis needed?

5. To what extend should the tolerances of the unimportant factors be opened up?

6. What would have happened if the descending order of importance in selecting the factors had been reversed?

Answers

1. Stage 1 is successful because the two tests of significance have been passed.

> The three best levels are all better (in specifications) than the three marginal levels (out of specifications).
> D is 1050 − 738 = 312 ma; $\overline{\text{d}}$ is $\dfrac{17 + 29}{2}$ = 23; so the D:$\overline{\text{d}}$ ratio of 312:23 is much greater than the minimum 1.25. Stage 1 is successful; the only conclusion that can be drawn is that engineering chose the right factors. (But Stage 1 cannot determine which is the Red X, which is the Pink X, etc.)

2.

> The decision limits (best) are: 6 median best ± 2.776 (d/1.81) = 738 + 2.776 × 7.5/1.81 = 773 to 703.
> The decision limits (marginal) are: median marginal ± 2.776 (d/1.81) = 1085 to 101.
> An alternate method, the center line between the median of the best and marginal levels is $\dfrac{1050 + 738}{2}$ = 894.

Table 13-9. Variables Search: Engine Control Module

Factor description	Factor nominal value	Factor tolerance	Factor levels	
			Best (B)	Marginal (M)
A. Resistor: R85	0.68 Ohms	±5%	0.68 Ohms	0.65 Ohms
B. Power supply voltage: V_{cc}	5.0 Volts	±5%	5.0 Volts	4.75 Volts
C. Resistor: R77	100 Ohms	±1%	100 Ohms	99 Ohms
D. Resistor: R75	787 Ohms	±1%	787 Ohms	729 Ohms
E. Xsister: Q8 Saturation voltage	75 M.V.	150 M.V. Max	75 M.V.	150 M.V.
F. Resistor: R79	43 Ohms	±5%	43 Ohms	40.185 Ohms
G. Integrated circuit: 1C4	0 M.V.	±8 M.V.	0 M.V.	−8 M.V.

Offset voltage

Stage 1	All Factors at Best Levels	All Factors at Marginal Levels
	742 ma	1053 ma
	738 ma	1050 ma
	725 ma	1024 ma

Stage 2	Test No.	Combination	Results (ma)	Control limits	Conclusion
	1	$A_M R_B$	768		
	2	$A_B R_M$	1020		
	3	$B_M R_B$	704		
	4	$B_B R_M$	1051		
	5	$C_M R_B$	733		
	6	$C_B R_M$	1028		
	7	$D_M R_B$	745		
	8	$D_B R_M$	1018		
	9	$E_M R_B$	726		
	10	$E_B R_M$	1022		
	11	$F_M R_B$	733		
	12	$F_B R_M$	1020		
	13	$G_M R_B$	1031		
	14	$G_B R_M$	718		

Source: Motorola Inc., Schaumburg, Ill.

> On the basis of the decision limits method, factors A through F stay within their respective decision limits and are, therefore, not important. Also according to the alternate method, factors A through F do not cross the center line of 894 and are, therefore, not important.
> Factor G is the only one that goes outside both decision limits. It also crosses the center line, so it is a lone, solid Red X.
> There are no significant interaction effects, based on the rule that if a main factor is unimportant, its associated interaction on effects can also be proven to be unimportant. (See Figure 13-5, which shows two factors in this case study, A, and B, with four possible combinations—$A_M B_M$, $A_M B_B$, $A_B B_M$, and $A_B B_B$. The numbers are derived from Table 13-9. The existence of two parallel lines means the A_B interaction is virtually zero.)

3. See graphical plot (Figure 13-6).

4. A capping run is not necessary, because complete reversal was achieved with just one factor (G), nor is a factorial analysis needed, with only one factor that had with no interaction effects.

5. Since factor G is the only Red X, the tolerances of the remaining 6 factors can be opened up to reduce costs. (This required further experimentation. The original Stage 1 and 2 experiments were performed by a technician in two days.) The IC offset voltage tolerance was cut in half, to ± 4 mv., with the supplier being shown how to reduce his process variability with DOE at lower costs. The tolerances for the ± 1 percent components are opened up to ± 5 percent. The tolerances for the four remaining components are not changed, mainly because there were no price advantages for the larger tolerances. *The total savings (preventive for quality im-*

Figure 13-5. Testing for a Two-Factor Interaction Effect

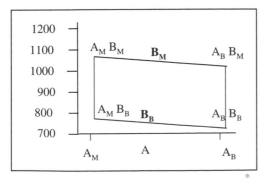

From Stage 1: $A_B B_B = 738$
$A_M B_M = 1050$

From Stage 2: $A_M B_B = 768$
$A_B B_M = 1020$

AB Interaction $= 0$

Figure 13-6. Variables Search: Engine Control Module— A Graphical Plot

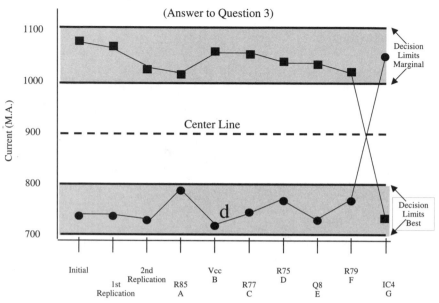

● All factors best, except A, B, etc., at their marginal levels in Stage 2.
■ All factors marginal, except A, B, etc., at their best levels in Stage 2.

provement) and actual for procurement cost reduction amount to $450,000 in the first year alone.

6. If the order of selecting components (factors) had been reversed, with the IC offset voltage (factor G) becoming the first, Stage 2 would have been reduced from 14 to just two experiments, because a complete reversal would have resulted by swapping G alone.

Since Variables Search is so important and so practical a technique, a few more case studies and workshop exercises are included in this chapter. These will illustrate Variables Search's versatility as well as some typical pitfalls that practitioners are liable to fall into while conducting Variables Search studies.

Case Study 2: Cracked Epoxy

This case study involves one of our clients in the Far East, who has been experiencing a problem in which the epoxy bonding a substrate and header was cracking during curing. The reject rate was around 10 percent and the problem had existed for three years. A DOE team elected to use a Variables Search experiment to solve the problem. (See Table 13-10.)

Green Y

A Likert scale of 0 to 10 was used to determine the degree of the epoxy crack—with 0 as no crack and 10 as a 100 percent crack.

Conclusions

1. The Red X was curing temperature, which had to be kept at 150°C.
2. The other factors were unimportant, but the clipping had to continue for other reasons.
3. The volume of epoxy and its viscosity could be reduced to reduce costs.
4. The reject rate went from 10 percent to zero.
5. The savings was: $40,296 (U.S.) per year.

Workshop Exercise 2: Screen Printing (Unsuccessful)

In a screen printing process, the weight of the paste had to meet a specification of 1.0 ± 0.1 gm. To reduce variability in production, a DOE team established a Variables Search experiment with six factors; 50 screen dots were measured in each experiment and the mean weight and standard deviation(s) calculated. The Stage 1 and Stage 2 results are shown in Table 13-11.

Questions

1. Was Variables Search the right starting point?
2. Were the right levels selected for the best and marginal levels?
3. Should there have been only one Green Y—namely, paste weight?
4. Was the sample size of 50 units appropriate?
5. Was the use of mean and standard deviation(s) values the right approach?
6. Was Stage 1 performed correctly?
7. Was Stage 2 performed correctly?
8. Should Stage 3 and 4 be performed?
9. Are the team's conclusions about the Red X and Pink X correct?
10. How would you conduct a proper DOE experiment?

Table 13-10. Case Study 2: Cracked Epoxy

Stage 1

| | | Factor level | |
| | | Best (B) | Marginal (M) |
Factor code	*Factor description*		
A	Curing temperature (°C)	150	120
B	Curing time (minutes)	30	45
C	Perpendicularity	0°	1.5°
D	Volume of epoxy (lead coverage)	100%	75%
E	Alignment of tuning hole	No clipping	Clipping
F	Epoxy viscosity (CPS)	199000	180000

Sample Size: 20 units: Weighted Defects = (No. of defective units × Likert Scale)

	Best (B)	Marginal (M)
Run 1	0	41
Run 2	0	29
Run 3	0	33

$D = 33; \bar{d} = 12/2 = 6; D/\bar{d} = 33{:}6.$ (So, greater than 1.25)

Stage 2

Experiment number	*Combination*	*Results*	*Importance*
1	$A_M R_B$	37	A: Red X
2	$A_B R_M$	0	
3	$B_M R_B$	0	B̸
4	$B_B R_M$	25	
5	$C_M R_B$	0	C̸
6	$C_B R_M$	19	
7	$D_M R_B$	0	D̸
8	$D_B R_M$	22	
9	$E_M R_B$	12	E: Pink X
10	$E_B R_M$	0	
11	$F_M R_B$	0	F̸
12	$F_B R_M$	27	

Note: / = not important.

Table 13-10. (Continued)

Stage 3: Capping Run 1

Combination	Result
$A_M E_M R_B$	30
$A_B E_B R_M$	0

However, factor E had to be kept to the marginal level to avoid misalignment between housing hole and warp coil turning hole. So, a second capping run was performed.

Capping Run 2

Combination	Result
$A_M E_M R_B$	24
$A_B E_M R_M$	0

Source: Motorola, Penang, Malaysia.

Answers

1. Since there are many paste dots to investigate per unit, Variables Search should have been postponed until a Multi-Vari could pinpoint the family.
2. Assuming that the best levels were reasonable, the marginal levels were way out, by factors of 2.5:1 in some factors. That is too much of a spread. In addition, one factor—screen lifting speed—was not quantified. "Slow" and "fast" should be objective measurements, not subjective descriptions.
3. It is conceivable that the size and shape of the paste dots could be as important as paste weight.
4. The sample size is much too large. If a Multi-Vari had been performed first, a sample of five locations in each unit (North, South, East, West, and middle) might have sufficed.
5. Mean values are not suitable. They dilute variations. Also, the use of standard deviations, yield percentages, and defect percentages involve large quantities of attribute-type data. They lack the sensitivity of variables data.
6. Stage 1 was not performed correctly. The original all-best and all-marginal levels were not replicated at all. They should have

Table 13-11. Workshop Exercise 2: Screen Printing

		Factor level	
Factor code	Factor description	Best (B)	Marginal (M)
A	Past viscosity (Mcps)	1.32	0.95
B	Squeegee speed (in/sec.)	1.6	3.8
C	Squeegee pressure (lbs.)	8	20
D	Screen overtravel (mils)	0	0.5
E	Screen wiping	Yes	No
F	Screen lifting speed	Slow	Fast

Stage	Test No.	Combination	Mean weight (gm)	Standard deviation(s)
1	1	All best	1.071	0.0123
	2	All marginal	0.965	0.0612
2	1	$A_M R_B$	0.9369	0.0180
	2	$A_B R_M$	1.1623	0.0177
	3	$B_M R_B$	1.1312	0.0359
	4	$B_B R_M$	0.9804	0.0237
	5	$C_M R_B$	0.9366	0.0241
	6	$C_B R_M$	1.2088	0.0387
	7	$D_M R_B$	1.0464	0.0326
	8	$D_B R_M$	0.9843	0.0368
	9	$E_M R_B$	1.0310	0.0157
	10	$E_B R_M$	1.0875	0.0197
	11	$F_M R_B$	0.9591	0.0261
	12	$F_B R_M$	1.1237	0.1059

been replicated twice. With the large standard deviations, the all-best levels do not outrank the all-marginal levels. That should have terminated the experiment and other factors should have been tried.

7. Disregarding standard deviation for the time being and concentrating only on the mean values, Stage 2 appears to indicate that factors B, (squeegee speed) and D (screen overtravel) have some importance. On the other hand, using standard deviation as the

Green Y, factors A (paste viscosity) and E (screen wiping) have
some importance. But there is too much "noise" in all of Stage 2
and not enough "signal" to draw any firm conclusions.
8. With Stage 1 a failure, Stages 2, 3, and 4 should not be performed.
9. The team's conclusion that B is the Red X and A is the Pink X are
only partially and speculatively correct for the mean and standard deviation Green Y's, respectively, as seen in Answer 7.
10. A proper DOE would start with a Multi-Vari, followed by a Prod-
uct/Process Search. Only after clues are generated from these
two DOE disciplines would a Variables Search be in order.

Case Study 3: Tombstone Defects (A Wrong Technique)

Tombstoning is a phenomenon that occurs on printed circuit boards when
one lead of a chip component is reflow soldered, but the other lifts up
and causes the horizontal component to stand vertically on the board, like
a tombstone. A company had improved its process so that the defect level
was down to 10 to 20 ppm (counting all components on the board). Its
goal, however, was 1 ppm or less! A Variables Search was tried with the
factors shown in Table 13-12. The DOE team recognized, belatedly, that
the sample size of 75 boards was much too small to capture a defect level
of 10 to 20 ppm. Even a sample size of 10,000 would not have captured
that low a defect level. Variables Search, therefore, was the wrong technique to use.

The team fell back on Paired Comparisons, accumulating eight good
boards and eight tombstoning boards (which occurred only once per day,

Table 13-12. Case Study 3: Tombstone Defects

Factor code	Factor description	Factor level	
		Best	*Marginal*
A	Paste weight gm	0.312	0.334
B	Placement accuracy	Centered	0.25 mm off set
C	Reflow profile:		
	(1) ramp rate	1.2°C/sec.	3.5°C/sec.
	(2) number of soaks	2	1
	(3) soak temperature	100°C & 175°C	100°C only
D	Paste type	Alpha	SCM
		1005205 A15	1005205 A20
	Results	0 ppm	0 ppm

Source: Motorola, Penang, Malaysia.
Note: Sample size = 75 boards.

on average, despite high production volume). They examined several characteristics of the chip components and the pads. The only repetitive difference was in paste-to-pad accuracy, with the good units having the paste for the chip components centered over the pad, whereas the bad units displayed a 0.3 mm offset (noncentering of the paste for the chip relative to the pad). The final solution was switching from a Sanyo in-time printer to an MPM printer with a greater paste-to-pad accuracy. The result? Zero tombstone defects sustained over several months of production.

Case Study 4: Contact Lens Cylinder Not Meeting Specifications

This case study is a good example of persisting with a combination of factors that produced only partial reversals in Stage 2, with complete reversal established in a final capping run.

In Chapter 11 on Paired Comparisons, Workshop Exercise 1 dealt with a contact lens that failed to meet optical specifications. The Red X in that exercise was identified as the cylinder dimension, which exceeded a maximum specification of 0.025 mm. A further Variables Search study was conducted to determine the important contributing factors. The results of Stage 1, 2, and 3 are shown in Table 13-13. (The actual best and marginal levels are not shown to protect company confidentiality.) Figure 13-7 is a more dramatic and graphic display of the results, using the decision limits for best and marginal levels, and the center line method to distinguish between important and unimportant factors.

Conclusions and Comments

1. Stage 1 was successful, with a D:$\overline{\text{d}}$ ratio of 11:1, which is greater than 1.25.
2. As Table 13-13 and Figure 13-7 show, factors B (back pressure) and D (mold temperature) are unimportant (although, technically, both fall just outside the upper decision limit of the marginal level).
3. The first capping run with factor A (melt temperature) and C (screw speed) produced a partial reversal, requiring another factor, E (hold pressure), to be swapped. Factor E went outside one decision limit (best), but not the other (marginal).
4. Therefore, a second capping run was performed with factors A, C, and E. This again resulted in a partial reversal, requiring another factor, F (hydraulic pressure), to be swapped. Factor F went outside one decision limit (marginal), but not the other (best).
5. Finally, a four-factor capping run of factors A, C, E, and F pro-

Table 13-13. Variables Search: Lens Molding

Purpose of test: Identify the Red X variable(s) that causes cylinder in the female mold to exceed .025 mm.

STAGE ONE

TEST *	TEST RESULTS		COMMENTS
	ALL-BEST	ALL-MARGINAL	
1-B and 1-M	.018 mm	.032 mm	
2-B and 2-M	.016 mm	.033 mm	
3-B and 3-M	.016 mm	.032 mm	

* The three all-best and three all-marginal run in random order.

$$D:d \qquad D=(B-M)/2 \qquad \bar{d}=0.002 + 0.001=0.0015 \text{ so } D/d \text{ is} > 1.25:1$$

$$D=0.032-0.016=0.016$$

STAGES TWO AND THREE

IDENTIFICATION OF VARIABLES BEING TESTED	VARIABLE SETTINGS		TEST RESULTS			
	BEST VALUE	MARGINAL VALUE	TEST #	ALL-BEST EXCEPT	TEST #	ALL-MARGINAL EXCEPT
Melt Temp.			A-1	.026 mm	A-2	.016 mm
Back Pressure (P17-21)			B-1	.015 mm	B-2	.035 mm
Screw Speed (D2)			C-1	.007 mm	C-2	.026 mm
Mold Temp.			D-1	.015 mm	D-2	.035 mm
Hold Pressure (P7-16)			E-1	.024 mm	E-2	.031 mm
Hyd. Pressure (P4)			F-1	.014 mm	F-2	.020 mm
Capping - Melt T & Screw S			G-1	.030 mm	G-2	.012 mm
Capping - MT & SS Hold P			H-1	.020 mm	H-2	.013 mm
Capping - MT & SS Hold P & Hyd P			I-1	.038 mm	I-2	.011 mm
Capping - Hold P & Screw S			J-1	.039 mm	J-2	.015 mm
Capping - Hold P & Hyd P			K-1	.022 mm	K-2	.012 mm

Source: Ciba Corp., Atlanta, Ga.

Figure 13-7. Variables Search: Lens Molding—A Graphical Plot

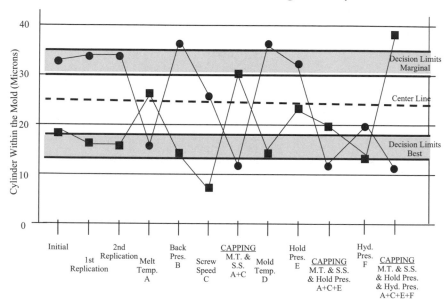

■ All factors best, except A, B, etc., at their marginal levels in Stage 2 and 3.
● All factors marginal, except A, B, etc., at their best levels in Stage 2 and 3.

Source: Ciba Corp., Atlanta, Ga.

duced a great reversal, indicating interaction effects among them that needed to be quantified with a factorial analysis.

6. *Actually, when there are more than three factors, it is better to conduct a 2^4 full factorial experiment as a follow-on to Variables Search rather than just number-crunching with a factorial analysis.*

Workshop Exercise 3: Spot Welding—Two Parameters (i.e., Two Green Y's), Mechanical and Visual

This workshop exercise demonstrates the use of Variables Search to optimize two or more outputs or responses or Green Y's. *It also illustrates actions that can be taken if the input factors that are optimum to produce one Green Y are not the best factors to use for another Green Y.*

A Variables Search experiment was used to improve a spot welding process that had an unacceptable defect rate. Two Green Y's were considered important. The first was mechanical: A good spot weld is defined as one that leaves a plug at least 1/4" in diameter when the spot weld is broken apart after welding. The second was visual—minimum weld distortion. For the latter Green Y, a Likert scale was established, with 1 being the best and 10 the worst. Scores of 5 or less were considered acceptable, those with 6 or more were rejectable. Five weld parameters were listed, as shown in Table 13-14.

Questions

1. Were the two Green Y's quantified and measured?
2. Were the six experiments in Stage 1 conducted in a random sequence?

Table 13-14. Workshop Exercise 3: Spot Welding

Factor Code	Factor Description	Factor level	
		Best	Marginal
A	Weld count	15	22
B	Hold time (sec.)	25	37
C	Squeeze time (sec.)	25	37
D	Weld pressure (PSI)	25	35
E	Weld % of current	80	90

Stage	Test	Combination	Mechanical	Visual
1	All-best		Pass	1
	All-marginal		Fail	9
	All-best		Pass	1
	All-marginal		Fail	10
	All-best		Pass	2
	All-marginal		Fail	8
2	$A_M R_B$		Pass	4
	$A_B R_M$		Fail	6
	$B_M R_B$		Pass	3
	$B_B R_M$		Fail	10
	$C_M R_B$		Pass	2
	$C_B R_M$		Fail	9
	$D_M R_B$		Fail	1
	$D_B R_M$		Pass	8
	$E_M R_B$		Pass	7
	$E_B R_M$		Fail	5

Source: Craftsman Co., Melrose Park, Ill.

3. Which were the unimportant factors? Why?
4. Which were the important factors? Why?
5. Are the important factors for one Green Y the wrong factors for the other Green Y?
6. Should the capping run have been conducted?
7. If the answer to question 5 is "yes," what further steps should be taken?

Answers

1. Both Green Y's were quantified—the mechanical with a variable (minimum 1/4" diameter plug), and the visual with a Likert scale. However, it would have been better if the actual mechanical values had been shown, rather than "pass" or "fail."
2. Stage 1 should always be conducted in random sequence (see Chapter 15). Otherwise, uncontrollable or "noise" factors, which could vary in a cyclical manner, or have shifts or trends in themselves, can bias the results. In this example, the sequence was randomized, but not shown.
3. Stage 2 shows that factors A, B, and C are unimportant—no reversal from the readings of Stage 1—for both the Green Y's.
4. and 5.

> Factor D is important, with D_B giving good results for the mechanical Green Y, but poor results for the visual Green Y.
> Factor E is important in a direction opposite from factor D, with E_B giving poor results for the mechanical Green Y, but good results for the visual Green Y.

6. A capping run should have been conducted. This was not done.
7. There are four approaches:

> A capping run with all factors best and all factors marginal could have been repeated, duplicating Stage 1. This is not conventional, but if the all-best factors gave good results and the all-marginal poor results (as they did in Stage 1), it would indicate that E_B could be considered a minor influence (Pale Pink X) and that D_B was a dominant influence (Red X).
> A time capping run with (1) $D_B E_M R_M$ and (2) $D_M E_B R_B$ should have been conducted. If the results duplicated Stage 1, it would have indicated that D should be maintained at its best level and E should be at its marginal level for best results for both Green Y's.
> If the capping run indicated a deterioration of one or both Green

Y's, a 2 × 2 factorial would be needed as a follow-up with a different combination of levels—say 28 and 32 psi for factor D, along with 83 and 86 for factor E—to see if both the mechanical and the visual Green Y can be optimized through one of these four combinations.

> If the 2 × 2 factorial was not successful, an evolutionary optimization (see Chapter 16) would be needed to determine the optimum values of D and E for both the mechanical and the visual Green Y.

Variables Search: Software Applications

Variables Search has also been used in software applications, as illustrated by the following case study.

Case Study 5: Software Applications

In a new microcontroller test fixture, with ultraviolet erasable microcontroller function and memory testing capability, a Variables Search experiment was designed to check the microcontroller memory content and functionality. The structure of the software program consists of

1. PROM content,
2. timer, and
3. RAM and I/O Tests.

On every execution, the master UVC8 sends a portion of the test (data bytes) to the slave UVC8 RAM. Upon receiving the data, the slave UVC8 runs a self-test and then transmits the results back to the master UVC8 before the next portion is executed. The results are indicated through four LEDs labeled Blank, Nonblank, Good, and Bad.

Four types of UVC8 conditions were selected, each consisting of two levels, as shown in Table 13-15.

A Combination of Variables Search and Paired Comparisons as a Derivative DOE Technique

In recent years, the authors have developed a DOE technique, derived from the principles of Variables Search and Paired Comparison. It has proved useful in certain unusual situations in product work and in administrative work.

Table 13-15. Case Study 5: Software Applications

Factor code	UVC8 condition	Levels	
		True (t)	False (f)
A	Blank	Blank	Nonblank
B	Nonblank	Nonblank	Blank
C	Programmable	Programmable	Nonprogrammable
D	Nonprogrammable	Nonprogrammable	Programmable

Test	Combination	Results
1	A_fR_t	True
	A_fR_t	False
2	B_fR_t	False
	B_tR_f	True
3	C_fR_t	False
	C_tR_f	True
4	D_fR_t	False
	D_tR_f	True

Conclusion: The Red X was the blank test portion, thus eliminating the possibility from other test portions.

After the debugging process was completed and the program was simulated on the emulator, the UVC8 was retested using both the current test fixture and the new fixture (for production). The results:

Test	Fixture pair	Result
Blank	1 & 2	True
Nonblank	1 & 2	True
Programmable	1 & 2	True
Nonprogrammable	1 & 2	True

Conclusion: The program is fully functional and the new fixture can be introduced into production.

Product Applications

What happens if a product that is assembled is so complex that

1. A nondestructive Paired Comparison cannot be performed on good and bad units, and;
2. A destructive Paired Comparison cannot be performed as a follow-up test, to examine differences in components or subassemblies because they would be ruined in the process of disassembly?

In such instances, select best and marginal components "a priori"—before the fact, i.e., before assembly and build—say, 20 to 40 assemblies with 10 to 20 best components and 10 to 20 marginal components. Then, after complete assembly, select eight of the best Green Y's and eight of the worst Green Y's and perform a Tukey test on the original component values associated with the eight best and eight worst assemblies. If a total end-count of 6 or more results for each of these components, between their original best and marginal values, then those components are important; if the total end-count is less than 6, those components are not important.

An alternative would be to build 30 assemblies, made up of components ranging in values from say, 0 to ±3 sigma in tolerances from a target value and then selecting the eight best and eight worst Green Y's. Next would be a paired comparison Tukey test for each of the different components to determine total end-counts, as above. This alternative is the less preferred method, because it does not concentrate on the best and worst component values—the Variables Search approach—and has therefore, less sensitivity in terms of potential results.

Variables Search/Paired Comparison Case Study 1: Travel Motor

A large manufacturer of construction equipment had been experiencing an unacceptable failure rate in the field of a travel motor well within its warranty period. In order to capture a similar failure mode well ahead of exposure to the field and to its customers, it devised an overstress test, with accelerated speed, that could detect failures within the first 20 to 80 hours of operation. The Green Y was hours to catastrophic failure.

A failed motor would be so badly damaged that disassembling the motor would only reveal ruined parts and subassemblies. Hence, Paired Comparisons of good and bad motors using either nondestructive or destructive measurements were not possible.

It was decided to build 30 motors with eight "best" parts and eight marginal parts. The part characteristics suspected to cause the problem were:

> Spherical surface of the barrel
> Spherical surface of the part plate
> Spherical surface match lap between barrel and part plate
> Dowel pin length
> External barrel spline size
> Internal barrel spline
> Spline run-out
> Spring hold depth

The motors were assembled and subjected to the accelerated over-stress test. The test produced six good and 10 failed motors. Five of the eight part characteristics listed above showed Tukey end-counts of 6 or more, with the spherical surface match lap between the barrel and plate being the Red X. Further work was conducted on the material of the part plate.

The total investigation took five months, but the results were dramatic. There were no more field failures of the motor during the entire warranty period and even beyond this period.

Variables Search/Paired Comparison Case Study 2: Instrument Intermittency

A maker of highly complex instrument (with mechanisms more intricate than a Swiss watch) was experiencing an unacceptably high defect rate in the field because of intermittency and lack of correlation at certain levels within the instrument range. After considerable effort, a more stringent final test was devised within the factory to simulate field failures with just one hour of a stress test.

Failed instruments could not be taken apart so that various components and subassemblies could be examined with paired comparisons, because the several adjustments during the testing of the product would be negated.

A Variables Search/Paired Comparisons DOE technique was used to assemble six instruments with 13 best components/parameters/adjustments and six with 13 marginal ones as follows (large quantities would have been preferable but the instrument maker had production deadlines to meet):

> Cleanliness (10,000 classroom vs. ordinary working conditions);
> Surface finish on gears and pivots;

> Tooth shape;
> Gear mesh adjustment;
> Anti-backlash gears;
> End play on shafts;
> Jewel quality;
> Gear eccentricity;
> Lubrication;
> Diaphragm cross load;
> Balance;
> Gear dimensions;
> Alignment sequence.

The assembled instruments were then final tested and stress tested to produce five good and seven bad units. The values of each component/parameter/adjustment were examined in a Paired Comparisons/Tukey test.

The details of the results are confidential, but four of the 13 components/parameters had a total end-count of 6 or more, including the necessity to go to a superclean room (10,000, or eventually, a 1,000 classroom). The results were zero field failures, with throughput having been increased fourfold by eliminating the three to four dreary cycles of test-rejection-rework and retest, etc.

Variables Search/Paired Comparisons in Administrative Applications

Chapter 11 cites examples in which the Paired Comparisons technique can be eminently suitable for a number of nonproduct applications, such as sales and marketing, human resources, services, dealerships, farms, schools, hospitals, and governments.

They are based on "a posteriori"—after the fact considerations; i.e., the parameters or factors distinguishing eight good or eight bad Green Y's (such as people) had been determined as causes after the problem was stated. For example, in Case Study 4 in Chapter 11 ("High Turnover of Temporary Employees"), factors such as commuting distance, perceived quality of supervision, level of education, etc., were established in retrospect as possible causes.

If it seems necessary to inject two distinct levels of commuting distance, or two distinct levels of education, or two distinct levels of turnover rates on previous jobs a priori, i.e., before the DOE experiment, to see their relative effects on temporary employees, the Paired Comparisons technique can be replaced by Variables Search to design the best and marginal levels of various factors and then see the effect—favorable or unfavorable—on the people (Green Y). Using this technique Case Study 4 could have been redesigned and slightly modified, as shown in Table 13-16.

Next, let us assume that 20 to 40 temporary hires, having characteristics A through E of the best levels, are placed in the best work situations—F, G, and H. Likewise, 20 to 40 temporary hires, having characteristics A through E of the marginal levels, are placed in the marginal work situations—F, G, and H.

The human resources department could monitor both groups for, say, the period of one year or more, (and, of course, interviewing in-depth the individuals who may have quit earlier as they were leaving). Then the department could select the eight who stay the longest and the eight who leave the earliest, and perform a Paired Comparisons/Tukey test on each of the above characteristics to see which have an end-count of 6 or more (and therefore are important) and which are not. If none of the above characteristics turn out to be important, new characteristics may have to be explored. If several of the characteristics are unimportant, time and money need not be spent on them. Only the important characteristics must be nurtured and strengthened.

Analogy With Medical/Pharmaceutical Research

Medical studies are frequently conducted on a large population of people to determine the effects of a particular drug, such as aspirin, anticholesterol medication, etc., over a long period of time. The population is divided into two groups; one is given the particular drug, the other a

Table 13-16. Variables Search/Paired Comparisons: Administrative Applications

Factor code	Factor descriptions	Best level	Marginal level
A	Commuting distance (miles)	<10	>15
B	Driver's license	Yes	No
C	Level of education (number of years of schooling)	<12	>12
D	Past turnover rate in other companies (number/year)	<1	>2
E	Perception of pay vs. other companies	Higher	Lower
F	Work shift	Constant	Rotating
G	Quality of supervision	Empowering	Autocratic
H	Treatment vis-à-vis permanent employees	Equal	"2nd class citizen"

placebo. The groups are then monitored for a particular effect (a Green Y), such as heart attacks, over months and even years. Reports are then compiled, indicating that the group that took the drug regularly were or were not significantly more likely to have heart attacks than the group that took only the placebo (without either group knowing what they were taking). Such studies have a few shortcomings.

1. There is only one Green Y (output), e.g., a heart attack.
2. There is only one input variable of interest—drug versus placebo.
3. The studies involve large populations—generally 1,000 to 5,000 people.
4. Other input variables such as differences in age, health conditions, dietary habits, environmental factors, climate, and a host of other personal variables that could be important enough individually and collectively to bias the results, may not be separated.
5. The experiment is conducted over a long period of time, so each of the above variables could change with people and with time.
6. The results are measured in relatively small percentage improvements.

The authors are not medical experts, but it should be possible to use modified Variables Search/Paired Comparisons experiments in these medical studies.

1. There could be more than one Green Y—e.g., heart attack, stroke, blood pressure, bleeding, and other side effects of concern.
2. The major input variable of interest could remain—drug versus placebo.
3. Other causal factors could be separated into best and marginal, as shown in Table 13-17.

The sample size would only be 40 to 80 drawn from people possessing characteristics of the best levels and 40 to 80 drawn from those possessing characteristics of the marginal levels. Each group would be equally split between those administered the drug and those given the placebo.

At the end of a specified trial and monitoring period, eight of the people that had the best results (before and after tests) and eight that had the worst results (deterioration) would be selected. A Paired Comparisons/Tukey test, on each of the above factors, would then be made. Only those with a total end-count of 6 or more (90 percent confidence or greater) would be considered important.

Thus, with a very much smaller sample size, more meaningful and more valuable results would be registered, with a degree of confidence

Table 13-17. Variables Search/Paired Comparisons: Medical Applications

Factor code	Factor descriptions	Best level	Marginal level
A	Drug	Yes	Placebo
B	Age (years)	<65	>65
C	Sex	Female	Male
D	Weight (lbs.)	10 to 20 under	20 to 40 over
E	Diet	Prescribed	Uncontrolled
F	Smoking	No	Yes
G	Cholesterol levels	Low	High
H	Family history of disease	None	Present
I	Environment	Low Pollution	High Pollution

surpassing greatly those of conventional practices. This proposed technique has not been tried, but negotiations are under way with a pharmaceutical company to launch this cost cutting, time saving, and quality enhancing methodology.

Administrative Case Study: Appliance Servicer

The repair service industry is notorious for its shoddy work, price gouging, unethical charge-backs to the manufacturer, indifferent dealers, careless installers, nonmotivated servicers, and dissatisfied customers! Add to this, some 20 to 40 percent of the service calls result in a category called "no apparent defect" (NAD) or "no trouble found" (NTF), which generally leave customers even more frustrated.

An appliance manufacturer, faced with high repair costs within the warranty period, decided to establish criteria for selection of its dealers and their servicers. It decided to use a Variables Search/Paired Comparisons approach. It selected a large metropolitan area where several of its dealerships were located.

The output or Green Y was the satisfaction index of its final customers, i.e., the consumers. (The index was based on (1) the importance [I] of a number of parameters dealing with performance, installation, service, price, etc.; (2) the customer's rating of each parameters [R]; (3) the score of each parameter [I × R]; (4) an overall score, expressed as percent satisfaction, from 0 to 100.) The input factors spanned dealer, installer, servicer, and product characteristics, as shown in Table 13-18. Two levels—best and marginal—were selected for each factor. Fifteen of the best and 15 of the marginal dealers, based on reputation and inputs from the manufacturer's sales force, were selected.

Table 13-18. Variables Search/Paired Comparisons: Appliance Server

Factor code	Factor descriptions	Best level	Marginal level
	Dealer		
A	Size	Small	Large
B	Representation	Single manufacturer	Several manufacturers
C	Sales personnel turnover rate	Low	High
	Installers/Servicers		
D	Turnover rate	Low	High
E	Training	High	Low
F	Level of education	High	Low
G	Pay	High	Low
H	Bonus for achieving high customer satisfaction index	Yes	No
	Product		
I	Complexity	Low	High
J	Reliability	High	Low
K	Installation/servicing difficulty	Low	High
L	Built-in diagnostics	Yes	No

Customer satisfaction index scores from consumers are now being monitored for one year and eight of the best dealerships and eight of the worst dealerships selected for Paired Comparisons/Tukey test ranking. (Preliminary results point more to shortcomings in the manufacturer's product reliability and serviceability, rather than to weaknesses in the dealer/installer/servicer links originally suspected.)

Questions for DOE Teams as Guidelines

(Questions on Green Y determination and accuracy are the same as in previous DOE techniques.)

1. Are clue-generation techniques used to identify and concentrate on the important variables in drawing up a list of such variables for Stage 1?
2. Have computer simulation or circuit analysis techniques been used to determine the selected variables? (Such techniques must always be followed up with Variables Search, using actual hardware as an insurance policy.)

3. Is the list of variables selected truly ranked in order from the most likely down to the least likely? (This could significantly cut down the number of experiments required in Stage 2.)
4. Has the best level of each variable or factor been determined as the target value of each factor, if previous history indicates a low level of defect?
5. Has the best level of each variable or factor been determined on the basis of improvements over its current level, if previous history indicates an unacceptable rate of defects?
6. Has the marginal level of each variable or factor been determined as its current level so that there can be a step-up for the best level?
7. If there is uncertainty about the best or marginal levels of a particular factor, is a trial B versus C test (see Chapter 15) used as a preliminary step to determine which level is better (B) and which level is worse (C), keeping the other factors constant during this trial run?
8. How have sample sizes been determined? Has a conscious effort been made to select a variable for the Green Y, or at least to convert an attribute Green Y into a variable using a Likert scale? The object is to keep sample sizes small.
9. Make sure that Stage 1 is not skipped—a common mistake.
10. Make sure that Stage 1 is done with three all-best and three all-marginal runs, not just one all-best and one all-marginal.
11. Make sure that the three all-best and three all-marginal runs are done in *random order* (see Chapter 14 on randomization).
12. Is the test of significance, in Stage 1, successful? (D:$\bar{\text{d}}$ ratio>1.25).
13. If not, is Stage 1 tried again with a partially modified set of levels of some factors or a modified set of the factors themselves?
14. Are decision limits for the best and marginal levels in Stage 1 calculated?
15. Or, at least, has a center line been drawn between the median of the best and the median of the marginal levels to distinguish between important and unimportant factors?
16. In Stage 2, is there a correct determination of the importance of each factor—important (Red X), unimportant, or somewhat important?
17. If the result in Stage 2 is a partial reversal, has another factor(s) been determined as also of partial importance and have the two or more factors been combined to test for complete reversal?
18. Has a capping run been performed to verify important or unimportant factors?

19. Has a factorial analysis been constructed to quantify the important main effects and interaction effects?
20. Is there a sequel to the Variables Search experiment to see how far the tolerances of the unimportant factors can be opened up in order to reduce costs?

Questions for Top Management to Review DOE Team Projects

1. Why was the Variables Search methodology chosen in preference to other techniques like the Full Factorial, the Fractional Factorial, Taguchi Orthogonal Array, computer simulation, etc.?
2. How long will—or did—the experiment take?
3. Were the results an improvement over the present level of the Green Y?
4. Was there more than one Green Y and, if so, were there conflicts in the importance of some factors for one Green Y versus those for another Green Y?
5. How were these conflicts resolved?
6. Was a capping run performed?
7. How many factors were important? Was a factorial analysis constructed? What was the relative quantification of the main effects and interaction effects?
8. Was there a follow-up to Variables Search with techniques such as Scatter Plots, B versus C, Positrol, and Process Certification?
9. Was Variables Search extended to open up the tolerances of the unimportant factors to reduce costs?
10. What were the results of Variables Search—in terms of quality improvements, cost improvements, and cycle-time improvements?

14
··

The Full Factorial: Purest Technique for Separating and Quantifying Each Interaction Effect

Chapter 13 introduced the Full Factorial as the purest of all formal DOE techniques, because it can neatly and correctly separate and quantify each main effect, each second-order, third-order, fourth-order, and higher order interaction effect. (In fact, Sir Ronald Fisher—the pioneer researcher and grandfather of Design of Experiments—used only the Full Factorial—and without the use of computers. He never sullied his work with the short-cut of fraction factorials!) This chapter will explore the use of the Full Factorial—its limitations, objectives, principles, and methodology—and provide examples through case studies and workshop exercises. (See Figure 7-1 for its place in the detailed problem-solving roadmap.)

Limitations

As discussed in Chapter 13, the Full Factorial requires 2^n experiments for a randomized, replicated, and balanced design, where n is the number of factors or variables being investigated. For values of n at 5, 6, 7, 8, 9, and 10, a Full Factorial would need 32, 64, 128, 256, 512, and 1,024 experiments, respectively. An inordinate amount of time is required to conduct so many experiments, and the possibility of errors and uncontrollable, extraneous (or noise) factors increases exponentially. So, from a practical point of view, the Full Factorial is limited to four factors or less. Variables Search, then, becomes the experiment of choice for five to 20 factors.

Objectives

1. To determine which of 2, 3, or 4 variables—culled from a large number of variables through one or more of the four clue-generation techniques—are important and which are unimportant.
2. To open up the tolerances of the unimportant variables to reduce costs.
3. To quantify the magnitude and desired direction of the unimportant variables and their interaction effects, and to tighten the tolerances of these variables to achieve a C_p, C_{pk} of 2.0 and more.
4. While the Full Factorial can be used as a problem-solving tool, the temptation to use it at the very start of a problem investigation should be resisted. Preference should be given, instead, to one or more of the four clue-generation tools as a first order of business.
5. However, at the start of a design, where prototype quantities may not be enough to run clue-generation tools, and where the design group can investigate no more than four variables, the Full Factorial can and does become the primary DOE technique.

Principles

Three principles are essential in most DOE studies—balance, replication, and randomization.

Balance

The power of a Full Factorial is that every one of the four (or fewer) chosen variables is tested with all levels (generally two) of every other variable. Thus, all possible combinations of variables and levels are tested in a balanced design, allowing for the systematic separation and quantification of all main effects and interaction effects. The rule for a balanced design is that there must be only one less contrast, or column, than there are experiments. It is this rule that is violated by fraction factorial apologists.

Replication

In an experiment, it is impossible to include all uncontrollable causes or factors or variables. These causes can add up to "noise" or inconsistencies in results, as opposed to the pure "signal" of the selected factors. The purpose of replication (i.e., repeating) in each combination, or "cell," is to determine the variation or inconsistency within each cell. If the inconsistency is too great, (say, more than 10 percent of two readings within each cell), the noise of the experiment "muddies up" the signal and it should be discarded in favor of another experiment under more controlled conditions.

So, a 2^2, 2^3, and a 2^4 experiment should be replicated or repeated twice to determine the signal-to-noise ratio and the validity of the experiment. An exception to replication is that when there are 16 cells in an experiment, a Tukey test with an end-count of 6 or more, can be conducted for each column to determine the confidence of replication. With this rule, a 2^4 factorial, with 16 cells, does not require replication. A 2^3 factorial, with only eight cells, should be repeated once more (i.e., two readings per cell); while a 2^2 factorial, with only four cells, must be run three more times to get four readings per cell.

Randomization

The principle of randomization is best illustrated with a series of games.

> Ask an audience of at least 20 people to choose one of four numbers—either 1, 2, 3, or 4—and write down each person's selection. The great majority will choose "3." The authors have repeated this test in over 33 countries, widely dispersed in geography, culture, and religion. The number chosen, 98 percent of the time, is 3.
> Ask members of a similar audience to choose any piece of furniture that comes to mind. The majority will choose "chair."
> As a similar audience to choose a flower. The majority will choose "rose."

We human beings have certain biases, feelings, hunches, and opinions that tend to select a certain response. There is also an element of herd instinct. In any case, we do not have the ability to choose numbers at random. If we did, 25 percent would have chosen "1," 25 percent "2," 25 percent "3," and 25 percent "4."

But, one may ask, what has this got to do with Design of Experiments? The answer is that the order or sequence of experiments must not follow a set pattern. For instance, as Chapter 15 will show, if there are three B's (better product) and three C's (current product), a logical sequence would be to test the three C's first, then make the change and run three B's, as shown.

Start $>$ C1,   C2,   C3   :   B1,   B2,   B3

————————————————————— Finish

But that could introduce biases into the experiment. There could be:

> ➤ A shift over time in extraneous factors, or noise factors, such as temperature, humidity, static electricity, etc., say, with the C's tested in the morning and the B's tested in the afternoon.

> ➤ A trend over time in the above extraneous factors.

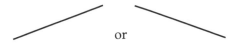

> ➤ A cyclical pattern over time in these extraneous factors

Any of these extraneous changes could introduce "noise" that could unduly influence the results of a change from C to B.

Hence, the experiments must be run in random order. The purpose of randomization is to give these noncontrollable or noise factors an equal chance of entering or not entering an experiment. One of the severe criticisms leveled at Taguchites is that they do not believe in randomization—another cardinal sin. The only condition under which randomization can be bypassed is when the difficulty of switching back and forth on a new versus old process or method could introduce variations greater than the differences between the two processes being tested.

There are three methods of selecting random numbers:

1. One is to use a random number table, such as the one shown in Table 14-1, which was compiled by Cambridge University. No one number has any relationship to any other number. The procedure is to select six or more numbers in a random sequence. Throw a pencil or dart at Table 14-1. Let us say it lands at the number 60. Then go either from left or right, or right to left, or up to down, or down to up or even diagonally. Suppose we go from left to right and read off six numbers that we designate as three B's and three C's. We then arrange the six numbers in a sequence, with the smallest (or largest) tested first, as shown:

Table 14-1. Table of Random Numbers

80 14 67 29 70	44 69 53 51 58	40 45 4 31 85	25 6 31 74 14	55 13 34 95 34
48 58 6 90 36	35 19 94 38 13	25 42 21 79 44	94 13 4 56 70	27 67 42 34 39
69 63 85 3 17	82 5 22 26 54	84 78 47 0 91	29 87 90 47 74	32 27 54 83 66
39 65 78 11 40	48 40 23 30 25	45 32 15 9 3	12 14 4 28 68	89 49 73 50 87
61 18 41 7 27	3 83 48 10 88	22 66 22 32 45	30 6 86 5 80	33 72 10 21 7
15 66 33 12 4	90 82 6 33 70	83 57 49 96 12	47 9 73 18 89	80 80 95 24 73
79 12 39 88 47	37 8 18 99 69	31 89 46 64 6	50 48 47 81 51	66 16 10 83 50
27 95 81 3 65	75 84 46 62 60	92 95 15 44 89	41 61 31 28 11	56 61 47 62 37
34 62 68 17 22	27 56 90 53 45	21 84 83 43 71	57 86 34 64 31	55 72 44 19 75
57 16 83 35 96	13 39 71 72 93	42 3 71 92 50	63 24 59 37 34	49 80 31 87 49
3 74 9 96 37	29 11 25 26 30	44 85 78 39 31	50 75 7 35 22	78 66 71 82 30
21 49 58 38 12	72 74 55 91 52	59 25 79 39 10	73 73 13 38 19	56 79 10 23 6
11 8 72 1 8	11 19 88 12 53	3 46 91 4 72	58 26 90 69 37	96 69 43 77 71
7 92 88 46 16	1 14 31 9 43	85 28 54 31 99	1 21 42 89 87	90 5 10 66 1
70 35 91 61 58	51 71 83 74 61	91 8 15 42 95	96 23 86 42 82	44 16 97 91 51
69 65 46 7 6	41 49 47 49 35	47 5 54 15 36	8 80 8 71 18	28 87 3 32 67
91 11 32 74 42	38 72 55 49 63	27 68 23 4 70	8 52 87 6 76	45 25 35 4 66
90 12 32 72 44	80 14 83 88 71	74 88 72 99 80	46 29 2 19 95	90 4 84 79 97
39 91 70 7 15	72 84 78 86 96	33 50 5 30 39	55 86 65 96 26	55 90 14 49 77
42 16 79 69 40	1 93 70 59 12	30 30 45 26 5	67 29 77 7 2	7 14 59 57 49
16 49 20 58 56	75 44 82 68 78	34 55 25 55 37	96 71 4 43 34	21 37 49 68 10
8 73 64 39 27	99 97 54 58 63	98 71 95 15 19	90 55 54 11 34	10 72 30 18 38
85 2 70 67 40	94 74 38 49 33	29 82 94 51 6	8 89 74 42 81	95 25 29 27 0
18 45 98 50 14	3 57 15 14 90	52 60 45 92 97	33 44 90 94 76	95 81 33 17 49
77 27 24 53 8	73 76 28 93 74	49 62 57 47 67	55 47 33 23 3	43 47 19 9 73
43 40 76 93 60	45 2 81 51 24	56 89 90 75 88	1 13 31 66 69	45 60 7 7 76
5 67 50 60 7	69 77 74 54 37	32 28 7 96 40	37 38 57 53 63	73 0 96 7 19
30 35 40 31 60	53 58 76 92 77	86 97 4 13 34	29 59 96 9 75	54 54 85 24 91
38 40 85 73 33	27 79 42 41 54	39 73 48 45 4	32 62 9 1 70	37 75 20 71 31
26 53 35 39 64	82 61 1 55 35	71 77 76 41 17	23 60 78 37 37	61 9 73 92 72
56 83 50 74 40	22 50 35 34 40	35 7 41 34 35	14 66 78 87 83	43 77 88 59 57
37 47 15 8 1	65 9 41 94 52	40 19 62 84 64	43 89 21 77 54	56 94 57 17 72
3 93 15 95 92	40 20 5 92 91	97 99 45 4 43	87 80 30 32 52	96 97 84 7 66
32 66 85 76 53	14 4 51 43 11	69 70 35 32 11	39 91 95 55 55	85 36 5 79 0
82 82 59 19 21	24 71 64 65 81	11 45 14 31 73	97 11 66 62 5	67 87 68 89 20
42 57 30 94 10	98 25 52 45 93	69 16 76 34 62	9 32 93 6 11	69 36 79 37 13
41 56 71 3 9	35 21 28 22 8	74 78 81 76 21	83 3 93 54 37	76 35 43 53 50
20 24 77 27 5	9 21 7 20 52	14 11 1 89 54	22 96 29 26 82	73 94 85 32 0
19 62 31 92 88	76 14 49 65 8	71 69 91 66 86	56 66 50 13 74	55 54 25 78 23
48 40 52 61 27	67 1 4 20 62	52 33 44 51 79	40 45 74 83 59	83 32 80 43 13

C_1	C_2	C_3	B_1	B_2	B_3
60	45	92	97	33	44
④	③	⑤	⑥	①	②

The correct random order would be B_2 first, then B_3, C_2, C_1, C_3, and B_1.

2. A second method is to use a calculator. Select five single-digit numbers, say, 4, 1, 8, 3, and 9. Punch in the divide sign and select

five other single-digit numbers, say, 2, 8, 6, 7, and 3. Punch in the equal sign, and you get 1.45917762354. Select a random order sequence of 1, 4, 5, 9, 7, and 6 (ignoring a repetitive single digit). Mathematically, a division operation generates a sequence of random numbers.

3. A third method is to use a calculator with a random number function that automatically generates a set of random numbers.

Randomization is not required in Multi-Vari or Paired Comparisons or Product/Process Search studies, because a deliberate sequence with time is the objective. However, for Components Search and Variables Search, the sequence in Stage 1 should be randomized (i.e., the all-good/all-best should not be tested first, followed by the all-bad/all-marginal, or vice versa). Randomization is also required in a Full Factorial experiment, in B versus C studies (see Chapter 15), in Scatter Plots and Surface Response Methodology (see Chapter 16) or in Scatter Plot/Multi-Vari studies to determine the accuracy of instrumentation.

Methodology

The example given is for a 2^4 Full Factorial. The procedure is simpler for a 2^2 or 2^3 Full Factorial.

Green Y

Use the same careful rules in selecting the Green Y as in Variables Search (Chapter 13), namely, looking for an earlier Green Y, the accuracy of the measuring instrument to be at least five times the specification tolerance of the Green Y, and converting an attribute Green Y into a variable with a Likert scale.

The Matrix

1. Select four input variables or factors to be investigated, based on the same methods outlined in Variables Search. Designate them as A, B, C, and D.
2. Select two levels for each factor. The first level, labeled ($-$), is usually but not necessarily the current level for that factor. The second level, labeled ($+$), is assumed to produce better results, but again, not necessarily. A practical alternative is to measure the actual range of the factor or part used in the shop every day,

when many of the best parts can be designated (+) and the not-so-good parts (−).

3. Draw up a matrix (see Table 14-2) showing the 16 combinations by which each factor is tested with each level of every other factor.

4. Randomize the sequence for testing each combination or cell.

5. Run an experiment with each combination in the sequence indicated by the random order table and record the Green Y (output) in each cell.

6. Repeat Steps 4 and 5 using another random order for the second-test sequences.

7. Calculate the average of the two readings in each cell.

8. If the differences between the two readings in each cell are great (larger than, say, ±10%) the "noise" in the experiment is too great. Other factors or other levels may have to be selected or the uncontrollable (noise) factors may have to be brought under better control through Process Certification (see Chapter 18).

9. Do not draw any conclusions based on optimum results in one cell alone. This ignores valuable data in the remaining 15 cells. By comparing all the cells that are (+) to those that are (−), we get a magnifying effect that permits a higher confidence in the appropriate level of each factor and the relationships between main effects and interaction effects.

10. For the 32 sets of readings, add all the average cell readings where A is (−) and all the cells where A is (+). The difference between A(−) and A(+) is due to factor A alone, because all other factors—B, C, and D—balance one another, that is, they have added or subtracted a constant to, or from, both levels, thereby not changing the original difference. Similarly, add all the average cell readings where B is (−) and where B is (+). The difference is due to factor B alone. In like manner, calculate the difference between C(−) and C(+) averages and D(−) and D(+) averages.

11. Construct an Analysis of Variance (ANOVA) table and, if needed, a graphical analysis to display interaction effects (explained in the following case study).

Case Studies and Workshop Exercises

Case Study 1: Motorola Wave Soldering

Fifteen years ago a direct labor team—who had had only one seminar on DOE from this author—undertook to improve a wave solder process that

Table 14-2. Wave Solder 2⁴ Factor Full Factorial Experiment

Green Y: Number of solder defects

		(A) Flux			
		(A-) A19		(A+) 880	
		(B-) Speed 4 ft/min	(B+) Speed 6 ft/min	(B-) Speed 4 ft/min	(B+) Speed 6 ft/min	
(C-) Angle 5°	D-) Pre-Heat 60°F	**1** - - - - 21 (19) 17	**3** - + - - 14 (15) 16	**2** + - - - 104 (108) 112	**4** + + - - 8 (8) 8	→150
	D+) Pre-Heat 220°F	**9** - - - + 17 (16) 15	**11** - + - + 64 (61) 58	**10** + - - + 1 (1) 1	**12** + + - + 0 (0) 0	→78
(C+) Angle 7°	(D-) Pre-Heat 160°F	**5** - - + - 4 (4) 4	**7** - + + - 43 (45) 47	**6** + - + - 44 (41) 38	**8** + + + - 3 (3) 3	→93
	(D+) Pre-Heat 220°F	**13** - - + + 32 (33) 34	**15** - + + + 14 (13) 12	**14** + - + + 10 (10) 10	**16** + + + + 0 (0) 0	→56
		↓ 72	↓ 134	↓ 160	↓ 11	

(Left margins: C) Angle, (C-) Angle 5°, C+) Angle 7°)

$$\left.\begin{array}{l}\textbf{A -} = 72 + 134 = 206 \\ \textbf{A +} = 160 + 11 = 171\end{array}\right\} \quad \text{A– is worse than A+ by 35 defects.}$$

$$\left.\begin{array}{l}\textbf{B -} = 72 + 160 = 232 \\ \textbf{B +} = 134 + 11 = 145\end{array}\right\} \quad \text{B– is worse than B+ by 87 defects.}$$

$$\left.\begin{array}{l}\textbf{C -} = 150 + 78 = 228 \\ \textbf{C +} = 93 + 56 = 149\end{array}\right\} \quad \text{C– is worse than C+ by 79 defects.}$$

$$\left.\begin{array}{l}\textbf{D -} = 150 + 93 = 243 \\ \textbf{D +} = 78 + 56 = 206\end{array}\right\} \quad \text{D– is worse than D+ by 109 defects.}$$

(-) A19 FLUX (+) 880 FLUX
(-) 4'/MIN (+) 6'/MIN
(-) 5° ANGLE (+) 7° ANGLE
(-) 160° PREHEAT (+) 220°

Source: Motorola Inc., Seguin, Tx.

was running at a defect level of 10,000 ppm for poor solderability. The team's very ambitious goal was to reduce the defect level to 200 ppm—a 50:1 improvement. (In the early 1980s, no wave solder processes anywhere in the world were running below a defect level of 10,000 to 15,000 ppm.)

The team decided on a Full Factorial experiment, with four factors and two levels each, as follows:

Factor code	Factor description	Factor level (−)*	Factor level (+)
A	Flux type	A19	A880
B	Belt speed: feet/minute	4	6
C	Angle of incline	5°	7°
D	Preheat temperature: °F	160	220

*The (−) levels represented current levels.

The results are shown in the Full Factorial matrix (Table 14-2). The procedure is outlined in the matrix section of the methodology. It indicated that all four (−) factors representing current process levels were worse than the (+) factors. However, in order to determine interaction effects, a full analysis of variance (ANOVA) had to be constructed, using the guidelines explained in the introduction to Variables Search in Chapter 13. The construction of the ANOVA table (Table 14-3) is as follows:

Table 14-3. ANOVA Table: Wave Solder 2^4 Factor Full Factorial Experiment

Cell Group	Factors (Main Effects) A	B	C	D	Two-Factor Interaction AB	AC	BC	AD	BD	CD	Three-Factor Interaction ABC	ABC	ABC	ABC	Four-Factor Interaction ABCD	Output
1 (1)	−	−	−	−	+	+	+	+	+	+	−	−	−	−	+	19
2 a	+	−	−	−	−	−	+	−	+	+	+	+	+	−	−	108
3 b	−	+	−	−	−	+	−	+	−	+	+	+	−	+	−	15
4 ab	+	+	−	−	+	−	−	−	−	+	−	−	+	+	+	8
5 c	−	−	+	−	+	−	−	+	+	−	+	−	+	+	−	4
6 ac	+	−	+	−	−	+	−	−	+	−	−	+	−	+	+	41
7 bc	−	+	+	−	−	−	+	+	−	−	−	+	+	−	+	45
8 abc	+	+	+	−	+	+	+	−	−	−	+	−	−	−	−	3
9 d	−	−	−	+	+	+	+	−	−	−	−	+	+	+	−	16
10 ad	+	−	−	+	−	−	+	+	−	−	+	−	−	+	+	1
11 db	−	+	−	+	−	+	−	−	+	−	+	−	+	−	+	61
12 adb	+	+	−	+	+	−	−	+	+	−	−	+	−	−	−	0
13 cd	−	−	+	+	+	−	−	−	−	+	+	+	−	−	+	33
14 acd	+	−	+	+	−	+	−	+	−	+	−	−	+	−	−	10
15 bcd	−	+	+	+	−	−	+	−	+	+	−	−	−	+	−	13
16 abcd	+	+	+	+	+	+	+	+	+	+	+	+	+	+	+	0
	−	−	−	−	−	−	+	−	+	+	+	+	+	−	+	
Total	35	87	79	79	211	47	33	189	115	35	73	139	127	181	39	

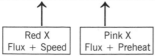

Red X
Flux + Speed

Pink X
Flux + Preheat

1. In the "cell group" column, enter the cell combinations. The conventions are:

> ‣ Cell 1 (1) means all factors, A, B, C, & D are (−).
> ‣ Cell (a) means all factors are (−), except A.
> ‣ Cell (b) means all factors are (−), except B.
> ‣ Cell (ab) means all factors are (−), except A and B, and so on.

2. In the main factor columns, enter the appropriate (−) and (+) signs for the factors A, B, C, and D.
3. In the output column, enter the average of the outputs recorded in each cell from Table 14-2.
4. In the two-factor interaction columns, multiply, algebraically, the signs of A and B in cell 1 (1) and record the sign of the product in the AB column. Here, because A and B are both (−), the product sign for AB is (+). Similarly, determine the algebraic products of A and C, B and C, etc., and record them in the appropriate two-factor interaction column in each row.
5. In the three-factor interaction columns, multiply the signs of the appropriate three factors ABC, ABD, etc., and record the signs of the products in the appropriate three-factor column in each row.
6. Do the same for the four-factor interaction column by multiplying the signs of the appropriate four factors ABCD. Record the sign of the product in the appropriate four-factor column in each row.
7. In column A, add all the outputs where A is (−), and add all the outputs where A is (+). Note the difference between these two sums in the last row, labeled "Main and Interaction Totals." Place a (−) sign above the A total since the A (−) sum is 35 points larger than the A (+) sum. This means that A (−) is worse than A (+) by 35 points—the same results as in Table 14-2.
8. The last row displays, in precise quantified form, the contribution of each main factor as well as each two-factor, three-factor, and four-factor interaction—both in magnitude and in direction (+) or (−).

This is shown in Table 14-3, which indicates that none of the four main factors is nearly as important as a two-factor AB interaction (the Red X), a two-factor AD interaction (the Pink X), and a three-factor BCD interaction (the Pale Pink X).

The last step is to plot the major interaction effects (Figure 14-1). The procedure is as follows:

1. For the AB interaction, observe the A and B columns jointly. Add all the outputs of those cells where A and B are both (−). Add all

Figure 14-1. Wave Solder Experiment: A Graphical Portrayal of Interaction Effects

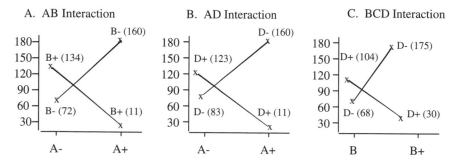

A. AB Interaction   B. AD Interaction   C. BCD Interaction

the outputs where A is ($-$) and B is ($+$). Add all the outputs where A is ($+$) and B is ($-$). Add the outputs where A is ($+$) and B is ($+$).

2. For the AD interaction, repeat step 1, observing the A and D columns jointly.
3. For the BCD interaction, repeat Step 1, observing the B, C, and D columns jointly.
4. Plot the results of the four corners for the AB interactions: A$-$, B$-$; A$-$, B$+$; A$+$, B$-$; and A$+$, B$+$ (Figure 14-1A).
5. Similarly, Figures 14-1B and 14-1C show the results of the AD and BCD interactions.

Interpretation of Tables 14-3 and Figure 14-1

We can now interpret the physical meaning of the results.

> In factor A (flux type), the 880 flux (new) is better than the A19 flux (old).
> In factor B (belt speed), the faster speed (6 ft./min.) is better than the slower speed (4 ft./min.).
> In factor C (angle of incline), the higher angle (7°) is better than the lower angle (5°).
> In factor D (preheat temperature) 220° is better than 160°.

However, none of these main factors are as important as several of their interaction effects:

> The interaction between flux and belt speed (AB), is the Red X, indicating that A and B should be kept at their $+$ levels. This is confirmed in Table 14-3—211 more defects if A and B were both ($-$)—and in Figure 14-1, which indicates a very strong interaction effect. (Two parallel lines mean no interaction effect; two nonparallel lines mean a decided interaction effect; and two crossing lines,

as in Figures 14-1 A, B, and C, mean very strong interaction effects.) For best results (lowest defects), A and B should be kept at their + levels.

> Similarly, the AD interaction is the Pink X—189 more defects if A and B were both (−). This is confirmed by the strong crossing lines of Figure 14-1B. For best results (lowest defects) A and D should be kept at their + levels.

> Similarly the BCD interaction is the Pale Pink X—181 more defects if A, B, and C move (−). This is confirmed by the strong crossing lines of Figure 14-1C. For best results B, D, and D should be kept at their + levels.

Confirmation Experiment: Capping Run

With A, B, C, and D at their (+) levels, a capping run was performed on 17 new boards. With 800 connections per board, the defect rate dropped to 220 ppm, not quite the 50:1 improvement that was the team's objective, but a 45:1 improvement. Nobody, not in the U.S., not in Europe, not in Japan, had achieved such low defect levels for wave soldering in those early 1980s. (Today, however, with more DOE work, Motorola has achieved defect levels below 10 ppm on a steady state basis, and other companies have registered similar successes.)

The team went on to implement similar parameter modifications on 12 other wave solder machines in the plant; they eliminated 20 touch-up operators and an equivalent number of inspectors, for a yearly savings of $750,000. The team leader, who was a maintenance technician, became so enthused about DOE that he would, on his own initiative, run one or two DOE experiments per week; he rose to become the primary experimenter and coach in the 1,800-employee Texas plant.

Workshop Exercise 1: Paint Yields

In a large appliance factory, yields in a porcelain paint process were unsatisfactory, fluctuating between 68 percent and 82 percent. The plant's engineers were convinced that the yields varied greatly during different times of the year—low in the summer and higher in the winter. The plant manager was dissatisfied even with the higher winter yields. He estimated that each one-percent improvement in yield would save $100,000 per year. This author was requested to help solve this chronic problem. A task force was set up to conduct a DOE experiment after a concentration on process certification (see Chapter 18). Because the task force was so convinced that the higher temperatures and the higher humidity in the plant were the cause of the yield losses, a simple 2^2 factorial (Figure 14-2)

Figure 14-2. Paint Yields: A 2^2 Full Factorial

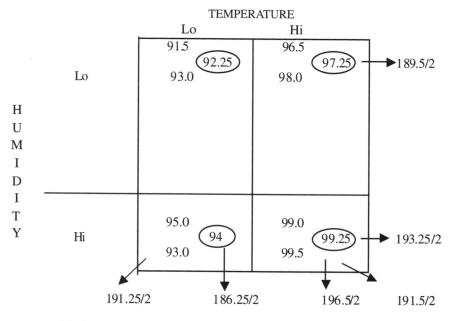

was established, with two levels of temperature and two levels of humidity. (The exact levels are not stated to protect confidentiality.)

Questions

1. What are the contributions of temperature and humidity and any interaction effects?
2. What is the contribution of signal versus "noise" in the experiment?
3. Was the initial opinion of the task force on temperature and humidity confirmed?
4. What was the real Red X?
5. What are the conclusions to be drawn and the lessons to be learned?

Answers

1. Temperature (T) Contribution $= \dfrac{196.5 - 186.25}{2} = 5.125\%$

   Humidity (H) Contribution $= \dfrac{193.25 - 189.5}{2} = 1.87\%$

   Interaction (T × H) Contribution $= \dfrac{191.5 - 191.25}{2} = 0.125\%$

2. The lack of repeatability in each cell varies from 0.5 percent to 2 percent, with all yields over 90 percent. So the signal-to-noise ratio is very high and very acceptable. (To be technically correct, each cell in a 2^2 Full Factorial should have four, not two, readings for full replication, but the high signal-to-noise ratio already achieved with one replication enabled us to skip this last step.)

3. The initial opinions of the task force about the importance of temperature and humidity were right in terms of the two factors, but dead wrong in terms of direction. The higher temperature actually provided higher yields, not lower ones, and the higher humidity provided somewhat higher yields, not lower ones. Further, the temperature contribution to yield improvement was almost three times that of humidity.

4. To the amazement of the team, none of the four temperature-humidity combinations produced yields under 90 percent. They had never experienced yields this high ever! The real Red X, therefore, was the establishment of a process certification (see Chapter 18) discipline—a regimen of nailing down all quality peripherals, such as equipment preventive maintenance, calibration, monitoring of controls, clean-up, housekeeping, etc., ahead of the 2^2 factorial experiment.

5. The morals of the story are: First, let the parts and the process (not the engineers) do the talking. Second, *make sure that good manufacturing practices, such as maintenance, calibration and clean-up, are in place before the start of an experiment, to ensure that these uncontrollable noise factors are kept to a minimum and do not interfere with the purity of the signal.*

Postscript

The plant engineers did not want to believe the results of the task force. "Wait till summer fully arrives," they said. "The yields will go down again." The summer came and went. The yields never fell below 90 percent! The savings to the plant were over $1.5 million. The task force's new goal is to achieve yields of 99 percent with further DOE studies.

Case Study 2: Moire Effect Minimization

In a new development of a computer monitor, a design team had to minimize the moire effect on the screen. Known as a scan moire, the problem is a wavy pattern caused by the shadow mask pattern and the horizontal line pattern.

The desired specification (Green Y) is 1 mm maximum in size for the moire effect. Readings in prototype units were measuring 2 mm and more. Scan moire depends on the horizontal scanning frequency and can be reduced by an appropriate choice of this frequency. However, the monitors must operate over a range of scanning frequencies.

Four factors, as shown below, were selected, based on a circuit analysis, for a 2^4 Full Factorial experiment to determine the best combinations to minimize scan moire.

Factor code	Factor description	Factor level	
		(−)	*(+)*
A	Resistor (R_1)	22r	5 r 6
B	Resistor (R_2)	470r	220r
C	B+ Voltage (V)	7	6
D	Q4 Transistor gain (H_{fe})	12.6	16.9

Table 14-4 shows the Full Factorial matrix, with two Green Y's—moire size and collector current (I_c)—run at a high horizontal scanning frequency. Tables 14-5 and 14-6 show similar matrices, run at middle and low frequencies, respectively.

Tables 14-7, 14-8, and 14-9 show the ANOVA tables for each of the three frequencies with only one output (or Green Y)—moire size. In the interest of brevity, the ANOVA tables for collector current are not shown. The results for the Red X, Pink X, etc., were similar when collector current was the Green Y to results when moire size was the Green Y.

Analysis

1. ANOVA Tables 14-7, 14-8, and 14-9 all show that factor A (resistor R1) is the Red X for all three horizontal scanning frequencies. Therefore, to minimize moire size, A should be kept at its (+) level. This also holds true for the second Green Y—collector current (I_c), even though the ANOVA tables for I_c are not shown.
2. The AD interaction is a Pink X for all three horizontal scanning frequencies. The AD interaction is higher at the (−) level rather than the (+) level, which would normally indicate that A and D should both be kept at their (+) levels. However, a graphical plot of the AD interaction for all three frequencies (not shown) indicate that D(−) has a less steep (less disruptive) slope than D(+). So D is better kept at its (−) level.
3. Factor C is not important, except in the highest frequency ANOVA

Table 14-4. Full Factorial Matrix: Moire Size—High Frequency
2 Green Y's: Moire Size and Collector Current (I$_c$)

112.5k/90 Hz					Measures	
Experiment number	Factors Main Effects				Moire size (mm)	I$_c$ (mA)
	A	B	C	D		
1	−1	−1	−1	−1	2	195.94
2	1	−1	−1	−1	0	182.99
3	−1	1	−1	−1	1.5	192.95
4	1	1	−1	−1	0	170.74
5	−1	−1	1	−1	2.5	195.98
6	1	−1	1	−1	0.5	182.71
7	−1	1	1	−1	2	193.20
8	1	1	1	−1	0	170.27
9	−1	−1	−1	1	2.5	198.98
10	1	−1	−1	1	0	185.11
11	−1	1	−1	1	4	203.05
12	1	1	−1	1	0	186.66
13	−1	−1	1	1	30	201.58
14	1	−1	1	1	0	185.16
15	−1	1	1	1	40	200.87
16	1	1	1	1	0	185.94

Measured data at high frequency.

Source: Philips Corp., Chungli, Taiwan.

    table. In any case, C(−) gives lower moire sizes than C(+). This is confirmed by graphical plots (not shown).

4. Factor B is not important for any of the three frequencies and can be kept at a level that is economical.

The optimum levels, therefore, are A(+), B(+), C(−), and D(−).

Results

    A capping run on the optimum levels demonstrated that moire sizes were all well below 0.5mm—more than a 40:1 improvement—and C$_p$'s were over 3.0.

Commentary on Case Study 2: Moire Effect Minimization

1. Even though the project involved a new design, there were sufficient quantities to justify use of Components Search or Paired Comparisons for easier, faster results.

Table 14-5. Full Factorial Matrix: Moire Size—Middle Frequency
2 Green Y's: Moire Size and Collector Current (I_c)

106.2k/85 Hz					Measures	
Experiment number	Factors Main Effects				Moire size (mm)	I_c (mA)
	A	B	C	D		
1	−1	−1	−1	−1	1.5	186.26
2	1	−1	−1	−1	0	173.68
3	−1	1	−1	−1	1	183.75
4	1	1	−1	−1	0.5	167.14
5	−1	−1	1	−1	1.5	185.71
6	1	−1	1	−1	0	173.58
7	−1	1	1	−1	1.5	184.90
8	1	1	1	−1	0.5	166.85
9	−1	−1	−1	1	2	188.65
10	1	−1	−1	1	0	177.18
11	−1	1	−1	1	2	191.89
12	1	1	−1	1	0	179.59
13	−1	−1	1	1	2.5	192.67
14	1	−1	1	1	0	184.91
15	−1	1	1	1	2.5	192.87
16	1	1	1	1	0	178.17

Measured data at middle frequency.

Source: Philips Corp., Chungli, Taiwan.

2. There was no replication in any of the 16 cells of the matrix. However, a Tukey test on the important factors in the ANOVA tables
would indicate that for the A and AD factors (Red X and Pink
X) the total end-counts are 16 and 7 respectively—well above the
minimum 6, for confidence levels over 90 percent.
3. A scatter plot (see Chapter 16) to determine the correlation between the two Green Y's—moire size and collector current—was
performed. It showed very good correlation between the two
Green Y's at the high and middle frequencies, but not at the low
frequency.

Workshop Exercise 2: Drilling Operation

In a metal fabrication shop, the cross-drilling of two holes 9/64" in diameter through both walls of a piece part resulted in a heavy exit burr and

Table 14-6. Full Factorial Matrix: Moire Size—Low Frequency
2 Green Y's: Moire Size and Collector Current (I_c)

31.5k/70 Hz					Measures	
Experiment	Factors Main Effects				Moire	
number	A	B	C	D	size (mm)	I_c (mA)
1	−1	−1	−1	−1	1.5	120.06
2	1	−1	−1	−1	1	114.76
3	−1	1	−1	−1	1	119.80
4	1	1	−1	−1	0.5	114.01
5	−1	−1	1	−1	1.5	120.75
6	1	−1	1	−1	1	114.89
7	−1	1	1	−1	1	120.95
8	1	1	1	−1	0.5	113.91
9	−1	−1	−1	1	3	117.11
10	1	−1	−1	1	0.5	117.43
11	−1	1	−1	1	3	118.81
12	1	1	−1	1	0	118.13
13	−1	−1	1	1	3	118.67
14	1	−1	1	1	0.5	117.43
15	−1	1	1	1	2.5	118.45
16	1	1	1	1	0	110.90

Measured data at low frequency.

Source: Philips Corp., Chungli, Taiwan.

large hanging flags in over 50 percent of the parts. All shipments had been rejected by the customer even after each part was blown out with high pressure air. A 2^4 Full Factorial was designed on four parameters likely to have caused the problem.

		Factor level	
Factor code	Factor description	(−)	(+)
A	Spindle speed (rpm)	2,850	5,000
B	Drill type	GT100	Guhring
C	Drill feed (in. / rev.)	0.001	Gold
D	Coolant type	Water-soluble mist	Cutting oil

Table 14-7. ANOVA Table: Moire Size—High Frequency

| Group | Factors Main Effects | | | | Two-Factor Interactions | | | | | | Three-Factor Interactions | | | | Four-Factor Interactions | Moire size (mm) |
	A	B	C	D	AB	AC	BC	AD	BD	CD	ABC	ABD	ACD	BCD	ABCD	
1	−1	−1	−1	−1	1	1	1	1	1	1	−1	−1	−1	−1	1	2.0
2	1	−1	−1	−1	−1	−1	1	−1	1	1	1	1	1	−1	−1	0.0
3	−1	1	−1	−1	−1	1	−1	1	−1	1	1	1	−1	1	−1	1.5
4	1	1	−1	−1	1	−1	−1	−1	−1	1	−1	−1	1	1	1	0.0
5	−1	−1	1	−1	1	−1	−1	1	1	−1	1	−1	1	1	−1	2.5
6	1	−1	1	−1	−1	1	−1	−1	1	−1	−1	1	−1	1	1	0.5
7	−1	1	1	−1	−1	−1	1	1	−1	−1	−1	1	1	−1	1	2.0
8	1	1	1	−1	1	1	1	−1	−1	−1	1	−1	−1	−1	−1	0.0
9	−1	−1	−1	1	1	1	1	−1	−1	−1	−1	1	1	1	−1	2.5
10	1	−1	−1	1	−1	−1	1	1	−1	−1	1	−1	−1	1	1	0.0
11	−1	1	−1	1	−1	1	−1	−1	1	−1	1	−1	1	−1	1	4.0
12	1	1	−1	1	1	−1	−1	1	1	−1	−1	1	−1	−1	−1	0.0
13	−1	−1	1	1	1	−1	−1	−1	−1	1	1	1	−1	−1	1	30.0
14	1	−1	1	1	−1	1	−1	1	−1	1	−1	−1	1	−1	−1	0.0
15	−1	1	1	1	−1	−1	1	−1	1	1	−1	−1	−1	1	−1	40.0
16	1	1	1	1	1	1	1	1	1	1	1	1	1	1	1	0.0
Effect	−84	10	65	68	−11	−64	8	−69	13	62	−9	−12	−63	9	−8	

Red X → A

Pink X → C, D, AC, AD, CD

Source: Philips Corp., Chungli, Taiwan.

Table 14-8. ANOVA Table: Moire Size—Middle Frequency (106.2k/85Hz)

	Factors Main Effects				Two-Factor Interactions						Three-Factor Interactions				Four-Factor Interactions	Moire
Group	A	B	C	D	AB	AC	BC	AD	BD	CD	ABC	ABD	ACD	BCD	ABCD	size (mm)
1	−1	−1	−1	−1	1	1	1	1	1	1	−1	−1	−1	−1	1	1.5
2	1	−1	−1	−1	−1	−1	1	−1	1	1	1	1	1	−1	−1	0
3	−1	1	−1	−1	−1	1	−1	1	−1	1	1	1	−1	1	−1	1
4	1	1	−1	−1	1	−1	−1	−1	−1	1	−1	−1	1	1	1	0.5
5	−1	−1	1	−1	1	−1	−1	1	1	−1	1	−1	1	1	−1	1.5
6	1	−1	1	−1	−1	1	−1	−1	1	−1	−1	1	−1	1	1	0
7	−1	1	1	−1	−1	−1	1	1	−1	−1	−1	1	1	−1	1	1.5
8	1	1	1	−1	1	1	1	−1	−1	−1	1	−1	−1	−1	−1	0.5
9	−1	−1	−1	1	1	1	1	−1	−1	−1	−1	1	1	1	−1	2
10	1	−1	−1	1	−1	−1	1	1	−1	−1	1	−1	−1	1	1	0
11	−1	1	−1	1	−1	1	−1	−1	1	−1	1	−1	1	−1	1	2
12	1	1	−1	1	1	−1	−1	1	1	−1	−1	1	−1	−1	−1	0
13	−1	−1	1	1	1	−1	−1	−1	−1	1	1	1	−1	−1	1	2.5
14	1	−1	1	1	−1	1	−1	1	−1	1	−1	−1	1	−1	−1	0
15	−1	1	1	1	−1	−1	1	−1	1	1	−1	−1	−1	1	−1	2.5
16	1	1	1	1	1	1	1	1	1	1	1	1	1	1	1	0
Effect	−14	0.5	1.5	2.5	1.5	−1.5	0.5	−4.5	−0.05	0.5	−0.5	−1.5	−0.5	−0.5	0.5	

Red X → A (Effect −14)

Pink X → AD (Effect −4.5)

Source: Philips Corp., Chungli, Taiwan.

Table 14-9. ANOVA Table: Moire Size—Low Frequency

Group	Factors Main Effects				Two-Factor Interactions						Three-Factor Interactions				Four-Factor Interactions	Moire size (mm)
	A	B	C	D	AB	AC	BC	AD	BD	CD	ABC	ABD	ACD	BCD	ABCD	
1	-1	-1	-1	-1	1	1	1	1	1	1	-1	-1	-1	-1	1	1.5
2	1	-1	-1	-1	-1	-1	1	-1	1	1	1	1	1	-1	-1	1
3	-1	1	-1	-1	-1	1	-1	1	-1	1	1	1	-1	1	-1	1
4	1	1	-1	-1	1	-1	-1	-1	-1	1	-1	-1	1	1	1	0.5
5	-1	-1	1	-1	1	-1	-1	1	1	-1	1	-1	1	1	-1	1.5
6	1	-1	1	-1	-1	1	-1	-1	1	-1	-1	1	-1	1	1	1
7	-1	1	1	-1	-1	-1	1	1	-1	-1	-1	1	1	-1	1	1
8	1	1	1	-1	1	1	1	-1	-1	-1	1	-1	-1	-1	-1	0.5
9	-1	-1	-1	1	1	1	1	-1	-1	-1	-1	1	1	1	-1	3
10	1	-1	-1	1	-1	-1	1	1	-1	-1	1	-1	-1	1	1	0.5
11	-1	1	-1	1	-1	1	-1	-1	1	-1	1	-1	1	-1	1	3
12	1	1	-1	1	1	-1	-1	1	1	-1	-1	1	-1	-1	-1	0
13	-1	-1	1	1	1	-1	-1	-1	-1	1	1	1	-1	-1	1	3
14	1	-1	1	1	-1	1	-1	1	-1	1	-1	-1	1	-1	-1	0.5
15	-1	1	1	1	-1	-1	1	-1	1	1	-1	-1	-1	1	-1	2.5
16	1	1	1	1	1	1	1	1	1	1	1	1	1	1	1	0
Effect	-13	-3.5	-0.5	4.5	0.5	0.5	-0.5	-8.5	0.5	-0.5	0.5	-0.5	0.5	-0.5	0.5	

Red X → A (−13)

Pink X → AD (−8.5)

Source: Philips Corp., Chungli, Taiwan.

302

Green Y

The attributes of burrs versus no burrs and flags versus no flags was converted into a Likert scale of 0 to 4. The defect score in each cell was the number of each type of defect multiplied by the scale.

	Scale
Minimal burr—nondefective	S0
Slight raised burr	S1
Raised burr plus one hanging burr—easily broken off	S2
Raised burr plus two or more flags	S3
Excessive hanging burr and multiple flags	S4

One hundred pieces were run in each cell, and the sequence was randomized. A new drill was used in each experiment to eliminate tool wear. The factorial matrix is shown in Table 14-10 and the ANOVA table in Table 14-11.

Questions

1. Were 100 pieces necessary for each cell?
2. What were the benefits of grading the defects on a 0 to 4 scale?
3. Based on the results of a single cell, what are the best levels to use?
4. Based on the ANOVA tables, which are the Red X and Pink X factors?
5. What are the optimum levels to use for each factor?
6. Does the graphical plot for interactions confirm these choices?

Answers

1. If the defect rate had been small, say, 5 percent or less, 100 pieces for each cell would have been justified. With a defect rate of 50 percent and the magnification afforded by the Likert scale, 10 units would have sufficed.
2. There were two benefits to grading. (1) The spread in defect scores was magnified, from 7 to 396. This could have reduced the sample size in each cell, as described in Answer 1. (2) If a particular type of defect (Green Y) had to be separated, e.g., burrs alone or flags alone, the matrix could easily have separated these two Green Y's.
3. Based on a single cell, the best levels would be A $(+)$, B $(-)$, C $(+)$, and D $(+)$. As it turned out eventually from the ANOVA

Table 14-10. Full Factorial: Drill Experiment

		(A) Spindle speed			
		(A-) 2850 R.P.M.		(A+) 5000 R.P.M.	
		(B-) GT 100	(B+) Guhring Gold	(B-) GT 100	(B+) Guhring Gold
(C-) 0.001	(D-) Mist	1 | 9 * S1: 37 S2: 42 S3: 3 S4: 2 Tot: (168)	2 | 3 S1: 9 S2: 26 S3: 54 S4: 7 Tot: (251)	3 | 14 S1: 42 S2: 35 S3: 3 Tot: (121)	4 | 5 S1: 18 S2: 30 S3: 50 Tot: (228)
	(D+) Oil	5 | 11 S1: 49 S2: 41 S3: 1 S4: 2 Tot: (142)	6 | 10 S1: 1 S3: 1 S4: 96 Tot: (396)	7 | 7 S1: 34 S2: 42 S3: 6 S4: 1 Tot: (140)	8 | 6 S1: 3 S2: 7 S3: 46 S4: 44 Tot: (128)
(C+) 0.003	(D-) Mist	9 | 8 S1: 50 S2: 43 S3: 7 Tot: (157)	10 | 13 S1: 15 S2: 35 S3: 45 S4: 4 Tot: (236)	11 | 12 S1: 53 S2: 17 S3: 3 S4: 0 Tot (96)	12 | 15 S1: 62 S2: 30 S3: 2 Tot: (128)
	(D+) Oil	13 | 2 S1: 22 S2: 7 Tot (36)	14 | 16 S1: 35 S2: 49 S3: 10 S4: 1 Tot: (167)	15 | 4 S1: 5 S2: 1 Tot (7)	16 | 1 S1: 11 Tot: (11)

(C) Drill Feed

Notes: The first square in each cell corner represents the cell number.
The second square in each cell represents the run sequence.

table, this combination was the best. But the full ANOVA exercise is necessary so that the very useful data in the remaining 15 cells are not thrown away.

4. From the last row of the ANOVA table, the factor with the highest reading is C, and its best level should be the opposite of (−), i.e. (+). The next highest factor is B, and its best level should be (−).
5. The optimum levels, based on the readings and signs in the last row of the ANOVA table, are A (+), B (−), C (+), and D (+).
6. The graphical plot can be interpreted as follows: In the CD interaction, C (+), D (+) give the lowest defects. (It could be argued that D (−) should be used because the D (−) slope is less steep than

Table 14-11. Full Factorial: Drill Experiment—ANOVA Table

| Cell Group | Factors Main Effects | | | | Two-Factor Interactions | | | | | | Three-Factor Interactions | | | | Four-Factor Interactions | Output |
	A	B	C	D	AB	AC	BC	AD	BD	CD	ABC	ABD	ACD	BCD	ABCD	
1	-1	-1	-1	-1	1	1	1	1	1	1	-1	-1	-1	-1	1	168
2	1	-1	-1	-1	-1	-1	1	-1	1	1	1	1	1	-1	-1	251
3	-1	1	-1	-1	-1	1	-1	1	-1	1	1	1	-1	1	-1	121
4	1	1	-1	-1	1	-1	-1	-1	-1	1	-1	-1	1	1	1	228
5	-1	-1	1	-1	1	-1	-1	1	1	-1	1	-1	1	1	-1	142
6	1	-1	1	-1	-1	1	-1	-1	1	-1	-1	1	-1	1	1	396
7	-1	1	1	-1	-1	-1	1	1	-1	-1	-1	1	1	-1	1	140
8	1	1	1	-1	1	1	1	-1	-1	-1	1	-1	-1	-1	-1	331
9	-1	-1	-1	1	1	1	1	-1	-1	-1	-1	1	1	1	-1	157
10	1	-1	-1	1	-1	-1	1	1	-1	-1	1	-1	-1	1	1	236
11	-1	1	-1	1	-1	1	-1	-1	1	-1	1	-1	1	-1	1	96
12	1	1	-1	1	1	-1	-1	1	1	-1	-1	1	-1	-1	-1	128
13	-1	-1	1	1	1	-1	-1	-1	-1	1	1	1	-1	-1	1	36
14	1	-1	1	1	-1	1	-1	1	-1	1	-1	-1	1	-1	-1	167
15	-1	1	1	1	-1	-1	1	-1	1	1	-1	-1	-1	1	-1	7
16	1	1	1	1	1	1	1	1	1	1	1	1	1	1	1	11
Main and Interaction Contribution	-491	881	-939	-155	-213	-217	-389	-13	-279	-637	-135	-167	-19	-231	+7	

Figure 14-3. Full Factorial: Drill Experiment

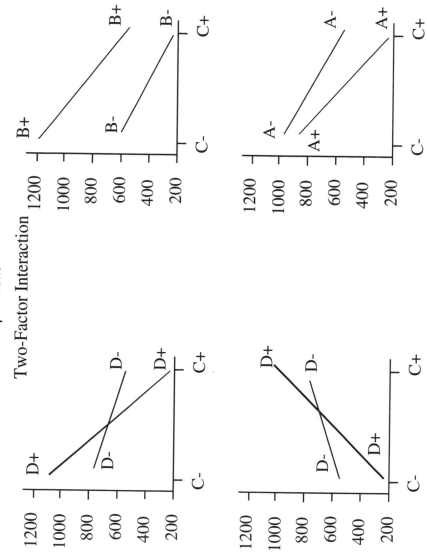

Two-Factor Interaction

the D (+) slope, but in actual production there is no danger of D (the coolant) wandering off to another type of coolant. Similarly, in the BC interaction, C (+), B (−) gives the lowest defects as well as the lowest slope. In the BD interaction, B (−), D (+) gives the lowest defects, and D(+) is chosen for the same reason as the CD interaction. In the AC interaction, A(+), C(+) gives the lowest defects and the two slopes are about equal, indicating very little interactions.

Conclusion

These results were contrary to engineering expectations, where the lower drill feed rate was thought to be better. With the combination of the higher drill feed rate, the GT100 drill type, the higher spindle speed, and the cutting oil, the defect rate dropped to zero.

Questions for DOE Teams

1. Were all the good manufacturing practices—such as equipment preventive maintenance, instrument calibration, control of the various environments, housekeeping—nailed down ahead of the Full Factorial experiment to reduce noise factors and increase the signal-to-noise ratio?
2. Were the principles of balance, replication, and randomization adhered to?
3. Were the (−) levels for each factor the current levels and the (+) levels felt to be a decided improvement over the current levels?
4. Was each cell in the factorial matrix repeated or replicated, and was the sequence of testing randomized?
5. Was there reasonable consistency in the two readings of each cell (i.e., a high signal-to-noise ratio); or, if there were 16 cells in the experiment, was a Tukey test calculated on the important parameters?
6. Was there a follow-up on Variables Search with B versus C, Scatter Plots, Positrol, and Process Certifcation?

Questions for Management

1. Was the discipline of Process Certification (see Chapter 18) used before the Full Factorial experiment to ensure good manufacturing practices and a high signal-to-noise ratio for the experiment?

2. Why was the Full Factorial approach chosen instead of the Variables Search technique?
3. On what basis were the factors for the experiment selected?
4. Were the disciplines of an ANOVA table and graphical plots of interaction effects used?
5. What were the results of the experiment, in terms of quality, cost, and cycle-time improvements?
6. What were the lessons learned that can be passed on to future teams?

15
B versus C: An Excellent Validation Technique

The Importance of Validation

A central weakness in all problem-solving practices is assuming that an improvement, once made, is substantial, real, and permanent. The history of problem-solving exercises is littered with initial successes followed by failures soon after. No attempt is made to go back to conditions before the improvement and see if the problem has been recreated.

The best way to confirm the magnitude and permanency of the improvement is to go back to the pre-improvement product or process or method and ensure that the problem has been reproduced. Then, switch to the new improved product, or process, or method, and ensure that the problem has disappeared. Do this at least twice more. It is like turning on a light switch. Turn the problem on, turn the problem off. Turn the problem on, turn the problem off again. Only then can the experimenter develop sufficient confidence about the permanency of the improvement.

Disc Brake Case Study

An example will illustrate why such verification is important. A manufacturer of aircraft disc brakes was experiencing a crisis in the quality of the product. The company's customer had almost disqualified the company as a supplier. But the company rallied. It had gone through a "black belt" training program by an outside contractor. The black belt team designed a classical fraction factorial experiment; solved the problem, and projected a savings of almost $5 million per year. But, one month after the improvements had been introduced, the problem returned in spades! Had the team designed a follow-on verification experiment, it would have discovered that the solution was unstable and far from permanent.

This author was then hurriedly called in by the company to solve the problem. The fraction factorial approach was scrapped. A fresh start was made, first, with Paired Comparisons, then Product/Process Search and verified with a B versus C to confirm the permanency of the improvement.

What Is B versus C?

The symbols B and C stand for two different products, processes, methods, or business policies/practices, where C is labeled the current product and B is, supposedly, a better product. But B and C could be two alternate processes, alternate methods, or alternate policies. The task is to determine which is better.

B versus C is a nonparametric comparative experimentation, where no assumption of normality is necessary for either the B or C product or process distribution. The term nonparametric refers to the third type of data—rank data—discussed in Chapter 12. The power of nonparametric ranking is that it needs only extremely small sample sizes—typically three B's and three C's—to compare two products, processes, or methods and determine, with a very high degree of confidence, which one is better. See Figure 7-1 for its place in the detailed problem-solving roadmap.

Objectives

B versus C should be used as a verification tool rather than as an initial problem-solving tool. The basic purpose of this technique is to determine which of two products or processes is better in terms of quality and reliability, with confidence of 90 percent or higher, using very small sample sizes. Its additional objectives are:

1. To predict how much better a given product or process is than another, with confidence of 90 percent or higher.
2. To assure the permanency of an improved product or process over a previous one.
3. To select one product or process over another, even if there is no improvement in quality, because of some other tangible benefit, such as cost or cycle time.
4. To evaluate more than just two products, processes, materials (B, C, D, E, etc.) simultaneously.
5. To extend B versus C to almost any field of human endeavor.
6. To serve as a poor man's Gallup poll in preliminary surveys.

Principles

1. *Process Capability Studies.* These studies are usually used to compare two processes—a current one (C) and a possibly better one (B)—with 50 to 100 units run on each process. The results could be any one of four frequency distributions (Figure 15-1).

> In Figure 15-1A, there is no difference between B and C, this is called the null hypothesis.
> In Figure 15-1B, B is better than C, but there is some uncertainty about the improvement, with an area of overlap, where some C

Figure 15-1. Four Distributions of B and C Processes

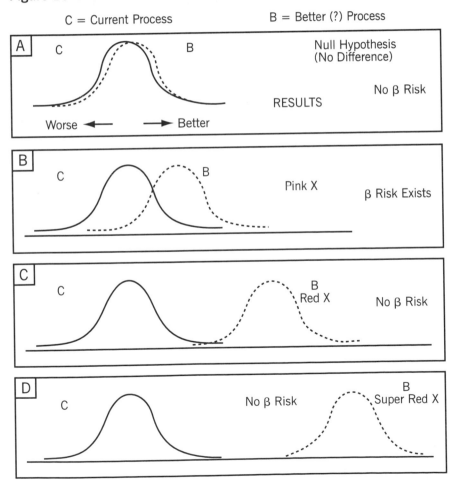

C = Current Process   B = Better (?) Process

A   C   B   Null Hypothesis
                           (No Difference)

                           No β Risk
                   RESULTS

Worse ◄——   ——► Better

B   C   B   Pink X   β Risk Exists

C   C   B
                        Red X   No β Risk

D   B
     C   No β Risk   Super Red X

units are actually better than some B units. This may be a Pink X or Pale Pink X improvement.
> In Figure 15-1C, the worst B units are equal to the best C units—a Red X improvement.
> In Figure 15-1D, the worst B units are much better than the best C units—a super Red X improvement.

But such a process capability, with a total of 100 to 200 units, would require a great expenditure of time, money, and manpower.

2. *The "Six-Pack Test."* In all of our DOE techniques, we aim for simplicity, graphics, and effectiveness. We also aim for small sample sizes. In B versus C, we speak of a "six-pack test"—with three Coors and three Budweisers! This, of course, is just a memory jogger—a humorous and easy way to remember the most popular sample sizes in B versus C tests: three B's and three C's—"a six-pack test."

3. *The Laws of Combinations.* Conventional statistics indicate that it is the absolute size of a sample drawn from a population that determines how closely the sample represents the population. The larger the absolute size (not the percentage of the population) the closer it is to the population. How, then, can a tiny sample size of three B's and three C's come close to representing each of two populations? The answer lies in the power of the laws of combination, given by the formula:

$$\text{Number of combinations} = \frac{n!}{(n-r!)r!}$$ where n = the total number of units, r = the total number of units of one type, and (n − r) = the total number of the old type.

With three B's and three C's, the number of combinations =

$$\frac{6!}{3!3!} = \frac{6\times5\times4\times3\times2\times1}{3\times2\times1\times3\times2\times1} = 20.$$

Therefore, there are 20 ways of arranging three B's and three C's without repeating the same order of combinations, as shown below.

	1	2	3	4	5	6	7	8	9	10	11	12	13	14	15	16	17	18	19	20
↑ Best	B	B	B	B	B	B	B	B	B	B	C	C	C	C	C	C	C	C	C	C
	B	B	B	C	C	C	C	C	C	C	B	B	B	B	B	B	C	C	C	C
	B	C	C	B	C	B	B	C	C	C	B	B	B	C	C	C	B	B	B	C
	C	B	C	B	B	C	C	B	B	C	B	C	C	B	B	C	B	B	C	B
Worst	C	C	C	C	B	B	C	B	C	B	C	B	C	B	C	B	B	C	B	B
↓	C	C	B	C	C	C	B	C	B	B	C	C	B	C	B	B	C	B	B	B

So, if three B's and three C's are ranked in descending order—from best to worst—in a B versus C test, there is only one way out of 20 that the three B's would rank above the three C's entirely due to chance, entirely due to the fickle finger of fate! That means there is a 1 in 20 chance that an observed improvement that all three B's are better than all 3 C's is false, and that in actuality there is no improvement. A 1 in 20 chance is a 5 percent risk, even if three B's outrank three C's, that there is no improvement. Conversely, there is a 19 in 20 chance, i.e., a 95 percent confidence, if three B's outrank three C's, that there is definitely an improvement of B over C.

4. α *and* β *Risks*. An experimenter can make two decisions based on what the experiment says versus the actual (but unknown) situation, as shown below:

Decision Based on Actual Experiment	Real (But Unknown) Situation	
	B is better than C	B is the same as C
	Yes	No
B appears better than C	OK	Type I Error α risk
B appears to be same as C	Type II Error β risk	Ok

If the experiment indicates that B is better than C (three B's outrank three C's), then the experimenter is rejecting the null hypothesis (H_o) of B being the same as C. If, in reality, B is truly better than C (in the real, but unknown situation), the right decision was made by the experimenter. If, however, there is actually no improvement, the experimenter will have committed a Type I error; its probability is called the α risk.

If the experiment indicates a mixed rank, where not all three B's outrank all three C's, i.e., B is the same as C, the experimenter is not rejecting the null hypothesis. If, in reality, B is not better than C, the experimenter has made the right decision. But if B is actually better than C, the experimenter will have committed a Type II error; its probability is called the β risk.

The α risk, therefore, is defined as the risk of rejecting the null hypothesis, i.e., assuming improvement where no improvement exists. The β risk is defined as the risk of accepting the null hypothesis, i.e., assuming no improvement when a desirable improvement does exist.

In simpler terms, the α risk is used to detect whether B is better than C. The β risk is used to detect whether the *degree of improvement* of B over

C is sufficient or not. Figure 15-1 shows a β risk only in Figure 15-1B where there is an overlap and uncertainty of improvement. Figures 15-1C and 15-1D have no overlap and no β risk. Figure 15-1A has certainty, but of *no* improvement and no β risk.

Methodology

Table 15-1 is the authoritative guide, based on the laws of combination, in determining sample sizes and the appropriate α and β risks for B versus C tests.

Risk and Confidence Levels

Select the appropriate risk or confidence levels. The complement of risk is confidence.

> * Moderate importance—up to a cost of $10,000—0.10 or 10 percent risk (90 percent confidence).
> * Higher importance—up to a cost of $100,000—0.05 or 5 percent risk (95 percent confidence).
> * Critical importance—up to a cost of $100 million and a few lives lost—0.01 or 1 percent risk (99 percent confidence).
> * Supercritical importance—many lives lost—0.001 or 0.1 percent risk (99.9 percent confidence).

Sample Size for B's and C's

Select the appropriate number of samples of the B and C products/processes within each confidence basis. Because C is the current process, there are likely to be more C units available for testing than the newer B units.

However, a simple guideline for most B versus C experiments in industry is to use the six-pack test—three B's and three C's, with an α risk of 5 percent (or a confidence of 95 percent.) It has the advantage of (1) ease of remembering (3 and 3), and (2) it gives the smallest total number of units to test.

Importance of Randomization

A very important precaution is to randomize the sequence of testing, as described in Chapter 14. Running the three C's first and then switching to the three B's—a logical sequence—can bias the results, because the

Table 15-1. B versus C Sample Sizes and α, β Risks

(Based on No Overlap rule)
α Risk: Risk of rejecting the null hypothesis (no difference).
β Risk: Risk of accepting the null hypothesis when improvements exist.

Consequences of a Wrong Decision	No. of Randomized (Sets of) Tests B's	C's	Values of K (Differences Between Means) β Risk = 0.50	0.10	0.05
α Risk Confidence 0.001 0.999	2	(43)	3.0* / 3.9*	4.0 / 5.1	4.3 / 5.5
Super Critical	3	16	2.5 / 3.2	3.6 / 4.5	3.9 / 5.0
> Many lives lost	4	10	2.3 / 2.9	3.4 / 4.3	3.8 / 4.8
> Food poisoning	5	8	2.2 / 2.9	3.4 / 4.3	3.7 / 4.7
> Nuclear reactors	6	6	2.2 / 2.8	3.3 / 4.2	3.7 / 4.7
α Risk Confidence 0.01 0.99	2	13	2.3 / 3.0	3.4 / 4.4	3.8 / 4.6
Critical	4	7	2.0 / 2.6	3.2 / 4.1	3.6 / 4.6
> A few lives lost	4	5	2.0 / 2.5	3.1 / 4.0	3.5 / 4.5
> Up to $100 million	5	4	2.0 / 2.5	3.1 / 4.0	3.5 / 4.5
α Risk Confidence 0.05 0.95					
Important	1	19	2.5 / 3.2	3.6 / 4.6	3.9 / 5.0
> Up to $100K	2	5	1.7 / 2.2	3.0 / 3.8	3.4 / 4.3
	3	3	1.6 / 2.0	2.9 / 3.7	3.3 / 4.2
	4	3	1.7 / 2.2	3.0 / 3.8	3.4 / 4.3
α Risk Confidence 0.10 0.90					
Moderate	1	9	2.1 / 2.6	3.2 / 4.1	3.6 / 4.6
> Up to $10K	2	3	1.4 / 1.8	2.7 / 3.5	3.2 / 4.0
	3	2	1.4 / 1.8	2.7 / 3.5	3.2 / 4.0

Source: Copyright 1988 Red X Technologies, Inc.
*Upper case values where $\sigma_B = \sigma_C$
**Lower case values where $\sigma_B \neq \sigma_C$ (generally, when $\sigma_B = 1.5\,\sigma_C$ or $\sigma_C = 1.5\,\sigma_B$)

uncontrollable or noise factors are not given an equal chance of either entering or not entering the experiment.

Rank Order

Use variable data. Or at least convert attribute data in gathering B's and C's to variable data, using the Likert scale. Avoid percentages of defects or percentages of yields. Then rank the units, B and C, from the best to the worst.

Decision Rule

There are two approaches in B versus C decision:

> *No-Overlap Rule.* This allows no overlap. More properly referred to as the no overlap end count, the three B's must all outrank the three C's (or vice versa). Then B is judged to be better than C, with 95 percent confidence (or vice versa). But the no-overlap rule must be invoked "a priori," i.e., before the experiment. If only one or two B's outrank the C's (i.e., if there is an overlap in the rankings), B is not considered better than C, nor is C considered better than B. Given the small sample size and an overlap, there is not enough confidence that B is an improvement over C.
> *The Overlap/End-Count Rule.* This is the famous Tukey Test, discussed at length in relation to Paired Comparisons and Product/Process Search. In several industrial situations, it may be preferable to allow some overlap and still keep the risk of wrong decisions very low. As an example, if the ranks of five B's and five C's are:

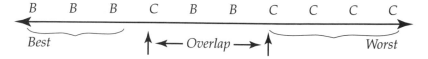

The B end-count = 3; the C end-count = 4; and the total end-count = 7. Here, an overlap (of 3) exists. But, again, the overlap rule must be invoked in advance. Further, the number of samples for B and C are larger—6 or more for each. The sample size for B, i.e., n B, can be smaller or larger than the sample size for C, i.e., n C. But the ratio of n B to n C should not be greater than 3:4 (or 4:3). The risk and confidence levels are the same, as indicated in the discussions of Paired Comparisons and Product/Process Search.

Risk (α)	Confidence	End-count ($\geq$)
0.10	90%	6
0.05	95%	7
0.01	99%	10
0.001	99.5%	13

β Risk: Determining the Magnitude of Improvement of B Over C

It is not enough to know whether B is better than C. It is economically and technically useful to predict, before the experiment, the desired magnitude of the real improvement. The β risk associated with this magnitude is assessed by the separation between the mean of the B units and the mean of the C units. This separation or delta (Δ) distance is measured in $K\sigma_C$ units, where K is a stipulated number selected in advance by the experimenter and σ_C is the standard deviation of the C units. (There may be too few of the B units to determine its σ_B standard deviation accurately.) Table 15-1 shows the K values for β risks of 0.5, 0.1, and 0.05 (or confidences of 50 percent, 90 percent and 95 percent). The upper case values for K assume that $\sigma_B = \sigma_C$. The lower case values for K assume that $\sigma_B \neq \sigma_C$ (either could be greater than the other).

As an example, if three B's and three C's are tested, and all three B's outrank all three C's, then we have 95 percent confidence that the B's are better than the C's. But how much better? For this, we move to the right side of Table 15-1 and obtain the value of K in the 3B, 3C row for 0.1 risk (i.e., 90 percent confidence). Assuming $\sigma_B = \sigma_C$, the value of K from Table 15-1 is 2.9. If the average of the C units is $\overline{X}_C$ and that of the B units is $\overline{X}_B$, then the separation: $\overline{X}_B - \overline{X}_C$ should be equal to or greater than 2.9 σ_C to obtain a 90 percent confidence that this improvement will be detected (or only a 10 percent risk that the improvement will go undetected). Figure 15-2 illustrates this graphically.

Case Studies and Workshop Exercises

Case Study 1: Cracked Epoxy

In Chapter 13, on variable search, Case Study 2 described the successful outcome of a situation in which the epoxy bonding a substrate and a header was cracking during curing. The Red X was curing temperature, which produced zero defects at 150°C, but was producing a 10 percent defect rate at 120°. In addition, the volume of epoxy and its viscosity, both unimportant, could be reduced to reduce material costs.

Figure 15-2. β Risk: Determining the Magnitude of Improvement of
              B Over C

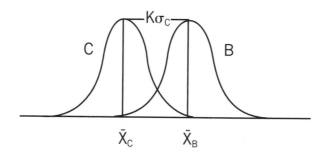

where: $\bar{X}_C$ is the average of the C product/process;
       $\bar{X}_B$ is the average of the B product/process;
       σ_C and σ_B are the standard deviations of the C and B units, respectively;
       K = 2.9 for a confidence of 90%, if $\sigma_B = \sigma_C$; and
       K = 3.7 for a confidence of 90%, if $\sigma_B \neq \sigma_C$.
K σ_C is the minimum separation required for $X_B - X_C$.

To ensure that the improvement with the higher temperature was permanent, as well as to observe any epoxy cracking that occurred when the volume and viscosity of the epoxy were reduced, a B versus C confirmation experiment was conducted on three B units and three C units, as follows:

Parameter	B Process	C Process
Curing temperature (°C)	150°	120°
Volume of epoxy (lead coverage)	60%	75%
Epoxy viscosity (CPS)	150,000	180,000

The Green Y, as before, was a Likert scale for epoxy crack, with 0 as no crack and 10 as a 100 percent crack. The score was weighted defects = number of defective units × Likert scale.
    The ranking of three B's and three C's (run in randomized sequence) were:

Unit Type	No. of Defects	Defect Type Likert Scale	Weighted Defect Score
B	0	0	0
B	0	0	0
B	0	0	0
C	1	2	2
C	1	4	4
C	1	5	5

This validated that the B process was better than the C process, with 90 percent confidence. It also validated that the reduced levels in epoxy volume and viscosity did not degrade performance.

Workshop Exercise 1: Wire Bond Strength

A B versus C experiment was conducted to determine if a process change (B) had improved the strength of wire bonds (through a calibrated pull test) in an IC chip, as compared to the current process C. The following had been decided before the start of the experiment:

1. An α risk of 5%.
2. A β risk of 5%.
3. No overlap permitted.
4. The standard deviation of B was 3.0 gm.
5. σ_B was assumed equal to σ_C.

The results of the three B tests, followed by three C tests (gm.) were:

B: 225, 223, 219
C: 217, 212, 210

Questions

1. Is the B process better than C? With what degree of confidence?
2. Assuming that the test was redone and the sequence of testing was: $B_1, C_2, C_1, B_3, C_3, B_2$, is the B process better than C? With what degree of confidence?
3. Calculate the separation between $\overline{X}_B$ and $\overline{X}_C$.
4. Is the magnitude of the B process improvement over C enough? With what degree of confidence?

Answers

1. No, No, No! The B versus C test sequence was not random. There-fore, the test is invalid and totally useless.
2. Now that the testing has been done in random order sequence, it is valid and the three B's outrank the three C's, with 95 percent confidence (5% risk).
3. $\overline{X}_B = 222.3$; $\overline{X}_C = 213$; so, $\overline{X}_B - \overline{X}_C = 9.3$.
4. The minimum separation of $\overline{X}_B - \overline{X}_C = K\sigma_C$. Since $\sigma_B = \sigma_C = 3$ and the β risk is 5 percent, $K = 3.3$, so, $K\sigma_C = 3.3 \times 3.0 = 9.9$. Since the actual separation of 9.3 is less than the required mini-mum separation of 9.9, the magnitude of the B process improve-ment over C for a confidence of 90 percent is inadequate.

Case Study 2: The Press Brake

In the Variables Search Case Study 1 on the press brake, a B versus C confirmation experiment was conducted to assure that the improve-ments—associated with metal bow and holding of the material—were indeed permanent. The Green Y was the dimension tolerance that pre-viously could not be held within $\pm 0.005''$ and that through variables search had been reduced to $\pm 0.002''$. The B versus C testing was done in random order and was expressed in deviations from nominal in multiples of $0.001''$. The α risk chosen was 5 percent (95 percent confidence), and the overlap method (Tukey test) was used because some of the C results might be better than B, and an overlap was likely to occur. Twelve B's and 13 C's were selected as the sample sizes. The results, in random sequence, are shown in Figure 15-3.

Increasing B and C Sample Sizes to Reduce Uncertainty of Predicting the Magnitude of B Improvement Over C

In the no-overlap decision when running three B units and three C units, if the three B's all outrank the three C's, there is 95 percent confidence that the B product is better than C. If the reverse is true, with the three C's outranking the three B's, there is also 95 percent confidence that C is better than B. But if this end-count is less than six (i.e., not all B's are better than all C's), any improvement can only be estimated by the sepa-ration distance between $\overline{X}_B$ and $\overline{X}_C$. For 95 percent confidence (β risk of five percent) and assuming $\sigma_B = \sigma_C$, K from Table 15-1 is 3.3, and so the minimum required separation between $\overline{X}_B$ and $\overline{X}_C$ is 3.3 $\overline{X}_C$. But such a

Figure 15-3. Case Study 2: The Press Brake

C

2, 5, 5, 4, 6, 9, 7, 1, 6, 4, 8, 2, 1

B

2, 0, 1, 2, 2, 2, 1, 1, 0, 1, 2 , 2

In descending rank order, the results were:

0	B		B end-count = 3
0	B		
0	B		
1, 1, 1	B	1, 1 C	Overlap
2, 2, 2, 2, 2,	B	2, 2 C	
		4, 4 C	
		5, 5C	
		6, 6 C	C end-count = 9
		7 C	
		8 C	
		9 C	

Note: Total end-count = 3 + 9. So the confidence was 99.5 percent—greater than the required 95 percent—that the B process was an improvement over the C process.

minimum separation may be too wide in actual practice. Here, the required K of 3.3 is too large.

In order to restore the same confidence when the actual separation of $\overline{X}_B$ and $\overline{X}_C$ is small, the required K must be reduced. This can be done if the sample size of each of the three B's and each of the three C's can be increased to, say, 2 to 10 units, and the average of each of the B's and each of the C's can be calculated. (Randomization between the B's and C's is in order but not within each B or C.) That means that a total of six to 30 B's and six to 30 C's may be required, a trade-off for the lower separation required for $\overline{X}_B - \overline{X}_C$. The needed sample size is determined by the Central Limit Theorem:

$$\sigma_{\overline{x}} = \frac{\sigma_x}{\sqrt{n}},$$ where n is the required sample size and $\sigma_{\overline{x}}$ and σ_x are the standard deviation of the sample and the population, respectively.

Rewriting the above formula: $\sqrt{n} = \dfrac{\sigma_x}{\sigma_{\overline{x}}}$ or $n = \dfrac{\sigma_x^2}{\sigma_{\overline{x}}^2}$. (Equation 1)

Substituting K for σ

The set size $n = \dfrac{\text{Table } K^2}{\text{Required } K^2}$ (from Table 15-1).

The minimum separation between $\overline{X}_B$ and $\overline{X}_C$ is $K\sigma_{\overline{x}}$ (see Table 15-1).

For 95% confidence, K (from Table 15-1) is 3.3. So the minimum separation is 3.3 $\sigma_{\overline{x}}$. If we want a lower separation, and K is reduced to 2:

From Equation 1: $n = \dfrac{3.3^2}{2^2} = \dfrac{10.89}{4} = 2.72 \approx 3$.

This means that each of the three B's must be increased to three units, for a total of nine B units, and each of the three C units must be increased to three units, for a total of nine C units, to get a lower K and permit a lower required $\overline{X}_B - \overline{X}_C$.

Table 15-2 has been constructed from Equation 1. It shows that to reduce K values and thus accommodate a lower separation, the sample sizes for each B and each C have to be increased. The table is based on a β risk of 5 percent (or 95 percent confidence). There would be slightly different sample sizes for β risks of 10 percent or if $\sigma_B = \sigma_C$.

For example, in Workshop Exercise 1 on wire bond strength, it was shown that the minimum separation of 9.9 between $\overline{X}_B$ and $\overline{X}_C$ was not met. If the sample size of each B and each C had been increased to 2, K would be reduced from 3.3 to 2.33 and the minimum separation required would be 2.33 $\times$ 3 = 6.99. Then, the actual separation of 9.3 would be sufficient with 95 percent confidence.

Table 15-2. Sample Size Increase to Narrow $\overline{X}_B$–$\overline{X}_C$

Minimum Required Separation $\overline{X}_B$–$\overline{X}_C$	Sample Size (n) Needed for Each of 3 B's and 3 C's
K = 3.3	1 B, 1 C
K = 2.33	2 B's, 2 C's
K = 2.0	3 B's, 3 C's
K = 1.65	4 B's, 4 C's
K = 1.47	5 B's, 5 C's
K = 1.34	6 B's, 6 C's
K = 1.26	7 B's, 7 C's
K = 1.16	8 B's, 8 C's
K = 1.10	9 B's, 9 C's
K = 1.03	10 B's, 10 C's

Modified Tests to Determine That C Is Worse Than B

The Tukey test, as discussed in this and previous chapters, is essentially independent of sample size as long as the good versus bad, (+) versus (−) or B versus C ratios are somewhat equal and do not exceed a 3 to 4 ratio (are within 25 percent of one another in size).

But the Tukey test is a two-tailed test, i.e., B can be worse than C or C can be worse than B. If, however, the only concern is to make sure that B is not worse than C, we can modify the Tukey end-counts to reflect only those situations in which C is worse than B. Here, too, the laws of combination and the multiplication theorem can be invoked.

As an example, if we have four B's and four C's, the probability that the worst unit is a C is: $^4/_8$. The probability that the second worst is also a C is $^4/_8 \times ^3/_7$. The probability that all four worst units are C's are:

$$\frac{4}{8} \times \frac{3}{7} \times \frac{1}{5} = 0.014$$

So the risk here is 0.014 or 1.4 percent, and the confidence is 98.6 percent. Similar calculations can be made to arrive at Table 15-3.

Expanding the Number of Alternatives Beyond Two (Beyond B and C)

So far, this chapter has dealt with only two choices or two alternatives—a B and a C. But more products/processes/methods than just these two can be simultaneously evaluated; e.g., B, C, D, E, F, G, etc., using an extension of the Tukey test approach and increasing the number of samples for each B, C, D, E test.

Table 15-3. Minimum End-Counts for C's Being Worse Than B's
(When the B:C sample ratio is 1:1)

Confidence	No. of C's	Minimum Bottom End-Counts for C
Critical	5 to 6	5
99%	7 to 19	6
	20 to ∞	7
Important	3	3
95%	4 to 15	4
	16 to ∞	5

Table 15-4, based on this Tukey test extension, shows the total minimum end-count (top and bottom) needed to assure the appropriate confidence:

> two levels of confidence: 99% and 95%;
> 2, 3, 4, 5, and 6 choices; i.e., B and C and up to B through G; and
> different sample sizes, n, for *each* choice.

Workshop Exercise 2: Choice Between Four Suppliers

Four suppliers—B, C, D, and E—were being evaluated by a manufacturer for surface finish on a critical part used in its assembly. A B versus C versus D versus E experiment was performed, requiring a confidence level of 95 percent. Four units were selected from each supplier and a rank order established, as shown in Table 15-5. Four possible outcomes are listed in columns 1, 2, 3, and 4.

Table 15-4. Rank Order for More Than Two Choices (i.e., B, C, D, E, etc.)

Confidence	\multicolumn{10}{c}{*Number of Choices/Alternatives (B, C, D, E, etc.)*}

Confidence	\multicolumn{2}{c}{*2*}	\multicolumn{2}{c}{*3*}	\multicolumn{2}{c}{*4*}	\multicolumn{2}{c}{*5*}	\multicolumn{2}{c}{*6*}
	n	*Min EC*	*n*	*Min EC*	*n*	*Min EC*	*n*	*Min EC*	*n*	*Min EC*
	6 to 14	9	4 to 9	12	4	14	4	17	3	18
	15	10	10 to 12	13	5	15	5	18	4	20
			13	14	6	16	6	19	5	23
99%					7	16	7	21	6	24
					8	17	8	24	7	26
					9	18	9	24	8	28
					10	19	10	25		
	4	6	4	9	3	12	3	13	3	16
	5 to 13	7	5 to 7	10	4, 5	13	4	15	4	18
			8 to 10	11	6, 7	14	5	16	5	20
95%			11 to 13	12	8	15	6	18	6	23
					9	16	7	19	7	25
					10	17	8	21	8	27
							9	22		
							10	24		

Table 15-5. Ranking of Four Suppliers: Workshop Exercise

		Column 1	*Column 2*	*Column 3*	*Column 4*
Best	1	B	B	B	B
	2	B	C	E	B
	3	E	D	B	B
	4	B	D	E	C
	5	B	D	C	B
	6	C	B	D	E
	7	D	C	B	E
	8	C	D	E	C
	9	E	B	D	C
	10	E	C	C	E
	11	C	B	D	D
	12	E	E	C	E
	13	D	E	D	C
	14	C	C	B	D
	15	D	E	C	D
Worst	16	D	E	E	D
Total End-count					

Questions

1. Calculate the end-count of the best supplier in each column.
2. If the results were those shown in Column 1, what conclusions would you draw?
3. If the results were those shown in Column 2, what conclusions would you draw?
4. If the results were those shown in Column 3, what conclusions would you draw?
5. If the results were those shown in Column 4, what conclusions would you draw?

Answers

As Table 15-4 shows, the minimum end-count for 95 percent confidence and four choices is 13.

1. As shown in Table 15-6, Column 1, there are 2 B's on top and 11 C, D, and E's at the bottom. So, B has an end-count of 13 (2 + 11) ranks. So B is significantly better than suppliers C, D, and E.

Table 15-6. Ranking of Four Suppliers: Answers

		Column 1		Column 2		Column 3	Column 4	
Best	1	End-Count for B B		B ⌐E.C for B		B	For B B	
	2	B	End-Count for D	C		E	B	
	3	E		End-Count for E D		B	B	End-Count for D
	4	B		D		E	C	
	5	B		D		C	B	
	6	End-Count for B C		B		D	E	
	7	D		C		B	E	
	8	C		D		E	C	
	9	E		B		D	End-Count for B C	
	10	E		C		C	E	
	11	C		B		D	D	
	12	E		E	End-Count for B	C	E	
	13	D		E		D	C	
	14	C	End-Count for D	End-Count for E C		B	D	End-Count for D
	15	D		E		C	D	
Worst	16	D		E		E	D	
Total End-Count: EC		For B: 2 +11 = 13 For D: 6 + 2 = 8		For B: 1 + 5 = 6 For E: 11 + 2 = 13		For B, C, D, E 0	For B: 3 + 11 = 14 For D: 10 + 3 = 13	

As shown further in Table 15-6, Column 1, there are 2 D's at the bottom and six non-D's at the top. So D has an end-count of 8 ranks, not enough to be called the worst supplier.

2. In Column 2, there is one B at the top and 5 non-B's at the bottom. So B has an end-count of 6 from the top, not enough to be called the best supplier. In Column 2, there are two E's at the bottom and 11 non-E's at the top. So E has an end-count of 13 ranks from the bottom, so E is significantly the worst supplier.

3. In Column 3, the round end count: for B = 1 + 2; for C = 5 + 1; for D = 5 + 3; for E = 1 + 1; so none of the suppliers have an end-count even close to the minimum 13. Hence, there is no significant difference between any of the four suppliers.

In Column 4, there are 3 B's on top and 11 non-B's at the bottom; there are 10 non-D's at the top and 3 D's at the bottom. So, B and D have end-counts of 14 and 13 from top and bottom, respectively. Hence B is significantly the best and D the worst supplier.

A Special B versus C Stress Tests to Failure

B versus C is a versatile technique for validating improvements in industrial problem solving. However, there are three areas in which the traditional B versus C techniques discussed so far may be inadequate:

1. When it is difficult to convert an attribute Green Y into a variable, even utilizing the Likert scale. For example, when a product or process has so many defect modes, say, seven to 20, that it becomes impractical to attach a Likert score to such defects, either singly or collectively, then the defects must be combined into an overall defective percentage or yield percentage. In such cases, three B's and 3 C's, or even larger samples for each B and each C, may not be adequate to detect differences between two such defect percentages or yield percentages.

2. When the defect levels in both the B and C product/process are so small, say 50 ppm and below, that three B's and three C's or even larger samples for each B and each C may not be sensitive enough to detect differences between B and C.

3. When the problem does not manifest itself as a quality problem in the plant, but develops as a reliability problem later on in the field in the hands of a customer after months of use.

For all of these situations, a special technique is to develop a Green Y called stress test to failure. This technique is part of a powerful reliability tool called Multiple Environment Over Stress Test (MEOST), introduced in Chapter 3 and explained in detail in Chapter 22.

Briefly, it means stressing, say, three B's and three C's, with one or more environments or stresses and continuing to overstress beyond design limits until all the B's and all the C's fail. The Green Y then becomes stress to failure or time to failure. If the three B's all require a higher stress to failure or a longer time to failure than all three C's, there is 95 percent confidence that the B product/process is better than the C. Similarly, the magnitude of the improvement can be estimated. Of course, care must be taken to ensure that the failure mode is realistic and parallels historic failure modes in the field. It should not be an artificial failure that is not likely to occur in the field.

Here, too, it may be sufficient to prove that a new material, B, introduced because it is less expensive, is not any worse than the old C material.

Case Study 3: Gear Train Motor

A manufacturer of an instrument used in off-the-road vehicles had a very low failure rate, 120 ppm per year, on a motor driving a gear train. It wanted to substitute a motor from another supplier that had met all of the specifications of the motor from the current supplier. The projected cost savings of $225,000 per year made it economically attractive. But the engineers were concerned about reliability after six to 12 months of use in the rough environments in which off-the-road vehicles regularly operate. The current failure rate of 120 ppm was totally acceptable to the company's customers.

Normal B versus C evaluations would not suffice because of the low failure rate of the present motor and the several months needed to detect failures. Therefore, a B versus C test for 99 percent confidence was established, and five current (C) motors and four new (B) motors were selected. The Green Y was determined to be time to failure when all nine motors were subjected to simultaneous multiple environments (stresses), including vibration, shock, extremes of temperature, humidity, and dust. The stresses were gradually escalated, even beyond design stress, until failures were observed on all nine units. Randomization was not needed because all nine motors were tested in the same multiple environment chambers at the same time.

The results in terms of hours to failure were:
C Motors: 148, 163, 182, 225, 237.
B Motors: 171, 196, 203, 221.

After rank ordering the C's and B's indicated that the B motors were no worse that the C's in terms of reliability, they were authorized for use. After use of the B motors in the field for two years, the failure industry proved to be 132 ppm per year—an insignificant increase from the original level of 120 ppm of the C motors.

Industrial Applications for B versus C

Applications of the B versus C technique in industry are as interesting as they are diverse. There are two outcomes: (1) B is better than C with a desired confidence level (generally 95 percent or higher); (2) B is not better than C, but is no worse than C from a quality perspective. Table 15-7 lists several applications for each outcome.

For example, one of the very important uses of B versus C introduced by this author was his insistence that every engineering change made in current production with a B versus C test to confirm either a quality improvement or to certify that there was no quality deterioration.

Of course, adherence to the "six-pack test"—three B's and three C's—should not be slavish. In some cases, the overlap approach is more appropriate than the no-overlap, even though it means somewhat larger sample sizes. In some cases, increasing the sample size of each B and each C (to two to 10) *reduces the uncertainty of the magnitude of the B improvement*. In some cases, it is only necessary to prove that C is worse than B. Then, only the bottom end-counts for C matter. In some cases, the number of alternatives can be increased from two (B and C) to three to six or even

Table 15-7. Applications of B versus C Trials

When B Is Better Than C	When B Is No Worse Than C
› Design changes	› Cost reduction
› Process changes	› Cycle-time improvement
› Manufacturing method changes	› Variability reduction
› Reliability, life trials	› Safety
› New equipment	› Easier manufacturability
› New supplier/materials	› Ergonomics (user friendly)
› Yield improvement	› Space reduction
	› Environment improvement
	› Less expensive tooling
	› Less capital equipment
	› Increased uptime
	› Machine efficiency
	› Opening tolerances
	› Eliminating an operation/test

more. And finally, stress test to failure can be a powerful extension of the B versus C methodology in reliability evaluations or forcing the separation of very small defect levels in B versus C.

Administrative Applications for B versus C

Outside of the realm of products and manufacturing, the applications of B versus C techniques are almost limitless. Whenever any two (or more) alternatives need to be evaluated, B versus C can be put to good use. Table 15-8 lists just a few of many, many possible applications. Companies

Table 15-8. Applications of B versus C in Administrative Services

› Focus groups, clinics, panels
› Surveys: marketing, political, economic, social, health
› Advertising
› Sales promotion, sales forecasting
› Job enrichment: vertical and horizontal
› Company policies: working conditions, fringe benefits, insurance, flextime, etc.
› Hospitals: admission, emergency rooms, nursing, billing, etc.
› Schools: recruitment, scholarships, methods of instruction, methods of learning, etc.

spend millions of dollars in advertising, marketing, and sales promotions. In the political arena, surveys are conducted on candidate preferences, with sample sizes ranging from 500 to 2,000 people. A faster, simpler, and less costly B versus C technique in such situations can give an early indication of trends and preferences, which—if necessary—can be followed by more conventional methods.

Case Study 4: Automobile Styling

In testing product alternatives, companies traditionally introduce them in test markets; run advertisements in newspapers, on radio and on television; or conduct extensive customer preference surveys. All of these practices do have value. But results are not known until hundreds of thousands or millions of dollars have been spent.

One car company decided to try a preliminary B versus C test on two styling approaches for its cars. In its focus group evaluations, it presented the two styling alternatives to 20 panelists. Each was asked to rate the two styles on a Likert scale of 1 to 10, with 10 being the best and 1 the worst. Based on the panelists' ratings, Style 1 appeared superior to Style 2, with a total end-count of 11, representing a confidence level of 99 percent.

The car company did not believe in the power of the technique or in the high confidence it generated. It followed up the B versus C test with more traditional market research and came to the same conclusion after having spent over $45,000 on a market research study.

B versus C in Opinion Surveys: A Poor Man's Gallup Poll

This author, in his public and private seminars, has tested the waters for a B versus C determination of the choice between two political candidates in a close contest for public office or between two controversial issues. It is intended to be more of a game interlude than a serious methodology.

Generally, two to 16 people are chosen at random from the participants and asked to cast their secret ballots for one or the other of the two candidates or two issues, along with a Likert scale from 1 to 10 (with 10 being the best and 1 the worst) to rate the intensity of preference for the selected candidate. I've had 80 percent success in predicting the winning candidate or issue in dozens of such contests. The exercises, labeled "A Poor Man's Gallup Poll," is more for fun than a serious substitute for a rigorous poll. But it does illustrate the dramatic power of small numbers and innovative techniques. (I have not had the inclination to pass this technique on to the Gallup or Roper organizations!)

Questions for DOE Teams as Guidelines for B versus C

1. Is the B versus C test used only as a verification technique to assure the permanency of an improvement made with previous DOE techniques?
2. Is the use of a B versus C test discouraged as a means of trying out a proposed or hoped-for improvement, without prior use of other DOE techniques? The reason is that such hoped-for improvements are based on opinions, hunches, guesses, and theories of technical personnel. Given the track record of engineers in their ability to guess at root causes, going directly to a B versus C test would likely result in failures—and failures more than once.
3. How was the α risk (or corresponding confidence) level determined?
4. Was the no-overlap or the overlap method selected? Why?
5. How was the appropriate number of B and C units determined?
6. Was the sequence of testing the B and C units randomized?
7. In determining whether there was improvement of B over C, was there also concern about the magnitude of the improvement?
8. What β risk was selected? Why?
9. If the object was to reduce the uncertainty of the magnitude of the improvement of B over C, was an appropriate lower K value selected and the sample size of each B and C unit correspondingly increased?
10. If the objective was to prove that the C's were worse than the B's, was the number of C's and the minimum end-count for the C's determined from the appropriate table?
11. If there were more than two choices or alternatives—such as B, C, D, E, etc.—was the appropriate table used to determine the sample size for each B, C, D, E unit and the minimum required end-count?
12. Is a stress-to-failure used to assess improvement of B over C if the Green Y can only be measured in yield or defect percentages; or if the defect rates of B's and C's are very low (below 500 ppm); or if the problem is one of field reliability rather than plant quality?
13. Would other economic/ergonomic/environmental factors justify going to B even if there is no quality improvement over C?
14. Have any B versus C studies been considered in administrative and service areas of the company?

Questions for Top Management in Reviewing
DOE Team Projects

1. Has the temptation to use B versus C as a initial DOE been resisted?
2. Is the primary use of a B versus C tool to verify the permanency of a product/process improvement?
3. Why were the appropriate confidence levels chosen $(1 - \alpha$ risk$)$?
4. How were the appropriate sample sizes determined?
5. Was the sequence of the B versus C tests randomized?
6. Were there more than two alternatives to be evaluated (e.g., B, C, D, E, etc.), and were the appropriate techniques used?
7. Were stress-to-failure methods used in cases such as very low defect rates and to assess reliability differences and still employing B versus C techniques?
8. Even though B was not an improvement over C for quality, was it still used for economic and environmental reasons?
9. Have B versus C techniques been employed in white collar/service work?

Part V
. . . .
DOE Optimization

16. Scatter Plots to Achieve Realistic Specifications and Tolerances

17. Response Surface Methodology (RSM): To Optimize Interactions

Part III dealt with five clue-generation techniques for problem solving—the Multi-Vari, the Concentration Chart, Components Search, Paired Comparisons, and Product/Process Search. These techniques show how to "talk to the parts." They provide powerful and meaningful clues, without disrupting production. Part IV followed with more formal DOE problem-solving techniques, where the objective is product/process characterization. This meant separating the important variables from the unimportant ones. This is done by Variables Search, if there are five or more input variables to investigate, and by Full Factorials, if there are four or fewer. But that is not the end of the road. Then comes the important step of ensuring that the improvements achieved through these problem-solving methods are permanent—B versus C tests.

But that is still not the end of the road. Problem-solving and Product/Process characterization must be followed by Product/Process Optimization. This means establishing the optimum target values, specification limits, and tolerance for the previously characterized (i.e., important) input variables. Part V deals with various techniques for optimization:

> Scatter Plots
> Response Surface Methodology (Sm), including
> > Evolutionary Operation (EVOP)
> > Simplex EVOP
> > Random Evolutionary Operation (REVOP)
> > Steepest Ascent

16

Scatter Plots to Achieve Realistic Specifications and Tolerances

Objective

The objectives of the Scatter Plot are to

1. Establish realistic specifications and realistic tolerances
2. Tighten the tolerances of the important variables to achieve high C_{pk}'s
3. Open up the tolerances of the unimportant variables to reduce costs. The place of this technique in the problem-solving roadmap is shown in Figure 7-1.

The Importance of Realistic Specifications and Tolerances

Why are specifications and tolerances so important, and why should they be realistic? The reason is simple—high costs. Table 16-1 lists the unacceptable costs associated with loose tolerances. Table 16-2 lists the unacceptable costs associated with tight tolerances.

Table 16-1. Unacceptable Costs Associated With Loose Tolerances

> Loss of market share	> Competitive disadvantage
> Customer defections	> Government fines
> Law suits	> Environmental infractions
> Product recalls	> High service call rates
> Poor field reliability	> High warranty costs

Table 16-2. Unacceptable Costs Associated With Tight Tolerances

> No correlation with customers' real needs	> More Material Review Board appeals
> High scrap and rework	> Higher supplier costs
> Higher 100% inspection and test	> More accurate instrumentation to meet 5:1 ratio of product instrument
> More analyzing costs	
> Tighter tool tolerances	
> Shorter tool life	> More frequent equipment calibration
	> More fights between production and quality

Yet, how do some engineers establish specifications and tolerances:

1. They pull numbers out of the air. This is called *atmosphere analysis!*
2. They carry over the same numbers from old designs and old drawings.
3. They use tight tolerances to protect their hides. They are less likely to be criticized by management for tight tolerances and higher costs than for the product not working.
4. They use boilerplate, pre-digested tolerances.
5. They slavishly follow supplier recommendations.
6. They use worst-case scenarios for tolerances.
7. They do not consult with customers on what is important or unimportant to them.

The result is that 90 percent of specifications and tolerances are wrong. This is best illustrated with a case study.

Case Study: Edge Defects in Contact Lenses

A manufacturer of contact lenses was convinced that cosmetic edge defects in the contact lenses had to be rooted out. These defects included scratches, chips, inclusions, etc., around the periphery of the lens. It was difficult to see these edge defects with the naked eye. Operators and inspectors had to use high-power microscopes to sort out the defects; to make sure that the final product had no defects before going to customers, each lens had to go through four to five inspection stations—a brute force quality approach.

The company had spent millions of dollars in this purification practice, yet it was losing market share to its competitor. In a "reverse engineering" study, it found—to its amazement—that the competitor's lenses had far more edge defects than its own lenses. A marketing study was then initiated to determine why patients preferred the competitor's lenses. The study revealed that the edge defects were of little concern to the lens wearer because they were only on the periphery of the lens; could not be seen with the naked eye, and did not affect vision, which is concentrated around the center of the lens. The competition's superiority lay in (1) closer adherence to the lens prescription and hence better vision; (2) greater wearing comfort. The company rapidly changed its concentration from edge defects to prescription accuracy (achieved C_{pk}'s of 2.5 and higher) and to wearing comfort, and restored its market share within 18 months.

Principles

> Specifications and tolerances, in the final analysis, have to be traced back to the real requirements of the customer. (If the customer can express such requirements only in a vague and subjective manner, more formal techniques such as Quality Function Deployment (Chapter 3), or focus groups, panels, and clinics should be employed to quantify the requirement.)
> While more sophisticated techniques, such as regression analysis or multiple regression analysis, can be used, Scatter Plots offer the oft-stated advantages of all our DOE techniques—of simplicity, graphics, and effectiveness.
> The amount of vertical scatter is a measure of the total contribution of all the input variables to the Green Y, other than the input variable or in the Scatter Plot. (See the section on methodology.)
> Scatter Plots should be used only if previous DOE experiments, such as Variables Search or Full Factorials, indicate that there are no strong interactions between two or more important input variables. If there are, Response Surface Methodology (see Chapter 17) should be employed.

Methodology

In a DOE study such as Variables Search, let us assume that a best level of a particular Red X variable gives a better result and its marginal level a poorer result. But how do we know that the better result is truly the best level? Could a level on one side or the other of this level give even better results? The purpose of a Scatter Plot is to fine tune this and determine the very best level of Red X, i.e., the design center, as well as its realistic tolerances to ensure zero defects.

The Scatter Plot is a graphical technique in which 30 readings* representing 10 or more levels of a range of values of an independent variable are plotted, in a random time sequence, against the corresponding range of values of a dependent Green Y. If there is good correlation—a thin parallelogram—the independent variable is a Red X or strong Pink X, and its most appropriate target value and tolerance can be graphically determined. If there is little correlation—a fat parallelogram—the independent variable is not important and its value and tolerance can be placed at levels that are the most economical.

Scatter Plots are best illustrated by the graphs in Figure 16-1. Let us assume that the effect of an independent variable T, temperature, on a dependent variable (Green Y), say, a dimension, is to be observed. The temperature is now varied,† say, from 80°C to 140°C, at intervals of 2°C, and the corresponding dimension Green Y noted. Typically, plotting could result in pictures A, B, C, or D. In plot A, there is strong evidence of a positive (thin pencil-line) correlation between temperature and the Green Y (dimension). There is no influence on the Green Y other than temperature, which can be called a Red X variable. The same is true in plot B, where temperature is also a Red X variable, but the slope of the correlation line is negative instead of positive. In plot C, there is correlation, but it is weaker. If two parallel lines are drawn, we get a parallelogram effect. Even if the temperature were held constant at, say, 110°C, there is variation in the Green Y. That variation cannot come from temperature because it is held constant. The vertical intercept in plot C, therefore, represents the contribution of all input variables other than temperature to the Green Y. The larger the vertical intercept, the less is the contribution of the input variable, temperature T. In picture D, there appears to be no correlation at all.

Figure 16-2 shows other examples of scatter plots. Plot A shows good correlation, but it is not linear. Correlation does not have to be linear. Plot B shows a poor correlation if only the middle of the picture is considered, but if the range of the input variable is extended on both sides we get a reasonable correlation. Plot C would show little correlation if all the data points were considered together. But there appear to be three separate and stratified correlations, indicating three influences.

---

*The 30 readings can be grouped into a minimum of eight to 12 levels.
†Scatter Plots are used when there are no strong interactions between input variables. So, as each input variable is being varied, the other variables are kept at constant levels.

Figure 16-1. Typical Scatter Diagrams

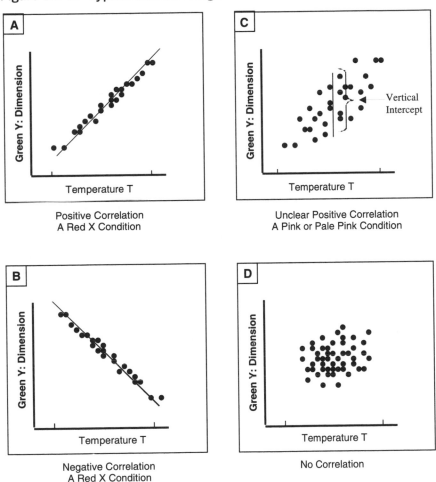

Positive Correlation
A Red X Condition

Unclear Positive Correlation
A Pink or Pale Pink Condition

Negative Correlation
A Red X Condition

No Correlation

Quiz No. 1

Figures 16-3A and 16-3B show two separate scatter plots of an input variable X and its associated Green Y. Is there correlation in either case?

Quiz No. 2

Does X show a greater influence on the Green Y in Figure 16-4A than in Figure 16-4B?

Figure 16-2. Unusual Scatter Diagrams

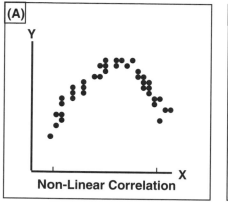
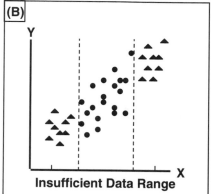

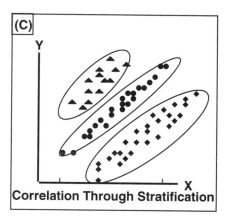

Figure 16-3. Vertical and Horizontal Scatter Plots

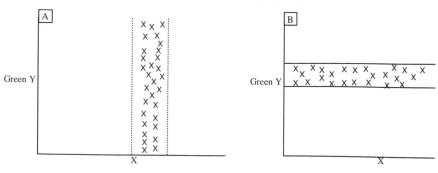

Figure 16-4. Scatter Plots With Different Tilt Angles

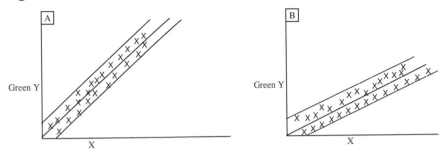

Quiz Answers

1. There is no correlation either in Figure 16-3A or Figure 16-3B. In Figure 16-3A, there is a huge change in the Green Y, even though the input variable X is constant. So the variation in the Green Y must come from other input variables, not X.

In Figure 16-3B, there is no variation in the Green Y, despite large variations in X, the input variable, so X has no influence on Y.

The point of this exercise is that there must be tilt in the scatter plot in order to have correlation. Neither a vertical plot nor a horizontal plot has correlation.

2. The influence of X on the Green Y is not necessarily more important in Figure 16-4A than in Figure 16-4B. Figure 16-4A does have a 45° slope and Figure 16-4B a lower slope, but slopes depend on the scales you use for X and the Green Y. Tilt is more revealing about correlation than about slope, because the latter can be changed, depending on the scale chosen.

Determining Realistic Specifications and Tolerances

1. Select the Green Y and its maximum and minimum specification limit always referencing such limits to what is required by the customer.

2. Determine from previous DOE techniques the Red X and Pink X input variables that need optimizing. Make sure that the Red X and Pink X variables have been verified as permanent improvements, using B versus C tests.

3. Make sure that the interaction effects between these important input variables are not present or are negligible. If not, go to Response Surface Methodology instead of Scatter Plots.

4. Select a range of values (or levels) for the Red X variable that is likely to fine-tune the Green Y. Run 30 such values of the Red X and note the corresponding Green Y values.

5. Plot the results (see Figure 16-5). If there is *tilt* in the graphics plot and only a small vertical scatter, the Red X is further validated. If there is little or no tilt and the vertical scatter is large, the variable is not a Red X or Pink X and is unimportant.

6. Draw a median line, called the line of regression, through the 30 plots. Draw a line on either side of the median and parallel to it. The two lines should be equidistant from the median and containing all but one of the 30 points should fall between them. The vertical intercept through this created parallelogram is the variation in the Green Y due to all input variables added together, other than the Red X variable. This vertical intercept should be no more than, say, 20 percent of the Green Y specifica-

Figure 16-5. Determining Realistic Specifications and Tolerances With Scatter Plots

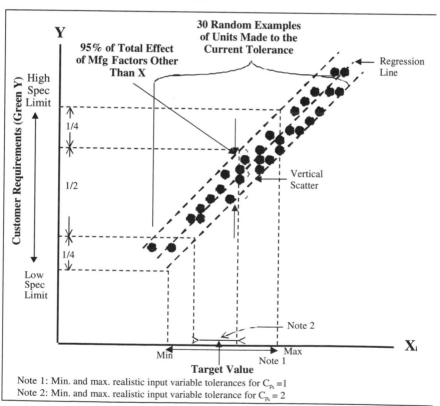

Note 1: Min. and max. realistic input variable tolerances for $C_{p_k} = 1$
Note 2: Min. and max. realistic input variable tolerance for $C_{p_k} = 2$

tion to justify the input variable being labeled the Red X. If the vertical intercept is 20 to 50 percent of the Green Y specification, the input variable is probably a Pink X or a Pale Pink X.

7. Next draw a horizontal line from the upper specification limit of the Green Y to intersect the top line of the parallelogram; then draw a line at this intersection point perpendicular to the Y axis up to the X axis. This represents the maximum realistic tolerance for the Red X input variable. Any value of the Red X to the right of this maximum results in a rejection of the Green Y specification (above the upper specification limit).

8. Similarly, draw a horizontal line from the lower specification limit of the Green Y to intersect the bottom line of the parallelogram; then draw a line at this intersection point perpendicular to the Y axis and up to the X axis. This represents the minimum realistic tolerance for the Red X input variable. Any value of the Red X to the left of this minimum results in a rejection of the Green Y (below the lower specification limit).

9. The middle of the maximum and minimum levels of the Red X is the target value of the Red X. These maximum and minimum values will assure a C_{pk} of 1.0 vis-à-vis the customer specification width.

If, on the other hand, a C_{pk} of 2.0 is desired vis-à-vis the customer specification width, the latter should be divided into four equal quarters. Two lines should be drawn from the middle half of the specification width to the upper and lower parallelogram lines, along with perpendiculars from the intersections to the X axis. These will determine the maximum and minimum values of the Red X to assure a C_{pk} of 2.0 rather than just a C_{pk} of 1.0.

10. These correct maximum/minimum and target values for the Red X should be compared against existing values and tolerances and the necessary changes made to ensure zero defects and 100 percent yields.

Case Study 1: Ignition Amplifier

In the manufacture of an engine ignition amplifier, production was experiencing a greater than 10 percent defect rate in a critical parameter, off-time, which determines the amount of time in milliseconds (m.s.) that the ignition is turned off in a rapid cycle of off-and-on switching. Previous studies had indicated that resistors R_3 and R_4 were the Red X and Pink X, respectively, and that there was little interaction between them.

Scatter Plots were drawn, measuring off-time as the Green Y and varying values of the two resistors (Figure 16-6).

The Scatter Plot for resistor R_4 confirms that R_4 was a Pale Pink X. The parallelogram has tilt, but it is fat, with the vertical intercept at about

Figure 16-6. Scatter Plot Case Study: The Ignition Amplifier

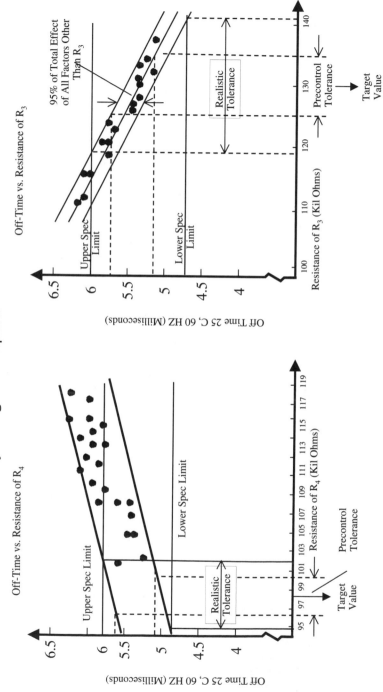

Source: Motorola, Schaumburg, Ill.

344

60 percent of the allowed Green Y specification width of 1.2 m.s. (4.8 to 6.0 m.s.), indicating that 60 percent of the Green Y variation was caused by all factors other than R_4. Further, the plot shows graphically that the original resistance of 110K ohms ± 10 percent was wrong and was a likely cause of the high defect rate. The plot indicates that the realistic tolerance should be 94 to 102K ohms, with a target value of 98K ohms to achieve a minimum C_p of 1.0. However, for a C_p of 2.0, the Green Y specification width could only vary from 5.1 to 5.7 m.s., requiring R_4 to be no less than 96K ohms and no more than 100K ohms, i.e., 98K ohms ±2 percent.

The Scatter Plot for R_3 confirms that it is the Red X: The parallelogram is thin and the vertical intercept is only about 15 percent of the Green Y specification width of 1.2 m.s. This means that only 15 percent of the Green Y variation is caused by factors other than R_3. But here again, the Scatter Plot clearly shows that the original resistance of R_3, 120K ohms ± 10 percent, is wrong, and led to a high defect rate for the ignition amplifier. The graph shows that the realistic tolerance should be from 118.5K ohms to 141.5K ohms, with a target value of 130K ohms, to achieve a C_{pk} of 1.0. If a C_{pk} of 2.0 is desired, the range should be from 124K ohms to 135K ohms, or 130K ohms ±4 percent. The final values for R_3 and R_4 were a compromise between the ideal target values and the availability of the closest step values provided by the supplier. After the resistor values were adjusted, the defect rate dropped to zero.

Workshop Exercise 1: Infrared Soldering

Yields at the infrared soldering of the central processing unit (CPU) in a complex electronic module were historically poor. Three process variables—preheat temperature, viscosity of the solder paste, and flatness of the CPU leads—were identified as important and the interactions between them were negligible.

Scatter plots, varying each of the above variables and measuring yield percentages, were drawn (Figure 16-7).

Questions

1. Is preheat temperature important? Why?
2. Is viscosity of the solder paste important? Why?
3. Is flatness of the CPU leads important? Why?
4. In the chart depicting the Red X, what is the contribution of all the other variables to the yield percentages?

Figure 16-7. Scatter Plot Workshop Exercise 1: Infrared Soldering

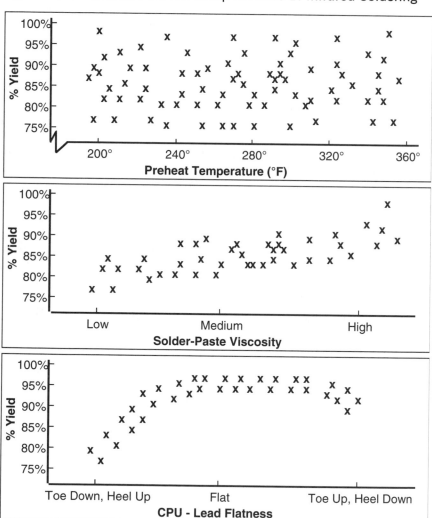

5. If a minimum 90 percent yield is desired, what should be the level of the three variables being evaluated?

Answers

1. and 5. See Figure 16-8. Preheat temperature is not important. The Scatter Plot has no tilt and the vertical intercept is large, meaning the contribution of all the other input variables

Figure 16-8. Scatter Plot Workshop Exercise 1 Answers: Infrared Soldering

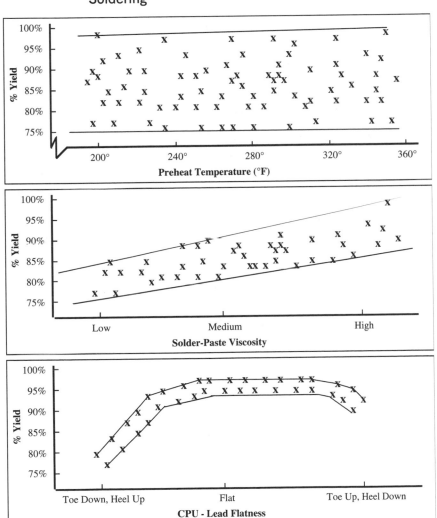

Source: Astec Co., Manila, Philippines.

is huge. For a minimum 90 percent yield: Preheat temperature could be kept anywhere between 200° and 360°; but
for economic reasons should be kept at 200°.

2. and 5. Viscosity of the solder paste is somewhat important—a
Pink X or a Pale Pink X. The Scatter Plot has tilt (although
slight), the parallelogram is somewhat horizontal, and the
vertical intercept is medium, indicating that 10 to 20 percent of the yield variation is due to other input variables.
For a minimum 90 percent yield, the viscosity should be
kept as high as possible.

3. and 4. The flatness of the CPU is very important—a Red X. The
Scatter Plot, though nonlinear, (Scatter Plots do not have
to be linear) has a small vertical intercept, indicating that
only five percent of the yield variation is due to other
input variables. For a minimum 90 percent yield, the CPU
leads should be flat. However, since it is impossible for all
64 leads to be perfectly flat, the toe-up, heel-down direction is better, because its slope is gentler than the steep
ski-slope of the toe-down, heel-up direction.

Case Study 2: Cylinder Prescription versus Lens Axis

In the manufacture of a contact lens, a study was initiated to determine
the relationship between cylinder prescription (optical accuracy) and the
axis of the lens from both the "plus" group of lenses and the "minus"
group of lenses. Ten lenses were selected in each group from six different
axes (30, 60, 90, 120, 150, and 180).

Figure 16-9 shows the resulting scatter plot of the "plus" group of
lenses and Figure 16-10 that of the "minus" group of lenses.

Conclusions

For the "plus" lenses, the scatter plot shows little tilt, except for a slight
bow in the 90 to 120 axes. Further, the readings for each axis show a
large variation in the actual cylinder prescription—a spread of 40. This
indicates that the axis is hardly a factor in the cylinder prescription variations.

For the "minus" lenses, the Scatter Plot shows a definite trend, with
the 90 and 120 axes having a decided increase in the actual cylinder prescription, as compared to the 30, 60, 150, and 180 axes. However, here too
there is quite a spread in the 10 readings at each axis—a variation of 30

Figure 16-9. Effect of Axis on Cylinder Rx (Plus Lenses)

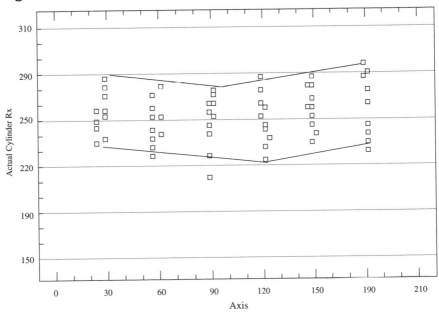

Source: Ciba Corp., Atlanta, Ga.

Figure 16-10. Effect of Axis on Cylinder Rx (Minus Lenses)

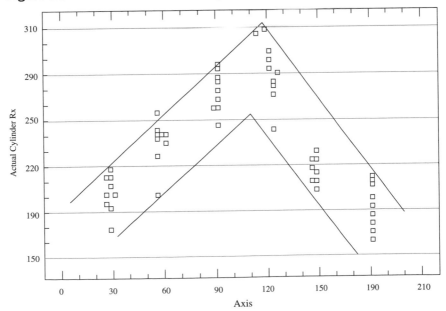

Source: Ciba Corp., Atlanta, Ga.

to 40 in the cylinder prescriptions. There is some other factor that needs to be investigated to explain this variation.

Workshop Exercise 2: Digital Circuit

An output voltage in a digital circuit must be kept in the "on" or 1 condition to be considered acceptable. The "off" or 0 condition is considered unacceptable. Previous studies had identified a 1,000 ohm resistor in the digital circuit as the Red X. Its tolerance was specified at ±1 percent.

A scatter plot was constructed to check both the resistor value and its tolerance.

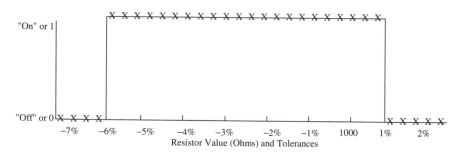

Questions

1. Is 1,000 ohm the right value? If not, what should be the target value for the resistor?
2. Is the ±1 percent tolerance right? If not, what should be the right resistor tolerance?

Answers

1. In this example, we have only attributes (1 good and 0 bad), so there is no tilt in the plot. At exactly 1,000 ohms, the resistor would give good results. But it is not centered. The range is from −6 percent to +1 percent, so the center or target should be 7/2 or −3.5 percent, i.e., at 965 ohms.
2. The tolerance of ±1 percent is too tight. It can be opened up to ±3.5 percent for a C_{pk} of 1.0 or to ±1.75 percent for a C_{pk} of 2.0.

Use of Scatter Plots in Administrative Applications

As with so many of the other DOE techniques, Scatter Plots have been used extensively in administrative and service applications—in industry,

Table 16-3. Scatter Plots: Administrative Applications

Output (Green Y)	Input Variable	Degree of Correlation
Gross domestic product	Power consumption	Close, until recently
Gross domestic product	Water consumption	Close, until recently
Per-capita income	Level of education	Strong
Income levels	Reputation of school	Strong
Cancer deaths	Level of smoking	Strong
Highway traffic deaths	Speed limits	Strong
Traffic deaths	Driver alcohol levels	Strong
Scholastic achievement	School funding	Indeterminate
Scholastic achievement	Class size	Indeterminate
Inner-city poverty	Head Start Program	Strong
Company longevity	Company ethics	Strong
Customer loyalty	Employee loyalty	Strong

government, schools, and hospitals, in fact, wherever the correlation of two parameters—an output or dependent variable (Green Y) and an input or independent variable—needs to be established. Some typical examples are given in Table 16-3.

Case Study 3: Customer Satisfaction versus Customer Loyalty versus Profit

It has been an article of faith in industry that higher levels of customer satisfaction produce higher profits. Yet, recent studies have shown that there is no correlation between customer satisfaction and company profitability. In fact, 15 to 40 percent of customers defect soon after they indicate, in company surveys, that they are satisfied. This is borne out in a Scatter Plot study conducted by the appliance industry; as Figure 16-11 shows, the correlation between customer satisfaction and customer loyalty is poor. By contrast, the same study shows a strong correlation between customer loyalty and company profits (Figure 16-12). The difference is that customer satisfaction studies measure what customers say, while customer loyalty measures what they do.

Multiple Regression Analysis

Scatter Plots and their more mathematical counterpart—regression analyses—are useful if there are only two variables—a dependent output and an independent input. Often, however, there are several (multiple) causes

Figure 16-11. Customer Satisfaction Not a Predictor of Customer Loyalty

Source: Keki R. Bhote, *Going Beyond Customer Satisfaction to Customer Loyalty,* New York: American Management Association, 1997.

affecting a given output. Then a more rigorous mathematical model—multiple regression analysis—is needed to show the relationship between these variables.

Example

An airline wanted to determine which of several independent variables would cause a person to choose that airline for repeat flights. A multiple regression analysis yielded the following results:

Variable	Cumulative Adjusted R-Square
Frequent flier program	0.43
Convenience of flight times	0.62
On-time arrival	0.75
On-board service	0.82
Baggage handling time	0.85

Figure 16-12. Close Correlation Between Customer Loyalty and Profit

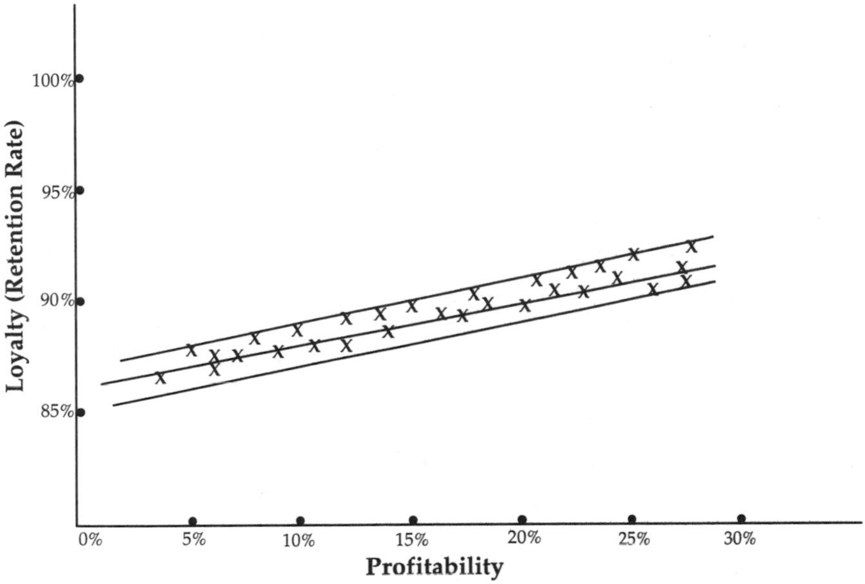

Source: Keki R. Bhote, *Going Beyond Customer Satisfaction to Customer Loyalty,* New York: American Management Association, 1997.

This indicated that 43 percent of the variance in a passenger's airline selection was based on the attractiveness of its frequent flier program and that an additional 19 percent was based on the convenience of its flight times. The remaining factors only slightly influenced selection of the airline.

Questions for DOE Teams as Guidelines for Scatter Plots

1. Have previous DOE experiments such as Variables Search been performed to characterize a product before attempting to optimize the product with scatter plots?
2. How were the current specifications and tolerances established? How were they challenged?
3. How well were the specifications related to the customer's requirements?
4. Were techniques like Quality Function Deployment, focus groups, panels, and clinics used to assess true customer requirements?
5. Were 30 readings of the input variable used in a minimum of

eight to 12 levels. (The absolute minimum would be 20 readings and six levels of the variable.)

6. Was the sequence of testing the readings and levels of the input variable randomized?
7. In capturing a Red X input variable, is the vertical intercept a small percentage of the total customer specification width?
8. Are the realistic tolerances based on a C_{pk} of 2.0 rather than a C_{pk} of 1.0?
9. If there are three or four input variables with strong interaction effects, has a Response Surface Methodology technique been considered instead of a Scatter Plot?
10. If there are several input variables, has a multiple regression analysis been considered as an alternative to a Scatter Plot?

Questions for Top Management

1. Are current specifications and tolerances directly related to customer requirements? Were customers contacted to determine such requirements? How?
2. Were the 30 readings in the Scatter Plot randomized in time sequence?
3. If there are interaction effects between two or more input variables, was a Response Surface Methodology technique tried?
4. Has the Scatter Plot approach been extended to administrative applications?

17

. . . .

Response Surface
Methodology (RSM): To
Optimize Interactions

Objectives

> The purpose of scatter plots, detailed in the last chapter, is to determine the best levels of noninteracting input variables to optimize a Green Y.
> The purpose of Response Surface Methodology (RSM) is to determine the best combination of levels of two or more interacting input variables (identified in previous DOE experiments) to achieve a maximum, minimum, or optimum Green Y. (Response, output, and Green Y are synonymous terms.) For the place of RSM in the problem-solving roadmap, see Figure 7-1.

Approaches

There are a number of empirical, statistical, and mathematical approaches to optimization and RSM—

> Evolutionary Operation (EVOP),
> Simplex;
> Random Evolutionary Operation (REVOP); and
> Steepest Ascent.

Fortunately, as we have emphasized throughout this text, it is not necessary to be a statistician or a mathematician to use these techniques. This chapter will focus on nonmathematical, graphical approaches that can easily be implemented with no more than three to 20 iterative trials.

The Steepest Ascent approach will not be discussed, because its mathematical rigor is not necessary in 90 percent of RSM applications.

The Concept: A Mountain Climbing Analogy

The concept of Response Surface Methods is best explained by an analogy to mountain climbing. Figure 17-1 is a two-dimensional contour plot of a mountain, where identical altitudes around the mountain are shown by contour lines. There is a gradual ascent until the peak is reached. RSM attempts, similarly to find this peak—or, in DOE terms, the optimum response (or optimum Green Y),—in a series of sequential mountain climbing experiments, EVOP, Simplex, REVOP, and Steepest Ascent are different paths to this summit. *Response Surface* is the mathematical or graphical representation of the connection between important, interacting input variables and a dependent output or response or Green Y, such as yields, impurities, etc. Green Y's of equal value are portrayed as contours, similar to the altitude contours on a mountain.

Evolutionary Operation

EVOP is the simplest of the RSM optimization techniques. The most basic EVOP experiments use two interacting input variables and one response variable or Green Y.

Procedure

Stage 1. A start is made with two levels of one input variable (above and below a previously determined good level for that variable) run with two

Figure 17-1. Mountain Climbing

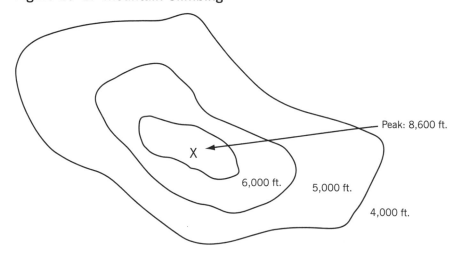

levels of the other input variable. This results in a 2^2 full factorial experiment. The response or Green Y of the four cells is plotted as a box. An additional experiment at the midpoints of the levels of the two input variables is also run to determine if there could be a peak within the box. This reading is called the center point. *Stage 2.* Moving in the direction of the highest Green Y in the box created by Stage 1, a second 2^2 full factorial experiment is tried with adjacent levels of both input variables. The box representing the four cells is again plotted, along with its center point. This may result in a higher Green Y. The procedure is recreated with Stage 3, 4, and 5, etc., until the peak or optimum Green Y is reached and no further improvements are registered in any direction.

Case Study: Maximizing Process Yields—Schottky Diodes

Two factors, time and temperature, were determined to be important and interacting in a Schottky Diode process that had previously been characterized in a variables search experiment. The yield (Green Y) was at 82 percent. The next step was to run an EVOP experiment to determine the levels of time and temperature that would result in the maximum yield. Figure 17-2 shows the four stages of EVOP.

Stage 1

The start of EVOP was the good levels of these two factors, as determined by the previous variables search experiment. For the time factor,

Figure 17-2. EVOP Experiment to Optimize Schottky Diode Yield

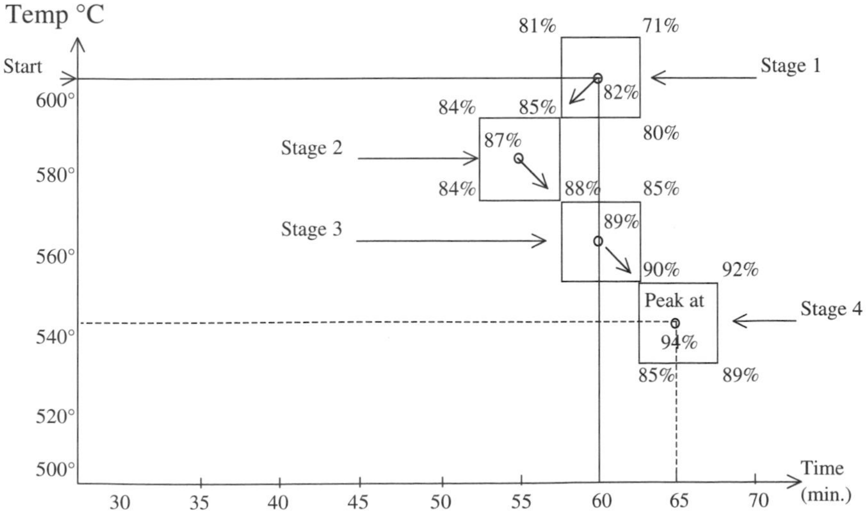

Source: Motorola, Phoenix, Ariz.

this was 60 minutes and for temperature, 600°C. A 2^2 factorial was next run at two adjacent higher and lower times of 56 and 64 minutes along with two adjacent higher and lower temperatures of 590° and 610°. (It is advisable to replicate this 2^2 factorial three more times to test for residual error or noise in the experiment. The 16 readings of the experiment can be tested for significance with a Tukey test. This more rigorous approach is skipped by many experimenters who are more concerned with averages than with the variance of the readings.) Figure 17-2 shows Stage 1 producing yields of 80 percent, 77 percent, 81 percent, and 85 percent at the four corners of the box.

Stage 2

The lower left reading of 85 percent is the highest. EVOP rules then require Stage 2 to move in a diagonal direction from the center of the box to the high end of 85 percent and beyond. The results of the second 2^2 factorial show yields of 85 percent (original), 84 percent, 84 percent, and 88 percent, along with 85 percent at the higher point. The higher yield at the southeast corner of Stage 2 than at the center suggests that EVOP be continued in a southeast direction. *Stage 3 and Stage 4.* The next Stages, 3 and 4, continue the process until at the end of Stage 4, a peak is reached at a yield of 94 percent, with the four corner readings all being lower than the center reading, indicating that the optimum time for the process if 66 minutes and the optimum temperature is 540°.

The total number of experiments in this case study (excluding replication) was 17. Generally, a EVOP experiments use a minimum of two stages and a maximum of seven stages.

Pitfalls to Avoid

1. Do not use EVOP as a screening experiment. The interacting input variables should be pinpointed ahead of EVOP by characterizing the product or process using clue-generation techniques and Variables Search or Full Factorials.
2. Do not use EVOP if there are more than four interacting input variables. In such a situation, Random Evolutionary Operation would be a better RSM technique.
3. The input factors should not be attributes. They should be continuously variable.
4. The changes in each input variable in any stage of EVOP should be kept small. Large changes are liable to miss the peak response and could result in back tracking.
5. Randomize the sequence of the 2^2 factorial in each stage to avoid

bias and give the noise factors an equal chance of entering or not entering the experiment.

6. Wherever practical, replicate the 2^2 factorial at each stage to determine residual error (i.e., the noise versus the signal).

7. Do not pursue an endless search for the peak Green Y. For example, the difference between a 94 percent yield in the case study and, say, a 100 percent or even 97 percent yield may be only marginally desirable relative to the cost, time, and effort necessary to achieve such incremental improvements.

8. Do not resort to the more mathematical models used in Steepest Ascent practices within RSM, if simple EVOP experiments will do the job with direct-labor people at less cost and with less expenditure of time. Much effort is needlessly spent in distinguishing linear from quadratic responses in an attempt to go from 99.5 percent to 100 percent.

9. Make sure that the product/process is not changing with time. If it is, either EVOP should be repeated or an investigation should be conducted using a combination of DOE and MEOST to determine the causes of such variation.

10. Make sure that in optimizing a particular Green Y, some other Green Y associated with performance or cost or reliability is not adversely affected.

Expanding EVOP to Three Interacting Input Variables

The same principles of EVOP apply if there are three or four interacting input variables to optimize a Green Y, rather than just two.

Figures 17-1 and 17-2 were two-dimensional visualization (2 factors) of three-dimensional outputs. To assess a third interacting input variable, a three-dimensional visualization is needed to explain the output or Green Y moving into the fourth dimension.

Figure 17-3 is a two-dimensional diagram with three input variables, A, B, and C, with the response surface, or Green Y, being in the fourth dimension.

Here, Stage 1 EVOP experiments are conducted with three factors, or variables—A, B, and C, each with two levels, (−) and (+). Now eight corners are samples instead of four, along with the center (at the midlevels of A, B, and C). As long as one or more of the eight corners of Figure 17-3 give better results than the center and the other corners, all three input variables are varied in the desired direction to move the "test cube" toward a better contour of the four-dimensional surface. When the center reading, after a series of such evolutionary 2^3 factorial moves, becomes better than any of the eight corners of the final cube, the Green Y is opti-

Figure 17-3. EVOP Visualization With Three Input Variables

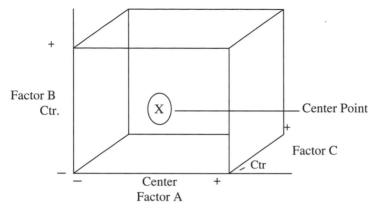

mum or very close to optimum. Table 17-1 is a tabular representation of the eight corners of Figure 17-3 and the center point, shown as a factorial matrix. It is essentially a 2^3 full factorial with a center point added at the midpoints of factors A, B, and C.

Expanding EVOP to Four Interacting Input Variables

To optimize a Green Y with four interacting input variables, a four-dimensional visualization is needed to explain a Green Y in the fifth dimension. This is impossible to portray graphically, but the same factorial matrix concept can be used. It requires a 2^4 full factorial matrix with a center point added as shown in Table 17-2.

Table 17-1. A Factorial Matrix for EVOP With Three Input Variables

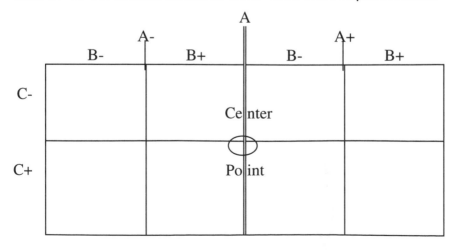

Table 17-2. A Factorial Matrix for EVOP With Four Input Variables

		A- B-	A- B+	A+ B-	A+ B+
C-	D-				
C-	D+			Center Point	
C++	D-				
	D+				

There are now 16 corner readings and one center point at the middle levels of factors A, B, C, and D. Again, a series of 2^3 factorials is conducted, until the center point becomes better than any of the 16 corners of the final matrix to reach the optimum Green Y.

Simplex

Even though EVOP is a simple, graphical, and step-by-step hill climbing journey to the "summit" of a Green Y, it can result in a large number of experiments. For example, if there are seven stages, each with a 2^2 factorial experiment and a center point, 28 experiments are required, even without replication.

Simplex is a more sophisticated technique that requires fewer experiments. Consequently, Simplex tends to be more efficient than EVOP, and reaching the summit is faster. Simplex designs require (n + 1) points in each stage, where n is the number of interacting input variables. Like EVOP, Simplex is best illustrated with a case study, involving two input variables.

Case Study: Paint Process Optimization

In a large paint shop, a previous variables search experiment had identified two parameters—powder particle size (regrind to virgin ratio in coded unit) and oven temperature (in coded units) as interacting variables. The variables search had achieved a yield of 84 percent. To increase the yield even further—to a target of 97 percent—an optimization DOE, utilizing Simplex, was initiated. Figure 17-4 shows the three stages of

Figure 17-4. Simplex Experiment on Paint Process Optimization

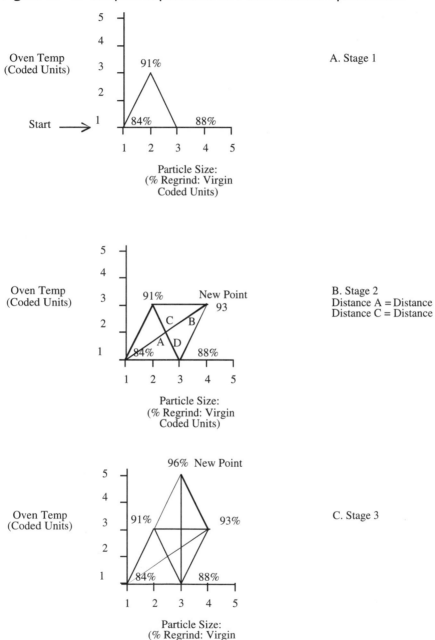

A. Stage 1

B. Stage 2
Distance A = Distance
Distance C = Distance

C. Stage 3

Simplex experiment. The start is the yield of 84 percent reached as a result of variables search.

Stage 1

Two levels of the temperature variable and three levels of the particle size variable were tried. The triangle results of Stage 1 show that the starting yield of 84 percent was the lowest, while the other two yields were 87 percent and 91 percent.

Stage 2

Optimizaiton proceeded by moving in the direction of the desired response. This was accomplished by deleting the Simplex point with the lowest yield—84 percent—and forming another Simplex with the two remaining points of the Stage 1 triangle. (A number of algorithms have been developed for determining the third point of the new Stage 2 triangle. The simplest technique is to form a straight line connecting the two remaining points.) The new trial is on a line going from a deleted point, bisecting the line through the remaining points and extending it to a distance equal to the distance from the deleted point to the bisected line.* Figure 17-4B shows a line from the deleted simplex point of 84 percent, bisecting the 91 and 85 percent yield line and arriving at the higher yield of 95 percent.

Stage 3

The lowest yield of Stage 2—88 percent—was deleted and a Stage 3 triangle created (Figure 17-4C) with yields at 91 percent, and the apex at 96 percent. It would have been possible to keep going with more stages, but in the interests of time and costs, a yield of 96 percent was declared sufficient. It is interesting to note that a comparable EVOP approach would have required 12 experiments for the three stages, whereas the Simplex approach required only $3 + 1 + 1 = 5$ experiments.

Random Evolutionary Operation

Evolutionary Operation (EVOP), while efficient and thorough, can become time-consuming and costly when the number of interacting input

---

*If the new point is lower than the other two points in the Simplex charting, the rule is to go back in the direction of the previous Simplex. Sophisticated computer programs have also been developed for Simplex techniques.

variables exceed four. This problem led to the development of Random Evolutionary Operation (REVOP). The theory, essentially the same as EVOP, introduces random directions to locate the direction of improvement. Practitioners of REVOP state that optimum Green Y's can be attained in 16 to 20 trials.

Procedure

1. Attempt to reduce the truly interacting input variables or factors to less than three or four, if possible, using factorial analysis, in a variables search or full factorial experiment. This eliminates the need for REVOP.
2. If Step 1 is not possible, list the input factors and determine the practical ranges of each factor, based on safety, cost, prior experience, customer/government requirements, etc.
3. Determine the random direction and random amount of change to be made in each factor.
4. Determine the maximum portion of the range to be used in one trial for each factor.
5. Select a starting point, based on good levels from previous experiments.
6. Plot the results of the first random change. If the result is favorable, continue in the same direction.
7. If it is unfavorable, reverse direction.
8. Select another random direction if the result is neither favorable nor unfavorable, or both are unfavorable.
9. Continue these steps until about four successive random, unfavorable directions and amounts have been selected (along with the corresponding four reverse directions also being favorable). The chances are that an optimum Green Y has been reached.

Figure 17-5 is a graphical plot of a REVOP experiment, involving five input variables—temperature, pressure, time, concentration, and volume—where the objective is to maximize an output or response.

Questions for DOE Teams as Guidelines in Response Surface Methodology (RSM) Projects

1. Is RSM used only as a last step in the search for the Red X—and only after a product/process has been characterized?

Figure 17-5. Graphical Plot of a REVOP Experiment

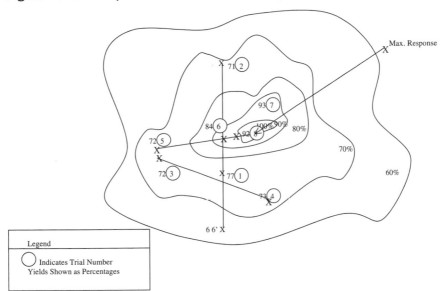

2. Has the presence of two or more important interacting input variables confirmed in earlier DOE experiments to justify RSM?
3. What was the rationale in choosing among the different approaches to RSM—namely EVOP, Simplex, REVOP, and Steepest Ascent?
4. Are the level changes in each input variable deliberately kept small?
5. Are the 2^2 factorial experiments in EVOP randomized and replicated?
6. Is there a reasonable compromise between reaching an absolute peak Green Y and the expenditure of time, manpower, and money?
7. Are the simple, graphical approaches to RSM preferred over complex mathematical models?
8. Is there a reliability problem—changes in the Green Y with time and stress? If so, is a combination DOE/MEOST approach being considered to resolve the problem?
9. Are there other Green Y's to optimize besides the one chosen?
10. In optimizing one Green Y, is another suboptimized, in which case compromises within the input variables may have to be made?

Questions for Top Management During
DOE Team Project Reviews

1. Is RSM really needed as the last step in the DOE project?
2. What is the cost of RSM in relation to the benefits from Green Y improvements?
3. Can RSM be taught to line operators and nontechnical people?
4. Is the simple, graphical approach emphasized over costly mathematical approaches?
5. How is a conflict between optimizing two or more Green Y's—each requiring different levels of input variables—resolved?

Part VI
The Transition From DOE to SPC: Vital Disciplines

18. Positrol: Freezing Process Gains

19. Process Certification: Eliminating Peripheral Causes of Poor Quality

Parts III, IV, and V dealt with a versatile toolbox of DOE techniques that, together, can solve any chronic quality problem—and, more important—prevent such problems in the first place.

However, that is still not the end of the road. Before we can go on to statistical process control (SPC)—which is, at best, a monitoring and maintenance tool, not a problem-solving tool—two very important disciplines must be exercised. *No textbook on quality even mentions them and the vast majority of quality professionals are blissfully ignorant of their place and power.*

> The first of these is Positrol, which freezes the process—specifically its *gains*—following DOE.
> The second is Process Certification, which systematically audits and corrects a number of peripheral causes of poor quality that might be lurking in the factory and might not be factored in to a DOE experiment. In fact, collectively, such factors can negate any experiment by the accumulation of noise factors to such an extent that the results can be rendered inconclusive or wrong.

More and more, the authors are coming to the conclusion that Process Certification should be a prerequisite to any DOE as well as a follow-on to DOE.

18
· ·
Positrol:
Freezing Process Gains

The Concept

One of the weaknesses of industry is that its engineers and technicians attempt to control a process by checking the product it produces. That is too late. An analogy, in nautical terms, would be to steer a boat by looking at the wake it produces! A process—like a product—has idiosyncrasies, inherent variables that must be identified and analyzed with DOE tools.

> ➤ The clue generation technique of product process search is a DOE technique that can separate important process variables from unimportant ones.
> ➤ Variables Search and Full Factorials take DOE further to distill the important variables and their interaction effects.
> ➤ Scatter Plots and Response Surface Methodology establish realistic specifications and realistic tolerances for each important variable.

But all of this work comes to naught if these important variables and their tolerances are not controlled in day-to-day production—locked up, frozen. We have seen scores of companies where good DOE work resulted in drastically reduced defect levels, only to find in subsequent production that the defects crept back in again.

The Positrol Plan

A regimen—called the Positrol* Plan—must be established to ensure that important variables (the *"what,"* characterized and optimized through

*The term *Positrol* is coined from *Positive Control.*

369

previous DOE experiments, are kept under tight control with a *"who,"* and *"how,"* a *"where"* and a *"when"* plan. The place of Positrol in the problem-solving roadmap is shown in Figure 7-1.

The plan determines *who* should be monitoring, measuring, and recording each important process parameter. The *how* determines the correct instrumentation to measure these important parameters (observing the 5:1 rule, which specifies that the accuracy of the instrument should be at least five times the accuracy [i.e., tolerance] of the parameter). The *where* should be the optimum location of measuring the process parameter, so that it truly reflects its correct value. The *when* is the frequency of measurement, determined initially by engineering judgment, but later by precontrol (see Chapter 21).

Table 18-1 is an example of a Positrol plan prepared after the successful 2^4 full factorial wave solder study detailed in Chapter 14. The Positrol plan must be scrupulously followed by the process technicians, maintenance people, and line operators—*with no deviation or shortcuts*. If the important parameters and their tolerance have been painstakingly established with DOE, they should be adhered to, unless additional DOE studies can improve quality or yields even further.

The Positrol Chart

Once a Positrol plan is prepared, it must be followed by a Positrol chart that is a running log maintained at the process, with high visibility. It should be filled out by the designated person (who) and monitored periodically by the supervisor, the process engineer, and quality control.

Table 18-1. Positrol Plan for a Wave Solder Process

Parameter (What)	Spec. and Tolerance	Measurement			
		Who	How	Where	When
Preheat temp.	220°F ± 5°	Automatic	Thermocouple	Chamber entrance	Continuous
Angle of incline	7° ± 20%	Process tech.	Angle scale	Tilt post	Each model change
Belt speed	6 ft./min ± 10%	Process tech.	Counter	Board feed	Each model change
An 880 flux density	0.864 gm./cc ± 0.008	Lab tech.	Specific gravity meter	Lab	Once/day

Source: Adi K. Bhote, Motorola, Scottsdale, Ariz.

Table 18-2 is an example of a Positrol chart on a sputtering machine used to metallize glass with a layer of chrome, nickel, and gold on one side of the glass, and with chrome and gold on the other side. Previous history on the sputtering machine indicated continual "in-and-out" defects for metal adhesion on the glass. The process engineer would twiddle one knob after another in an effort to control adhesion, but would end up "chasing his own tail" and become thoroughly confused as to what to do. DOE studies identified four factors—power, gas pressure, speed, and vacuum—as important. Scatter plots established the maximum realistic tolerances for each of these parameters. A chart was maintained by the operators four times a day on this three-shift operation. With DOE, the defects were reduced to zero. With Positrol they were maintained at zero!

In many cases, it can be more economical to use Pre-Control (see Chapter 21) than a Positrol chart. Pre-Control has the advantage of being able to lengthen the period between checks on each process parameter if the time between two successive corrections is sufficiently long. There is another advantage to using Pre-Control for processes rather than for product. When defect levels for a product fall much below 100 ppm, control charts are useless. But even use of Pre-Control to check product characteristics can become costly. The answer then is to control the product by monitoring the process (rather than the other way around), with Positrol and Pre-Control to monitor key process parameters.

In more modern processes, usually microprocessor based, process parameter tolerances can be designed into the process so that Positrol becomes automatic, eliminating the need for either a Positrol chart or Pre-Control.

Reasons for Retrogression

Why do good initial results of DOE retrogress, slide backwards, go up in smoke? There are several reasons.

1. Experimenters have not validated the improvements of DOE with B versus C tests (Chapter 16).
2. Experimenters, usually technical types, turn over the maintenance of a process to their maintenance people, setup people, technicians, and line operators with little guidance on the importance of Positrol in maintaining the gains achieved.
3. These operators mean well. They are, for the most part, genuinely anxious to do a good quality job. But they are not part of the DOE solution and believe, in their minds, that they have the process down pat and can do better than the engineers.

Table 18-2. Positrol Chart on a Metal Sputtering Machine

Process: Metallization Machine: 903 Week Ending: 6-20

Machine Parameters			Monday				Tuesday				Wednesday				Thursday				Friday				Saturday			
			6a	12p	6p	12a	6a	12p	6p	12a	6a	12p	6p	12a	6a	12p	6p	12a	6a	12p	6p	12a	6a	12p	6p	12a
Power (W)	800-900	Cr	820	800	820	820	820	832	865	820	820	820	820	820	800	882	861	861	861	861	861	861				
	4700-4900	Ni	4848	4830	4779.2	4779	4772	4772	4797	4779	4779	4779	4817.5	4817.5	4765	4772	4817	4770	4855	4855	4819.5	4819				
	2300-2400	Au	2400	2400	2400	2400	2370	2370	2370	2510	2370	2370	2370	2370	2370	2370	2370	2340	2340	2340	2340	2340				
	1050-1150	Cr	1066	1066	1066	1066	1066	1066	1066	1066	111	1111	1127.5	1127.5	1227	114	1127	1127	1148	1148	1148	1148				
	2300-2400	Au	2400	2400	2400	2400	2370	2370	2370	2570	2370	2370	2570	2570	2370	250	2370	2340	2340	2340	2340	2340				
Gas Pressure (n)	3.0	Cr	3.0	3.0	3.0	3.0	3.0	3.0	3.0	3.0	3.0	3.0	3.0	3.0	3.0	3.0	3.0	3.0	3.0	3.0	3.0	3.0				
	3.0	Ni	3.0	3.0	3.0	3.0	3.0	3.0	3.0	3.0	3.0	3.0	3.0	3.0	3.0	3.0	3.0	3.0	3.0	3.0	3.0	3.0				
	9.5	Au	9.5	9.5	9.5	9.5	9.5	9.5	9.5	9.5	9.5	9.5	9.5	9.5	9.5	9.5	9.5	9.5	9.5	9.5	9.5	9.5				
	9.5	Cr	9.5	9.5	9.5	9.5	9.5	9.5	9.5	9.5	9.5	9.5	9.5	9.5	9.5	9.5	9.5	9.5	9.5	9.5	9.5	9.5				
	9.5	Au	9.5	9.5	9.5	9.5	9.5	9.5	9.5	9.5	9.5	9.5	9.5	9.5	9.5	9.5	9.5	9.5	9.5	9.5	9.5	9.5				
Speed (IPM)	4.0	Cr	4.0	4.0	4.0	4.0	4.0	4.0	4.0	4.0	4.0	4.0	4.0	4.0	4.0	4.0	4.0	4.0	4.0	4.0	4.0	4.0				
	7.5	Ni	7.5	7.5	7.5	7.5	7.5	7.5	7.5	7.5	7.5	7.5	7.5	7.5	7.5	7.5	7.5	7.5	7.5	7.5	7.5	7.5				
	7.0	Au	7.0	7.0	7.0	7.0	7.0	7.0	7.0	7.0	7.0	7.0	7.0	7.0	7.0	7.0	7.0	7.0	7.0	7.0	7.0	7.0				
	5.5	Cr	5.5	5.5	5.5	5.5	5.5	5.5	5.5	5.5	5.5	5.5	5.5	5.5	5.5	5.5	5.5	5.5	5.5	5.5	5.5	5.5				
	7.0	Au	7.0	7.0	7.0	7.0	7.0	7.0	7.0	7.0	7.0	7.0	7.0	7.0	7.0	7.0	7.0	7.0	7.0	7.0	7.0	7.0				
Vacuum 3x10⁻⁶			3×10^{-6}	3×10^{-6}	3×10^{-6}	3×10^{-6}	3×10^{-6}	3×10^{-6}	3×10^{-6}	3×10^{-6}	3×10^{-6}	3×10^{-6}	3×10^{-6}	3×10^{-6}	3×10^{-6}	3×10^{-6}	3×10^{-6}	3×10^{-6}	3×10^{-6}	3×10^{-6}	3×10^{-6}	3×10^{-6}				
			3×10^{-6}	3×10^{-6}	3×10^{-6}	3×10^{-6}	3×10^{-6}	3×10^{-6}	3×10^{-6}	3×10^{-6}	3×10^{-6}	3×10^{-6}	3×10^{-6}	3×10^{-6}	3×10^{-6}	3×10^{-6}	3×10^{-6}	3×10^{-6}	3×10^{-6}	3×10^{-6}	3×10^{-6}	3×10^{-6}				
Checked by																										
Number of runs at end of each shift			12	14			10	9			5	9			7	8			9	8						
Comments/problem cause																										

Source: Motorola, Schaumburg, Ill.

4. These process technicians are, by nature, "diddle artists" and cannot keep away from control knobs.
5. There is lack of discipline in the plant.
6. There is diffused responsibility for results.
7. Line operators are made to feel that Positrol is a "spy system" monitoring them rather than a spy system for process behaviors.

In one sense, the discipline of Positrol parallels the discipline of ISO-9000, in which a procedure is to be followed to the letter. The big difference, however, is that ISO-9000 is imposed before a process has been improved with DOE. What good does that do? *It simply freezes the defects, while Positrol freezes the improvement!*

The importance of Positrol is best illustrated with a case study.

Case Study 1: The Pick-and-Place Machine

In a reputable multinational company, the Singapore plant had retained this author as a consultant to drastically improve its outgoing quality. The main thrust was DOE. Working with this company, in periodic visits, we had improved its outgoing quality from 15,000 ppm to 120 ppm in two years. One of the processes—a pick-and-place machine—which picks components off a tape and reel and transfers them to a printed circuit board at a fast clip of 100 parts per minute—had a defect rate of 3,000 ppm. Our DOE team had reduced the defect rate to 60 ppm.

But on my next visit, the plant manager mentioned that the defect rate, while not as bad as earlier results, had now jumped up to 500 ppm. Taking him in tow, I said: "Let's go talk to the parts." At the pick-and-place station, a chart had plotted the defect history on a daily basis. On some days, the defect rate was zero; on others 1,000 ppm, 200 ppm, or 500 ppm. It was like a sawtooth plot, indicating that the machine was not being controlled. I asked: "Where is your Positrol chart?" The plant manager repeated my question to the process technician. His face was blank. The plant manager had known of the importance of Positrol. He had attended my DOE seminar for two days.

The incident prompted a discipline to be established throughout this plant. Every machine was equipped with a Positrol chart prominently displayed, enabling the gains made by their scores of DOE projects to be locked in. A further testimony occurred a few years later. When Singapore labor became too costly, a feeder plant was created in Indonesia, across the Malacia Straits with several of the processes were moved there. Management was worried about setbacks with a new country, a new plant, and new people. But with each process having been characterized, optimized, and frozen, the transfer went so smoothly that Singapore's yields were replicated within a week.

Workshop Exercise 1: P.C. Board Soldering

In a large television manufacturing plant, DOE was used to reduce the defect rate on solder connections from 12,000 ppm to 85 ppm. A Positrol plan was then established, as shown in Table 18-3, to monitor key process parameters.

Questions

1. What approach might you have used on this product and its associated wave solder process?
2. What modifications would you use on the Positrol Plan?

Answers

1. and 2. The Positrol plan indicates that there are 15 process parameters that are important and need to be maintained with Positrol. That appears to be too large a list. A start could have been made with product process search as the preferred DOE technique to narrow down the list of 15 process parameters. The list could have been further reduced by variables search to the four or five truly important parameters.

Three additional case studies—in three widely separated processes—show how Positrol can become an important step, following process characterization using DOE.

Case Study 2: CNC Lathe

Positrol Plan: (Tolerances of Parameters Not Stated). See Table 18-4.

Case Study 3: Plastic Injection Molding Machine

See Table 18-5.

Case Study 4: Die Casting

See Table 18-6.

Questions for DOE Teams as Guidelines for Positrol Projects

1. Has the process been investigated with a Product Process Search to pick up clues on important process parameters?

Table 18-3. Workshop Exercise: Positrol for P.C. Board Soldering

Specification

Equipment		Materials	
Model:	EPM CDD 300E	Solder alloy:	SN 60 PB 40
Products:	UV 900 double-sided boards	Flux:	ZEVA 590
Method:	No cleaning	Diffusion oil:	COBAR 808
Air:	Dry air with filter		

Positrol Plan

Parameter (What)	Specification	Measurement			
		Who	How	Where	When
Flux	0.814–0.83 (PC Liner 0.818–0.826)	MC Opr	Density Meter	FX Tank	3X/Shift
Spray Fluxer Pressure	1.6–1.8 Bar	MC Opr	Regulator	Machine entrance	3X/Shift
Spray Fluxer Drum Rotation	6.5–7.5 rpm/8.0–9.23 Sec/Rev	MC Opr	Stop watch	Flux drum	3X/Shift
Flux Spray Angle	85–90 degree right	Tech/AE	Angular gauge		Daily PM
Preheat Temperature	90C–110C	Tech/AE	Mole profile	Entrance to exit	Weekly
Solder Level	27 mm to 28 mm with pump on	Tech/AE	Rules/Level sensor	Solder bath	4X/Shift
Nozzle Gap	0.8–0.9 mm	Tech/AE	Feeder gauge	Chip nozzle	Daily PM
Chip Wave Height	1 to 1.5 glass gauge division	MC Opr	Glass Gauge	Chip wave	3X/Shift
Main Wave Height	2 to 3.0 glass gauge division	MC Opr	Glass Gauge	Main wave	3X/Shift
Solder Temperature	245C to 250C	MC Opr	Thermo meter	Main wave solder	3X/Shift
Tuner Base to Top of Chip Nozzle	10.5 mm to 11.5 mm	Tech/AE	Vernier caliper	Chip wave nozzle	Weekly PM
Tuner Base to Top of Main Nozzle	5.5 mm to 6.5 mm	Tech/AE	Vernier caliper	Main wave nozzle	Weekly PM
Conveyor Speed	50 to 55 seconds per meter	MC Opr	Stop watch	1 meter on cov/chain	3X/Shift
Different Pump Oil	25–35 Gamma/4-W	Tech/AE	Oil pump	Main wave	3X/Shift
Carrier Washing	15 car on line	Prodn Opr	Ultrasonic machine	Flux room	4X/Shift

Source: Phillips, Singapore.

375

Table 18-4. Case Study 2: CNC Lathe

What	Who	How	Where	When
Coolant	Automatic	Reflectometer	Nozzle	Every 4 hours
Feed	Automatic	Tachometer	Internal	Continuous
Speed	Automatic	Tachometer	Internal	Continuous
Cutting tool	Operator	Visual: 10x magnification	Tool holder	Every ½ hour

Source: S.K.F., Gottenburg, Sweden.

Table 18-5. Case Study 3: Plastic Injection Molding Machine

Parameter What	Spec. & Tolerance	Who	How	Where	When
Mold temperature	140°–150°F	Asst. foreman	Pyrometer	On cavity surface	Twice/shift
Boost pressure	540–560 PSI	Asst. foreman	Pressure gauge	At machine	Twice/shift
Holding pressure	570–590 PSI	Asst. foreman	Pressure gauge	At machine	Twice/shift
Melt temperature	520°–530°F	Asst. foreman	Pyrometer	In melt	Once/shift
Drying of material	180–200 sec.	Asst. foreman	Temperature gauge	At dryer	Twice/shift

Source: Pine River Plastics, Warren, Mich.

Table 18-6. Case Study 4: Die Casting

Parameter What	Spec. & Parameter	Who	How	Where	When
Metal Temperature	800° ± 20°	Operator	Thermo-couple	At press	Twice/day
Shot pressure	800–1000 PSI	Operator	Gauge	At press	Each setup
Hydraulic press pressure	800–1000 PSI	Operator	Gauge	At press	Each setup
Coolant	Full	Operator	Visual	At press	Twice/day
Spray mold release	Full	Operator	Visual	At press	Once/day

Source: Racine Die Casting, Racine, Wisconsin.

2. Has a Variables Search and/or a Full Factorial followed Product/Process Search to characterize the process?
3. Has a Scatter Plot/Response Surface Methodology followed Variables Search and/or Full Factorial to optimize the process?
4. Have realistic specifications and tolerances been established on each important process parameter (the what) as the start of a Positrol plan?
5. Have the *who*, the *how*, the *where*, and the *when* of the measurement of each important parameter been established?
6. Is a Positrol chart established following the Positrol plan?
7. Is Pre-Control used to monitor and control important process parameters, especially when product defect levels associated with the process are below 100 ppm?
8. Are line operators, maintenance teams, and technicians warned never to deviate from the Positrol chart and to desist from their usual tendency to "diddle and adjust" unless a further DOE is deemed necessary?
9. Are Positrol charts prominently displayed for all to see and for immediate action if process parameters go out of control?
10. Are there warning lights or other audiovisual signals to alert operators and management to out-of-control parameters?
11. Are warning limits built into the process, using microprocessor technologies so that the process shuts down automatically if the process parameters got out of control?
12. Are line operators assured that Positrol is not a management system to spy on their performance, but a system to monitor how well the process is behaving?

Questions for Top Management During DOE Project Reviews

1. Is there a clear distinction between the need for ISO-9000, which tends to *freeze defects*, and Positrol, which is designed to *freeze improvements?*
2. Has management explained to all line operators, maintenance teams, technicians, etc., that Positrol is not meant to check their performance, but to check the performance of the process and its consistency?
3. Is there a periodic, roving check by management, at different levels, to see if the discipline of the Positrol chart is being maintained?
4. Is Pre-Control used in conjunction with Positrol to monitor selected process parameters?
5. Can warning lights and other audiovisual signals be designed to alert line operators to out-of-control process parameters?

19

Process Certification: Eliminating Peripheral Causes of Poor Quality

Murphy's Law

If St. Patrick is the patron saint of Ireland, St. Murphy must, undoubtedly, be the patron saint of industry! In fact, the humorous, but very real, foundation of Process Certification is Murphy's Law—the universal adage that states: "If something can go wrong, it will." Murphy's Law is omnipresent in industry. The challenge of Process Certification is to disarm Murphy's Law.

The major causes of variation can be drastically reduced with DOE. But there are still a number of peripheral causes of poor quality, scores of little Murphies running around that can trip up a process before and after DOE studies. They must be captured and incarcerated. The policeman needed for this capture is Process Certification. Its place in the detailed problem-solving roadmap is shown in Figure 7-1. (Note: *It should also be used before DOE studies.*)

A Generic List of Peripheral Causes of Poor Quality

Table 19-1 is a generic list of the various peripheral causes that can contribute to poor quality. It can be divided into five broad categories:

> Management/supervision inadequacies;
> Violation of good manufacturing practices;
> Plant/equipment inattention;
> Environment neglect; and
> Human shortcomings.

Table 19-1. List of Peripheral Causes of Poor Quality

(1) Management/Supervision Inadequacies	*(2) Violation of Good Mfg. Practices (GMP)*

> Pervasive fear among line workers
> Worker ideas stifled
> Error cause removal not encouraged
> Dictatorial line supervision
> No intradept. or cross-functional teams
> High people turnover
> High absenteeism
> No gain sharing
> Little or no training
> Little or no Poka-Yoke
> No operator certification
> Multiskilled operators not encouraged
> No reach-out goals
> Measurements
  > Cost of poor quality not measured
  > Yields/cycle time not tracked
  > C_p, C_{pk} not measured
> Little feedback of results
> No audio/visual quality alarm signals
> Data pollution—little action on data
> No worker authority to shut down poor quality line
> No Positrol
> Supervisors chasing parts; excess paperwork
> Push for quantity over quality
> Lack of recognition for job well done
> Poor working conditions
	> Standard Operating Procedures (SOP) not written or too difficult
	> Poor safety for workers and products
	> Poor ergonomics
	> Sloppy housekeeping
	> Process flow vs. product flow
	> Push vs. pull systems
	> Setup, changeover time too long
	> Excess inventory on floor; crowded aisles
	> Tools difficult to access
	> Frequent model changes
	> Frequent line stops
	> Partial builds
	> Unclear, confusing, contradictory instructions
	> Excessive network

Table 19-1. (Continued)

(3) Plant/Equipment Inattention	(4) Environmental Neglect	(5) Human Shortcomings
> Total Product Maintenance not used > Poor ratio of preventive maintenance to "fix when broke" > Inattention to: > Lubrication > Machine noise > Machine vibration > Overheating > Voltage surges > Conveyor speeds > Corrosion > Air hose pressures > Instrumentation: > 5:1 accuracy not met > No traceability to national standards > Calibration infrequent/not done > Inadequate ventilation > Poor fail/safe controls > No airlocks for outside air	Lack of: > Temperature control > Humidity control > Water purity > Air purity > Dust control > Chemicals control > Lighting adequacy > Vent control > Electrostatic discharge protection > Electromagnetic compatibility protection > Smoking prohibition	> SOPs not followed > Lack of discipline > "Diddle artists" > Rugged individualism over team cooperation > Personal problems brought to work > Alcoholism/drugs > Unreasonable union demands

The list is by no means all-inclusive. It is intended as a checklist and as a guideline for Process Certification teams as they conduct pre-DOE and post-DOE audits. Some of the items in each category are self-explanatory. Others need a little elaboration.

Management/Supervision Inadequacies

Dr. W. Edwards Deming has said that one of the most corrosive elements in industry is the *rampant fear among employees of speaking out.* Workers, next to parts themselves, are the most productive source of clues for problem solving, but if their reservoir of ideas is not tapped, a valuable resource is lost. Further, workers need to be "in on things," to feel wanted. Otherwise, they withdraw into their noncommunicating, nonparticipating shells.

Error Cause Removal (ECR) is one way to get workers to record quality problems. They do not need to provide solutions, but encouraging them to point out such problems is a first step toward getting them involved and toward problem solving.

Operator Certification is a necessary discipline, especially for difficult processes and assemblies. It consists of training, followed by tests and certification of the operator for that particular process. There should also be periodic recertifications of the operator to make sure that correct methodologies are not bypassed. Often, a matrix is maintained, listing the names of each operator and the various processes for which they are certified.

Among quality measurements, the cost of poor quality is the most important macroscopic parameter. Including items such as warranty, scrap, analyzing, repair, inspection, test, and excess inventory—all non–value-added items—the cost of poor quality accounts for 10 to 20 percent of sales that are a total waste. *More specifically, poor quality costs a company $100 to $200 per employee per day!* More detailed measurements include the tie-in between yields (with a target of 100 percent) and cycle time (with a target of no more than twice direct labor time) and other measures, such as total defects per unit (TDPU), in which all the defects from the start of a production line to the finish are added up and divided by the total number of units passed; and C_p and C_{pk} for important product/process parameters.

Violation of Good Manufacturing Practices (GMP)

Good manufacturing practices are well known in industry. They are reinforced by programs such as Quality Circles, Small Group Improvement Activities (SGIA), Kaizen, Glass Wall Management, and ISO-9000, etc. These programs should be utilized to determine:

> ➤ Whether Standard Operating Procedures (SOP) are necessary.
> ➤ If necessary, whether they are too difficult or too bureaucratic for operators to follow.
> ➤ That they are included in simple terms.
> ➤ Whether the operator inputs into the SOP are encouraged.
> ➤ Whether operators follow instructions—but only when necessary.
> ➤ Whether Positrol is enforced.

➤ Whether SOPs are periodically audited for simplification, accuracy, and compliance.

Within the last 10 years, Lean Manufacturing, based on the Toyota production system, is increasingly coming into vogue. Its disciplines include focus factories, product versus process flow, pull systems, small lot sizes, short setup times, etc. Lean Manufacturing also emphasizes product quality, process quality, and short cycle time, which are part and parcel of its design.

Plant/Equipment Inattention

The overall discipline of this category is Total Productive Maintenance (TPM), which was discussed in Chapter 3. Most Western industries are ignorant of its use and enormous benefits. As a result, the attitude on processes and machines is: "If it ain't broke, don't fix it!" Ratios of preventive maintenance to corrective measures are less than 1:10, rather than the other way around. Line operators should be encouraged, in teams, to undertake a much larger share of preventive maintenance reinforced with DOE techniques.

Further, just as parts give clues, so do processes and machines. Machine noise, heat, vibration, and other telltale signs are early warnings of future trouble.

The whole subject of metrology also needs to be visited. We have already established the rule that the accuracy of the instrument must be at least five times the specification tolerance of the product being measured. In addition, the test equipment calibration must be traceable to national standards. The frequency of calibration and adherence to such timetables must be monitored.

Environmental Neglect

In many plants, environmental controls are not on the screen of production management thinking. Room ambient temperatures, humidities, static electricity discharged, etc., are accepted with whatever variation nature provides. Yet, any one of these environmental conditions can have a drastic impact on product quality in many products.

Take dust as an example. In the semiconductor industry, dust is the sworn enemy of quality. It is measured in terms of particles of foreign matter greater than 0.5 microns in one cubic foot of air. In the surgical ward of a hospital, the allowable figure is 10,000 particles. In the semiconductor industry, the maximum number of foreign particles allowed several years ago was 1,000. Today, rooms are being built that require no more than 1—10,000 times as clean as the surgical ward of a hospital!

Human Shortcomings

Employees, for the most part, are not the problem. Quality gurus like Deming and Juran state that 85 percent of quality problems are the responsibility of management, with only 15 percent are the responsibility of workers. But there can be a tendency among workers to skirt discipline, to develop shortcuts, to speed up production, to "diddle" controls—all with good intent, but at the expense of good quality. Such tendencies should be monitored and corrected by supervision.

Process Certification Methodology

1. Process Certification is best conducted by an interdisciplinary team, consisting of, say, members from development or engineering, quality, manufacturing engineering, and production, as well as any other departments that are familiar with the process to be certified.
2. The team consults the generic list of quality peripherals described above or prepares a more limited list that is specific to that process.
3. It then proceeds to audit the process, making sure that all the potential quality peripheral problems are resolved and nailed down in a thorough "process scrub" before certification is granted to the process.
4. In terms of timing, the older recommendation was to do process certification after DOE and Positrol, but before the introduction of SPC as a maintenance tool. The current recommendation of the authors is to *do a preliminary audit of the process, even before the start of DOE and to do a post-DOE audit as well*. The reason is that a process may contain many of these peripheral quality problems to begin with. If they are not solved, they could add to the "noise" of the experiment to such an extent that the "noise exceeds the signal" of the DOE study. A process "scrub" ahead of DOE would assure the success of the DOE study.
5. Only with everything in place after Step 4, is the process given certification status to begin unit no. 1 in production.
6. Periodically—preferably once or twice per year—the process should be recertified by the team, so that the old peripheral quality problems do not reappear and new ones do not creep in.

Case Study 1: SCAP Metallization

In a Silicon Capacitance Atmosphere Pressure (SCAP) sensor product, a sputtering machine deposits metal layers on two sides of a glass plate. The following process certification check list was drawn up by the process certification team:

1. Are a Positrol plan and a Positrol chart in place for the sputtering machine?
2. Are environmental controls for temperature and humidity in place?
3. Are there safety controls in place for storing and using chemicals?
4. Are the operators clear on their performance goals?
5. Are there clear instructions for the operators?
6. Are there quality targets and shut-down criteria when targets are not met?
7. Are the cleaning procedures for glass adequate and unambiguous?
8. Is there a calibration procedure and frequency for all test equipment?
9. Is the effectiveness of an engineering change validated with a B versus C experiment before the change is incorporated?
10. Is there a gold control and salvage policy and procedure in place, and is it adhered to?

Case Study 2: Punch Press

In a machine shop, the following process certification checklist was established after a DOE study:

1. Are a Positrol plan and Positrol chart on the important parameters identified in the variables search equipment?
2. Are there periodic checks on the raw material for thickness, hardness, width, and camber—the list to be checked on every lot?
3. Do the dereeler and stock straightener have preventive maintenance schedules?
4. Is the stock feeder adjustment checked?
5. Is the buckle detection in place?
6. Press controls:

> Is the ram adjustment made?
> Is the RPM correct?
> Is the part ejection mechanism in order?
> Is the counterbalance pressure correct?
> Are the safety circuits functioning?

7. Die set (tooling)

> Are the sharp cutting details checked?
> Is the forming detail checked?
> Is the clamping pressure correct?

8. Is lubrication in order?
9. Is the deburring within specs?
10. Is the degreasing under control?

Comment

The DOE experiment on the press brake, as described in the chapter on Variables Search, indicated two important variables that had to be closely controlled. But, as indicated above, there are still a number of "little Murphies" that have to be guarded against on this process to achieve zero defects and C_{pk}'s of over 2.0 on a continuum of time.

Workshop Exercise 1: Porcelain Paint Process

In the chapter on full factorials, Workshop Exercise 1 dealt with a porcelain paint process whose yields had been traditionally poor—between 63 and 82 percent. Temperature and humidity were two possible causes suspected by the DOE team, because yields were somewhat higher (around 82 percent) in the winter months and somewhat lower (around 63 percent) in the summer months.

The workshop exercise described a 2^2 factorial initiated by this author. The results were amazing. None of the four combinations of two temperatures and humidities produced yields below 91.5 percent! The DOE team could not believe the excellent results—regardless of temperature or humidity.

Questions

1. What was the real Red X?
2. What were the lessons learned from this exercise?

Answers (1 and 2)

> The 2^2 factorial showed that the higher temperature was actually producing higher yields than the lower temperature, contrary to the DOE team's theory.
> The higher humidity was actually producing higher yields than the lower humidity, also contrary to the DOE team's theory.
> Temperature contributed three times as much as humidity to higher yields.
> Neither temperature nor humidity was the real Red X.
> *The real Red X was the Process Certification audit and the "scrub" that cleaned up the peripheral quality problems the audit discovered before the DOE experiment was started.*
> The plant manager had taken this author on a line tour to explain the paint process. He was proud of the sophisticated equipment. But on the line tour, I observed many lapses of good manufacturing practices—housekeeping, calibration of equipment, control of adjustments, etc. The plant manager was embarrassed. I recommended that, before the team started the DOE study, a process certification audit be conducted by the team and the little Murphies apprehended, captured, and put away, as a first order of business.

Table 19-2 shows the results of the Process Certification audit. The situation was even worse than anyone had anticipated. It took a solid three weeks to do the Process Certification scrub to remove the deficiencies, however, the scrub *eliminated many of the "noise" factors that would otherwise have entered the 2^2 factorial experiment and muddied up the purity of the signal.*

The lesson to be learned from this eye-opening exercise for this plant is that *a Process Certification audit should be conducted before a DOE study* to establish a purer and relatively noise-free baseline and give the DOE study a chance to succeed.

Workshop Exercise 2: Poor Yields on Memory Chips

In a U.S. semiconductor plant making memory chips, yields could not go over 75 percent despite many attempts at problem solving. Yet the company's joint venture plant in Japan, producing similar memory chips, was experiencing yields of at least 95 percent.

A fact-finding team was sent to the Japanese plant to investigate possible causes for the yield difference. It could discover no difference in the

Table 19-2. Process Certification Audit Findings: Paint Process

1. Hangers not aligned or missing
2. Hangers rubbing wall at exit of powder room
3. Base coat hand spray (no auto guns)
4. Air gauges show low pressure
5. No level controls in booths
6. Guns leak in back
7. Pumps leaking
8. Transfer leaks
9. Powder escaping from final filters in universal booth
10. Transfer room walls need insulation
11. Rust on parts in washer
12. Washer temperature 20° too low
13. Washer conveyor needs seals
14. Too many line stops (5 in one hour)
15. Conveyor surges
16. Conveyor rail needs cleaning
17. Cooling tunnel floor dirty
18. AC return air in wrong location
19. Transfer area understaffed
20. Hanger banger full of powder
21. Hoses on universal booth too long
22. Insufficient supply of spare parts
23. No Azo screens or Azo waste container
24. Outside air infiltration

designs, processes, materials, or test equipment. The clean rooms also had identical maximum foreign particle requirements.

Question

What was the Red X difference and how was it discovered?

Answer

Frustrated in its inability to find the root cause for the yield differences in the two plants, the company decided on a "walk through" of the Japanese plant to record any differences in operating practices, starting at the beginning of a work day. It flow-charted the various steps of fabrication, assembly, and test. Again, no significant differences were found between the U.S. and Japanese practices, except for two very pertinent observations:

1. The Japanese workers would enter the superclean room at exactly the same time in the morning, go out at exactly the same time at the morning break and reenter at exactly the same time after the break. They would do the same at other breaks, such as lunch. The U.S. workers would straggle into the superclean room at somewhat different times, go out individually for a cup of coffee or for a smoke several times before the first break and do this repeatedly throughout the shift. As a result,

the doors to the clean room let in the dust-filled outside air far more frequently than in the Japanese plant.

2. After each break, the Japanese workers sat at their work stations with their arms folded, doing no work for a full five minutes, before resuming their tasks. This is to let the dust settle *physically.* The loss of five minutes of productivity was more than made up by the higher yields. The reason for this perplexing practice is that human beings give off dust particles at the rate of over 100,000 per minute. That figure jumps to over one million when people are walking or moving. Allowing the dust to settle before work proceeds on sensitive semiconductor devices is now standard practice. The team returned to the United States, instituted these process certification audit improvements, and achieved yields of 95 percent and higher.

Questions for DOE Teams as Guidelines for Process Certification As Well As for Management During DOE Project Reviews

Process Certification Audits and Scrubs

1. Is an interdisciplinary team formed to develop a checklist of items to observe on a process before the start of an audit?
2. Does the team conduct such a Process Certification audit *before the start of DOE studies* to remove or reduce noise factors in the DOE work?
3. Does the team do a Process Certification scrub to remove the causes of the several peripheral quality problems?
4. Does the team do a Process Certification reaudit after the DOE study?

Management/Supervision

1. Is there an atmosphere of *fearless communication* between management and the workers?
2. Are workers given adequate training on the job and in problem solving using simple DOE tools?
3. Is Error Cause Removal (ECR) formally in place to allow workers to point out recurrent quality problems?
4. Are workers certified to handle skilled jobs on one or more critical processes, and are they periodically recertified?
5. Is Poka-Yoke instituted so that workers receive signals from sen-

sors that a mistake is about to be made and can be corrected a priori?

6. Are a Positrol plan and a Positrol chart in place on the process and are they being scrupulously maintained?
7. Are quality metrics such as Cost of Poor Quality; yield/cycle time charts; total defects per unit; and C_p, C_{pk} in place to track improvement?
8. Is teamwork encouraged with disciplines such as Quality Circles and Kaizen?

Good Manufacturing Practice

1. Are Standard Operating Practices (SOPs) in place where necessary? Are they easy to follow? Are worker inputs solicited in formulating SOPs?
2. Are Lean Manufacturing concepts such as pull systems, product flow, small lot sizes, and short setup times introduced and practiced?

Metrology

1. Are instrument accuracies traceable to the Bureau of Standards or other national agencies?
2. Is there a calibration timetable on all important instruments, and is it followed and audited?

Total Productive Maintenance

1. Is Total Productive Maintenance in place and is Factory Overall Effectiveness measured for each process?
2. What is the ratio of preventive maintenance to correction on each process?
3. Are there audiovisual alarm signals as indications of process problems?
4. Are there built-in diagnostics for the process with self-correcting mechanisms?

Environment

1. Are ambient environments such as temperature, humidity, static electricity, etc., considered in Process Certification audits and DOE studies?
2. Are dust, air, water, gases, and chemical controls in place?

People

1. Are workers forbidden to "diddle" with controls and adjustments once a comprehensive DOE has been established on the process, along with Positrol?

Part VII
· ·
Statistical Process
Control: For Monitoring
Quality

20. Control Charts: A Technique Whose Time Has Gone

21. Pre-Control: A Technique Whose Time Has Come

Statistical Process Control (SPC) has been widely touted as the hallmark of the quality movement—"the silver bullet" that can miraculously solve chronic quality problems. Yet, although thousands of companies have embraced it in the last 20 years, it has produced disappointing results, with C_p's and C_{pk}'s barely reaching 1.0.

Part VII of this book states that there is an important use for SPC—but not as a problem-solving tool. It should only be used after quality variation and quality problems are resolved with DOE. Its main function is to so monitor a vastly improved product or process that the problems do not reappear. It serves mainly as a maintenance tool.

There are two branches of SPC:

> Control Charts—the older and less effective technique; and
> Pre-Control—the newer and statistically far more powerful technique.

They are examined in Chapters 20 and 21, respectively.

20

Control Charts: A Technique Whose Time Has Gone

The Roller-Coaster History of Control Charts

Developed by Walter Shewhart more than seventy years ago, control charts quickly became a bridge between the academic world of the laboratory and the practical world of production. It was widely used in World War II production. But in the post–World War II period, as America became the only economic superpower, industry felt it did not need these statistical techniques.

By the late 1970s, however, the U.S. industrial lead had vanished. NBC produced a television documentary: "If Japan Can, Why Can't We?" Its theme was that Japan's quality was outstanding because it had SPC and control charts, while the United States was backward because it didn't. It did not know that several years earlier, Japan had abandoned control charts as ineffective! NBC's documentary, nevertheless, became a historical continental divide between a pre-SPC era and an SPC era. Control charts were recalled from exile and received a coronation.

It has been a tyrannical reign, with several original equipment manufacturers customers, especially Ford, demanding use of control charts as a passport to doing business with them. Yet, control charts have failed miserably in solving problems and reducing variation. Industry has spent billions of dollars on control charts, but the return on investment is in the millions—about 0.1 percent in 15 years! One could do better at a failed S&L bank! The reason: They are meant only to maintain an already improved product or process achieved through DOE.

The Weaknesses of Control Charts

Because of the huge volume of published materials on the control chart[17] its theoretical underpinnings, its formulas, and its mechanics are bypassed in this text. Instead, we will concentrate on the inherent weaknesses of control charts, which are best illustrated with two case studies.

Case Study 1: A Bushing

In a machine shop operation, a bushing had to be fabricated to a length of $0.500'' \pm 0.002''$. Table 20-1 shows the data from which the $\overline{X}$ and R charts of Figure 20-1 were constructed.

These charts show that all the subgroup averages ($\overline{X}$) are within upper and lower control limits, as are all the subgroup ranges (R). This shows that the trial control chart, which incidentally took 60 readings, 32 calculations, and $1^{1}/_{2}$ shifts to complete, indicated that the process was stable, (otherwise called a constant cause system). So full production could go forward to fabricate hundreds of thousands of units.

Table 20-1. Control Chart Data on Bushing Length

Bushing Length Specification
$= .500'' \pm .002''$

Sample #	8am	9	10	11	12pm	1	2	3	4	5	6	7
1	.501	.501	.502	.501	.501	.500	.500	.500	.501	.502	.501	.500
2	.501	.501	.501	.502	.501	.500	.501	.501	.501	.502	.502	.500
3	.500	.501	.502	.501	.501	.502	.501	.501	.501	.501	.501	.501
4	.501	.501	.501	.500	.501	.502	.501	.501	.501	.502	.501	.502
5	.502	.502	.501	.500	.501	.502	.500	.500	.501	.501	.501	.501
Sample of X	2.505	2.506	2.507	2.504	2.505	2.506	2.503	2.503	2.505	2.508	2.506	2.504
X_1	.501	.5012	.5014	.5008	.5010	.5012	.5006	.5006	.5010	.5016	.5012	.5008
R_1	.002	.001	.001	.002	.000	.002	.002	.001	.000	.001	.001	.002

Sum of $X_1 = 6.0128$
Sum of $R_1 = 0.0115$

$$\overline{\overline{X}} = \frac{\Sigma X}{N} = \frac{6.0128}{12} = .50107 \qquad \overline{R} = \frac{\Sigma R}{N} = \frac{.015}{12} = .00125$$

Control Limits:

$$\overline{\overline{X}} \pm A_2\overline{R} = .50107 \pm (.58)(.00125)$$
$$UCL = .50180$$

For Sample Averages: $LCL = .50034$

$$UCL_R = D_4\overline{R} = (2.11)(.00125) = .00264$$

For Range: $LCL_R = D_3\overline{R} = (0)(.00125) = 0$

Figure 20-1. Bushing Length: X̄ and R Charts

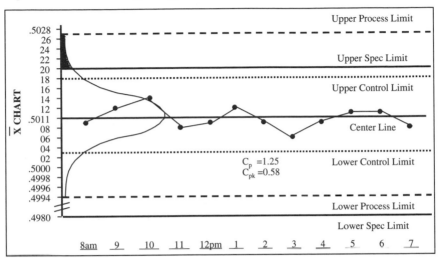

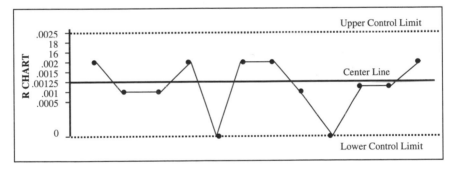

Source: Wilson Sporting Goods Co., Chicago, Ill.

Yet, if specification limits are drawn, as shown in Figure 20-1, it can clearly be seen that the upper control limit for averages, X̄, is dangerously close to the upper specification limit for individual readings. Even a lay person, without statistical insights, can reason that if average values are so close to a specification limit, the individual values that make up the average can go beyond that limit. (Many Control Chart purists do not allow specification limits to be shown on the chart because they fear that such a practice would inhibit the necessity for continual process improvement, which they believe can magically be achieved by the mere construction of control charts!)

More precisely, the projected spread of individual values can be calculated by the formulas for process limits:

Upper Process Limit = $\overline{\overline{X}} + 3\sigma^1 = \overline{\overline{X}} + 3\overline{R}/d_2$
Lower Process Limit = $\overline{\overline{X}} - 3\sigma^1 = \overline{\overline{X}} - 3\overline{R}/d_2$
Where: σ^1 is the population standard deviation
$\overline{\overline{X}}$ is the grand average of the subgroup averages
$\overline{R}$ is the average of the subgroup ranges
d_2 is a constant for a given subgroup size; for a subgroup size of 4, d_2 is
2.059, for a subgroup size of 5, d_2 is 2.326.

Figure 20-1 depicts these process limits. It clearly shows that the
upper process limit is 0.007″ above the upper specification limit, indicating that 7 percent of the bushings are likely to be defective (the shaded
portion of Figure 10-1). *So here is a control chart indicating that all is well and
that production can continue at full speed, when, in actuality, the process is
likely to produce a totally unacceptable rate of defective parts.* Again, in most
control chart work, process limits are not even known, much less calculated or used to gauge process capability. In fact, if the C_p and C_{pk} of this
process were calculated, they would be a poor C_p of 1.25 and a disgrace-
ful C_{pk} of 0.58! What a dramatic condemnation of Control Charts!
    In the quality control literature, a β risk is defined as the risk of ac-
cepting product that should be rejected and an α risk is the risk of rejecting an acceptable product. (In this case study, the β risk is 7 percent). It
can be proven that the β risk, under certain conditions, can be as high as
30 percent.

Case Study 2: Sensor Capacitance

An electronic element for sensing atmosphere pressure in an automobile
had a capacitance requirement of 31 to 45 pico-farads (pf). Figure 20-2
shows the $\overline{X}$ and R control charts for the process.
    In contrast to the charts in first case study, both the $\overline{X}$ and R charts
show points outside of the upper and lower control limits. The process
was declared out-of-control and stopped. Yet, production claimed that it
had produced over 100,000 units in the last 1-1/2 years without a single
reject in the outgoing quality audits or at the customer's plant. A glance
at the subgroup data would reveal that no individual reading is even
close to either the upper specification limit of 45 pf or the lower limit of
31 pf. Further, the projected process limits for the individual readings are
41 and 35 pf—well within the specification limits. (The projected process
spread is slightly narrower than the spread of the actual individual readings because the chosen subgroup size of 10 is unusually large.)
    Here we have an opposite condition from the one shown in the first
case study—a control chart declaring that the process should be shut
down, when production had every logical reason to continue! As a matter

Figure 20-2. Sensor $\overline{X}$ and R Charts

Spec: 31 to 45 pf

$\overline{X}$ = 37.2 pf; R = 2.2; UCL$_X$ = 37.88; LCL$_x$ = 36.52; UCL$_R$ = 3.95; LCL$_R$ = 0

Upper Process Limit = 41.0; Lower Process Limit = 35.0

C_p = 2.0; k = 0.58; C_{p_k} = 1.92

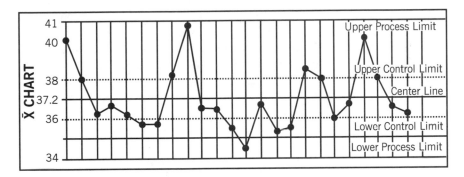

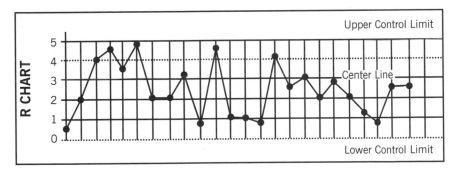

Source: Motorola, Schaumburg, Ill.

of fact, the C_p and C_{pk} of this process were 2.0 and 1.92, respectively—a world class quality level reached 15 years ago!

Slipshod Control Chart Practices

In actual practice, there are many more violations of control chart rules and guidelines than there is conformance. Here are some of the ways in which companies—especially suppliers, who are forced at economic gunpoint, to use Control Charts—get around the bureaucracy.

1. No action is taken on out-of-control charts. Somehow, merely charting them implies compliance.
2. Line operators, supervisors, and technicians don't have a clue on what to do when a point goes outside control limits, so they file away piles of control charts to furnish proof that they exist.
3. There is an explosion of control charts dealing with every conceivable parameter—important or not—as if mere quantity could compensate for meaningful content.
4. The walls of a plant are littered with control charts, with plants vying to see who can win the prize of having the most charts. (The record in one plant was 2,000 charts.)
5. In more than 75 percent of control charts, the initial trials to determine control limits are never recalibrated. Once drawn, they are cast in stone.
6. In a few cases, there is outright "fudging" of control charts—"creative charting" a day before a customer's quality representative is to visit the plant.
7. There is a mistaken belief that a constant cause system pervades a product or process if the control chart shows that all $\bar{x}$ and R points are within control limits. In actuality, there is no such thing as a stable process. Designs change, processes change, materials change, environments change, people change, and equipment changes. The only thing constant in industry is change!
8. Control charts are prepared with no specification limits drawn and hence no reference to reject levels; no process limits are calculated and hence there is no reference to C_p and C_{pk}'s or α and β risks; no $1\sigma_{\bar{x}}$, $2\sigma_{\bar{x}}$ limits to detect trends.

Questions for DOE Teams and Top Management

Because Control Charts have outlived their usefulness, DOE teams should not waste their valuable time on control chart questions as a memory jogger, nor should top management review progress on control chart work. Top management should, instead, allocate time, money, and manpower to more useful projects.

21

• •

Pre-Control: A Technique
Whose Time Has Come

Pre-Control is newer, simpler, more user-friendly, less costly, and statistically more powerful than control charts could ever be. A later section in this chapter will show that Pre-Control has all the advantages of control charts and none of their disadvantages. Because Pre-Control is less well known, however, it is presented in greater depth than control charts. Its place in the problem-solving roadmap is shown in Figure 7-1.

The Discovery of Pre-Control

Pre-Control was developed by the consulting firm of Rath and Strong in the 1950s for a major Fortune 500 company that had became disenchanted with cumbersome and ineffective control charts.

Pre-Control's founder, Frank Scatherwaite, is a brilliant statistician who established its theoretical underpinnings in a comprehensive paper more than 40 years ago. Unfortunately, just as Pre-Control was gaining recognition (this author introduced Pre-Control at Motorola in the late 1950s), the U.S. industry, flushed with economic success in the post–World War II years, threw out all statistical methods, control charts and Pre-Control included. Then, as SPC became fashionable again in the 1980s, and control charts came back into prominence, Pre-Control started to reappear on the statistical horizon.

There still appears to be a rear-guard resistance to Pre-Control on the part of a few prominent companies, living in the buggy-whip age instead of entering the jet age. But their ranks are decidedly thinning. Fifteen years ago, the ratio of control chart users to Pre-Control users was 99:1; today the ratio is 80:20. And, in the 21st century, as the simplicity and effectiveness of Pre-Control is better publicized, control charts will, increasingly, be relegated to history as in Japan, and Pre-Control will become the principal maintenance tool in the SPC world.

The Mechanics of Pre-Control in Four Easy Steps

The mechanics of Pre-Control are so simple that they can be taught to anybody—line workers, suppliers (and even engineers!) in less than 10 minutes. There are only four simple rules to follow:

Rule 1. Establishing Pre-Control Lines (Limits)

(a) For a two-sided tolerance, divide the specification width* of the Green Y parameter by 4 and mark off 2 points through the middle half of that width; i.e., one-quarter of the width from the low specification limit and one-quarter from the high specification limit. And, voilá, you immediately have the two control limits for Pre-Control, called Pre-Control lines, or P-C lines for short (see Figure 21-1A). (Pre-Control does not require a normal distribution or any assumption concerning the shape or stability of that distribution.)

How simple and elegant is this Rule 1 for Pre-Control! All you have to know is how to divide by 4 and you immediately get your P-C lines. That is why this technique is called Pre-Control. You get your control limits before you even begin production. How different from control charts, for which

> ➤ You must run 100, 200, or 300 units for one, two, or three days.
> ➤ You then get only *trial* control limits.
> ➤ And you must constantly recalibrate those trial limits every two weeks or so because there is no such thing in industry as a stable system.
> ➤ You must go through another 100, 200, 300 units for one, two, or three days for each such recalibration.

The area between the two P-C lines is called the green zone. The two areas between each Pre-Control line and the specification limits are called the yellow zones, and the two areas beyond the specification limits are called the red zones.

(b) For one-sided tolerance (upper specification limit only)

Where there is only an upper specification limit and no lower limit, divide the distance between the upper specification limit and zero in half to construct a single P-C line at the center, as shown in Figure 21-1B.

---

*It is assumed, of course, that the correct specifications and tolerances have been established with DOE using optimization techniques detailed in Part VII.

Figure 21-1. Pre-Control Rules

Simple Pre-Control Rules:

1a. Draw two precontrol lines in the middle half of the specification width.

1b. Draw a single precontrol line midway between the upper spec limit and 0.

1c. Draw a single precontrol line midway between the lower spec limit and the target value.

2. To determine process capability, 5 units in a row must be within P-C lines (green zone). If not use DOE.

3. In production, sample 2 units consecutively and periodically.

4. Frequency of sampling.

   Divide the time interval between two stoppages by 6.

Condition	Action
1. 2 units in green zone	Continue
2. 1 unit in green and 1 unit in yellow zone	Continue
3. 2 units in yellow zone	Stop*
4. 1 unit in red zone	Stop*

*To resume production, 5 units in a row must be within the green zone.

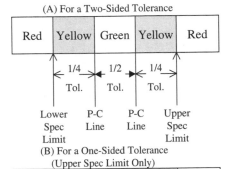

(A) For a Two-Sided Tolerance

| Red | Yellow | Green | Yellow | Red |

← 1/4 Tol. → ← 1/2 Tol. → ← 1/4 Tol. →

Lower Spec Limit | P-C Line | P-C Line | Upper Spec Limit

(B) For a One-Sided Tolerance
(Upper Spec Limit Only)

| Green | Yellow | Red |

← 1/2 Tol. → ← 1/2 Tol. →

Zero (Good) | P-C Line | Upper Spec Limit

(C) For a One-Sided Tolerance
(Lower Spec Limit Only)

| Red | Yellow | Green |

← 1/2 Tol. → ← 1/2 Tol. →

Lower Spec Limit | P-C Line | Target Value

Source: Rath & Strong, Boston, Mass.

(c) For one-sided tolerance (lower specification limit only)

Where there is only a lower specification limit and no upper limit, divide the distance between the lower specification limit and the target value or design center in half and construct a single P-C line at the center, as shown in Figure 21-1C. (Alternately, some Pre-Control practitioners use the average value of the Green Y parameter instead of the target value, but this requires prior knowledge of this average value and is not as accurate as using the target value.)

Rule 2. A Shortcut to Determine Process Capability

Process capability is usually determined by taking a sample of 30 to 100 units from a given process, after which C_p and C_{pk} can be calculated. Pre-

Control's second rule offers a shortcut in which a sample of only five consecutive units are taken from the process. Only if all five fall within the green zone can it be concluded (see Pre-Control theory section) that the process capability is a minimum C_{pk} of 1.33 and, possibly, much higher. That gives a signal that production can get started. If, however, even one of the five consecutive units falls outside the green zone, the process is not in control, and production is not allowed to start. The appropriate action should be a DOE study to identify and reduce the causes of variation.

Rule 3. Pre-Control in Production: Sample Size; Continuing/Stopping

Once production starts, the sample size is two consecutive units drawn periodically (see Rule 4) from the process. The following rules apply for continuing or stopping Pre-Control sampling:

1. If both units fall in the green zone, continue production.
2. If one unit falls in the green zone and the other in the yellow zone, the process is still in control. Continue production.
3. If both units fall in the same yellow zone, it is an indication of drift. Stop production momentarily to make process adjustments (based on process parameters identified in previous DOE studies). If the two units fall in opposite yellow zones, it is an indication of a major shift. Stop production and conduct an investigation into the cause of variation.
4. If even one unit falls in the red zone, you have a known reject and production must be stopped to investigate the cause of the reject.
5. Whenever production is stopped (as in Rules 3 and 4) and the cause identified and corrected, you must go back to Rule 2; i.e., five consecutive units must fall within the green zone before production can resume.

Rule 4. Frequency of Sampling

The frequency of sampling of 2 consecutive units is determined by dividing the average time period between two stoppages (i.e., between two pairs of yellows) by 6. In other words, if there is a stoppage (two yellows) at 9:00 A.M. and the process is corrected and restarted soon after, followed by another stoppage at 12:00 noon (two yellows again), the three-hour period between the two stoppages is divided by 6 to indicate that sampling should occur every half-hour. If, on the other hand, the period between two stoppages is three days, the frequency of sampling is reduced to once every half-day (or every four hours). Pre-Control, therefore—in the best traditions of quality control—provides a carrot and a stick, a carrot of very little sampling for very good quality, and a stick of very frequent sampling (hence, cost) for poor quality.

The choice of six samplings between two stoppages represents a compromise between the time and cost of more frequent samples and the risk of producing out-of-tolerance product (see the section on Pre-Control theory).

Special Circumstances Requiring Modifications of Pre-Control Steps

1. A Constant Sampling Frequency. Some Pre-Control practitioners ignore the rule on sampling frequency, which varies depending on quality levels, and use a constant sampling frequency, such as two consecutive units every hour. The rationale is that changing sampling frequency may be confusing to line operators and not conducive to a constant throughput. However, if the sampling frequency is never increased for poor quality, the β risk—i.e., the risk of accepting bad product when it should be rejected—is increased. And if the sampling frequency is never decreased for very good quality, the costs of Pre-Control checks go up unnecessarily.

2. A Ceiling on Sampling Frequency Increases. The frequency of sampling, using Rule 4, cannot go on being increased indefinitely. For example, if the sampling frequency is—at the start—two units per hour, and two yellow pairs appear within three hours of one another, the sampling must be increased to two units per half-hour (3/6). Now, if there are then two more yellow pairs within one hour of each other, the sampling frequency must be further increased to two units every 10 minutes (1/6). The next extrapolation of this logic could be two units every minute! Such a scenario would indicate, even to a novice, that the whole process is horribly out of control and the Pre-Control must be stopped and a strong dose of DOE employed immediately. A guideline could be established that whenever the sampling frequency exceeds, say, 15 minutes, an out-of-control condition is declared and a DOE study must be initiated.

3. A Floor on Sampling Frequency Decreases. The opposite scenario can also occur, in which the quality levels permit less frequent sampling. What if the period between two yellow pairs is one month? Then the frequency of sampling could theoretically be 22 days/6 or roughly once every four days. That is too long a period to go without a Pre-Control sample. As a practical rule, sampling should not be reduced to less than once per day, regardless of how good the quality level may be.

4. *Going From Frequent Sampling to Less Frequent Sampling.* Let us say that a deteriorating quality level has forced more frequent sampling—say, from two units per hour to two units every half-hour. Assuming that good quality is now restored, when can the lower sampling frequency be reinstituted? One approach would be to take the next six samples at the rate of two units every half-hour. If there are no more yellow pairs, the original sampling frequency of two units per hour can be reinstituted. If another six samples at this frequency produce no more yellow pairs, the new sampling frequency can be two units every two hours, and so on, until the floor of sampling once per day is reached.

5. *Pre-Control Guidelines During Production Discontinuities.* Production discontinuities can be a major cause of quality deterioration and Pre-Control must be sensitive to such changes. Examples of large discontinuities include model changes, setup changes, tooling changes, startup after lengthy downtimes, and infrequent runs of a given product. Whenever a major discontinuity arises, Pre-Control should go back to Rule 2—namely taking five units consequently to see if all the readings fall within the green zone to assure good process capability.

6. *Pre-Control for Defect Levels Below 100 ppm.* Good as Pre-Control is, and superior though it be to control charts, there is a limit to its usefulness for product defect levels below 100 ppm. A periodic sample size of two may not be large enough, even if such sampling is done very frequently, to be able to detect defect levels as low as 50, 10, or 5 ppm, which several companies are now attaining. Under these conditions, *the best way to control the product is to control the process that is producing it.* Pre-Control can then be applied to controlling and monitoring key process parameters rather than product parameters. An alternative is to increase the sample size of two to two sets, with 5 to 20 units in each set.

The Theory of Pre-Control

Based on the mechanics of Pre-Control, what are its Alpha (α) and Beta (β) risks?

α Risk

The α risk is the risk of rejecting a good process. Figure 21-2 is a worst-case scenario of a process in which the specification width is equal to the process width, i.e., a C_{pk} of 1.0. Assuming a normal distribution, the area of the curve in the green zone is 86 percent, and the area in each yellow zone and red zone is 7 percent (from a table of normal distributions).

Figure 21-2. Pre-Control: α Risk

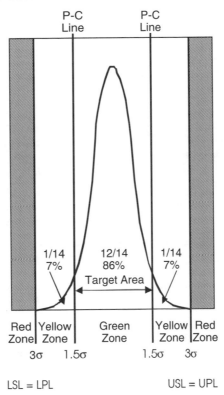

So the probability of one unit falling in one yellow-red zone is 7 percent. The probability of another unit landing in the same yellow-red zone is also 7 percent. So, using the multiplication theorem, the probability of both units landing in the same yellow-red zone is 7% × 7% = 0.49%. This means that the probability of two units landing in the same yellow-red zone is roughly 1 in 200. But there are four ways in which two units can be in the two yellow-red zones—two in one yellow-red zone; two in the opposite yellow-red zones; one in the left yellow-red zone & one in the right yellow-red zone; or one in the right and the next in the left. Therefore, the total probability of two units falling outside of the Pre-Control lines is 1 in 50, or 2 percent. In other words, there is a 2 percent risk of over-correction; that there is nothing wrong with the process and that two units have both fallen outside the Pre-Control lines entirely by chance. But there is a 98 percent probability that this is not due to chance (or a 98 percent confidence that a correction is needed).

If the C_{pk} is 1.33, the red zones shrink to zero and the yellow zones shrink to 4.6 percent, so the probability of two units landing in the same yellow zone is 4.6% $\times$ 4.6% = 0.21%. Again, there are four ways in which two units can be in the two yellow zones, so the probability of two units landing outside the Pre-Control lines entirely by chance is 0.21% $\times$ 4 = 0.84%, giving an even lower risk of overcorrection than with a C_{pk} of 1.0.

β Risk

The β risk is the risk of accepting a rejectable process. Table 21-1 is a tabulation of the various β risks, expressed as a percent defective, for C_p's of 1.0, 1.33, and 0.8 and C_{pk}'s of 1.0, 0.83, 0.67, and 0.5 for each C_p. The C_{pk}'s are based on an $\overline{X}$ shift from a target value of 0σ, 0.5σ, 1.0σ, and 1.5σ, respectively.

> P_{red}, P_{yellow}, and P_{green} are the percentages of the total area (100 percent) in a normal distribution for the red, yellow, and green zones, respectively, in each C_p, C_{pk} column. They are derived from a table of normal distributions.
> P_{go} = q is the probability of not getting a pair of yellows or one red = 1 − (probability of getting 2 yellows + probability of 1 red) (The probability of getting two yellows is 7% $\times$ 7% (see α risk) or 0.49%. Since there are four ways of getting two yellows, P_{yellow} = 0.49% $\times$ 4 = 1.96%. The probability of getting a red on one side or the other = 0.135% + 0.135% = 0.27%. So, P_{go} = 1 − (1.96% + 0.27%) = 1 − 2.23% = 97.77%.)
> P_A = q^6 is the probability of not getting two consecutive yellows in six pairs of two units between two stoppages.
> APQ (similar to AQL in sampling plans) is the expected average quality defect level and is q $\times$ P_{red}; i.e., 87.29% $\times$ 0.27% = 0.23%.

The Enormous Statistical Power of Pre-Control

Table 21-1 clearly shows the statistical power of Pre-Control and its great superiority over control charts.

> If C_{pk}'s of 1.33 are attained, the β risk—the risk of accepting bad product—drops to zero.
> For C_p's of 1.33, the highest β risk occurs at a point where $\overline{X}$ is two standard deviations (2σ) away from a target value (not shown in Table 21-1) and is only 0.34 percent.
> For C_p's of 1.0 and a C_{pk} of 1.0, the β risk is only 0.23 percent.

Table 21-1. Tabulation of β Risks for Processes With Varying C_p's and C_{p_k}'s

Parameter	C_p	$D(\sigma)=0$ $C_{p_k}=1.0$	$D(\sigma)=0.5$ $C_{p_k}=0.83$	$D(\sigma)-1.0$ $C_{p_k}=0.05$	$D(\sigma)-1.5$ $C_{p_k}=0.033$
P_{RED}		0.27%	0.64%	2.28%	6.68%
P_{YELLOW}		14.00%	17.51%	29.19%	43.45%
P_{GREEN}	1.0	85.73%	81.85%	68.53%	49.87%
$P_{GO} = q$		97.77%	95.60%	86.97%	68.21%
$P_A = q^6$		87.29%	76.58%	43.27%	10.07%
APQ = β Risk		0.23	0.49%	0.99%	0.67%
		$C_{p_k}=1.33$	$C_{p_k}=1.1$	$C_{p_k}=0.89$	$C_{p_k}=0.67$
P_{RED}		0.00%	0.02%	0.13%	0.62%
P_{YELLOW}		4.56%	7.28%	15.87%	30.25%
P_{GREEN}	1.33	95.44%	92.70%	84.00%	69.13%
$P_{GO} = q$		99.77%	99.42%	99.22%	89.37%
$P_A = q^6$		98.63%	96.57%	95.41%	52.69%
APQ = β Risk		0.00%	0.02%	0.12%	0.33%
		$C_{p_k}=0.8$	$C_{p_k}=0.66$	$C_{p_k}=0.54$	$C_{p_k}=0.4$
P_{RED}		1.64%	3.06%	8.11%	18.41%
P_{YELLOW}		21.38%	25.60%	35.35%	43.73%
P_{GREEN}	1.33	76.98%	71.34%	56.54%	37.86%
$P_{GO} = q$		92.18%	87.41%	71.95%	47.45%
$P_A = q^6$		61.35%	44.60%	13.87%	1.14%
APQ = β Risk		1.01%	1.36% (APQL)	1.13%	0.21%

Legend:

$D(\sigma)$ = is the number of standard deviations separating $\overline{X}$ from a target value.

P_{RED}, P_{YELLOW}, P_{GREEN} = the percentages of the total area (100%) in the red, yellow, and green zones, respectively.

P_{GO} = q is the probability of 1 − probability of landing in yellow and red zones.

$P_A = q^6$ is the probability of acceptance (i.e., not getting two consecutive yellow pairs of two units in the interval between two process stoppages.

APQ = Average Percentage Defective = $P_A \times P_{RED}$; APQL = Max. Percentage Defective.

Source: Rath & Strong, Boston, Mass.

> For C_p's of 0.8, the highest β risk occurs at 0.5 standard deviation (0.5σ) away from a target value and is only 1.36 percent.
> *In short, if a C_{pk} of 1.33 is assured, which is the basis of Rule 2 in the mechanics of Pre-Control, there is virtually no risk of a bad product ever being accepted.*
> With C_{pk}'s of 2.0 (not shown in Table 21-1), Pre-Control has such a margin of safety that hundreds and thousands of units can be run without a single defect. The record was 30 million units!
> And to summarize the α risk—the risk of rejecting a good product—is only 2 percent.

Charting Pre-Control: Easing the Operator's Burden

Unlike the case with control charts, a graphical record is not mandatory in Pre-Control. The process operator has the simplest of rules:

> Two greens or one green and one yellow—continue.
> Two yellows in the same yellow zone—adjust.
> Two yellows in opposite yellow zones or one in red zone—stop.

There is no need to distract the operator with long and painful data entries. However, if a Pre-Control chart is required for historic purposes or as proof of control to a customer or from a supplier, the operator can just make slash-mark entries prepared on preprinted forms demarcating the green, yellow, and red zones. Figure 21-3 is an example of a Pre-Control chart used to control the thickness of chrome, nickel, and gold deposits on glass in a sputtering machine. From 15 pairs of the readings, C_p and C_{pk} values are easily calculated. There is no need for manual calculations, hand-held calculators, or expensive computer programs—an important advantage of small suppliers who do not want money thrown at a process with expensive and ineffective control charts.

Tackling Multiple Quality Characteristics

Pre-Control is also a far more economical tool than control charts in controlling multiple quality characteristics (multiple Green Y's). As an example, if the variation in a 36-cavity mold must be monitored in an injection molding machine, the number of readings required to establish even trial control limits in a control chart would be 5,400. By contrast, Pre-Control could determine process capability with five readings for each cavity, or a total of 180 readings.

Figure 21-3. Pre-Control Chart: Metalization

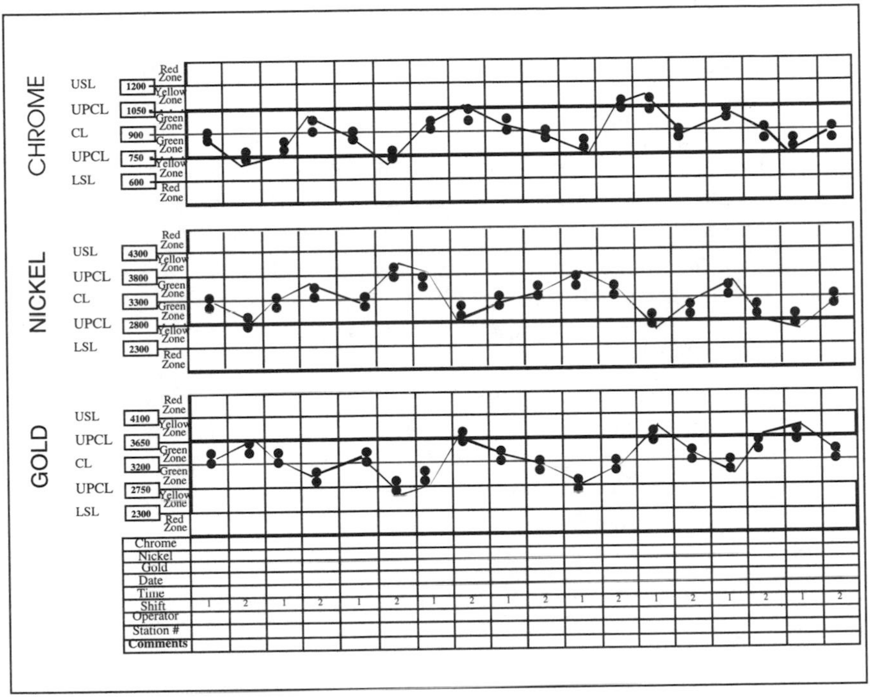

Source: Motorola, Schaumburg, Ill.

Further, it is not necessary to monitor all Green Y's after initial process capability is confirmed on each. Only the most important or the most varying Green Y's need to be periodically sampled. As an example, in the case of the 36-cavity mold, only the two or three cavities with large variations need to be constantly monitored. The rest could be monitored infrequently or not at all.

Reasons Why Some Companies Are Opposed to Pre-Control

As stated earlier, there are still several companies are opposed to the use of Pre-Control. Some of them threaten to disqualify those suppliers intelligent enough to discard control charts and adopt Pre-Control. There are several reasons:

> ➤ Most of these companies have not been exposed to the simplicity and elegance of Pre-Control.

› Their quality departments do not have the statistical depth to compare the weakness of control charts to the statistical power of Pre-Control.

› A higher lever authority in these companies has mandated control charts and people at lower levels are too scared to blurt out that the "emperor has no clothes."

› Most of these companies have not run parallel studies to see how Pre-Control can shut down a bad product much faster and continue a good product much longer than control charts.

› Some companies claim that the use of specification limits prevents continuous improvement. Superficially, this may be a valid point. In control charts, as improvements are made, control limits do get closer and narrower. But there is no law that says that the specification limit goal-posts cannot be moved inward in Pre-Control. Intelligent practitioners of Pre-Control often use the tighter process limits as internal specification limits to draw the half-tolerance Pre-Control lines. So, as process C_{pk}'s increase, so can the narrower Pre-Control lines track such improvement.

There are three ways to deal with obstinate and rigid customers who insist on control charts over Pre-Control.

1. Ask them to prove the statistical superiority of control charts. Use Chapters 20 and 21 to marshal your response.
2. Run a parallel study on a typical process, using both control charts and Pre-Control. Prove to yourself the greater sensitivity of Pre-Control in rejecting a bad product and continuing with a good product.
3. Use Pre-Control, with a sample size of two units, for internal control. Then add two more units to the sample size to make a subgroup size of four, and construct a control chart to satisfy external customer requirements. But this last step should only be used if the two previous recommendations fail to dislodge an unreconstructed customer.

A Capsule Comparison of Pre-Control and Control Charts

We are now in a position to truly compare the weaknesses of control charts versus the strength of Pre-Control. Table 21-2 is a detailed comparison. Only a few characteristics need some elaboration.

The Use of Averages

Control charts use averages for $\overline{X}$ and $\overline{\overline{X}}$ values. But averages can be deceptive, as illustrated by the story of a hunter. He spotted a duck on a pond, took aim, and fired. He missed. The bullet went slightly to the left of the duck. So he took aim and fired again. He missed again. This time the bullet went to the right of the duck. But, on the average, the duck was dead! Averages tend to dilute the variation found in individual values. Pre-Control, using only individual values, is much better at measuring the extent of the individual variations.

Feedback of Results

Control charts require the recording of many individual readings, their averages, their ranges, and extensive plotting before trends can be observed. That is a delayed reaction. It is too late. It is like substituting with control charts the steering wheel of a car in order to steer the car! Pre-Control, on the other hand, requires only two readings to stay on course or make corrections. It stimulates drivers' instinctive little tugs on the car's steering wheel.

Case Study 1: Wave Soldering

In the case study in the chapter on Full Factorials, a DOE team had reduced the solder defects on a printed circuit board from 10,000 ppm to 220 ppm. Following optimization, Positrol, and process certification, Pre-Control was initiated to assure that the 45:1 improvement would be maintained in ongoing production.

The DOE team decided on two measures. It increased the sample size of two units to two sets, each with 10 boards, in order to capture defect levels as low as 100 ppm. Second, it used a Likert scale to rate the severity of various types of solder defects. The types were further subdivided into oversolder defects and undersolder defects, as shown in Figure 21-4, to permit artificial two-sided tolerances. The severity of a defect type multiplied by the number of defects of that type gave a defect score. The specification limits were set at 100 ppm for oversolder and 100 ppm for undersolder, while the P-C lines were set at 50 ppm for oversolder and 50 ppm for undersolder.

The Pre-Control chart proved very useful. The operators liked its simplicity, as compared to the cumbersome control charts it replaced. An out-of-control situation could be spotted almost instantaneously, and the cause could be examined and recorded on the Pre-Control chart along

Table 21-2. Advantages of Pre-Control Over Control Charts

Characteristics	Control Charts	Pre-Control
1. Simplicity	› *Complex*—calculations of control.	› *Simple*—Pre-Control limits are middle half of specification width.
2. Use by operators	› *Difficult*—charting mandatory, interpretation unclear.	› *Easy*—green, yellow, and red zones, a practical approach for all workers.
3. Mathematical	› *Involved*—X, R, control limits, and process limits must be calculated.	› *Elementary*—must only know how to divide by 4.
4. Process qualification	› Twenty-five subgroups, each with four or five units, required.	› Five greens in a row assures minimum C_{pk} of 1.33.
5. Small production runs	› Useless for production runs below 500 units; sampling of 80 to 150 units before even trial limits can be established.	› Can be used for production runs above 20 units, Pre-Control lines predetermined by specifications (which can be narrowed).
6. Decisions	› *Delayed*—plots required and many points charted.	› Instantaneous—Green, yellow, or red.

7. Recalibration of control limits	> *Frequent*—no such thing in industry as a constant cause system.	> *None needed*, unless specification "goal posts" are moved inward.
8. Machine adjustments	> *Time-consuming*—any adjustment requires another trial run of 80 to 150 units.	> *Instant*—based on two units.
9. Frequency of sampling	> *Vague*, arbitrary.	> *Simple rule*—six samplings between two stoppages/adjustments.
10. Discriminating power	> *Weak*—α risk of rejection when there are no rejects, is high. β risk of acceptance when there are rejects, is high. Little relationship to specifications.	> *Excellent*—α risk of rejection is low; less than 2% under worst conditions; 0 with C_{pk} of 1.66. β risk <1.36% under worst conditions, 0% with C_{pk} of 1.66.
11. Attribute chart	> P & C charts do not distinguish between defect mode types or importance.	> Attribute charts can be converted to Pre-Control charts by weighting defect modes and an arbitrary rating scale.
12. Economy	> *Expensive*—calculations, paperwork, large samples, more frequent sampling, long trial runs.	> *Inexpensive*—calculations simple, minimum paperwork, small samples, infrequent sampling if quality is good, process capability determined by just five units.

Figure 21-4. Pre-Control Chart: Wave Solder Operation

Oversolder Code   **Demerits**

Oversolder Code	Demerits									
Solder short	+20			X						XX
Near short	+10									
Excess solder	+5									
Capping	+5									
Total				+20						+40

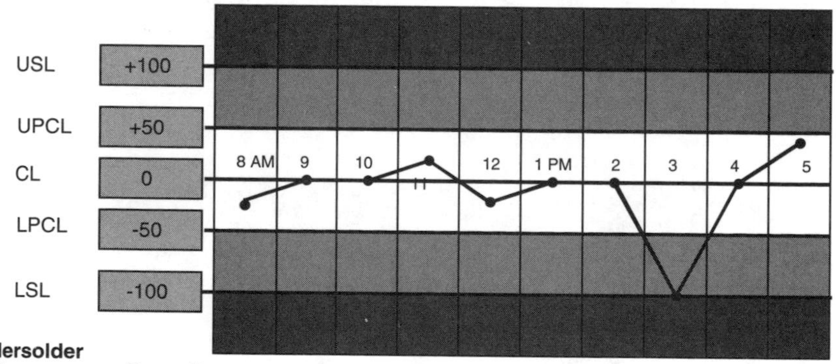

Undersolder Code   **Demerits**

Undersolder Code	Demerits									
Unsoldered connection	-100								X	
Insufficient solder	-20	XX								
De Wet	-20									
Blow hole	-5					XX				
Total		-40				-10			-100	

Source: Motorola Inc., Seguin, Texas.

with the adjustment or corrective action taken. Pre-Control became a way of life in the entire plant.

Workshop Exercise 1: Bushing

In the chapter on control charts, Case Study 1 dealt with a bushing that required a length of 0.500" ± 0.002". It showed that the control chart indicated a stable, in-control situation, even though the potential defect rate was 7 percent.

Questions

1. If Pre-Control had been used on this process, would it have detected an out-of-control condition, as opposed to control charts that did not?
2. How soon would Pre-Control have stopped this bad process?

Answers

1. The specification for the bushing was 0.500″ ± 0.002″. So the Pre-Control lines would be at 0.500″ ± 0.001″. Table 20-1, in the chapter on control charts, shows that there are several pairs of individual readings that fall outside the precontrol lines, indicating that the process should have been stopped.
2. Rule 2 of Pre-Control states that, at the outset, five units in a row should fall within the Pre-Control lines to assure process capability. Table 20-1 indicates that in the very first sample of five units, two units are borderline at the P-C lines and one unit well outside the P-C line. *The bad process would have been stopped cold by Pre-Control at the very start and not allowed to continue for 60 readings in control charts, along with a wrong decision to continue production.*

Workshop Exercise 2: Sensor Capacitance

In the chapter on control charts, Case Study 2 depicts a sensor capacitance that had a specification of 31 pico-farads minimum to 45 pico-farads maximum. Figure 20-2 shows the control chart data and the X and R charts. It indicates that the sensor capacitance is horribly out of control and should be stopped forthwith.

Question

If Pre-Control had been used to monitor this product, would an out-of-control condition have existed and would an order have been issued to stop production?

Answer

The Pre-Control limits in this example would be 34.5 and 41.5 pf. There is not a single reading that goes beyond these P-C lines, let alone two readings. The C_p of this process is 2.0 and its C_{pk} is 1.92, indicating very good process capability. *Pre-Control would never have stopped this excellent process, which control charts erroneously rejected.*

Workshop Exercise 3: The Wire Bonder

An automatic wire bonder, which bonds a wire the thickness of a human hair to the die and post of a transistor had been certified to start Pre-Control. The integrity of the wire bond is checked with a destructive pull test on the wire. The specification for bond strength, before the bond is lifted on either side, is a minimum of 6 gm and a maximum of 14 gm. The initial sample of five consecutive units to determine process capability had the following readings: 8.7 gm, 9.0 gm, 9.4 gm, 8.9 gm, and 10 gm.

Questions

1. What are the values for the Pre-Control lines?
2. On the basis of the sample of five units, is there good process capability?
3. How frequently (initially) should a sample of two consecutive units be tested for bond strength, assuming that when full production began, the period between two stoppages (two pairs of yellow) averaged 12 hours?
4. During subsequent production, the results of two consecutive sample units drawn periodically from the process were as shown on Table 21-3. (For the purpose of the exercise, waive the rule requiring five units in a row to fall within the green zone to reestablish process capability.) What action would you take on each sample? Continue production or stop?
5. What nonrandom trends do you detect in Question 4? Explain your answer.
6. If there were no upper specification limit of 14 gm for bond strength, where would you draw the single Pre-Control line, assuming that the targeted bond strength was at 11.0 gm?

Answers

1. Pre-Control lines are at 8 and 12 gm.
2. All five units in the initial sample are in the green zone, so process capability is firmly established.
3. The sampling frequency should be 12/6, or every 2 hours.
4. Continue production on sample numbers 1 through 7 and 10 through 12. Stop production on sample numbers 8 and 9. (In ac-

Table 21-3. Workshop Exercise 3: The Wire Bonder

Sample No.	Unit 1	Unit 2	Action
1	9.4	9.0	_____
2	9.0	8.8	_____
3	8.9	8.6	_____
4	8.5	8.1	_____
5	8.4	8.0	_____
6	8.0	8.0	_____
7	8.0	7.6	_____
8	7.5	7.3	_____
9	13.0	13.0	_____
10	12.0	12.0	_____
11	11.6	11.4	_____
12	11.0	10.8	_____

tual practice, the process must be adjusted or corrected after sample number 8, and five more units must fall within the green zone before the sampling of two units is resumed. The same holds for sample number 9.)

5. There are three nonrandom trends: (1) Bond strengths are getting lower and lower until a correction is made after trial number 8. (Cause could be bond contamination or loss of bond energy.) (2) The second reading in each sample is almost always lower than the first. (3) Sample number 9 seems to be an overcorrection (bond strengths too high).

6. With the target at 11 gm and only a single lower specification limit, the single Pre-Control Line should be midway between the target of 11 gm and the lower specification limit of 6 gm, i.e., at 8.5 gm.

Questions for DOE Teams on Pre-Control

1. Have all the necessary DOE tools been employed to solve problems before SPC is initiated?
2. Have the disciplines of Positrol and Process Certification been utilized before the start of Pre-Control?

3. Have the correct specifications and tolerances been determined with customers, utilizing disciplines such as Quality Function Deployment, Scatter Plots, and/or Response Surface Methodology before tackling Pre-Control.
4. Has Rule 2 of Pre-Control been used to determine process capability (a minimum C_{pk} of 1.33)?
5. Have line operators been trained to conduct Pre-Control on their own processes and to record their findings in simple, preprinted Pre-Control forms?
6. Is process capability (Rule 2) reestablished at each major discontinuity during production or following a Pre-Control stoppage?
7. Is the sampling frequency varied depending on the time intervals between two stoppages?
8. Are there "ceilings" and "floors" established on the frequencies of such samplings?
9. Are only major parameters (Green Y's) tracked with Pre-Control?
10. Is there objective evidence presented to customers (or demanded from suppliers) in the form of Pre-Control charts to indicate the maintenance of excellent quality?

Questions for Top Management During DOE Project Reviews

1. Why do our customers prefer complex and ineffective control charts over simpler and more effective Pre-Control, and what actions have been taken to convince them of the need for the latter?
2. Have we stopped burdening our suppliers with the tyranny of control charts and coached them in the use of Pre-Control?
3. Do we present Pre-Control charts to our customers, periodically, as proof of our sustained good quality?
4. Do we demand Pre-Control charts from our suppliers, periodically, as proof of their sustained good quality?

Part VIII

. . . .

Linkage of DOE to Reliability

419

22

Multiple Environment Over Stress Tests: As Effective for Reliability as DOE Is for Quality

Quality versus Reliability

There is a fundamental difference between quality and reliability. Quality is the goodness of a product as it leaves the factory—at zero time. Reliability has two additional dimensions—time and stress. Time refers to product life. Stress refers to various stress or environmental factors, such as temperature, vibration, humidity, etc., that interact with one another, synergizing and accelerating field failures. So, even though quality and reliability are terms used synonymously, reliability is more important—to the customer, to warranty costs, to product recalls, and to liability law suits.

Fundamental Shortcomings in Traditional Reliability Practices

Unfortunately, current reliability practices are flawed. Yet, these weaknesses are regurgitated in reliability papers and conferences every year. Here are some of these practices:

> Attempts to predict unreliability, instead of concentrating on virtually eliminating field failures.
> Use of mathematical models, formulas, and computer software to forecast the reliability behavior of parts and products. These math-

ematical models are approximations at best and way off the mark
at worst. They are also confusing to the reliability practitioner.
> Use of brute-force testing in the mistaken belief that testing 200
  units for one week gives the same reliability estimate of testing one
  unit for 200 weeks!
> Slavish adherence to military reliability specifications that are 15
  years behind the times.
> Little use of derating (stress reduction) of parts.
> Not overstressing products and not combining environments in re-
  liability demonstrations.

Modest Reliability Advances

Some advances have been made in the last 20 years, but they are far from
benchmark reliability and should be sparsely used by the reliability practitioner.

1. *Reliability Prediction Studies:* Based on Mil-Handbook 217E; British
Telecom Handbook (BT); French National Center for Telecommunications
(CNET); and software programs such as "Predictor." These predictions
can miss actual field reliability by factors ranging from 25:1 (optimistic)
to 1:4 (pessimistic)—a 100:1 swing.

2. *Failure Mode Effects Analysis (FMEA):* More used in Japan and Europe than in the United States, an FMEA is—at best—an elementary,
paper study that only quantifies an engineer's guesses, opinions,
hunches, and theories.

3. *Institute of Environmental Science (IES) Guidelines:*

> They call for 100 percent screening in production.
> They limit temperature extremes in thermal cycling and the vibra-
  tion spectrum.
> Their surveys of "effectiveness" are basically a "popularity" as-
  sessment.

4. *Single Stress Tests:*

> Thermal cycling: low rates of thermal change, large numbers of
  cycles.
> Vibration: sinusoidal, single frequency.

5. *Single Environment Sequential Tests:*

> Multiple environments but applied sequentially, one at a time.
> Low stress acceleration.
> Interactions between stress completely missed.
> Reliability projections vary widely with each test.

Revolutionary Reliability Test Principles

Fortunately, the evolutionary reliability practices of the last 20 years are being jettisoned in favor of revolutionary techniques. The following principles are the underpinnings of this revolution.

> It is difficult, if not impossible, to predict field reliability with a high degree of confidence. Multiple Environment Overstress Test (MEOST)[18] can make this projection, but even this technique requires exposure in the field, for six months and for one year, before extrapolation of reliability for 5, 10, or 20 years can be made.
> Rather than worry about quantifying unreliability and failure rates, the objective is to eliminate failures, period. Then the reliability numbers will take care of themselves.
> The objective is not "success" testing. It is not to pass a test, so that the product gets into production quickly before it changes its mind! Rather it is to deliberately induce failures, because it is only through failures that the weak links of design can be smoked out.
> Every part has weak links. Some parts have a large guard-band between their ultimate stress-to-failure and a test stress. Others have a small guard-band. It is the latter—the weak links—that can be weeded out with stress well beyond design stress.
> Failures can be forced or accelerated with higher levels of overstress in order to shorten the time to failure as well as the variation in failure rates. Figure 22-1 shows how progressively higher stresses, up to MEOST, shorten the traditionally long and constant portion of the reliability bathtub curve that relates failure rates to time.[19]
> The ultimate stress is:

1. Combining individual environments (stresses) to stimulate failures caused by interactions. (As a simple example, temperature extremes alone may not cause failures. Humidity extremes alone may not cause failures. But extremes of both temperature and humidity can result in a synergy of failures.)

Figure 22-1. Bathtub Curve Showing Stress versus Expected Life Relationship

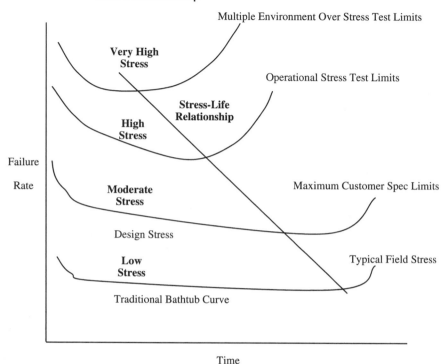

Source: Keki R. Bhote and James McLimm at Amway Corp., Ada, Mich.

2. Going well beyond design stress levels to stimulate failures.

This last principle is the foundation for MEOST.

Relationship of Failure and Stress

The level of stress in generating failures is governed by the Miner's Equation (or Power Law):

$D \approx ns^{\beta}$, where:
D = damage (failure) accumulation
$\approx$ = proportional to
n = number of stress cycles
s = stress
β = a power factor, generally from 1 to 12

For reliability, the β factor is generally 10, meaning that the degree of stress has 10 times the ability to detect failures as the number of stress cycles (usually, thermal cycles). Miner's equation is used both in thermal cycling and in vibration as stress agents.

Stress Acceleration in Thermal Cycling

Figure 22-2 shows how the number of thermal cycles to failure can be compressed if the rate of thermal cycling is increased.[19] For example,

> a 5°C/minute rate requires 400 thermal cycles to failure,
> a 25°C/minute rate requires only four thermal cycles to failure.

That is a 100:1 time compression!

Stress Acceleration in Vibration

Miner's equation applies not only to thermal cycling, but to all types of stress—mechanical, electrical, vibration, humidity, or any other stimulus. Figure 22-3 shows a S/N diagram (where S is stress and N the number of cycles to failure). The graph is derived from tensile fatigue tests on specimens.[20] It indicates that as tensile strength is increased linearly, the number of cycles to failure decreases exponentially (β is derived from

Figure 22-2. Thermal Cycling Rate (Stress) versus Number of Thermal Cycles

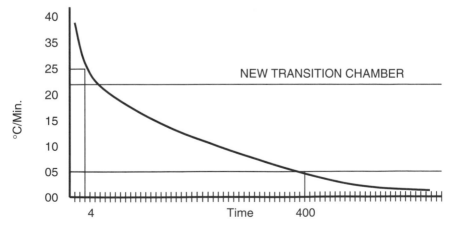

Source: Smithson S. "Effectiveness and Economics—Yardstick for ESS Decision," *Proceedings of the 1990 Annual Technical Meeting.* © Institute of Environmental Sciences and Technology, (847) 255-1561.

Figure 22-3. Tensile Strength to Failure versus Number of Fatigue Cycles Required

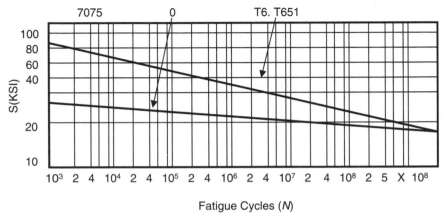

Fatigue Cycles (*N*)

Wrought Aluminum - Reverse Blending.

Legend:

0 =   Annealed

T6 = Thermally treated

Source: Steinberg, *Vibration Analysis of Electronic Equipment.* Copyright © 1973, John Wiley & Sons, Inc. Reprinted by permission of John Wiley & Sons, Inc.

the slope of the curve) for the T6 (thermally treated), nonannealed T651 aluminum.

> ➤ A stress of 40K PSI requires 2,000,000 cycles to fail,
> ➤ a stress of 80K PSI requires only 2,000 cycles to fail,
> ➤ an increase of tensile stress of just 2:1 causes a decrease in cycles (or time) to failure of 1,000 times.

This acceleration factor is much higher for mechanically induced fatigue than for electronically or thermally induced fatigue. Parts that fail in the field have some imperfection that causes an increase in stress. This stress concentration, caused by even a small imperfection, may be two or three times as high as in a perfect part. That stress increase can cause fatigue failure by several orders of magnitude, quicker in marginal parts than in robust parts with less inherent stress.

It is this ability to accelerate stress by factors of 2:1 and 4:1 that can acceler-ate time to failure by 10:1 in tests such as thermal cycling and by 1,000:1 in vibration. This is the key to effective reliability testing. Thermal cycling and vibration are two of the most important stress agents and are widely used by the best practitioners of reliability.

Table 22-1 summarizes the salient features of benchmark thermal cycling and Table 22-2 summarizes those of benchmark vibration.*

If Figure 22-1 could be extrapolated to a thermal cycling rate of 40°C/minute instead of 25°C/minute, the time would be one cycle or a time compression of 400:1. What a savings in throughput time and test equipment!

Highly Accelerated Life Tests (HALT)

In the last 15 years, a system called HALT has been used by several leading companies, especially in aerospace and electronic industries. It continues the revolution in stress testing.

Table 22-1. Salient Features of Benchmark Thermal Cycling

> High temperature gradients: 25°C/minute up to 60°C/minute.
  As few thermal cycles as possible. Continue until the "weakest link" parts fail.

> Highest possible temperature extremes—only 20% to 30% short of "fundamental limits of technology," (FLT) i.e., to destruct limits.

> Thermal shock: for components only (instant change from hot to cold).

> Use of liquid nitrogen to accelerate the rate of thermal cycling (as opposed to compressors)

> Air turbulence

> A minimum dwell time of 10 minutes at each temperature extreme.

> Continuous monitoring of Green Y's (output) parameters to detect intermittents.

Table 22-2. Salient Features of Benchmark Vibration

> Random vibration

> Tri-axial vibration system with 6 degrees of freedom.

> Six-axis stimulation (x, y, z, and three rotations) excites all product response modes simultaneously, providing vector acceleration in any orientation needed to stress potential defects.

> Response from 2 Hz to 2.5 KHz and higher.

> Minimum product vibration is 20 G (RMS)

*Vibration stress times are an order of magnitude or two less than thermal cycling, 5 to 10 minutes compared to hours for thermal cycling.

Principles

> - Not intended to predict field reliability.
> - Not intended to pass a stress test but to fail it.
> - Stresses a product right up to the fundamental limit of technology (FLT).
> - Purpose is to stimulate failures regardless of whether they occur in the field.
> - By stressing way beyond design limits, it causes weaker elements to fail, leaving strong ones intact.
> - The extreme overstress also shortens the time to failure.

Methodology

1. Determine the upper and lower destruct limit of each stress up to the fundamental limit of technology.
2. Select as many samples as possible.
3. Select stresses (usually thermal cycling and vibration).
4. Step stress one stress at a time.

> - Vibration in 25 percent GRMS steps.
> - Thermal in 5 to 10°C steps, starting with cold, then hot.
> - Voltage in steps equal to 20 percent of the operating margin.
> - Other stresses, as appropriate, in steps equal to 20 percent of their operating margin.

5. Continue step stress until at least half the samples fail.
6. Analyze each cause of failure down to root cause; take corrective action.
7. Continue step stress until the fundamental limit of technology is reached.
8. Go to next stress and repeat above steps.
9. Run combined stress, if needed (generally, thermal cycling and vibration).
10. Rerun the whole cycle, at the destruct level, a second or third time to evaluate corrections and design changes.

HALT: Pros and Cons

The most positive brief for HALT is its success over several years in at least those industries, especially aerospace, that have consistently used it. It has also been cost-effective in terms of faster time to production and to market, and in returns on investment.

On the other hand, it has not been as useful in smoking out mechanical weak links, especially on large products. Nor has it gone as far in eliminating field failures as MEOST (see comparisons in a later section).

But the most significant drawback—and the most controversial—is its insistence on pushing a single stress (or a combination of stresses) to its ultimate levels; i.e., right up to FLT. Figure 22-4 depicts the spread between product specification limits, operational limits, MEOST practical overstress limits and HALT destruct limits (which are the fundamental limits of technology) on a continuum of stress. First, some definitions of these limits are in order.

Definitions of Limits

1. *Destruct Limit* (DL), as used in HALT, is:

> That stress level reaching the fundamental limit of technology when the product falls apart.
> Or, that stress level when a *very small increase in stress* will cause a *very large increase in the number of failures.*

Figure 22-4. Specs. versus Operational (HASS) versus Max. Practical Over Stress (MEOST) versus Destruct Limits (HALT)

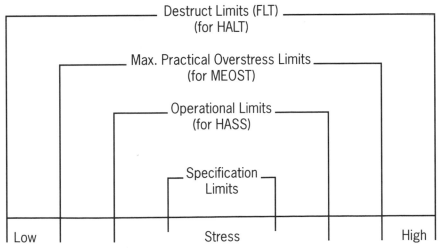

Legend: 1. FLT (Fundamental Limits of Technology) =
Destruct Limits − HALT Stress
2. Max, Practical Overstress = MEOST Stress
3. Operational Limits = HASS Stress

2. *Operational Limit* (OL) is a level of stress that will *damage weak parts but will not damage good parts.* OL is used in HASS (next technique).

3. *Maximum Practical Overstress Limit* (MPOSL) is a stress level with a sufficient guard band below a destruct limit to prevent the accumulation of artificial failures, generally 20 to 33 percent below the destruct limit.

MPOSL is used for Multiple Environment Over Stress Tests (MEOST). Stressing to the fundamental limit of technology (FLT) can introduce totally artificial (or silly) failures that would never occur in the field, even under extreme conditions. Chasing each lone, random, artificial failure is like chasing ghosts. It wastes time, manpower, and costs. Anybody acquainted with the physics of failure analysis can appreciate how difficult it is to probe for the root cause, and once finding it, to validate it by turning the cause on and off.

HALT successes are trumpeted by its adherents, while its failures are buried. Even among its successes, reliability improvements of 10:1, while impressive, have only reduced failures, not eliminated them as stated in HALT objectives. Other weaknesses of the technique are: using for the most part only two stresses (thermal cycling and vibration); large sample sizes for test; and inability to predict field reliability.

Table 22-3 provides a summary of the positive and negative features of HALT.

Highly Accelerated Stress Screening (HASS)

HALT is primarily used at the design stage of a product. HASS is, for the most part, a 100 percent test in production. Its salient features are: *Prerequisite:* full-fledged HALT in the design stage of a product. *Definition:* HASS is a test screen that uses stresses that are substantially higher than those used in the field (including shipping). The stress levels should be high enough to precipitate relevant defects that would appear in the field, but leave 80 to 90 percent of useful life in the rest of the product.

Table 22-4 is a capsule summary of the pros and cons of HASS stress tests in production.

Multiple Environment Over Stress Tests (MEOST)

History

The earliest application of MEOST was in the hectic, unreliable days of the Apollo series of space probes by the National Aeronautics and Space

Table 22-3. Pros and Cons of HALT Stress Tests

Pros	Cons
› Good track record in aerospace and electronic industries. › Better reliability improvement technique than most other methods. › Shortens overall design cycle time. › Shortens stress test time drastically. › Facilitates earlier production and field launch. › Reduces cost; very good R.O.I. › Can be used at all levels of product—from parts to subassemblies to systems. › Commercial test equipment available.	› Less successful for mechanical products, especially large sizes. › Reliability improvements not as spectacular as claimed. › The cost and time involved in analyzing every stress-induced failure down to root cause and correction is prohibitive. › Pushing stresses to the very limit of technology can create artificial failures that may never be replicated in the field. › Primary reliance is on two stresses: thermal cycling and vibration. › Large number of units recommended for test. › HALT cycle repeated for each design change. › Units not returned from the field for further failure probing. › Not capable of reliability prediction.

Administration (NASA) in the 1960s. The Russian space shots seemed to be soaring into the heavens, while the U.S. space shots were flopping into the Atlantic! Every piece of Apollo space hardware had failed, except the lunar module. It had to carry two astronauts to the moon and back. Had the lunar module failed, the moon would have been overpopulated by two people! But it did not fail, because it had been subjected to MEOST on terra firma.

Since then, MEOST has been used to dramatically improve reliability in helicopters, aircraft engines, automobiles, railroad cars, water treatment and air treatment systems, aerospace and commercial work. It was one of the reasons why Motorola's equipment, which is the main radio link between earth and distant probes to Mars, Jupiter, and Saturn, as well as in space telescopes like Hubbell, has flown millions of miles for five to 10 years and longer without failure. MEOST is currently being used in Motorola's ambitious Iridium project, in which 66 satellites pro-

Table 22-4. Pros and Cons of HASS Stress Tests

Pros	Cons
1. Proof of screen, a good validation of HASS principles. 2. "Seeded samples"—introducing deliberate defects to test HASS power of screening. 3. Screen time quick both for vibration and for thermal cycling.	➤ 100% HASS tests in production are a brute-force approach to reliability. ➤ There is no guarantee that all defects can be detected despite "Proof of Screen." ➤ There is not much confidence that useful product life has not been degraded by using HASS. ➤ Only one or two stresses employed—thermal cycling and vibration. ➤ Proof of screen, seeded samples, and optimization are long and cumbersome procedures that can add costs, increase production cycle time, and increase costs. ➤ No reliability prediction attempted or possible.

vide wireless telephone communications from any point on earth to any other point without telephone exchanges. This author introduced MEOST at Motorola in the 1970s and applied it to several projects, starting with its Automotive and Industrial Electronics Group, achieving reliability improvements of 200:1 and—in one important under-the-hood customer application—zero failures in seven years, with over 500,000 miles of vehicular use.

The Objectives of MEOST

1. Develop a stress test that achieves reliability well above all other techniques;
2. Duplicate in the stress test the same failures found in the field on similar products;
3. Sharply increase stress levels to force failures much earlier;
4. Develop a cost-effective test screen in production to prevent manufacturing and supplier defects from degrading the integrity of design;
5. Develop a reasonably effective method of predicting lifetime reliability;
6. Develop a method for evaluating the effectiveness of engineering changes in tandem with Design of Experiments (DOE);

7. Develop a method to solve chronic quality/reliability problems along with DOE;
8. Develop a method to tackle the persistent problems of "No Trouble Found";
9. Develop a method of reducing costs in products in tandem with Value Engineering; and
10. Take MEOST beyond a company to help its suppliers and its customers.

The Benefits of MEOST

1. It virtually eliminates field failures instead of trying to predict a product's *unreliability.*
2. With a six-month and a one-year field exposure, it can extrapolate a quantified figure for reliability, with 90 percent confidence, to satisfy management demands.
3. It reduces overall design-cycle time, manpower, costs, space, test equipment, and power consumption.
4. In launching a new product fast into the marketplace, it gains a decided edge over competition.
5. With DOE, it is a powerful tool for problem solving.
6. With DOE, it is a powerful tool for evaluating the effectiveness of engineering changes.
7. With Value Engineering, it is a powerful tool for future product cost reductions.

MEOST Methodology: A Roadmap

Preamble (The roadmap applies to parts, modules, assemblies, and systems.)

1. Determine adequacy of de-rating (stress reduction) of parts. De-rating means that design engineers should reduce the stress on parts by a minimum of 25 percent from the maximum ratings recommended by parts suppliers. The few pennies saved by pushing parts stresses to their maximum ratings can cost companies 100 to 1000 times as much in terms of field failures and customer dissatisfaction. Under no circumstances should a comprehensive de-rating study be bypassed.
2. List and prioritize field failures on similar products.

Stresses and Levels

1. List as many stresses/environments as are likely in the field.
2. Separate stresses likely to occur simultaneously from those likely to happen in isolation.

3. Prioritize the simultaneous stresses and shorten the list to five or six, if possible.
4. Ascertain the highest stress levels likely in the field (preferably with instrumentation).
5. Determine the engineering spec limits. Compare these to the customer-required stresses and the highest field stresses. Use the highest of these three stresses as the design limits.
6. Ascertain the fundamental limit of technology for each stress. This is called the destruct limits.
7. Ascertain the operating limits of each stress, defined as that stress level likely to cause failure of weak parts, but not of the rest of the product (generally, higher than the design limit by one-third the distance between the design limit and the destruct limit).
8. Ascertain the maximum practical overstress limit (MPOSL) of each stress (generally lower than the destruct limit by one-third the distance between the design limit and the destruct limit).

Sample Sizes

1. In prototype stages: 3 for reparable units; 5 to 15 for nonreparable units.
2. In pilot run and subsequent stages: 10 for reparable units; 30 for nonreparable units.

The Seven Stages of MEOST

Stage 1: Single Stress to Design Stress Limit

> Step stress: Start with thermal cycling or vibration.
> For thermal cycling: 10°C to 15°C steps at a rate of 40°C/per minute; dwell time: 10 minutes at each extreme, starting with cold, then hot cycle.
> For vibration: 25 percent GRMS steps.
> If no failures occur, go to Stage 2.
> If there is even a single failure of any failure mode, analyze and correct each failure. Validate by turning failure "on" and "off," using B versus C test. Then go to Stage 2.

Stage 2: Single Stress up to Maximum Practical Overstress Limit (MPOSL)

> Continue Stage 1 beyond design stress limit, on same units of Stage 1 if reparable, or on new units if not reparable, up to MPOSL. Do not go to the destruct limit.

> If no failures in overstress region:
>   > The stress type or stress rate is inadequate.
>   > The test has not been executed properly.
>   > The failures need multiple environments.
>   > The design is robust for that stress.
> If there is only one failure per failure mode, ignore the failure.
> If there are two or more failures per failure mode, analyze and correct the failure. Validate with B versus C.

Stage 3: MEOST to Maximum Practical Overstress Limit (MPOSL)

> Select multiple environments (see stresses and levels).
> Prepare a MEOST test plan: levels of stress and sequence (continuous or intermittent).
> Use the same units as in Stages 1 and 2, if possible, and combine stresses.
> Start at design stress, then step stress in 5 to 10 intervals up to MPOSL.
> The procedure is similar to that in Stage 2, but with multiple environments. A key measure of success in Stages 1, 2 and 3 is the ability to reproduce the same failure modes found in the field on similar products.
> Perform another round of Stage 3 effectiveness with "seeded defects" (deliberately introduced).
> A successful outcome indicates that the design is ready for a pilot run.

Stage 4: MEOST at Pilot Run

Purpose. To assure that design changes, tooling suppliers, processes, fixtures, etc., have not adversely affected design reliability.

> Run a Stage 4 MEOST, using Stage 3 guidelines, with new units.
> A successful outcome means the design is ready for full production.

Stage 5: Truncated MEOST in Ongoing Production

Purpose: To assure that reliability integrity in design is not degraded by manufacturing processes, workmanship, and materials.

Stresses: Select only two or three of the most important stresses discovered in Stage 3 for a truncated MEOST, but stress up to MPOSL.

Sampling Frequency: Never use 100% sampling. Sampling once per week (or once per month minimum). Use continuous sampling plans—up or down—to reduce the frequency for good results and increase it for poor results.

Sample Size: Same as Stage 4: 10 for reparable and 30 for nonreparable units

Proof of Truncated MEOST Effectiveness: After initial truncated MEOST, perform one round of Stage 5 with "seeded defects."

Stages 6 and 7: MEOST on Good Field Returns

> Recall good units from the field after: (1) six months in service (Stage 6); (2) one year in service (Stage 7).
> Get as much field history on these units; e.g., hours of use; operating conditions; historical log (if available).
> Subject these field-return units to Stage 3 of MEOST.
> Use as many samples as possible—at least 10 for Stage 6 and 10 for Stage 7.
> Project stress levels versus time in field (i.e., 0 time, 6 months and 12 months) on Weibull graph.

Extrapolate to see if target reliability is met with 90 percent confidence (Figure 22-5). In Figure 22-5, the vertical scale is combined stress; hence Stages 1 and 2, which use preliminary single stresses, are not shown. The horizontal scale is exposure time in the field. The Operating Rectangle is the time-stress area where there should be virtually no failures. This means that a product launched into the field and maintained at full design stress should have no failures for the targeted product life (say 10 years). In short, it should clear the black dot, the extreme point in the operating rectangle.

MEOST in Stages 3, 4, and 5 starts at design stress and zero (field) time and continues until the maximum practical overstress is reached. Let us say that the highest failure distribution (among the three stages) is A_1. Similarly, in Stage 6, after MEOST has been applied to good field units retrieved in six months and one year, the failure distributions are A_2 and A_3, respectively. Extrapolating the lower tails of these three failure distributions on a stress-versus-time Weibull plot would give a point at the target reliability life time of 10 years, higher than the Black Dot. On the other hand, if the failure distributions were B_1, B_2, and B_3 at zero time, six months, and one year, respectively, the extrapolations on a Weibull plot would not clear the Black Dot, indicating inadequate reliability—probably two to three years.

Table 22-5 provides a capsule summary of the seven stages of

Figure 22-5. Stress to Failure Over Time

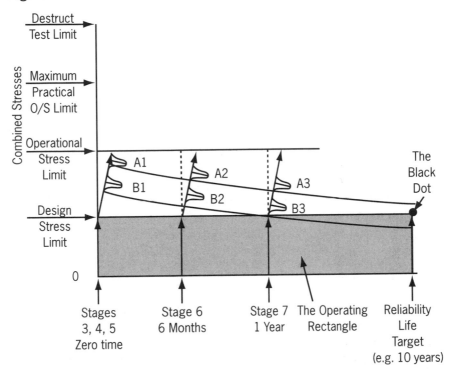

MEOST, depicting for each stage its place in the product launch, the type of stress, the stress level, the sample size, the number of failures allowed, and the frequency of testing.

A Comparison of Overall Effectiveness: HALT/HASS versus MEOST

After this comprehensive description of the principles, objectives, benefits, and methodologies of HALT/HASS and MEOST, a comparison of the effectiveness of these two major approaches to reliability improvement can now be made. It is assumed, of course, that other approaches—military, commercial, and international—have been left in the dust of the above two techniques.

Table 22-6 is a comparison of HALT/HASS vs. MEOST. A total of 20 features are compared. The table is self-explanatory. On almost all features, MEOST is superior to HALT/HASS.

Table 22-5. The Seven Stages of MEOST

Stage No.	Place in Product Launch	Stress Type	Stress Level[a]	Sample Size[b]	No. of Failures Allowed[c]	Frequency of Testing
1	Prototype	Single	Up to design limits	R: 3–10 N.R.: 5–15	0	Once
2	Prototype	Single	Up to MPOSL	R: 3 N.R.: 5–15	1	Once
3	Prototype	Multiple	Up to MPOSL	R: 3 N.R.: 5–15	1	Twice: second time with seeded defects
4	Eng./ Production[d] Pilot Run	Multiple	Up to MPOSL	R: 10 N.R.: 30	1	Once
5	Production[d]	Truncated multiple	Up to MPOSL	10 or as many as possible	1	1) Once/week or month 2) Also one round with seeded defects
6 & 7	Field	Multiple	Up to MPOSL	10 or as many as possible	1	1) After 6 mos. 2) After 1 year

[a]Stress Level: MPOSL = Maximum Practical Overstress Limit.
[b]Sample Size: R = reparable units; N-R = nonreparable.
[c]Failures Allowed: 0 or 1 refers to one failure mode only.
[d]Stages 3, 4, and 5, start at design stress and then step stress up to MPOSL.

The Close Linkage Between MEOST and Design of Experiments (DOE)

MEOST has increasingly been used by this author for tasks going beyond just reliability improvement. These tests are done in conjunction with DOE—a close and natural linkage.

1. Solving Elusive Problems

If a problem is elusive, such as intermittency or never being found in the factory, discovered only in the field, a combination of DOE and MEOST is the sure-fire approach.

The objective here is to take units in production and subject them to one or more stress tests in combination, until failures similar to what the customer sees occur. Now the time-to-failure or the stress-to-failure be-

Table 22-6. A Comparison of Effectiveness: HALT/HASS versus MEOST

Features	HALT/HASS	MEOST
> Reliability prediction ability	No	Yes; with two field returns at six months and one year
> Product diversity	Mainly aerospace and electronics	All
> Applicability to all product levels	Yes	Yes
> Highest stress level	Test to destruction	Max. practical over stress
> No. of environments/ stresses	Generally two	Generally three to six
> No. of failures allowed	None	None up to design stress Max. of one for each failure mode in overstress
> Interactions uncovered	Partial	Almost all
> No. of samples	"As many as possible"	Three to 10 for repairable products
> No. of rounds of tests in design	One for each design change	2: only for major changes
> Failure analysis/correction	Traditional	Design of Experiments
> Cost of failure correction	Costly, time consuming	No need for each solitary failure
> Validation of corrective action	Traditional	Nonparametric B versus C tests
> Shortening design cycle time	Yes	Even move
> Shortening design manpower/costs	Yes	Even move
> Pilot run evaluation	No specific action	Yes
> Production evaluation	HASS	Truncated MEOST
> Sample size in production	100%	Generally, 10; once/ month
> Seeding defects	Yes	Yes
> % of product life used up	Minimum 10%	None—only samples used
> Overall track record	Good	Very good

comes the response or output or Green Y. One or more of the above tech-niques can be employed to determine which input variables cause the problem. This author has solved a number of these exasperating prob-lems, seemingly illusive for his clients.

2. Tackling "No Trouble Found" (NTFs) or "No Apparent Defects" (NADs)

One of the most frustrating problems in industry and the most difficult to solve is a defect/failure category called "No Trouble Found" (NTF), "No Apparent Defect" (NAD) and other acronyms. Typically, these ac-count for 25 to 50 percent of field problems. Customers report a failure. The servicer or repair station finds nothing wrong. Sometimes the prob-lem is lack of customer understanding. Sometimes it is poor analyzing by the servicer. Sometimes it is an "intermittent." In any case, a traditional follow-up of such complaints can be time-consuming. It can be especially costly if a product liability suit is involved. A history of such cases indi-cates that 50 to 60 percent of NTFs are intermittents. The best way to tackle NTFs and intermittents, therefore, is to subject the unit(s) to MEOST, increasing stress levels until an intermittent failure becomes a *patent, permanent* failure.

3. Evaluating the Effectiveness of Engineering Changes

Engineers are notorious for making changes. Changes are designated by revisions A, B, C, etc. Frequently, the revision letters run the entire gamut of the alphabet and then start all over again with revisions AB, AC, etc.! Sometimes there are three or four sequential changes to solve the same problem.

Here, B versus C can be employed to evaluate each engineering change. B stands for a better design; C for the current design. It calls for testing three B's and three C's (done in a random order sequence) and then ranking the outputs from best to worst. If the three B's outrank the three C's in goodness, with no overlap, it can be claimed with 95 percent confidence that the B design is better than the C design.

These very small sample sizes—three and three—are adequate when the output (or response or Green Y) is a variable. But if it is an attribute, is expressed in high yield percentages, or has very low defect levels (say, 100 ppms or less), three B's and three C's are too small a sample. They do not have sufficient discriminative power to detect the difference between B and C. This is where the combination of a DOE technique (B versus C) with MEOST comes in. The object is to convert an attribute (or yields or defect levels that are also attributes) into a variable by subjecting both B's and C's to progressively higher and higher stress levels using MEOST. Then, the time to failure or the stress level to failure becomes a variable, making a sample size of three B's and three C's sufficient.

4. Cost Reduction

The primary purpose of MEOST is reliability improvement. Many skeptics, however, argue that carrying reliability to the ultimate is adding cost without compensating value, either to the customer or to the company. These critics don't get it. Quality and reliability have no finish line. They do not cost money; they save it. But can reliability levels attained by MEOST be maintained by reducing product cost? The answer is yes, and the answer is through MEOST.

Following Stage 6 and 7 of MEOST, when a stipulated reliability target is reached, a Stage 8 can be added as follows:

> ➤ Establish a cost reduction target for the product;
> ➤ Make a list of all the high-cost parts, modules, and subsystems;
> ➤ Prioritize the list, balancing the degree of cost reduction potential on each item against the danger of reliability retrogression, tooling, supplier risks, and cost of experimentation.
> ➤ Apply Value Engineering techniques[15] to each item, finding an alternate approach to provide the required function of the item without being restricted by the current design.
> ➤ With the alternate approach, test the validity of the design changes, using a combination of MEOST and B versus C.
> ➤ With time-to-failure and/or stress-to-failure as the output (or Green Y), rank the three B's (new, cost-reduced design) against the three C's (old but reliable design). If the three B's are not all worse than the three C's, the new cost-reduced design has not degraded product reliability.

Conclusion

This chapter offers the reliability practitioner a simple, nonmathematical, and yet highly timely and cost-effective approach, using the proven discipline of MEOST. However, in order to master the technique, the practitioner should start at the part, board, or module level and then expand the methodology to the system level and the supplier level.

Part IX
. . . .
A Logical Sequence in the Use of DOE Tools

23
....
Case Studies in Sequential DOE Tools to Solve Chronic Problems

Introduction: Difficulties Experienced by Beginning Practitioners in Implementing DOE

One of the concerns expressed by several of our client companies is that the introductory DOE seminars appear to be quite easy, nonmathematical and doable, but that the DOE tools are difficult to implement in real-life problem solving. There are a number of reasons for this seeming dichotomy.

1. The Root Cause Red X May Lie Five or Six Layers Deep

First, every problem—every Green Y—has a Red X cause. But one DOE study is seldom enough to discover the Red X. The uncovered Red X may itself be a new Green Y, a derivative problem that may require a second DOE study to uncover its underlying Red X. In some problem-solving exercises, two or three sequential experiments may be all that is required. In others, however, the *root cause Red X* may lie buried five or six layers deep, requiring five or six sequential experiments.

As an example, let us assume that a Components Search experiment uncovers a subassembly as the Red X. The subassembly may require a follow-on Components Search experiment to pinpoint a particular component as the Red X. If, now, this component is not capable of disassembly and reassembly, a Paired Comparison experiment may be necessary to identify the Red X parameter. This may require that the DOE study move to the component supplier to examine the problem with a Multi-Vari or a Product/Process Search experiment and so on.

2. Not Turning the Experiment "On" and "Off"

A second—and very prevalent—reason is not confirming the permanence of a DOE improvement with a validating B versus C test. Experimenters get so carried away with a perceived improvement that they assume the improvement is real and forever. History is replete with such optimism, only to be followed by subsequent disappointments that the improvement has vanished. The purpose of B versus C is to deliberately turn the problem on and off by going back and forth between the improved and the older product or process.

3. Not Establishing Realistic Tolerances

A third reason is the assumption of a "good" level, following a Variables Search experiment, for each important variable, without establishing a band of realistic tolerances around that central value, through an optimizing DOE study, such as a Scatter Plot or Response Surface Methodology. As a result, unrealistic tolerances in production can contribute to a lack of improvement.

4. No Positrol

A fourth reason is allowing a process to be controlled by the whim of an operator, technician, or maintenance person. Haphazard adjustments violate the rules of Positrol, which requires that each important process parameter, pinpointed in previous DOE studies, be safeguarded by a regimen of *who, where, how,* and *when.* The authors have found that the lack of the Positrol discipline is widespread despite sound use of prior DOE techniques.

5. No Process Certification (too much "noise" at the start of an experiment)

The importance of Process Certification to rein in numerous peripheral quality lapses cannot be overstated. *In fact, we believe that Process Certification should be conducted even before the start of a DOE study, so that the "noise" factors, such as poor manufacturing practices, environmental fluctuations, measuring instrument variations,* etc., can be kept within tight boundaries, to assure the success of the DOE study. Further, Process Certification should be reconfirmed after the DOE study and the recommencement of full production.

A Continuum of Linked DOE Tools

This chapter describes two comprehensive case studies that linked several of the DOE tools in a logical sequence to move toward zero defects. The outcome in each case was not achieved in a day or two. It took several sequential experiments. It took patience; it took discipline, it took perseverance. But the results were spectacular—1,000:1 quality improvement, savings of over $100,000 per year, a 4:1 reduction in cycle time, and a distinct advantage over competition. (Some specific details, including levels of the significant variables have been withheld to protect company confidentiality.)

Case Study 1: Wave Soldering

Product: Wave soldering
Defect level: 2,400 to 3,500 ppm; average: 2,970 ppm
Cost: $106,800/year
Defect modes: Solder shorts, 80%; unsoldered, 14%; insufficient solder and pinholes, etc., 6%
Problem duration: 14 months
Problem-solving
techniques to date: Process tweaking, brainstorming, cause-and-effect diagrams, and control charts

DOE Experiment 1: Multi-Vari

The start of DOE was a multi-vari, with four families of variation:

1. Time-to-time: 9:00 A.M.; 11:00 A.M.; 2:00 P.M.
2. Unit-to-unit: three panels; five boards per panel
3. Within board: left; midleft; midright; right
4. Defect type: solder shorts; unsoldered; other

Figure 23-1 shows the number of defects in chart form, with separation by family. With a total of 140 defects, the defect rate was 3,111 ppm, well above the rule of capturing a minimum of 80 percent of the 2,970 ppm defect rate.

> Figure 23-1A shows no significant variations from time to time or panel to panel.
> Figure 23-1B, by contrast, shows a very significant variation (5:1)

Figure 23-1. Multi-Vari Chart on a Wave Soldering Process
(Total Defect Count: 140)

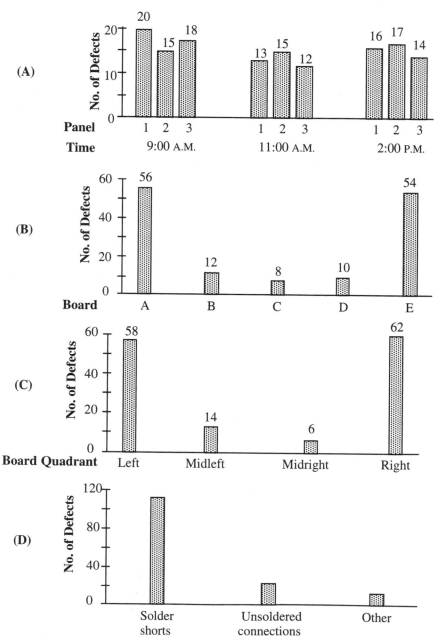

Source: BRK Electronics, Aurora, III.

between boards A and E, at the ends of the panel, which had many defects; and boards B, C, and D, in the middle of the panel, which had very few defects.

> Figure 23-1C also shows very significant variation (3:1 to 10:1) between the left and right quadrants of each board, which had many defects, and the two middle quadrants, which had very few defects.

> Figure 23-1D indicates that solder shorts are the dominant defect mode.

DOE Experiment 2: The Concentration Chart

The multi-vari clearly indicated that the largest number of defects (Red X family) were within-panel (at each end) and within-board. A concentration chart was constructed to depict the concentration of defects by hole location and component location within the panels and within boards. Each time period and each defect type was color-coded to facilitate the analysis.

The concentration chart (more popularly called the measles chart) revealed:

> The highest number of solder shorts were in the edge connector region at the right end of each board.

> A second concentration of solder shorts was in the IC leads at the left end of each board.

> These two solder-short types suggested that wave solder process parameters could be likely causes.

> The unsoldered connections, the number two defect mode, were concentrated in the same two hole locations.

DOE Experiment 3: Paired Comparisons of Boards

Four of the nine panels in Experiment 1 were selected to compare the "good" inner boards with the "bad" outer boards in each panel. Panel warp while going through the wave soldering was suspected, with the Green Y measured as the degree of warp.

Table 23-1 indicates that the outer boards had a repetitively higher warp (0.150" to 0.300") than the inner boards (0.008" to 0.015"), almost a 20:1 difference.

Corrective Action: The warp indicated that the panel fixturing was inadequate and that the temperature of the wave-soldering machine in the preheat zones could be too high. The panel fixtures were made stur-

Table 23-1. Paired Comparisons of Inner and Outer Boards

| Panel No. | Pair | Warp (From panel center to center of each board) | |
		Left board	Right board
1	Inner boards	0.008″	0.010″
	Outer boards	0.150″	0.0170″
2	Inner boards	0.010″	0.015″
	Outer boards	0.210″	0.250″
3	Inner boards	0.015″	0.012″
	Outer boards	0.300″	0.260″
4	Inner boards	0.013″	0.010″
	Outer boards	0.190″	0.160″

Source: BRK Electronics, Aurora, Ill.

dier with firmer anchoring, and the preheat zone temperature was lowered by 10°F.

DOE Experiment 4: Paired Comparison of Unsoldered Connections

Another paired comparisons study was performed on four boards where
there were repetitive unsoldered connections in the same location on each
board. These locations were compared with adjacent locations that had
perfect solder connections.

There were no differences between the "good" and "bad" solder
connections in terms of (1) plating in the holes or (2) solder coat on the
leads. But the "bad" solder connections had a higher hole-to-lead diameter ratio than the "good" solder connections by factors ranging from
1.4:1.0 up to 1.7:1.0.

Corrective Action: It was determined that a single drill bit size had
been used to drill the holes in the printed circuit boards. As a result,
components with small lead diameters were more prone to unsoldered
connections than the majority of components that had large lead diameters. Smaller drill-bit sizes were specified in the next fabrication of boards.

DOE Experiment 5: B versus C Validation

Next, a B versus C experiment was run to determine the effectiveness of
the corrective actions in Experiments 3 and 4.

C process: Current fixtures, preheat zones, and drill-bit sizes.

B process: Firm fixtures, 10°F lower preheat zones, and small drill-bit sizes for the affected hole locations.

Three C and three B panels were run over the wave solder machine in random order. The Green Y was the number of solder defects. The results were:

Panel	B_2	B_3	B_1	C_3	C_1	C_2
No. of defects	5	3	2	12	16	13

Conclusion: The B process was better than the C, with 95 percent confidence. The defect level had dropped from 3,111 ppm to 660 ppm, almost a 5:1 improvement.

DOE Experiment 6: Variables Search

At this point, a logical sequence in experimentation would have been the use of Product/Process Search to investigate the contribution of wave-solder process parameters to solder shorts. But Product/Process Search had not yet been developed, by the authors in those days so the team went on to conduct a Variables Search experiment. Table 23-2 shows the design of the experiment, with eight factors. Ten panels were selected at the best levels and 10 at the marginal levels. The results of the original all-best and all-worst and the two replications (run in random order) are shown in Table 23-2A (Design), Tables 23-2B (Stage 1), 23-2C (Stage 2); 23-2D (Capping Run); 23-2E (factorial analysis), and 23-2F (ANOVA) depict the remainder of the variables search experiment.

Conclusions

1. Stage 1 is successful, with a D:$\overline{d}$ ratio of 7:1, greater than the minimum of 1.25. This result means that the right factors were selected in the experiment.
2. Stage 2 indicates that factors A, B, F, G, and H are unimportant; hence, their interaction effects are also unimportant.
3. Factors C, D, and E are important and their interaction effects cannot be ignored. They should be quantified with a factorial analysis, which shows that a three-factor interaction, CDE, is the Red X, factor C is the Pink X, and Factor E is the Pale Pink X. For optimum results, B, C, and E should be kept at their best levels.

Table 23-2. Variables Search: Wave Solder

A: Design of Experiment

Code	Process parameter	Best level	Marginal level
A	Hot air knife pressure (psi)	14	10
B	Preheat zone temperatures	Profile 1	Profile 2
C	Flux density gm/cc	0.9	0.8
D	Conveyor speed (ft./minute)	4	6
E	Conveyor angle (°)	7	5
F	Solder temperature (°F)	480	450
G	Solder dwell time (sec.)	3.5	3.0
H	Flux foam height	1.2	1.0

B. Stage 1 (done in random order): Defects

All-best levels	All-marginal levels
4	42
5	46
2	51

Test of Significance

a) Three "all-best" better than three "all-marginal"
b) $D = 46-4 = 42$; $d = (9+3)/2 = 6$
   $D{:}\bar{d}$ Ratio $= 42{:}6\text{-}7{:}1; >$Min of 1.25

C. Stage 2

Factor combination	Green Y	Factor importance
$A_M R_B$	13	No
$A_B R_M$	38	
$B_M R_B$	12	No
$B_B R_W$	39	
$C_M R_B$	32	Yes, with
$C_B R_M$	15	another variable
$D_M R_B$	20	Yes, with
$D_B R_M$	21	another variable
$E_M R_B$	25	Yes, with
$E_B R_M$	22	another variable
$F_M R_B$	10	No
$F_B R_M$	40	
$G_M R_B$	9	No
$G_B R_M$	42	
$H_M R_B$	8	No
$H_B R_M$	38	

Decision Limits = Median $\pm$ 2.776 $\times$ d/1.81

Median $_{Best}$ = 4; Median $_{Marginal}$ = 46
So, Control limits (best) = 4 $\pm$ 2.776 $\times$ 6/1.81
= 13.2 & −5
Control limits (marginal) = 46 + 2.776 $\times$ 6/1.81
= 55.2 & 35.8
Center line between the two medians = 25

Table 23-2. (Continued)

D. Capping Run

Factor Combination	Green Y	Confirmed?
$C_M D_M E_M R_B$	43	Yes—R is unimportant
$C_B D_B E_B R_M$	7	Yes—R is confirmed as unimportant

E. Factorial Analysis

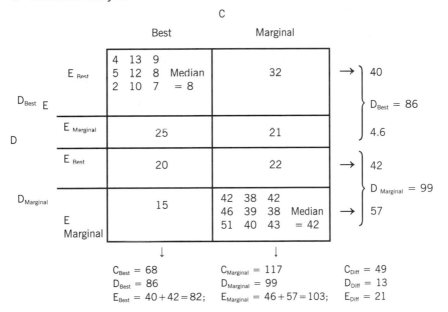

$$C_{Best} = 68 \qquad C_{Marginal} = 117 \qquad C_{Diff} = 49$$
$$D_{Best} = 86 \qquad D_{Marginal} = 99 \qquad D_{Diff} = 13$$
$$E_{Best} = 40 + 42 = 82; \qquad E_{Marginal} = 46 + 57 = 103; \qquad E_{Diff} = 21$$

F. Analysis of Variance (ANOVA) Table

C	D	E	CD	CD	DE	CDE	Output
+	+	+	+	+	+	+	8
−	+	+	−	−	+	−	32
+	+	−	+	−	−	−	25
−	+	−	−	+	−	+	21
+	−	+	−	+	−	−	20
−	−	+	+	−	−	+	22
+	−	−	−	−	+	+	15
−	−	−	+	+	+	−	42
−49	−13	−21	+9	−3	+9	−53	

Source: BRK Electronics, Aurora, Ill.

4. The defect rate had been reduced from the original 3,111 ppm to 660 ppm following the Paired Comparisons study. The Variables Search took the defect level down to approximately 80 ppm (4 × 10^6)/10 × 100 × 5, an improvement of 39:1.

DOE Experiment 7: B versus C Validation

Even though the capping run of the Variables Search experiment indicated success, it was felt that a B versus C verification of the improvement should be made 10 days later, on 10 B and 10 C panels run in random order.

C process:	Firm fixtures, low heat zone, smaller drill bits, standard wave-solder process parameters.
B process:	Same as above, except flux density at 0.9 gm/cc, conveyor speed at 4 ft./min., and conveyor angle at 7°.

Results: (total number of defects)

Panel	B_1	B_3	B_2	C_2	C_3	C_1
	3	3	4	25	31	29

Conclusion: The B wave-solder parameters were better than C, with 95 percent confidence.

DOE Experiment 8: Optimization Through a Full Factorial

Experiment 6 indicated a three-factor interaction between flux density (B), conveyor angle (E), and conveyor speed (D). The correct follow-on optimization experiment, in the presence of such interactions, would have been Response Surface methodology, possibly the Evolutionary Operation (EVOP) technique. The team, however, was not familiar with EVOP and elected to do a mini-optimization, using a 2^2 full factorial. Two of the most important factors from experiment 6 were chosen, with two levels each:

1. flux density: at 0.9 gm/cc (from the Variables Search experiment) and a possibly better level of 0.85 gm/cc
2. conveyor angle: at 7° (from the Variables Search experiment) and a possibly better level of 6°. Ten panels were run with each combination, along with replication and randomization. Figure 23-2 shows the results of the 2^2 full factorial (number of defects).

Figure 23-2. 2^2 Full Factorial on a Wave Soldering Process

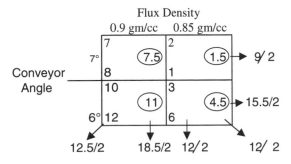

Flux density main effect = 18.5/2 − 6/2 = 9.25 − 3 = 6.25
Conveyor main effect   = 15.5/2 − 9/2 = 7.75 − 4.5 = 3.25
Interaction effect   = 12.5/2 − 12/2 = 6.25 − 6.0 = 0.25

Conclusions:

› Flux density should be changed from the original variables search best level of 0.9 gm/cc to 0.85 gm/cc.
› Conveyor speed, however, should remain at the original variables search best level of 7°.
› The interaction effect between these two factors is negligible.
› The combination resulted in a solder defect level of 30 ppm—a further 2.5:1 improvement and a reduction of 103:1 from the original 3,111 ppm.

DOE Experiment 9: Final Optimization With Scatter Plots

The full factorial of Experiment 8 showed that the flux density was the Red X and that solder defect ppms could be reduced even further by lowering flux density from 0.9 gm/cc to 0.85 gm/cc.

A scatter plot was the next logical step in the optimization process. Flux densities were varied over a range from 0.74 gm/cc to 0.90 gm/cc (the original Variables Search level). Figure 23-3 shows the scatter plot results, with the Green Y expressed directly in ppms. If a maximum defect level of 20 ppm is allowed, the scatter plot indicates that the flux density should be confined to levels between 0.78 and 0.84 gm/cc, with a target value of 0.81 gm/cc. For monitoring with pre-control, its P-C lines should be at 0.795 and 0.825 gm/cc.

Positrol

The three important factors—flux density, conveyor angle, and conveyor speed—identified in the variables search experiment were controlled with a Positrol plan (Table 23-3).

Figure 23-3. Flux Density Scatter Plot

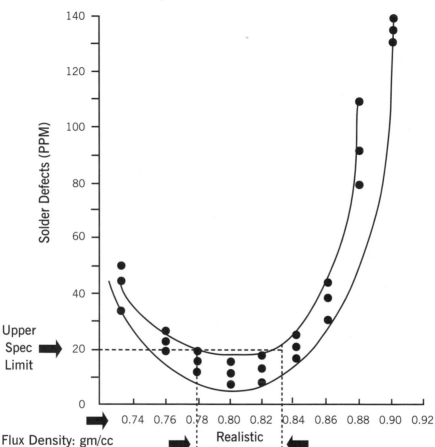

Source: BRK Electronics, Aurora, Ill.

Process Certification

Process Certification was the last discipline put in place to assure that peripheral quality issues do not derail the DOE gains. In many situations, *Process Certification should be conducted by an interdisciplinary team, before DOE studies, so that the uncontrollable "noise" of these quality problems does not overwhelm the purity of the DOE "signal."* This is especially important whenever it is suspected that good manufacturing practices are being violated. Table 23-4 is a checklist of quality peripherals associated with the wave soldering process that had to be audited by the interdisciplinary team before certification was granted.

Table 23-3. Positrol Plan: Wave Solder

What (key factor)	Who controls	How controlled	Where controlled	When (how frequently)
Flux density 0.1795 − 0.925 gm/cc	Solder technician	Specific gravity meter	Flux container	Once/hour
Conveyor angle 7° ± 10%	Solder technician	Machine setting	Conveyor	Once/day
Conveyor speed 4 ft./min. ± 10%	Solder technician	Counter	Conveyor	Each model change

Source: BRK Electronics, Aurora, Ill.

Case Study 2: Dome Tweeter Sensitivity

Product: Dome tweeter for automobile industry
Specifications: Sensitivity: 88.1 ± 1.5 db from 4.5 Khz to 20 Khz
Defect level: 40% requiring rework
Cost: >$100,000/year
Problem Duration: Since start of production several years ago

DOE Experiment 1: Components Search on Entire Assembly

See Table 23-5.

DOE Experiment 2: Paired Comparisons on Dome

See Table 23-6.

The Paired Comparisons test clearly showed:

> Moving mass as the Red X, with an end-count of 12.
> Position in air gap as a Pink X, with an end-count of 9.
> Mass coil as a Pale Pink X, with an end-count of 6.

DOE Experiment 3: Paired Comparison on Magnet

This experiment was performed on larger samples than needed. But Figure 23-4 shows a clear separation between the inductions of the good and the bad magnets, with the former rarely dipping below 9.0 gauss and the latter rarely going above 9.0 gauss. It was clearly the Red X for the magnet.

Table 23-4. Quality Issues: A Process Certification Check List

Operators
1. Are workers forbidden to make unauthorized adjustments to the process?
2. Are Positrol logs scrupulously maintained?
3. Are solder technicians certified and periodically recertified?

Management/Supervision
4. Is the climate of fear removed?
5. Is there DOE training for the operator?
6. Are there audiovisual quality alarm signals?
7. Do operators have authority to shut down a poor-quality line?

Good Manufacturing Practices
8. Is there a written Standard Operating Practice (SOP)?
9. Is the SOP too difficult to follow?
10. Is the SOP being used?
11. Is "housekeeping" perfect?
12. Are setup changes fast and accurate?

Equipment
13. Is Total Preventive Maintenance used?
14. What is the ratio of preventive maintenance to "fix when broke"?
15. Does instrumentation : product accuracy have a minimum 5:1 ratio?
16. Is instrument calibration in place?
17. Is there attention to lubrication, noise, vibration, overheating, voltage surges, etc.?

Environment
18. Are the temperature/humidity controls adequate?
19. Are chemical and dust control adequate?
20. Are water and air purity adequate?
21. Is electrostatic discharge protection (ESD) adequate?
22. Is smoking prohibited in the factory?

Summary of Wave-Soldering Case Study

Experiment	Average Defect Level (ppm)
1. At start	2970
2. Multi-Vari confirmation	3111
3. Following Paired Comparisons corrections (B versus C confirmation)	660
4. Following Variables Search	80
5. Following Full Factorial	30
6. Following Scatter Plot	<20

Table 23-5. Components Search on Dome Tweeter Sensitivity
BOB: 87.25 db; WOW: 85.2 db.

Component	Results
First and Second Disassembly/Reassembly	No change
Front swap	No change
Magnet swap	Partial
Dome swap	Partial
Magnet and dome swap	Complete reversal Red X

Table 23-6. Paired Comparisons on Dome Tweeters

Dome	Moving mass	Mass dome	Mass coil	Winding width	Position in air gap
#1 Good	0.156	0.072	0.081	2.2	0.35
#1 Bad	0.176	0.063	0.108	2.4	0.30
#2 Good	0.159	0.081	0.081	2.3	0.35
#3 Good	0.162	0.075	0.090	2.4	0.35
#3 Bad	0.179	0.081	0.100	2.2	0.30
#4 Good	0.162	0.076	0.086	2.2	0.35
#4 Bad	0.166	0.077	0.090	2.2	0.30
#5 Good	0.160	0.070	0.089	2.2	0.30
#5 Bad	0.173	0.078	0.092	2.35	0.25
#6 Good	0.160	0.078	0.088	2.35	0.35
#6 Bad	0.167	0.067	0.098	2.2	0.3
End-count	12	0	6	0	9

Source: Philips, Dendermonde, Belgium.

DOE Experiment 4: The Full Factorial

The DOE team went on to a 2^3 full factorial to quantify the relative importance of the moving mass and position in air gap in the dome and the induction of the magnets, as well as their interaction effects (see Table 23-7).

Conclusion

Additional DOE work had to be performed on all three factors, especially moving mass (the Red X), indicating a need to move to a lower mass.

Figure 23-4. Paired Comparisons: Induction Magnet

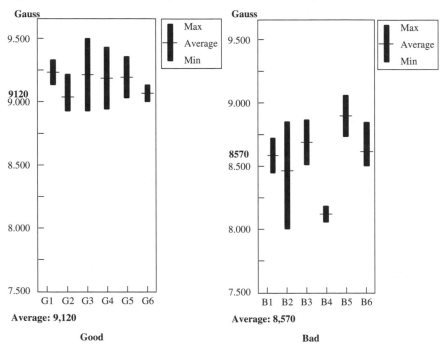

Average: 9,120   Average: 8,570

Good   Bad

Source: Philips, Dendermonde, Belgium.

DOE Experiment 5: Multi-Vari Study of Glue Weight on Dome

The identification of moving mass on the dome as the Red X led to a
Multi-Vari study (Figure 23-5) on the glue weight variations on the dome.
It showed that the dome-to-dome variation was the Red X family, rather
than time-to-time, with variations as high as 25 gm, or roughly a spread
of 20 percent in glue weight.

DOE Experiment 6: Multi-Vari Study of Glue Weight on Coil and Dome (not shown)

A similar multi-vari study was performed on the manual application of
glue and the resultant weight (Green Y) on both voice coil and dome. The
results were similar to those of Experiment 5, where the dome-to-dome
variation was again the Red X family, with a spread of 40 percent in glue
weight.

Table 23-7. Full Factorial: Dome Tweeter

Moving mass (C)

			Lo	Hi	
LO			87.7	86.0	
			(87.45)	(86.0) → 87.11	
	Induc-	Lo	87.2	86.0	→ 87.16
	tion (A)	Hi	88.5	86.9	
Position			(88.2)	(86.95)	
in			87.9	87.0	
air gap (B)		Lo	88.2	86.9	
			(88.1)	(86.9)	
			88.0	86.9	→ 87.9
	Induc-		89.2	87.8	
HI	tion (A)		(89.05)	(87.6) → 87.94	
		Hi	88.9	87.4	
			88.20	86.86	

Main effect: Moving Mass (C) = 1.34
Main effect: Position Air Gap (B) = 0.74
Main effect: Induction (A) = 0.83

Interactions   (Factorial analysis not shown)

AB	= 0.06
AC	= 0.01
BC	= 0.18
ABC	= 0.09

DOE Experiment 7: B versus C—Automatic versus Manual Applications of Glue

A B versus C experiment (overlap method) was run to determine if automatic application of glue would lead to a more uniform glue weight than manual application for both the dome and the dome/voice coil. The Green Y is the range or amount of spread in glue weight. Figure 23-6 shows a 3:1 reduction in spread (or a 3:1 improvement in C_p for glue weight on the dome and a 6:1 reduction in spread (or a 6:1 improvement in C_p) for glue weight on the dome and voice coil.

DOE Experiment 8: Position of the Voice Coil in the Air Gap

It was found that the voice coil position (Pink X) in the air gap was not in the middle of the air gap. Centering this parameter further improved speaker sensitivity and was confirmed with a B versus C test.

Figure 23-5. Multi-Vari: Glue Weight on Dome

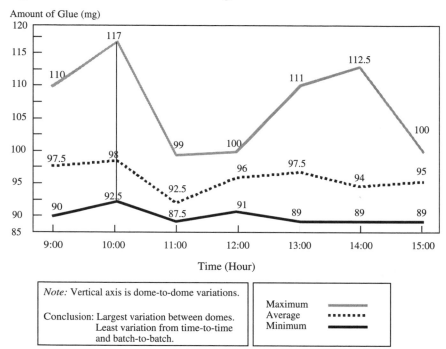

DOE Experiment 9: Change in the Magnetizing Unit (B versus C test)
===

The third (Pale Pink X) factor was the inductance. The full factorial indicated that a higher figure was in order. The magnetizing unit was modified and a B versus C was run on nine old (C) and nine new (B) units.
The Green Y is sensitivity (db). Figure 23-7 shows:

α Risk

> B is better than C.
> The Tukey test end-count is 14.
> That means that we have over 99 percent confidence in the im-
  provement

β Risk

> $\overline{X}_B$ is 87.75, $\overline{X}_C$ is 86.85.
> $\overline{X}_B - \overline{X}_C$ is 0.90.
> For 90 percent confidence, with $\sigma_B = \sigma_C$, K is 3.7.

Figure 23-6. B versus C: Automatic versus Manual Glue Application

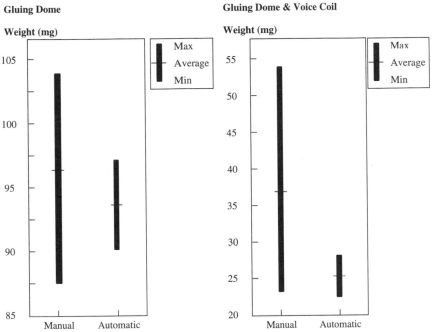

Gluing Dome

Gluing Dome & Voice Coil

With automatic gluing, the average can be adapted by adjusting air pressure on the glue nozzle, the variation remains mainly the same.
Automatic/semi-automatic is better because the sigma variation is smaller.

> So, the minimum separation of $X_B - X_C = K \sigma_C = 3.7K_C$.
> σ_C was estimated at 1/6, so minimum separation = 3.7/6 or 0.61, which is less than the actual separation of 0.9.
> So there is also a 90 percent confidence that B is sufficiently better than C.

DOE Experiment 10: Final Results

With all three changes—automatic glue application, voice coil centering, and higher induction in the magnetizing unit—the final sensitivity exceeded the maximum customer specification of 89.6 db.

Conclusion

The customer was delighted to receive the higher sensitivity, which was really pushing the state of the art. The customer was also very happy

Figure 23-7. B versus C: Before versus After Changing Magnetizing Unit

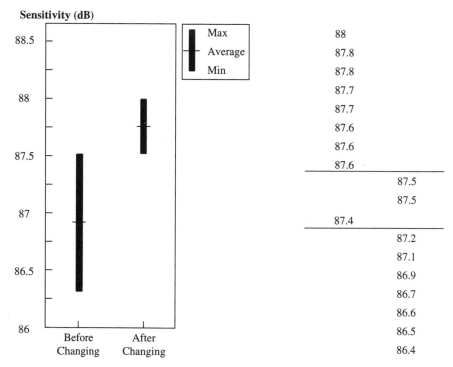

After changing: Higher induction and Sensitivity with smaller variation.

with the low spread—an increase in C_p from 0.6 to 3. Of the seven suppliers producing this product, the customer limited his suppliers to just two, with this company as the major supplier. The company not only saved over $100,000 per year, but its volume of business on this product increased 4.5 times!

Part X
From Classroom Instruction to True Learning on the Job

24. Learning by Doing

24
Learning by Doing

Practice, Practice, Practice

We repeat the story of a group of surgeons who visited us at Motorola to learn about our renowned Six Sigma process. One of the techniques discussed in the presentation was our success in benchmarking—finding the best company anywhere in the world with respect to a discipline or function or technique, determining its success factors, and incorporating or adapting them into your own company.

The surgeons decided that it was important to reduce cycle time in surgery. They visited an unusual benchmark outfit—the pit crew at the Indianapolis 500 car races, where four tires are changed in 12 seconds. Quite apart from the manpower and equipment, the pit crew shared the secret of their success—PRACTICE, PRACTICE, PRACTICE. The surgeons went back to the hospital and looked at every time element involved in their long and complex surgical processes. With repeated trials, they were able to cut the cycle time in half, doubling the number of surgeries performed per day with not one iota of deterioration of quality or health.

Diligent, disciplined, sustained practice is the key success factor in "Lean Manufacturing," in sports championships, in the Olympics. It is the key, also, to DOE success.

> Exposure to DOE is a prerequisite, but not enough.
> Reading this book is a head start, but only a beginning.
> Working with trained professionals and outside consultants is a shortcut to learning, but true learning and true comprehension comes only with practice, practice, practice.

The shop floor is chock-full of hundreds of opportunities for DOE. But, before the entire work force can be so energized, a DOE problem-solving culture needs to be built up, one step at a time.

467

Energizing a Problem-Solving Culture

Darryl Piersol,[22] a former IBM executive and professor emeritus of the University of Texas, created Figure 24-1 as a way to manage any complex change. It has five elements—vision, skills, incentive, resources, and action plans. All five elements must be present to effect a lasting culture change in industry. Applied to DOE, Figure 24-1 shows:

> *Without vision,* the outcome is likely to be mass confusion as different DOE initiatives pull in different directions. Only management can imagine that vision; "move that vision in directions never explored before," as Bob Galvin, one of the foremost captains of world industry, frequently states; and inspire people with that vision.

> *Without skills,* people will thrash around, trying a number of approaches, but ending up in anxiety and disappointment. This is especially appropriate in problem solving, where all approaches except our DOE are too complex and too difficult to implement.

> *Without action plans,* there will be no road map, and people will not have captured the *process* by which goals can be translated into results. The net outcome will be a series of false starts. For DOE, Table 7-1 and Figure 7-3 provide this essential road map.

> *Without resources*—i.e., manpower, money, and, above all, time—people will become frustrated and demotivated. This is one of the more frequent causes of DOE being abandoned for fire fighting. Somehow, management finds the time to attempt to solve the same chronic problem

Figure 24-1. Managing Complex Change

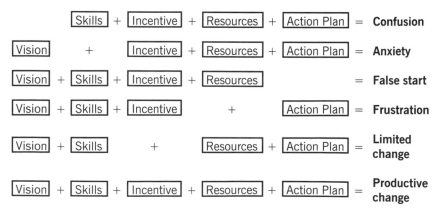

Source: Dr. Darryl Piersol, lecture at Motorola Management Institute.

several times, but not to do *one* comprehensive set of DOE studies to solve it forever!

> *Without incentives,* there will only be limited change. People need to become involved, to be in on things. Team synergy occurs only with individual buy-in.

However, the incentives need not be monetary. Recognition for a good job is fundamental. Motorola's 6,000 Total Customer Satisfaction (TCS) competition teams receive such top management recognition that their exuberance in pursuing team goals is almost too hard to tone down!

Given management vision, management resources, and management incentives, the DOE methods outlined in this text can provide problem-solving teams with the consummate skills and the action plans they need. These are clearly depicted in Table 7-1, a generic problem-solving framework—and in Figure 7-3—a problem-solving road map. In more specific terms, top management design engineers, quality professionals, production management, suppliers and line workers should step up to the plate. These steps are detailed below:

Step 1: Top Management Commitment and Involvement

Top management must, however, be weary of the oft-quoted statement that all good initiatives must start with them. When there are so many project balls in the air, a CEO has to be a veritable Houdini to juggle them. So, a CEO must choose priorities very carefully. We earnestly recommend that DOE be one of them—a key strategy. Figure 1-1, at the start of this book, graphically details the contribution DOE can make to business excellence. There is no area in the flow of product that DOE does not influence.

CEOs do not have to be experts in the use of these techniques, but they must know that they exist, must understand them, and must support them. More specifically, CEOs—and division managers, and plant managers—should:

1. Seek out a DOE goal "champion" in the ranks of top management who can become thoroughly immersed in DOE techniques and then pursue their implementation because of the vast payoff for the corporation. This person then becomes the *"process owner,"* the catalyst for a cultural transformation.

2. Make it mandatory for every technical person in the company to go through a one-day DOE seminar. It is a far better body-language signal to the staff if the top person attends the session all day, rather than just pronouncing holy invocations at the start.

3. Establish a steering committee to monitor progress. Its tasks are:

> Formulate quality/reliability improvement goals and target savings. (Keep track of training and experimentation costs, and measure them against savings. If a ratio of 10:1 of savings:cost is not reached, the entire effort is lagging. Recent public reports of companies, such as G.E., claiming a 3:1 benefit:investment would rate a C minus grade in our book.
> Identify the top quality and cost problems in the plant as well as in the field, and create projects for DOE teams to tackle.
> Create interdisciplinary DOE teams to tackle each selected project. (Joe Juran, one of the foremost quality "gurus" in the world, has flatly stated that the way to solve chronic problems and reduce the cost of poor quality is to select such projects and assign teams—there is no other way!
> Support the DOE teams with resources such as capital equipment and money, if needed. Most DOE projects do not require the expenditure of large sums of money. Make do with old equipment to the greatest extent possible. (An exception is Multiple Environment Over Stress Test, in which the high rates of stress acceleration require sophisticated equipment ranging from $50,000 up to $250,000.)
> Above all, support the DOE teams with time to experiment. Nothing demotivates a team more than pulling key people off DOE projects to fight fires and attend to routine work.
> Periodically—at least once a month and, preferably, once a week—review DOE team progress. Management typically sets goals and monitors results, but seldom reviews the all-important *process road* in converting goals into results. Steering committee exposure to DOE seminars and use of the checklists for teams and management at the end of each DOE technique chapter in this text will enable management and the steering committee to ask the right questions. Examination of due process will heighten management's own grasp of DOE, promote learning all around, and earn the respect of the DOE team members.

4. Create DOE workshops, as a follow-up to DOE seminars. The authors have used these workshops as a sure-fire way to accelerate learning.

> In these workshops, which typically are limited to one day, each DOE team leader presents the project, including:
> (1) Problem description (a succinct statement of the Green Y).
> (2) Its history: defect/failure level; estimated cost; duration.

(3) A flow chart associated with the location of the problem (along with physical samples, where possible).

(4) Possible causes of the problem.

(5) The approach taken to solve the problem prior to DOE.

(6) Why the particular clue-generation DOE technique has been selected (Multi-Vari, Components Search, Paired Comparisons, or Product/Process Search).

(7) Results of DOE to date.

Other team members also participate in each team presentation, adding perspective and insights.

> Next, the discussions are opened up to other DOE teams present at the workshop, even though they are not directly involved in the project. This is similar to design reviews in new product launch, where "alternate" development engineers play the role of devil's advocate in challenging the approach selected. Sometimes, this challenge deteriorates into a retreat into traditional problem solving by engineering judgement. But it is good to allow the technical dust to settle, so that all approaches can be aired.

> Finally, as outside consultants, the authors review each presentation—guiding, coaching, and encouraging each team to proceed to the next phase of the DOE project.

> A log of "lessons learned" is encouraged, so that future projects and future teams can learn from the mistakes, rather than such omissions being swept under the rug.

> After two to three such workshops, the company generally becomes self-sufficient, and DOE is made a way of life.

5. Create a cadre of DOE experts that can provide DOE continuity on a sustained basis. Some companies use the term "black belt" and "master black belt" to designate such experts. They define a black belt as one who has gone through formal DOE training and has demonstrated competency with a minimum of three or four successful projects. A master black belt is one who, in addition to completing DOE projects, can teach formal DOE classes.

6. Turn the whole factory loose on problem solving. While the "black belt" concept is sound, there is no need for an enlightened management to stop there. A company has only a limited number of technical people, who are already overloaded with new designs, new processes, total productive maintenance, fire fighting, supplier discontinuities, and paperwork.

Why not turn the whole labor force loose on problem solving. If the DOE techniques were hard to grasp, their use by direct labor, by the blue-collar worker, would, indeed, be an uphill, if not an impossible task. But, the DOE techniques detailed in this text are easy. In some ways, it is easier to instruct line workers in DOE than it is to teach them control charts. Having successfully implemented DOE down to the direct-labor level in scores of companies, the authors are confident that it would be eagerly accepted by line workers after suitable training, support, attention, and encouragement by management. The concluding case study illustrates the enormous benefits that accrued to a company that extended DOE to its direct-labor force.

7. Measure progress in DOE by:

> The number of technical people trained each month.
> The number of direct-labor people trained each month.
> The number of partnership supplier personnel trained each month.
> The number of projects undertaken in each of the above three groups.
> The monetary savings to the company, in terms of:
   (1) Quality improvements: cost of poor quality reduced; yields increased.
   (2) Reliability improvements: reduced warranty costs; recall costs; and product liability cost.
   (3) Cost reductions: product costs; supplier costs; total productive maintenance (TPM) costs through Factory Overall Effectiveness (FOE) increases.
   (4) Cycle time reductions: incoming materials, work-in-process, and finished goods.
   (5) Inventory reductions (increase in number of inventory turns).
   (6) Ratio of savings : investment (minimum: 5:1, maximum: over 100:1, average: 20:1).

Step 2: Conversion of the Design Engineer

If change must begin with top management, the systematic reduction of variation—an industrial evil—must begin with the design engineer. The vehicle is DOE. Yet, in many ways, the hardest missionary DOE work is in converting conservative engineers, far more difficult than with receptive production technicians and plant line workers who have to live with the engineer's product problems. The specific DOE-related disciplines in design include:

> Quality function deployment and mass customization to capture the "voice of the customer."

> Translating the customer's "voice" into realistic specifications and realistic tolerances instead of "atmospheric analysis."
> Designing to target values to achieve C_{pk}'s of at least 2.0.
> Using the powerful instrument of Variables Search to separate the important variables from the unimportant ones.
>> Tightly controlling the important variables to C_{pk}'s of 2.0 and more.
>> Opening up the tolerances of the unimportant variables to reduce costs.
> Forcing reliability improvements by forcing failures in design through Multiple Environment Over Stress Tests (MEOST).
> Recognizing that field failure is a dependant function of line failure on the production floor, which becomes the largest and earliest service center to apprehend and correct field failures.
> Avoiding the temptation of guessing at causes of problems and learning the language of "talking to the parts."

Step 3: Quality Management—From Policeman to Coach

The role of the quality professional is changing from one of whistle blower and perpetual pain in the side of production to one of coach, consultant, and teacher. But it is changing ever so slowly. Besides becoming the customer's advocate within the company, the quality professional—if he is to be of any use whatsoever to his engineering and production colleagues—must:

> Become an absolute expert in DOE to earn his keep. Without knowledge of DOE problem-solving tools, he can be of little help to the designer, to production, or to the line worker. Without the ability to help, he rapidly loses the respect of these line groups and is boxed into bureaucratic impotence.
> Become knowledgeable, if not expert, in the 10 powerful tools of the 21st century. Most quality professionals are not even aware of more than one or two of these tools, and even fewer practice them.
> Help to gather, analyze, and reduce the cost of poor quality as the single measure of macro-performance and ability to help.
> Understand the close tie-in between quality and cycle time, and work to fuse these disciplines.

Step 4: Production Management

Production management must start with a set of axioms:

> The line worker will perform as a highly motivated individual, unless ground down by poor management, with a bossy attitude or forced to work in an atmosphere of pervasive fear.

> The line worker's brain is as fertile as the manager's, given training, support, and encouragement.
> Inspection and test add no value to a product and should be drastically reduced.

To successfully implement DOE, production management must:

> Drastically reduce "fire fighting" quality problems in production by insisting that every important quality parameter on a new product entering production achieve a C_{pk} of 2.0. This is quickly and easily ascertained by Rule 2 of Pre-Control (five consecutive units must fall within the Pre-Control lines, i.e., in the green zone).
> Establish Positrol as an ironclad discipline to monitor process stability.
> Establish Process Certification as another ironclad discipline to rein in all quality peripherals.
> Maintain reduced variation and C_{pk} control with Pre-Control, not control charts.
> Verify the effectiveness of every engineering change with a B versus C quick, effective DOE study.
> Monitor progress with cost of poor quality; yields; defects per unit; C_p, C_{pk}; and cycle time (a target of no more than twice the direct labor time, also known as theoretical cycle time).

Step 5: Suppliers

Next only to design, suppliers account for the largest percentage of quality problems. The traditional approach that companies take is to bludgeon the supplier into compliance or find a new supplier. It is a dictatorial, remote-control approach. It does not work.

What is needed is a partnership between a customer company and its key suppliers. A cardinal principle in that partnership is that the customer-company must *help* the supplier improve his quality, cost, and cycle time. Why is that necessary? Because it is the best way to help your own company. In return for that help, the supplier must give a continual cost reduction every year. This should not be done by squeezing the supplier as companies tend to do, but by *helping the supplier actually increase his profit*. Only then is it a win-win partnership.

One of the most productive ways to help a supplier is through DOE. The customer's commodity teams must virtually live at the supplier's facility, teaching him, coaching him, solving his chronic quality problems. The measure of success is a drastic reduction in the supplier's cost of poor quality, which is then shared equitably between the two parties. This author has a proven track record of working with his client companies and their partnership suppliers to achieve 5 to 10 percent reductions each year in cost—a reduction over and above inflation.

Step 6: The Use of Skunk Works—An Unobtrusive Pilot Effort

But, what if Management, Design, Quality, and Production on support is lukewarm or not there. We have advocated our clients to form a small, unobtrusive "skunk works" team—dedicated to DOE—to try two or three DOE projects, without fanfare, measure the results and then present top management with the benefits. No reasonable management will turn down proven savings!

Step 7: The Untapped Gold Mine of Line Workers' Contribution

The last, but certainly not the least, step is to involve the entire direct-labor force in problem solving. The infrastructure for this initiative already exists, with companies increasingly turning to movements like Kaizen, Small Group Improvement Activities (SGIA), and Glass Wall Management. But we need to go beyond just infrastructure. We need to develop workers' skills, as indicated in Figure 24-1. We need to put simple but powerful tools in their hands—not elementary tools like cause-and-effect diagrams, brainstorming, and control charts, but effective tools, of which DOE is the easiest and most productive.

A case study will serve as an illustration of direct labor as a gold mine.

Case Study: Dendermonde, Belgium

A few years ago, I was called upon to introduce DOE to Philips Electronics in Dendermonde, Belgium. The precedent at Philips, one of the largest electronic companies in the world, was my success at Philips Singapore. The Dendermonde plant produces speakers for the automotive industry and for hi-fi customers.

The plant was losing money—a 15 percent red-ink each year. The workers were dispirited. There had already been a layoff of 300 people from a labor force of 800. The new plant management had to stop the hemorrhaging fast. It introduced a movement along the line workers called "Kill the Waste." It also felt that DOE was needed as an igniting spark.

I started DOE with a seminar for 40 of the plant's technical staff and on the second day's workshop, three DOE projects were outlined for solution. On my next visit, the three DOE projects had been successfully concluded and 12 new ones had been started. On my third visit, the DOE projects had grown to 30. In the technical areas, the plant was well on its way to success.

Based on my work with other companies, I suggested to the plant manager that a DOE seminar be given to the line workers as a start at opening up problem solving to the whole factory. He was reluctant. "They don't speak English, and you don't speak Flemish," he protested. But he selected 12 women, with a smattering of English from among the line workers to attend my one-day DOE seminar. All of them did well, solving simple workshop exercises similar to those that I give to technical groups. The women were so thrilled with their success that they pleaded for more detailed training for the entire work force. A capable manager was selected as the DOE goal champion to train the line workers.

DOE was then combined with the "Kill the Waste" initiative. Direct labor teams were formed. They selected their own team leaders, and the role of supervisors was changed to facilitators. Teams were given a half-hour each day, either at the start or at the end of a shift, to solve the previous day's problems, if possible on their own or with the help of the engineering staff, as needed. The question of a half-hour lost in terms of productivity did not even arise, because there was general agreement that the savings would far exceed the investment in time. The plant manager would personally attend as many of the team meetings as possible either at the start of a shift at 6:00 A.M. or late into the night.

The momentum built up. Three hundred of the 400 line workers were trained in DOE, with only three techniques emphasized—Multi-Vari, Components Search, and Paired Comparisons. The direct labor teams were able to solve 70 percent of the problems they confronted on their own power. In fact, they jokingly told the engineers: "Go do something else. We don't need you!"

The plant manager and his direct reports would review the DOE projects—both those of the technical staff as well as those of direct labor—every two weeks. At first, the statistics associated with the number of people trained, the number of DOE projects, and the savings in Belgium francs were plotted. The quality improvements registered ranged from 2:1 up to 100:1, with a median value of 15:1 and an average of 28:1. But, gradually, as DOE became a way of life, there was no need to justify its adoption.

The bottom line? After less than two years, the plant went from a 15 percent loss, as a percentage of sales, to a 4 percent profit!

Joy in the Workplace

Dr. W. Edwards Deming, the towering quality guru, frequently stressed that it was the role of management to create "joy in the workplace." When a worker spends at least half of his or her waking hours on the job, work should be fun.

Instead, what we typically see are workers as human robots, doing dull, repetitive, boring, dreary work day after day, week after week, month after month. And then we have the nerve to say that the average worker has lost pride in his work! Would any of our technical types, sitting in air-conditioned offices, trade places with workers on the line?

So the challenge for industry today is to:

> Remove fear from the minds of the workers who hunker down in their cocoons, afraid to stick their necks out.
> Train them, coach them in the simple but powerful tools they need.
> Pay attention to them—the Hawthorne effect. Listen to them, support them, encourage them. They know more about their own job than you do.
> Redesign/enrich their jobs by:
>> Combining tasks.
>> Forming natural work units and teams.
>> Establishing client relationships (the next operation as customer).
>> Building vertical job enrichment by giving them a progressively more operational management role.

In short, let us so transform the work place that we can truly change TGIF to TGIM—from "thank God it's Friday," to "thank God it's Monday!"

References

1. Schaffer and Thomson, "Successful Change Programs Begin with Results," *Harvard Business Review* 5/6, 1992.
2. Jay Matthews and Peter Katel, "The Cost of Quality," *Newsweek*, September 7, 1992.
3. Gilbert Fuchsberg, "Quality Programs Show Shoddy Results," *Wall Street Journal*, May 14, 1992.
4. A. Blanton Goddfrey, "Strategic Quality Management, Part 1," *Quality*, March 1990.
5. Keki R. Bhote, *Plan for Maximum Profit: The 12 Critical Success Factors That Guarantee Increased Profits from Total Quality*, Zurich: Strategic Directions, 1995.
6. Keki R. Bhote, *The Ultimate Six Sigma: The Pursuit of Business Excellence*, New York: American Management Association, forthcoming.
7. Keki R. Bhote, "A Powerful New Tool Kit for the 21st Century," *National Productivity Review*, Autumn 1997.
8. Bob Kine, *Better Designs in Half the Time*, Naiman Press, 1987.
9. Seiichi Nakajima, *T.P.M. Development Program: Implementing Total Productive Maintenance*, Cambridge, Mass.: Productivity Press, 1989.
10. Michael J. Spendolini, *The Benchmarking Book*, New York: American Management Association, 1992.
11. Nikkam Kogyo Shinbun, *Poka-Yoke: Improving Product Quality by Preventing Defects*, Cambridge, Mass.: Productivity Press, 1988.
12. Keki R. Bhote, *Next Operation as Customer: How to Improve Quality, Cost and Cycle Time in Support Services*, New York: American Management Association, 1991.
13. James Harrington, *Business Process Improvement*, McGraw-Hill.
14. Keki R. Bhote, *Strategic Supply Management: A Blueprint for Revitalizing the Manufacturer-Supplier Partnership*, New York: American Management Association, 1989.
15. Lawrence D. Miles, *Techniques of Value Analysis and Engineering*, McGraw-Hill, 1972.

16. J. Duncan Acheson, *Quality Control and Industrial Statistics*, 5th ed. Homewood, Ill.: Richard D. Irwin, Inc., 1986. (See p. 1007, Table D3)
17. Dorian Shainin and Peter Shainin, "Statistical Process Control," in *Quality Control Handbook*, ed. J. M. Juran and F. M. Gryna, section 24, McGraw-Hill, 1988.
18. Keki R. Bhote, "World Class Reliability through Multiple Environment Over Stress Tests (MEOST)," Asia Reliability Symposium, Hong Kong, February 1999.
19. Keki R. Bhote and James McLinn, "MEOST: An Approach to Quickly Evaluate Any New Product," Ada, Mich.: Amway Corp., March 8, 1996.
20. Stephen A. Smithson, "Effectiveness and Economics: Yardsticks for ESS Decisions," Proceedings of the Institute of Environmental Sciences, 1990.
21. Dave Steinberg, *Vibration Analysis of Electronic Equipment*, Wiley, 1973.
22. Darryl Piersol, *Managing Complex Change*, Endicott, N.Y.: IBM.

Index